THE UNOFFICIAL ECONOMY

The Unofficial Economy

Consequences and Perspectives in Different
Economic Systems

Edited by
SERGIO ALESSANDRINI
and
BRUNO DALLAGO
Università degli Studi di Trento

Gower

Published by
Gower Publishing Company Limited
Gower House
Croft Road
Aldershot
Hants GU11 3HR
England

Gower Publishing Company
Old Post Road
Brookfield
Vermont 05036
USA

British Library Cataloguing in Publication Data

The Unofficial economy : consequences and
  perspectives in different economic systems.
  1. Informal sector (Economics)
  I. Alessandrini, Sergio II. Dallago, Bruno
  339   HD2341

  ISBN 0-566-05131-1

Printed and bound in Great Britain by
Biddles Limited, Guildford and King's Lynn.

Contents

Part III ORGANIZATIONAL FORMS

Part IV CONSEQUENCES AND INCOME DISTRIBUTION

Preface

VITTORIO VALLI

In the last twenty years there has been in Italy a blosso-
ming of studies on the labour market and the unofficial
economy and a parallel steady increase of interest in the
field of comparative economic systems. It is not, therefore,
by chance if a research group of the University of Trento
has thought of engaging in the intersection of the two
fields. The result has been a comparative analysis on the
various forms of unofficial economy both in Western and
Eastern countries and the organization of a very fruitful
International Conference on the same subject. Is is not my
task to summarize and comment the several important contributions to the Trento Conference made by eminent scholars of
various countries. This is done very well by the editors of
the book in their introduction. I would rather like to make
some brief comments on the Italian situation in this field
of studies.

Between the end of the sixties and the beginning of the
eighties there was in Italy an impressive accumulation of
articles, reports and books on more or less the same pheno-
menom called in a variety of ways, as the 'irregular',
'unofficial', 'underground', 'submerged', 'informal', or
'parallel' economy, with its corollaries of 'black' or
'grey' labour, moonlighting, etc. All this apparatus originated in the rapidly increasing perception of the great
importance of the unofficial economy in the Italian case. At
the beginning, it seemed also to be a striking peculiarity
of the Italian system. Naturally, the phenomenon was considered to be present also in other countries, but on a much
more limited scale. The second aspect which it is important
to stress is that several Italian researchers, struck by the
emerging unexpected amplitude of the phenomenon, considered
it as a rapidly growing trend, spurred by extensive processes of decentralization of production carried out by the
enterprises in order to reduce labour costs and increase
flexibility. However, further progress in the research in
Italy and in several other countries partly corrected these
impressions. It was gradually perceived that the phenomenon
was a relevant one also in many other countries, although in
different forms and proportions. Moreover, we better understood the complexity and the variety of the world of Italian
micro-enterprises and of their connections with firms. It
also became clear that important forms of unofficial economy
had always existed in Italy and are a permanent feature of

the system, so that the first studies had probably overestimated the rise of the phenomenon in the first half of the seventies. A more precise and thorough analysis required further theoretical improvements and for other applied studies both on the Italian case and on a comparative basis. The former were mainly based on the labour market segmentation theory or on some complex fusion between theoretical tools framed by economists, sociologists and political scientists. The comparative studies were encouraged by the existence of a strong group of economists dedicated to the study of labour economics in Western and Eastern countries. We may recall among the former, Contini, Tarantelli, Vruno, Brusco, Salvati, Zenezini, Fuà, Ferri, Garonna, Del Boca, Frey, Dell'Aringa, etc. and, among the latter, Di Leo, Frateschi, Malle, Santacroce, Marcolungo, Dallago and several other authors. This field of research has already seen an extremely lively and fruitful debate, although many contributions, having been published only in Italian, are scarcely known abroad. The debate has been enhanced by the existence of two recently founded Associations: the Italian Association for the Study of Comparative Economic Systems (AISSEC) and the Italian Association for Labor Economics. The direction of future research is largely directed towards an attempt to combine the results of studies on the industry and the firm and studies on labour economics.

Vittorio Valli

Introduction

SERGIO ALESSANDRINI, BRUNO DALLAGO

Interest in the macroeconomic aspects of the unofficial economy began in the late Seventies. However, the phenomenon itself is not new, not even for social scientists, who discovered it earlier in many countries. Yet earlier studies considered only individual components and, with few partial exceptions, did not try to look for common features of the various components.

In recent years, the topic has reached a new stage, where its considerable diffusion across societies and economics has been recognized, although a lack of uniformity of definitions and taxonomy is still the main obstacle to a better knowledge.

A new insight has been the realization of the existence of apparently similar phenomena in Western, Eastern, and developing countries. An unofficial economy exists in each country and this means that its existence does not depend only on the characteristics of the economic and social system. At the same time, quality and quantity features of unofficial economies vary widely, which indicates the relevance of the features of the economic and social systems and of other (historical, traditional, geographical, etc.) factors.

This volume presents the papers given at the Trento seminar on the unofficial economy. More than 30 scholars from Europe, both East and West, the United States, and Israel met for two days to discuss the unofficial economy in different economic systems.

The aim of the seminar was to reunite some of the major experts in order to discuss the reasons for and consequences of the existence of an unofficial economy in both economic systems, and to attempt to make a first intersystemic comparison. This is, we believe, a necessary and important step on the way to a better knowledge of what the unofficial economy really is, what its causes and consequences are and what economic and social policy should make with it.

As far as we know, this is the first such attempt. Its originality is also stressed by the participation of economists, sociologists and anthropologists, discussing the same topic together. Of the many colourful and sensational terms often used to describe the phenomenon, we choose 'unofficial', which seems to be rather neutral and proved to be the best suited for the comparative purpose of the seminar.

The papers here published try to answer these questions

from various points of view. They have been organized in four sections, each giving some insights into a relevant aspect of the topic. They express a wide variety of standpoints and opinions, and this may also be seen in the variety of terms used, definitions adopted and specific phenomena considered.

A first group of papers deals with basic questions, from different points of view; their common aim is to identify the topic and to discuss the 'state of the art'. Here a clear picture is given of how much work has been done, how much has to be done and of the many difficulties stemming from confusions and lack of accuracy of definitions.

Peter WILES reviews in his paper the main problems met in defining the 'second' economy in general, and in particular when a definition valid for both Western and Eastern countries is looked for: definitions are system-dependent, as the Hungarian definition of the second economy illustrates. This means that, lacking a unique and comprehensive definition, measurement is also difficult, and quantitative comparison among various countries even more so. Wiles puts a strong accent on the moral aspects and of the consequences of the second economy on the national income: some second economy activities having an increasing effect, while others a decreasing one. Differences between the two - capitalistic and Soviet-type - economic systems are particularly clear and relevant when social and economic motivations are considered.

Jiri SKOLKA's paper is centered on Western countries and contains a critical review of what has been written on the 'hidden' economy. He criticizes the state of confusion surrounding definitions and the exaggeration of many quantitative estimates of the middle economy. Causes and consequences are also examined. Skolka correctly stresses the role of technical feasibility and productivity of the hidden activities compared to the official ones in determining which activities may be conveniently performed in a hidden way. The hidden economy has many complex consequences that do not permit a simple balance of its - positive or negative - role in the overall economy.

Ann WITTE considers only US studies and researches on 'unrecorded' activities in the United States. She takes into account only the production of goods and services, both legal and illegal, which is not recorded officially and whose existence stems from the inability of government to measure it. As far as legal production is concerned, her conclusion is that unrecorded activity involves mostly relatively disadvantaged people and areas, and therefore has a stabilizing and equalizing effect; a conclusion contrasting with others reached in various countries, but which seems to agree with Skolka's and Cassel-Cichy's studies in this volume. In the second part of her paper, Witte examines critically quantitative estimates worked out by governmental bodies in her country.

Edgar FEIGE's paper explicates a taxonomic framework of

the phenomenon and technically examines some of the empirical methods proposed to measure the size and growth of the
'underground' economy. He introduces two alternative concepts of the underground economy: economic and fiscal. Accordingly, an 'unrecorded economic income' exists and reflects an understatement of total economic income due to
underground economy, and an 'unreported fiscal income' that
represents an empirical understatement of total taxable
income. Feige critically discusses the most important official estimates of unrecorded income, comparing them with his
own. His conclusion is that official estimates understate
unrecorded income. Consequences of unrecorded income estimates for federal budget deficits are also examined and the
conclusion is reached that, should everybody abide by tax
laws, unreported income would be zero, and the 'full compliance budget' associated with full reports of incomes
would show a surplus.

Work is a major part of the unofficial economy and the
latter modifies the meaning of the former in contemporary
societies. Fedele RUGGERI's paper is centered on this topic
and his main conclusion is that the centrality of labor
still holds, but that it is now based on the connection
between the various forms of work and the reproduction of
the social relationships giving rise to those same forms. At
the same time it is also possible to speak of the disappearance of work: certain concrete forms of activity disappear,
while others continue to exist and still others come into
existence. It is in this context that the relationship
between official and unofficial economies has to be seen.
This relationship allows the bringing together of diverse
phenomena which, taken together, represent a certain way of
achieving an adjustment of social relations and their attendant tensions.

The second section of the volume comprises papers with a
specifically intersystemic comparative approach and others
presenting the main features of the unofficial economy in
one specific system. From this section a clear idea of
differences and similarities in different economic systems
is reached, throwing a new light on the understanding of the
phenomenon.

Dieter CASSEL and Ulrich CHICHY's paper points out both
general and specific causes of 'shadow' economies in the
framework of a neoclassical interpretation. The general
cause in both economic systems has to be looked for in the
economic role of the state, and in particular its allocative
function. System-specific causes are: in the West, the rising burden of taxation; in the East, cash-balance inflation. Specific causes determine the mix between official and
shadow economy and the latter's growth. However, in the two
systems a major difference exists as far as the role of the
shadow economy is concerned. It has a stabilizing role in
the West and economic policy should, as a consequence,
tolerate its existence - at least up to a certain degree. By
contrast, in the East the shadow economy has a destabilizing

effect and the economic policy has to fight it, in particular by widening the role of the market through comprehensive economic reforms.

Bruno DALLAGO tries to uncover the relationship between the economic system and the 'underground' economy. The paper compares the situation of consumers, workers, and firms and reviews the main components of the underground economy in the West and East, finding its causes in shortages as far as Soviet-type economies are concerned, and in the effort to decrease costs and increase demand by capitalist enterprises, and to increase personal incomes and find employment by families. The role of technical progress is also stressed. Underground enterprises have both advantages and disadvantages in comparison with regular enterprises, and often an integration develops between regular and irregular firms to mutual advantage. Underground activities have both positive and negative consequences, but their existence is unable to solve the main problems of the overall economy and often creates additional difficulties.

Zbigniew DOBOSIEWICZ's paper deals with the unofficial economy in North African countries and represents an interesting touchstone for the other papers dealing with different realities. From this paper, which is based mainly on the author's personal experience and 'field work' in those countries, we can understand how certain phenomena are diffused. According to him, unofficial economies are the result of the attempt by producers to diminish costs, particularly taxes, and the necessity of workers to find jobs. The latter is due to unemployment caused by social changes, such as urbanization, which have taken place in recent decades. This means that the unofficial economy is a transitory phenomenon, which will disappear with economic development. In the meantime, its role is positive, insofar as it permits the survival of many people, giving them employment, but its impact on production is less relevant because of low productivity characterizing unofficial activities.

Poland is a particularly interesting case study because of its widespread unofficial economy and recent economic and social developments. This is the subject of Zbigniew LANDAU's paper. He stresses the double nature of unofficial economy: certain components are common to all countries (e.g. tax evasion, smuggling), others are system-specific. As far as Soviet-type economies are concerned, four causes are prevalent: legislation, planning errors of prices and quantities, market situation (market shortages), relationship between government and state enterprises. In this period, the unofficial economy in Poland is particularly widespread because of the country's specific situation, due to the long economic and social crisis and the problems of transition to the economic reform. As far as consequences are concerned, the unofficial economy is seen as a factor increasing differences among social groups in income distribution.

In recent years, Hungary has experienced various changes in economic organization that have much in common with the unofficial economy. Éva SZITA discusses in her paper such new organizational forms that differ according to ownership rights, sector of activity, specific activities performed, people involved and personal income distribution. What is most interesting from our point of view is that these new forms "can hardly be considered attempts at the integration of the 'second economy' ...". These activities cause inflation, and inflation in turn fosters the development of the unofficial economy. Moreover, when the new organizational forms are successful, long-established errors of factory work organization are preserved. Overall, the introduction of new organizational forms proves to be ambivalent from an economic point of view, integrating to a certain extent many unofficial activities into the regular economy, and creating at the same time new opportunities for other unofficial activies.

The third section comprises both economic, sociological, and anthropological analyses of specific organizational forms in various national or regional, contexts. Papers in this section give an insight, each concentrating on one specific case study into the large variety of the phenomena listed under the heading of unofficial economy. Cases analysed in this section range from moonlighting traditions among shipyard workers in Northern Germany to the criminal economy of the Italian Mafia.

Gerald MARS amd Yochanan ALTMAN's papers cover various aspects of the second economy in Soviet Georgia. The approach is anthropological and is broadly based on case studies. The first paper deals with the organization of production and distribution of illicit goods through the careful study of a biscuit factory, whose irregular production is approximately 40% of the regular one. The authors examine the social and cultural bases of second economy operations and point out the micro-economic and social organization of the irregular activity. Such questions are discussed and illustrated as the way in which the enterprise involved in irregular production is able to circumvent the plan and obtain inputs both from inside the firm itself and outside it, and the way in which book-keeping is forged, and transportation and distribution of illicit goods is organized. In this way we obtain a vivid and clear picture from 'inside' of the working of the second economy in a Soviet situation, however peculiar, like the Georgian one.

The second paper continues the analysis by focusing on second economy distribution in Soviet Georgia. Attention is centered on four stores of different sizes and located in various areas of Georgia. In this context, too, the anthropological approach is extremely valuable in pointing out the role of cultural factors in promoting second economy. The store is a fundamental part of the latter, and its role is manifold. On the one hand, its irregular activity may take place either to the state's or the consumer's disadvantage. On the other hand, it benefits many people: from the store-keepers gaining a profit, through the workers obtaining premiums and rewards, to people in charge of controlling the correct working of the retail trade network (the police, in particular) who receive bribes and presents. The analysis of irregular selling practices reveals a complex network of activities, organizations, relationships deeply rooted both in a Soviet-type system and in traditional Georgian society. The analysis based on case studies and informant explanations permits the authors to work out five rules of informal trade which also set the boundary for the expansion of the second economy.

Perhaps the Mafia is the most typical component of the Italian illegal economy. However, its activity has recently spread to legal activities. Pino ARLACCHI examines in his paper the effects of the "La Torre Law" on Mafia crime and the Italian economy. Two new phenomena have emerged since the early Seventies within the Italian economy: the establishment of a vast illegal sector promoted and controlled by the Mafia and the increase in the number of Mafia firms and enterpreneurs in the emerging sectors of the economy in Southern Italy. The crucial element in the expansion of the Mafia's role in the Italian economy has been the close relationship between the legal and illegal sector of the economy. As a consequence, many Mafia firms operate in the legal sector, where they show a much greater availability of financial resources over regular firms, thanks to their illegal background. During its existence, still very short, the law has shown quite positive results, mainly because it has set up a barrier between the legal and illegal market. According to Arlacchi, this highly increases risks of illegal activities and may force Mafia groups to transfer resources from the illegal to the legal sector.

Bruno GRANCELLI's paper is centered on an interpretation of the Italian situation, in which the unofficial economy has a crucial role as an instrument of social and economic stabilization. Grancelli starts from a supposed 'anomaly' of industrial relations in Italy, where both 'neo-corporative' and 'neo-liberist' solutions seem to be impracticable, as the many deep and prolonged social conflicts show. The contrast with the fundamental stability of the social and economic situation is striking and traditional interpretations are unable to solve this dilemma. An answer can be found if we consider that a society is made up not only of collective actors but also of individual actors who are part of various social processes and who belong to different social groups. This means that official professions no longer decide the class position of individuals; rather, social actors tend to adopt a wide variety of instruments to improve their living conditions: it is in this context that the unofficial economy has a substantial role. Unofficial economy has therefore a stabilizing role within society and the unofficial economy has to be included in the building of a new analytical model.

The paper by JESSEN and others, presented in Trento by Walter SIEBEL, takes an opposite view. This paper denies that the 'informal sector' is growing and represents an alternative resource that helps the solution of labor market and socio-political problems. Instead, it increases inequality. It is interesting to note how differences in view and conclusions depend on the different methodologies and definitions adopted by the researchers and how far they reflect the different objects of analysis. Siebel's paper presents the results of an empirical research into household strategies, based on an interview project with 120 shipyard workers in Northern Germany. Here informal work is seen as a very common and rather traditional phenomenon, consisting of the work performed by industrial workers outside formal employment. Siebel finds that the informal economy does not represent an alternative to the official economy or a means for the transformation of the capitalistic system, but is rather an increasingly integrated part of the latter.

The consequences of unofficial economy, and in particular problems of welfare and income distribution are, dealt with in the fourth section. As already seen in the previous papers, unofficial activities can be divided in productive and distributive activities, according to their consequences. But unofficial activities that increase the production of goods and services have distributive effects both in the West and the East. Therefore, income distribution is a central topic of the unofficial economy, and is dealt with in the fourth section.

Gregory GROSSMAN presents a paper, written jointly with Vladimir TREML, discussing the methodology used in a major research project aimed at measuring and collecting information on the second economy in the Soviet Union. The paper is centered on methodological problems of measuring hidden personal incomes and the first results and information obtained from the research are presented. This is based on an extensive interview project with recent Soviet emigrés in the United States and the paper contains a description of the main characteristics of the sample and of the questionnaire utilized for the interviews. Preliminary results are also presented and discussed regarding hidden incomes obtained from private selling of foodstuffs both on the kolchozian and the underground market. Information is also given on incomes gained by selling goods that are produced by 'crypto-private' enterprises as 'socialist' and by speculating on goods in shortage. A regional breakdown of results is also provided.

The contradictory nature of the organizational changes introduced in Hungary in recent years, presented and discussed by Éva Szita, also appears in Andras HEGEDÜS's paper. As far as economic consequences are concerned, the legitimization and expansion of the second economy decreases shortage but increases inflation. The consequences for people's living standards are also both positive and negative, according to the social group concerned: overall, "the gap between the beneficiaries and the victims of the reforms is widening", and the education and leisure of people involved are affected. The legitimization and expansion of the second economy has also contradictory political consequences for pluralism and the power structure and is inconsistent with the existing ethos and the official ideology. These problems and contradictions raise the question of the feasibility of the implementation of such a reform in only one country and of the perspective of the Hungarian experiment. Hegedüs holds a cautious but optimistic view on both questions.

Arnold HEERTJE examines the welfare-economic aspects of the unofficial economy, which comprises both market transactions and transactions outside the sphere of the market. Heertje's attention is centered on the allocation of scarce resources, and in particular on the allocation taking place within economic units that belong to the unofficial economy. This internal allocation is caused by individuals' negative preferences for the interference of government and involves a positive welfare effect. Informal allocation is therefore an alternative to market allocation and depends on the transaction costs associated with market allocation (such as taxes and regulation) and the benefits of internal allocation (mutual trust). The analysis is then shifted to the consequences of disequilibrium that characterize modern Western economies because of rigidities in the economy. The unofficial economy is the result of mainly price rigidities. But within this economy a Walrasian price formation prevails. The market structure of the unofficial economy is that of perfect competition, and allocation is Pareto-optimal. Overall, we face a dual economy with a "schizophrenic character", where allocation is nearer to a Pareto-optimum, and the level of activity is higher than would be with no unofficial economy.

Ingemar HANSSON examines in his paper the more specific problem of tax evasion and its consequences. This is an important question in the debate on the unofficial economy, which is often seen as the main cause of the unofficial economy in the West. The paper examines optimal redistributive income taxation when an untaxed sector is considered. The untaxed sector consists of untaxed activities (such as household activities) and activities evading taxes. It is a two-sector, general equilibrium model of an open economy where two agents exist, I individual and a government collecting taxes and redistributing transfers. When the untaxed sector is considered, the optimal tax rate appears to be higher than when this sector is not taken into account, as in traditional models. The explanation is that the tax base acts as a signal for capacity in the untaxed sector, and income taxation provides insurance not only for variations in capacity in the taxed sector but also for variations in capacity in the untaxed sector.

Quite different from those argued for Heertje are the conclusions reached by Ivo BIĆANIĆ as far as a different, self-managed economy is concerned. Bićanić examines the causes and consequences of the unofficial economy on inequality in income and wealth distribution in Yugoslavia. The causes consist of the nature of the economic environment, the business cycle and short term economic policy, and the nature of the economic system. Overall, he finds that unofficial activities increase inequality, while other activities (such as moonlighting) decrease it. The paper is based on a survey of the main - published and unpublished - researches on the unofficial economy and income distribution in Yugoslavia: it outlines eight different types of the unofficial economy activities relevant for families (Bicanic does not deal with unofficial activities within enterprises).

Similar conclusions are reached by Leendert COLIJN, who presents a method of estimating the influence of macroeconomic disequilibrium on the size of the 'second' economy in Soviet-type economies. His approach may be defined as Keynesian mixed with some Kaleckian insights and is utilized - with the help of arbitrary parameter values together with official Polish data - to estimate only that part of the second economy caused by the existence of macroeconomic disequilibrium in the 'first' economy. It comprises also the legal private sector but does not consider second economy caused by partial disequilibria on the official market of consumer goods. The basic hypothesis is that, due to an exogenous shock, excess demand develops in the first economy and an inflationary gap arises which is in part spent in the second economy. The increase of second economy incomes turns out to be a multiple of the inflationary demand originated in the first economy and probably increases income distribution inequalities.

The picture of the 'state of the art' we obtain from these contributions is one of extremely lively and wide-ranging debate. A few firm conclusions have already been reached, while on other points the debate is still open. Our hope is that the Trento seminar and the present publication will contribute actively and fruitfully to a better definition and knowledge of the subject.

If this is the case, we feel even more grateful than we have been thus far to all those, people and institutions alike, who made possible the organization of the seminar and the publication of the present book. We are greatly indebted to the Department of Economics and the Department of Social Policy at the University of Trento, the Consiglio Nazionale delle Ricerche (CNR 82.01247.10 and CNR 84.00529.10), the Banca di Trento e Bolzano, the Regione Trentino-Alto Adige, and the Provincia Autonoma di Trento for having generously sponsored the organization of the seminar.

The Department of Economics at the University of Trento has also made possible the publication of the present volume with its financial assistance. A special thanks goes to Gerald Mars for his help in contacting the Publisher and to the latter for their readiness in accepting this volume for publication. Rosaria Prosser, Edit von Kismarjay and Marco Tomasi assisted us during the organization of the seminar. Last but not least, our thanks go to all the participants in the conference, for their active presence allowing an interesting and fruitful debate and exchange of ideas, and the contributors to the present volume.

Sergio Alessandrini
Bruno Dallago

PART I
THE PROBLEM AND ITS
IDENTIFICATION

The second economy, its definitional problems

PETER WILES

1.   It is my honour to present the first and dullest paper:
a   chapter of mere moral and financial accountancy.   But its
subject is not the least important.   For if we have no clear
definitions,   or at least personal sets of incompatible but
still clear definitions,   we do not know what we are talking
about.   Without such knowledge international conferences are
hardly   worth   holding.   My set of definitions is of   course
personal. It is not put forward to be imposed on others, but
rather   to ensure that,   having considered   this   particular
set, they understand the dangers. For instance, varied definitions   of the Hungarian 2E (*) put it at 15 and at 50%   of
GNP. But the same data are involved throughout.
    First some <u>moralizing adjectives</u>. The language of <u>l'Albion
perfide</u> is naturally rich in these.

1a.   <u>Illegitimate</u> is my over-arching word for the 2E, and is
      often shortened to 'black'.   The noun and the adjective
      mutually define each other.   The adjective includes and
      is exhausted by
1b.   <u>Illegal</u>:   what is contrary to the law,   however absurd,
      of the country under study; and -
1c.   <u>Illicit</u>:   what   is merely contrary to accepted economic
      <u>morality</u>, however absurd. So 'illicit' is also a local-
      ly   determined concept.   In colour terms illicit is   of
      course 'grey' while -
1d.   <u>Criminal</u> is strictly the same as illegal,   but the word
      is usually reserved for the 'jet-black' end of   illega-
      lity: <u>felonies</u> such as fraud, theft, violence and pro-
      ducing   or distributing really dangerous   drugs.   Other
      crimes,   such   as misdemeanours,   torts and breaches of
      contract (1), are much 'greyer'.

These are technical legal distinctions,   but in discussing
2E's they fit well enough.   The differences between a criminal and a Second Economist are extremely important, at least
in   the   eyes of the latter.   But they are sociological   and
legal rather than economic.
    Unreported activity includes nearly all of 1a - d,   except
where statisticians present estimates.   This they   sometimes
do.   They also often omit minor legitimate activities.   Thus
'unreported' is a very treacherous concept indeed, depending
on   local statistical practice.   For instance Italian labour
statistics   have   included   since 1976 a good   deal   of   the

21

labour in BVA. The 'household', '_informal_', or 'natural' sector is everywhere mostly unreported, but it is hardly anywhere illegitimate. It is very important, it is an entirely respectable subject of study, but it is only inside the 2E on the Hungarian definition (below). It is very misleading to group an activity that is itself 'whiter than white' along with crime and tax evasion.

Between one moralizing adjective and another there is always an indistinct area. This important point is so obvious we need only state it. 'Illicit' might include prostitution, the acceptance by officials of gifts _after_ they have done favours, the purchase of goods _suspected_ of being stolen, the purchase of marijuana for personal use only, etc. etc. The list is of course absurd and incongruous. Practical morality always is to the superficial observer.

2. But it would be a very grave error indeed to drain the 2E of _its moral, or rather immoral, content_. Rather would I say, all mere economic aspects pale into insignificance by comparison. Indeed all economic systems are based on a practical morality in addition to a larger and more theoretical ideology. If capitalism has lost the latter aspect with the invention of limited liability, it certainly still rests on the former. All systems do: they are unable to function without one, and indeed this practical morality is rather the same everywhere. It is a boy scout (or Pioneer) morality: love God (or Marx), honour the King (or Politburo), don't question the ideology (if any), work hard, pay your taxes, learn techniques, save money, obey the law, don't even do illicit things.

The fascination of the 2E is that despite its breach of this morality it aids economic systems to function. But it does also hinder them. Indeed in the writer's opinion the opportunity cost to the official economy, in terms of stolen labour time, stolen materials, the shrinking tax base and the consequently higher tax rates, the general damage caused by dangerous drugs, the expenses of theft and fraud prevention, is very big indeed. He questions strongly whether the 2E is ever a net economic advantage to the nation, even in the USSR. But this must be for another occasion; what is striking here is habitual neglect of moral issues by social scientists. Economists look right past them, as unscientific, or not in the paradigm, or unamenable to algebra; sociologists and anthropologists (below) deliberately relativize them out of existence. I maintain, even if _contra mundum_, that lawbreaking is nearly always bad, so the 2E is bad. So too are systems that drive ordinary people into such badness. Boy scouts, on the other hand, and Pioneers are good.

3. From the moralizing adjectives to the _statistical nouns_. These are all very commonplace economic or accounting terms.

3a. _Black value added (BVA)_: is work for the 2E in production and distribution, plus the cost of capital and the rent of the land. This concept includes also some bribes: those necessary to protect the process of adding black value.

3b. Black transfers: theft, including all simple cases plus the theft of employer's time and the theft of raw materials for or by Soviet craftsmen; bribes for all other purposes such as queue jumping, appointment, promotion, exit visas or the overlooking of some crime. See also 'benign plan violation', below.

3c. Black capital gains: are realized when those who hold some asset used in the 2E benefit from a price-rise which is due to no factor activity on their part.

BVA can work out at a very small part of this total. Thus in illegal gambling BVA is only the wages of the runners, the profits of the boss and the material office expenses. But gambling gains and losses are only transfers and work out at twenty times as much. Just like the official economy, the 2E consists exhaustively of events within one of the three categories above. Black transfers do not, of course, enrich the nation as a whole; neither do official transfers. Black capital gains are only a movement in some relative price. Duly deflated by a proper price index, the national income cannot gain. Only the BVA, of course, enriches the nation as a whole, so the distinction between BVA and the other two is the most important matter in all 2E studies. But even that is on the proviso that BVA is not performed by stolen labour time: a concept sufficiently important to be discussed at once.

3d. Stolen labour, then, is the non-performance of work during paid hours. This might be valued at the marginal hourly labour pay of the thief, or at the marginal loss to his employer. Clearly if BVA is created by stolen labour the thief gains but the national income may lose, for stolen labour has a high opportunity cost. Such theft is exceedingly common world-wide. It is undeniably a big part of the 2E, and also illegal. But most writers shy away from it. No doubt a big reason for this is that university professors, the main writers about the 2E, themselves engage mainly in this form of it, notably at international conferences. The fact that the wages (strictly we should not say the labour) are stolen means that they are a black transfer; and that productivity in the official economy is higher than we think.

3e. To stolen labour there corresponds the wear and tear on one's employer's machine, as one works it after hours; or of course the whole opportunity cost to him of working it in the 2E during normal hours - stolen services of capital.

4. What motives have we to behave 'illegitimately'? Obviously, profit, but that is too easy to say. First, man does not live by bread alone. He has other motives for illegitimacy. Minority nations (e.g. Georgians) are moved by nationalism and spite to cheat their conquerors (e.g. Russians). Again the law as such, the whole concept of

illegitimacy, can mean nothing to primitive peoples, who simply walk through the fences set up by 'civilized' men. They are not immoral by so doing.

Secondly, profit is far too broad a concept. The <u>sources of black profit</u> are:

4a.   <u>Tax evasion</u>. This is the oldest, the traditional and still the biggest source. Tax rates per article are ordinarily bigger than net profit rates per article; so if indirect tax is evaded profit rates are more than doubled. Tax rates per pound of net corporate profit are nowadays over 50 percent; so if direct tax is evaded profits are more than doubled. The general, secular increase of taxes has increased the total 2E. But note large, age-old production of particular heavily taxed goods in all societies. Moonshine and samogon are perfect examples.

Moreover, though tax evasion is a crime it is not severely punished, since it is so common and natural: the police and the judges have done it too. Long before there were price controls and tight detailed plans there were taxes. It is a prime error of non-specialists to attribute the Soviet 2E to price or quantity controls alone. Those are its more interesting causes. Its most important cause is simpler and older.

4b.   <u>Price control evasion</u>. This arises in a situation of 'shortage'. Shortage is a very treacherous and callous word. There is no shortage of food in the Ethiopian hinterland today, only famine: for prices have found their equilibrium. But in Addis Abeba there is a shortage, for price controls still function - and people live. A shortage can then arise when a Soviet planner misjudges the supply point (2) of a particular good; or in any society the combination of inflation with fixed prices sets up a queue of people, motivated by the num-

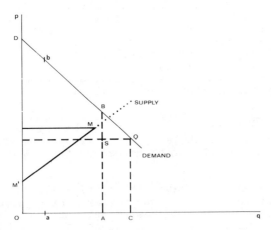

Figure 1. Price control evasion

ber of unbought goods SQ for which there is effective
demand. There is also a black price AB (see Figure 1)
which speculators can get if the frustrated purchasers
were all among the most desirous to purchase, i.e. the
original people whose demand curve for OA was DB (3).
There is thus a substantial profit to be made out of
reselling goods that have paid their tax, and not been
stolen. Shop assistants benefit hugely, but perform
very little work. So it is questionable if item 3b is
BVA at all, for nothing is added to national product.
Consumers bribe shop assistants, thus frustrating other
consumers: that is pure black transfer.

My inclination is to go along with this argument, and
confine the occasions when price control evasion generates BVA to those where, say, a region is starved of a
good by a price control that takes too little account
of transport costs - a common event. Then those who, in
their own cars or by devious public means, work to
transport the good are engaged in black distribution.
Naturally, too, a high black price with a low controlled price excites black production. But most of the effect is mere bribery, so only transfers.

Price control evasion is greatly increased, but not
entirely caused, by inflation which raises all demand
curves. Indeed inflation (in its monetary, not its
price raising aspects) plus price controls constitutes
suppressed inflation.

4c.   The evasion of Soviet-type output plans is thus reduced
to its proper size, or at least its proper statistical
size. Whatever its ideological importance, nothing
tells us that the Soviet 2E is bigger than the Colom-
bian 2E (marijuana). Obviously if the government com-
mands not only prices but also quantities there will
also be quantity control evasion. Many governments
impose quantitative maxima (including the zero maximum
on dangerous drugs); only a Soviet-type government
imposes quantitative minima. So our first problem is:

4c(i)   The deliberate shortfall from the minimum-output
target. This invariably leads to loss of bonus,
and to complaints from the (also nationalized)
customer whose plan includes our output as this
input. It is therefore only likely if there is
massive diversion of state resources into BVA, or
if shortfall is confined to a very narrow range of
the whole sortament of output, and so can be
defended by alleging technical difficulties, 'social' priorities, etc. In a word, deliberate
shortfalls need not detain us, however common
accidental shortfalls may be.

4c(ii) Deliberate overproduction over the whole range
of the sortament is the pipe-dream of every manager (4). But a great excess in one or two items
argues BVA: that diversion of state resources for
personal gain referred to above. Such an excess
will of course not be reported, its revenues will
be diverted and its costs concealed. It cannot be

overstressed that BVA with state resources, being
motivated by profit, is mainly motivated by tax
evasion or price-control evasion. The 'misjudge-
ment of the appropriate supply point' referred to
above, or even the suboptimal choice of relative
physical quantities which that implies (5), do not
bring about such massive profits as tax evasion
and suppressed inflation. The ordinary, old-fa-
shioned, non-Sovietological, explanations will not
go away.

4d. For logic and completeness we must include here the
production of forbidden articles. While this is over-
whelmingly dangerous drugs we must not forget arms,
pornography and samizdat. This category is of course
even bigger in many capitalist countries, especially
small ones that export dangerous drugs.

5. Benign Plan Violation (BPV) in the USSR is extremely difficult to range within a system of definitions. It is the
habit of Soviet managers to violate details in their extremely detailed plans in order to ensure the fulfilment of the
more important targets. Notably, they fail to fulfil every
minor output target in the sortament, they overspend their
wage fund and above all they acquire material inputs by
devious means.

All this is motivated by the search for a higher bonus,
but it is also probably in the interest of the state and the
society. And certainly all the extra output so achieved is
registered officially - for otherwise how could there be a
bonus? In the good old days of the early Stalin period, when
there was little corruption, even the 'devious means' of
beating the perpetual input shortage involved little bribery. One manager swapped particular goods with another; a
third used Party influence to hasten delivery.

In modern times all this is more efficiently conducted by
specialists (tolkachi) who use bribes. In any case BPV is a
necessary ingredient of the official system, whereas BVA
arises in all systems, and even in the USSR is mainly due to
taxation not planning. It seems then best to define the
bribes that are now essential to BPV as a hidden cost of the
official system, and to continue to exclude it from BVA.

That is by no means in order to play down its importance
and volume. It is only to put things in the right pigeon-
holes: the bribes connected with BPV are black transfers,
the thing itself is a sort of administration.

6. While we are discussing penumbral matters, it is important to consider ex post blackness. Illegality, even illici-
tude, is a matter of mens rea, one's intentions. A black
transaction is one intended to be black. The boundary is
here also very vague, and a quantitatively large part of the
2E can be found on it.

I go to a conference abroad, for the interest, the academic distinction conveyed and the incidental tourism; they
offer to pay my expenses only. The price is of course a
written contribution. But when the embarrassing moment comes

the envelope is found to contain not a cheque but cash, and
cash that covers also a non-negotiable <u>per diem</u>. As befits
my professional status, at least as conceived in foreign
countries, it is a very generous <u>per diem</u>, but it also
accidentally covers the second night of my stay when they
gave us all a festive dinner, and duplicates the lunch on
the first day that a native friend (not attending the conference) insisted on giving me at his home. One way or another
I am £50 to the good. So (a) do I report it for tax
purposes? If not then of course I have bilked the Inland
Revenue and that is an illegal (not illicit) black transfer.
But also (b), would I have gone at all if I hadn't thought
such an event probable - if I had expected a negative cash
flow instead? How <u>rea</u> was my <u>mens</u>? If the answer is again no
this was paid black work, and should be counted as BVA,
because in my guilty mind I wrote the contribution for about
£50. In any case of course, as pointed out above, I have
probably stolen labour from my university.

In the USSR the marginal rate of income tax on such earnings is high and progressive. This fact is commonly neglected by Sovietologists, and still more commonly by Soviet
citizens, of whom but an infinitesimal minority report legal
after hour earnings for income tax. They get away with it
because they are paid in cash (like British building repair
workers), and, it seems, because the tax authorities make no
serious effort to collect. So they fall under 'no to (a)'
and 'no to (b)'. So <u>all</u> private work is in a good sense BVA.

7. <u>Laundering</u> is the practice of concealing from the police
goods, services and money that are in the 2E, by passing
them off as official. In the West this is thought of mainly
as the laundering of black money (q.v.), but in fact the
'fence' (receiver of stolen goods) makes his vast and risky
profit precisely from the laundering of stolen goods, a
process indistinguishable from trading in them.

All black production is laundered when finally sold to the
population. But when the output is very great the black
retailing process is slow, inefficient and dangerous, so at
least in USSR it is common to launder the output already at
the wholesale stage. In few other countries, perhaps, is
this a mass phenomenon. The reason seems to be that so many
ordinary factories find it profitable, as nowhere else, to
create a part of their ordinary output (e.g. brandy bottles)
'on the left', out of raw materials that have been 'economized', and after working hours. This extra output is not
reported in order to earn bonus, but concealed in order to
evade tax. As there are more policeman per kilometer of road
than in other countries there is more danger in the transportation and ultimate retailing than in the production.
For the local policeman can and must be bribed; but one
cannot bribe the whole <u>oblast'</u> just in case some other
policeman conducts a spot check on vehicles, or one of one's
many black retailers is caught. So the liquor shop is
brought into the plot, documents are forged, and the whole
distribution process is regularized by retailing the bottles
off the shelf.

This kind of laundering raises many definitional questions. Clearly BVA is no longer the number of brandy bottles multiplied by the black price. The 'economized' raw materials, at least, have been stolen as before, from the legitimate wing of the enterprise, and present no new conceptual problem: BVA always includes the value of, or profit from, stolen inputs. But this is only as far as the Second Economists are concerned: on the national scale theft remains a black transfer, and the value of the theft must be recorded also as a 'loss', in Soviet statistical terminology, to the official economy. However on the output side we now face the official retail price, minus the official (and duly earned) retail gross margin. That leaves the work done in production and transportation, and the bribes to policemen and retail trade officials.

Laundering is not 'whitening'. This is the process, undertaken in Hungary and mooted in France and Italy, of deliberately withdrawing state controls, and lowering taxes, in order to give less cause for illegitimate behaviour, and thus to include many ongoing 2E activities within the official economy.

8. <u>Black Money</u> is whatever money is used to liquidate a particular black transaction. The black money arising in the great majority of transactions is automatically 'laundered' (q.v.) in the very next transaction, because these transactions are for <u>small</u> sums and in used notes, which the recipient can dispose of in the shops during one week. But very <u>large</u> sums, especially in new notes of large denomination but also even in bank accounts, excite the interest of the police as much as furniture, jewels, pictures, lathes, lorries etc. They present a severe laundering problem, which has given rise to a good journalistic literature in the USA (6). 'Large', black money is a predestined source of finance for black investment; it has nowhere else to go.

9. We now turn to ways of measuring the 2E.
9a. <u>The monetary approach</u>: The constant and easy laundering of a part of it means that the total of black money is extremely difficult to establish. Only the 'large' black money continually circulates within the 2E. Some of the 2E is of course barter, and it would be an error to assume that none of it was cheques. Again where money is inconvertible, or where black foreign trade is very important (marijuana, heroin, cocaine), a good deal of the 'large' black money is foreign money.

It need not be said that we have to know the velocity of circulation of black money before we can estimate along this route the total annual volume of the (non-barter) 2E. The velocity of cheque circulation, illegitimate and official put together, is of course easily known from bank clearing figures. Owing to Feige's work we have now a notion of the velocity of circulation, illegitimate and official, of all notes (USA). This is a giant step forward. But we have not, so far as I can determine, the slightest idea of the illegitimate and the official velocities taken separately, whether of notes or of cheques, at any time or in any place. This is the steep hurdle that the monetary approach must now take before it becomes more than merely promising. It would of course remain impossible to estimate BVA separately by this route.

9b. The 'Palermo' approach: This is to take regions or towns, in a count providing local statistics, and to compare, ideally by means of regression analysis, the visible consumption with the reported income. The gap (C - Y) is usually positive in all places, even before allowance is made for savings. But that ultimately depends on the efficiency with which consumption and income series respectively are collected. The C - Y gap in 'Palermo', where that city stands for the headquarters or heartland of the 2E (which, let us remember, includes crime), should be bigger than elsewhere. We then have a notion of the excess of BVA in the less honest over the more honest regions. We have now only to establish BVA in one region, say a minimum in the most honest: and we have a national total.

In the actual Palermo the gap is indeed very big. But this recently often reported fact seems impossible to document, and there are whole unstudied areas of mainland Italy where the more respectable side of the 2E is much more active than the Mafia; i.e. where BVA is a larger part of the total. For it must be remembered that Palermo benefits from positive interregional black transfers. Such net transfers increase regional consumption. Specifically in Italy, then, the Palermo approach is in its infancy.

Not so, if the author may say so, in the USSR, another country where the 2E is very localised. A very thorough, though in retrospect crude, attempt has been made there to use this approach, the 'localities' being the towns and the countryside of each republic, with Georgian towns representing 'Palermo' (7).

9c. The labour force approach: This, despite its Palermitan possibilities, is Italy's main contribution to 2E studies. One counts men, not money. An unusually high rate of apparent unemployment argues black employment, and the problem is to quantify the adverb 'unusually'. This method of course automatically isolates BVA, though it may well include full time petty thieves as workers in the 2E, and so in BVA.

9d. The Sociological, or Survey, approach: This is by questionnaires. They must of course be administered carefully, with pilot samples, cross checks, guaranteed anonymity, checks against other data, etc., etc. The best of these appear to be those of Ofer, Winokur, Grossman, and Treml, conducted on Soviet emigrés (see Grossman here). This approach distinguishes, of course, BVA, but should also yield the 2E total. To an applied economist it seems the most fruitful of all, since it is less expensive and more quantitative than -

9e. The Anthropological approach: Here the researcher

(usually Mars and/or Altman! - see their contributions here) lives in the subcriminal culture and pretends to conduct himself according to its norms. He learns in the end immensely much and comes back with many indispensable pieces of institutional knowledge - but no figures. This is because anthropologists refuse to put such questions, indeed personally dislike and mistrust them. Their discoveries must then be clothed in hard (or rather, alas, soft) estimates by other people.

9f. The Industry-by-Industry Approach: Some industries - dangerous drugs, building repairs, consumer durable repairs, the brewing and distilling of hard liquor - contribute far more to the 2E than the rest. It may suffice to tot up them alone, and guess a 10% residual, in order to arrive at total BVA (Wiles 1981).

In small Latin American drug exporters, black exports alone account for far the greatest part of BVA - and for a very high percentage of exporters (up to 50 percent) and so of GNP (up to 25 percent).

10. I conclude with the Hungarian definition. It is natural for accounting schemes to reflect this or that ideology. It is difficult, all the same, for the writer to detect his own. Certainly his wish is to produce one free of ideological preconceptions, resembling closely the universally agreed (8) national income terminology and applicable to all systems.

But the Hungarian definition is specific to economies of Soviet type (9). The basic Hungarian idea is the very same one that inspired the New Economic Mechanism (and this is why 2E studies can be printed in Hungary alone of Communist countries): we have created a superstructure, a pays légal, in which things are supposed to appear in such and such an approved way, but actually there survives beneath this the pays réel, where people use public and private property for their own ends - and when they do so that is the 2E. Sometimes the property they use is private, and so their actions are legal; sometimes they use public property, so they break the law (especially the plan). But the 2E is what people do spontaneously.

Words mean what we tell them to mean. While deploring the lack of clarity about definitions in the Hungarian literature accessible to me, I recognize everyone's right to use, after due warning, those that suit him. The 2E à la hongroise appears to contain, in my terms:

criminal theft (?);
theft of raw materials and labour time;
straight BVA;
black transfers other than theft (?), ie. mainly
    bribes;
BPV, in so far as it still exists in the reformed
    Hungarian system;
legal private production;
legal co-operative production; and
the 'household', 'natural', or 'informal' sector, even

though it is legitimate.

Note in these last three cases, the absolute rejection of moral criteria. It is not surprising that this very mixed bag adds up to 50 percent of GNP in the Hungarian case. My own modest definition, of a BVA alone (including theft of materials) that runs at 7 - 25 percent worldwide, is quite compatible.

The Hungarian definition, once cleared up, is by no means misleading or wrong. The answers to the questions, what is the total sum of the 2E, legal, individual and cooperative activity, and the informal sector, or what is the sum of value added under these three headings, would be very useful things to know. The concept of a 'grass-roots' economy is a perfectly valid one. It does indeed stand as a _pays réel_ against the _pays légal_ of public _and large private_ enterprises. It does encompass what people do if not 'organized', as Indian economists put it. It is not, of course, as Hungarians pretend, a specifically Communist phenomenon. It has very much in common with the concepts of economic sociologists like Jonathan Gershuny.

Definitions follow interests. The Hungarian definition suits students who want to know what happens where the government cannot reach. My definition suits those who want only to know how immoral people are, and what has been left out of the national income accounts that ought, by common definitions, to be in them.

Having heard at the conference many arguments against the application of the same definitions to Soviet-type as to market economies, I remain wholly unconvinced. The direct causative effect of the Soviet-type plan, and its pervasive suboptimalities, is indeed unique, but it is not big. The first motive is tax evasion, as everywhere else. The second biggest is surely the effect of being employed at all: the theft of labour time (or of wages). This too is universal. Perhaps Soviet-type institutions, especially the plan, come third (10). Fourth come the non-coincidence of the supply point with the demand curve; and while that is undoubtedly a far bigger feature of STE's than of ME's it is also very common in the public sectors of ME's. Let me only mention queues for minor operations in public health systems. Fifthly, many of the suboptimal allocations of normal consumer goods in a STE are after all compensated by suboptimal indirect tax rates, that reestablish market clearing prices. The whole informal sector is of course very similar everywhere - and legitimate everywhere (except in kibbutzim, armies and monasteries).

For international comparisons we might want simply to compare the untreated results of using these local concepts - in which case, notably, the USSR would be handicapped by its wider range of illegality. But we might also want to compare on the basis of some internationally constant concept, such as burglary or drug abuse - in which case the USA would have a bigger 2E than the USSR.

Let me again rub in what is to me the basic point. The sad fact is that men are bad. They surely differ _a little_ in the extent of their fundamental badness, and that is one consideration. But, also, different systems bring out their badness more or less, and that is another consideration. Thirdly, and worst of all, is the fact that in all this range of activity their badness has recently been increasing over time. It is not just that taxation, or Soviet-type planning, has been bringing out the old Adam, who was always in us. The old Adam is also growing.

NOTES

(*)   In this contribution 'Second Ebonomy' is abbreviated '2E'. The adjective is 'black'.
(1)   In English law a tort is an offence against society for which nevertheless the wronged person not the state must sue: assault, nuisance. A misdemeanour is a minor infraction such as parking in the wrong place or making too much noise. And strictly a crime is all felonies and misdemeanours plus some torts.
(2)   In a command economy money is passive, so there is no supply curve telling us the influence of price on output. There is only the point S, combining the output set by Gosplan and the price set by the State committee on prices. In a market economy a price control cuts off the supply curve M'M at M. Such a point as M would generate its own B and Q, and the whole analysis would still apply.
(3)   This is not the place to enter too thoroughly into this simple and pregnant diagram. Suffice it to say that the actual purchasers of OA may include some of those less desirous or less wealthy whose demand curve was BQ, so that AC and OA got mixed up. Then B would be higher, rising in the extreme case to ab (where Oa = AC), when only the people in Db were frustrated and now seek the good in the black market. If on the other hand only BQ were frustrated there would be no black market, for there would be no black supply.
(4)   Less so in the various experiments with planning-from-below. One can be penalized for having proposed too low a plan for oneself, and so overproducing too easily.
(5)   But does not entail. For the Gosplan might have set OA optimally, and the error could lie entirely with the Goskomtsen's choice of the price AS.
(6)   Thus (i) Swiss banks are the laundries <u>par excellence</u>, and their laundering capability is carefully supported by Swiss law; but (ii) a good way to launder high denomination, consecutively numbered notes is to have Mafia connexions with a casino, where you bet them and lose them in a few throws, but then make a 'surprising' win.
(7)   Wiles (1981).
(8)   I am entitled in this context to pass over the Soviet insistence on not counting 'unproductive' labour.
(9)   Cf. Gueullette (1981).
(10) Note that the Hungarian definition, being uninterested

32

in crime or immorality as such, has to exclude BPV and
its attendant bribery since they both belong to the
<u>pays</u>, so to speak, <u>légal</u>!

REFERENCES

DEZSENYI-GUEULLETTE, A., 'The Parallel Economy in the East:
the Hungarian Case', <u>Revue d'Etudes Comparatives Est-
Ouest</u>, June 1981.
WILES, P., <u>Die Parallelwirtschaft</u>, BIOS, Cologne 1981.

A few facts about the hidden economy

JIRI SKOLKA

"The weak and too slowly growing empirical foundation clearly cannot support the proliferating superstructure of pure, or I should say, speculative economic theory".

Leontief (1971)

1. DEFINITION OF THE HIDDEN ECONOMY

The terminology in the literature on the hidden economy is rich. Exact definitions are, on the contrary, rare. But discussion is impossible if the same term is given to different objects, or if one object has several terms.

1.1. Statistical definition of the hidden economy

In 1979 we were told that the hidden economy - hitherto almost unregistered - was exploding (Feige, 1979; Gutmann, 1979). Official statistics, which did not consider this explosion were accused of supplying economic policy with false data about growth, inflation and unemployment (1).

The level of economic activity in a country is measured in statistics by the gross domestic product. The estimates of its value, however, are never precise. These are always biased by errors and omissions, which depend on the experience and quality of statistical services of individual countries. In addition to such errors, the output of activities intentionally concealed from public authorities is also missing in the official figures on the gross domestic product.

These concealed activities compose the 'hidden economy'. According to the definition proposed by Blades (1982), the hidden economy consists of:

(i) Production of goods that is quite legal in itself, but that one or more parties involved try to conceal from the public authorities to avoid paying taxes or similar charges, (ii) production of illegal goods and services; and (iii) concealed income in kind".

35

The first item - the 'undeclared' legal production - has usually the largest share in the hidden economy. It is also the most frequently studied. It includes mainly 'moonlighting' and 'off-books business'. Moonlighting is concealed paid work by the employed carried out, independently and on their own account, after the official working hours. Off-books business includes cases where firms do not correctly declare their revenues or their expenditures in order to evade a part of the value added or corporate taxes. Is also includes barter exchange and clandestine employment (de Grazia, 1980, 1984). Clandestine employees get lower gross wages and do not pay wage tax and social security contributions.

Blades' definition of the hidden economy, proposed by a professional statistician, distinguishes between statistical errors and omissions (2) and bias caused by intentional hiding of activities. Blades also notes that a good statistical service using a profound system of checks and balances can trace a part of the hidden output (3). Blades' definition, however, has two weak points. The inclusion of illegal activities (4) can make the international comparability of data difficult (what is illegal in one country can be tolerated in another one), and motivations for the participation in the hidden economy are not fully considered. Avoidance of taxes and other charges is not the sole purpose of hidden activities. At least equally important is the aim of raising personal income (Klatzmann, 1979) through additional work.

The statistical definition of the hidden economy is a definition for developed market economies. Other definitions, which are also possible, may stress differences and similarities of economic systems, cultural and political traditions of countries etc., but are less suited for the measurement of the size of the hidden economy.

1.2. Phenomena similar to the hidden economy

The hidden economy, as defined above, is similar, but not identical to the 'informal economy' or 'tax evasion' in the Western economies, to 'the informal sector' in developing countries or to the 'black economy' in centrally planned economies.

The 'informal' economy includes the productive unpaid work (5) for one's own interest (i.e. household work, do-it-yourself, self-service activities and work in voluntary organizations). Except for a few items (own house construction, rents from owner-occupied dwellings and food production for own use), the output of the unpaid productive work is not included in the value of gross domestic product as defined by the UN System of National Accounts. In some cases, however, it is not easy to distinguish the output of the hidden economy from the output of the productive work for own use (6).

One of the main reasons why activities are concealed is to evade taxes, but the hidden economy and tax evasion are not identical. Some activities are concealed not to avoid taxes,

but to avoid other charges. (E.g. one of the aims of clandestine employment is to save social security and medical
insurance contributions (7)). Some cases of tax evasion have
a marginal impact on the value of gross domestic product.
(Examples: smuggling of goods to avoid customs duties; sales
of land or at a higher price than the declared one to avoid
the sales tax). And, finally, it is impossible to estimate
exactly the tax losses caused by the hidden economy. Additional income gained by tax avoidance is to a large degree
spent on the domestic market, and a part of the evaded taxes
flows back to the tax authorities (Peacock, Shaw, 1982).

The informal sector (8) in developing countries is subsistence activities transferred from rural areas to large
cities. The poor people living in slums are engaged in
productive work for their own support, in barter exchange
among themselves and in occasional work for the market. The
aim of activities in the informal sector is not to avoid
taxes (income taxation is anyhow low in developing countries), but to avoid hunger and poverty.

The main characteristics of the 'black' economy (9) in the
centrally planned economies (10) is its 'illegality' (Gábor,
1979). Almost all private business is illegal under central
planning. But laws can change. Hungary has in recent years
legalized small private business in the framework of the
'second economy' (11). The purpose of the 'black' economy is
to overcome failures of central planning by supplying scarce
goods and services, it is also stimulated by 'hidden' inflation (Brus, Laski, 1985). The black economy exists in various forms in all 'command economies' (Grossman, 1963). It
was common in the German economy during the Nazi era (W.
Eucken, 1948); in the centrally planned economies it exists
because of the 'economics of shortage' (Kornai, 1980).

2. SIZE OF THE HIDDEN ECONOMY

2.1. Variability and quality of estimates of the hidden eco-
nomy

Published rich information on the size of hidden economy can
be divided into two categories: (i) sources unknown, (ii)
sources known. The first one includes quantitative data, for
which the method of estimation, and even sometimes their
origin and author, are not given. The 'pseudo-statistics' on
hidden economy flourish in newspapers. These often exagge-
rated data are frequently quoted and requoted in articles
and reports until they are taken as good estimates. Then
they even appear in otherwise serious studies (12).

Estimates of the size of the hidden economy, for which
methods of estimation and data sources are known, have a
great variation. Their frequency distribution has two peaks:
there is one concentration above 10 percent of the GDP, and
another one around 4-5 percent of the GDP. Higher estimates
seem to be typical for businessmen and for theoretical

economists, lower estimates for professional statisticians (Buttler, 1984) (13).

The differences in the available estimates of the hidden economy depend largely on the estimation method. Of the numerous approaches three will be dealt with in this paper: (i) the monetary approach, (ii) evaluation of official statistics combined with plausibility assessment and (iii) estimates of the industry ·breakdown of the hidden economy. The first approach provides most of the high, spectacular estimates, the other two give insight into the causes of the hidden economy.

Almost all estimates of the hidden economy have one weak point in common: they pay little attention to methodological differences in the valuation of hidden production. This problem will therefore be also touched upon.

2.2. The monetary approaches

The 'simple' monetary approach to the measurement of the hidden economy studies either the ratio between cash and demand deposits (Gutmann, 1979) or the share of high denomination banknotes in the total volume of banknotes in circulation, or the relation between the cash in circulation and total transactions in the economy (Feige, 1979). A more sophisticated version of this approach investigates the relation between changes in the level of taxation and changes in the cash - money ratios (Tanzi, 1982, 1983). The monetary methods assume that transactions in the hidden economy are paid mainly in cash, and seldom by check or by bank transfer. This key assumption was, however, not convincingly proved (14).

The simple monetary methods give in general high estimates of the size of the hidden economy (15) (the world's top value was achieved for India (16)). Most of these results also indicate an explosion of the hidden economy in the seventies: according to Feige, the hidden economy in the United States amounted to 19 percent of GNP in 1976, to almost 27 percent in 1978 and to over 28 percent in 1979; according to Gutmann (1979), these shares were 10 percent in 1976 and over 13 percent in 1979. But there are also contrary results. For example the size of the hidden economy in the United Kingdom was estimated to have declined from 34.3 percent in 1952 to 7.2 percent in 1970 (Dilnot, Morris, 1981).

In Austria, the monetary methods were applied by Mooslechner (1983, 1984). Between 1955 and 1982 the ratio of cash to demand deposits had a slowly decreasing trend. The share of high denomination banknotes in total cash increased from 64 percent (1955/1959) to 86 percent (1975/1979) (but their ratio to demand deposits declined). The ratio of cash to total domestic demand and to the retail and wholesale turnover (both variables are a proxy for the volume of transactions) also decreased steadly. All this would allow the conclusion that in Austria the size of the hidden economy decreased slowly between 1955 and 1982. Mooslechner avoided such hasty reasoning and analysed the monetary data thoroughly. He has found that the ratio of cash to demand deposit was stable between 1955 and 1966, declined rapidly between 1967 and 1977 and increased after 1977. The upward shift in the last period was caused by changes in the level of demand deposits originating in shifts in portfolio patterns. The volume of cash has grown at a rather stable rate over the whole period 1955 to 1982 (17). The role of portfolio patterns in shaping the cash-money ratios was confirmed by the application of Tanzi's method to Austrian data: the tax level was not a significant and reliable explanatory variable for the cash-money ratios (18). Mooslechner's results for Austria do not allow estimation of the size of the hidden economy, but contribute to the growing criticism of the monetary approach (19). The monetary methods say a lot about what people do with their money, but very little about the hidden economy.

2.3. Evaluation of official statistics combined with plausibility assessment

A simple plausibility assessment of the likely size of the hidden economy was made by Blades (1982). He calculated, under the assumption that the size of the hidden economy amounts to 4 percent of GDP, how much an average household of 4 persons in several OECD countries would have to spend for goods and services produced in the hidden economy. This 'hidden' consumer spending was so high that Blades concluded that the 4 percent of GDP was the upper limit of the likely size of the hidden economy.

Broesterhuizen (1985) divided the reporting statistical units in the Netherlands into five groups: public institutions, large, middle sized and small firms (the dividing lines were 100 and 10 employees respectively) and units, for which the volume of output is estimated on the basis of tax statistics. The long experience of Dutch statistics shows that the error in the estimation of the value of output in these groups is different. It is nil in the first group, and increases up to the last one. Broesterhuizen considered several error intervals, and concluded that a size of the hidden economy over 5 per cent of the GDP is not very probable.

Carson (1984) concluded after analysis of the sources and methodology of the United States statistics in 1977, that 3 percent is the limit of the understatement of the US GNP caused by misreporting due to the hidden economy.

A combination of plausibility considerations with official statistics was used by Franz (1984, 1985) in Austria. Franz assumed that large production units cannot hide a large part of the output. His hypothesis was supported by the finding that the per capita net income of the owner of very small firms is lower than the net wage of employees in larger firms of the same branch. This 'income gap' diminishes with increasing size of the firm. Its size was used as a starting point for detailed estimates of the volume of the 'off-book' business. The estimates of the number of 'moonlighters' resulted from evaluation of detailed statistics about the occupational structure and regional concentration of certain professions. Franz concluded that the share of the hidden economy (more exactly undeclared legal production) in Austrian GDP was in 1976 around 3.5 percent. (Output of the hidden economy which was discovered by statistics and accounted in GDP - it amounts to 0.3 percent - is not included in this figure). Shares of the off-books business and moonlighters were roughly equal. The number of moonlighters in 'own occupation' was estimated around 240,000 (10 percent of total number of employed persons); the total number, including other, mainly occasional moonlighters (housewives, students, retired persons) was around 350,000. (Illegal production and concealed income in kind were not estimated).

2.4. Structure of hidden economic activities

Estimates of the size of the hidden economy in terms of GDP percentages say nothing about the composition of its output. But for the understanding of the causes of the hidden economy it is important to know in which industries the hidden economy flourishes and in which it does not exist.

The activity structure of hidden economic activities is known for several countries. In Austria, according to Franz (1984, 1985), off-books business was concentrated in retail trade, restaurants and hotels, and was also important in wood and in food manufacturing, transportation and freelance professions. For example, the estimated ratios of the value added of hidden activities to the official value added (less value added tax) were 17.7 percent in hotels and restaurants, 10.6 percent in construction, 6.9 percent in wood manufacturing, 4.4 percent in food processing, 5.0 percent in transport, 4.9 percent in private services and 4.2 percent in metalworking (A. Franz, 1985). Moonlighting was concentrated in occupations related to construction, transportation and in metal working (in particular in motor vehicle repair).

In Switzerland, (Weck-Hannemann, Frey, 1985) the share of the hidden economy in the output was between 5-10 percent in agriculture, construction, gastronomy, repairs, household services and cleaning, and between 2-5 percent in textiles and clothing, timber, furniture, retail trade, education, culture, leisure, health, and body care. The occupations most frequently represented in the hidden economy were (a share between 10-20 percent) gardeners, masons, painters, plasterers, waiters, cleaning personnel and domestic servants; and also (a share between 5-10 percent) farmers, carpenters, mechanics, solicitors, attorneys, medical and dental assistants.

In the United States, consumers expenditures for the output of the hidden economy were concentrated on home repair and additions, food, child care, domestic service, auto repair, sidewalk vendor goods, flea market goods, lawn and garden services, etc. The first four items had together a share of 80 percent of the hidden purchases (Smith, 1985).

In Spain, the hidden economy is significant in construction, production of textiles, shoes and leather products, in food production, in motor vehicle repair and in domestic services (Portela, Arango, 1983).

In France, clandestine employment and moonlighting are frequent in construction, clothing, small mechanics, industrial design, leather products, book-keeping, travelling salesmen, hair-dressing, agriculture and in seasonal occupations (Klatzmann, 1979; Sauvy, 1984).

In Great Britain, 11 percent of the British labour force meets the criteria for high potential participation in the hidden economy: farmers, construction workers and persons in the clothing trade. Another 40 percent have low but still noteworthy opportunities to enter the unofficial economy. Half of the labour force has almost nil opportunity to engage in the hidden economy (Rose, 1983) (20).

In Germany, the hidden economy was important in construction and car repair (Langfelt, 1983). In the Netherlands, hidden economy was frequent in the following activities: major repair of clothes, carpentry, wall decorating, painting, electrical installations, and repair and maintenance of cars (Renooy, 1984).

In Sweden, apart from the building sector, other sectors specially affected by clandestine employment were child-minding, domestic work, small trading, motor vehicle repairs, hotels and catering and transport. On the other hand, there seems to be practically no clandestine employment in the public sector, in industry or in public utilities (Quoted from de Grazia, 1984).

2.5. Valuation of the output of the hidden economy

Prices of goods and services delivered by the hidden economy are seldom known and must be therefore estimated (imputed). Price imputations are disliked by statisticians, but used in research on the informal economy, most frequently in estimates of the value of household work (21) (Goldsmith-Clermont, 1982, Suviranta, 1980-1982). If the volume of hidden activities is estimated in physical terms, it can be valued by the market prices of similar goods or services (assuming that the qualities of the hidden and marketed output are roughly identical). The substraction of the value of inputs - purchased on the market - gives the imputed value added on the hidden activity. The other method is to value work time in the hidden economy by an imputed wage rate. The imputed wage rate can be equal to the wage rate for a similar paid work, or to the average wage rate in the economy or the opportunity costs.

Different methods give different results. In studies on the hidden economy in Austria, the choice of valuation method was important in estimates of the value of the work of moonlighters and of house-owners in family house construction. The number of hours worked by moonlighters and house-owners was estimated in several surveys. These were valued alternatively by the wage rates paid to moonlighters (which are more or less known) and by the (higher) gross wage costs accounted by construction firms to customers. In 1979, the value of the work of moonlighters in construction of family houses was equal to 6.3 billion AS according to the first and to 9.5 billion AS according to the second valuation method (Neubauer, 1984). Both methods are variants of the 'input' approach. For National Accounts, the CSO (i.e. OeSZA - Austrian Central Statistical Office) estimates the value of the work of the house-owners (which implicitly includes also the work of the moonlighters), indirectly by the 'output' approach (OeSZA, 1982). The average price of a square meter in a dwelling in an apartment house is used for the valuation of finished family houses. This allows estimates of the value of work of both house-owners and moonlighters (which, however, are lower than those obtained by the 'input' method). In this specific case the difference of the results of the 'input' and 'output' approaches can be explained by two reasons. The price of a square meter in an apartment house is probably too low to be imputed to self-built family houses the quality of which is higher. The CSO data do not include most house repairs and improvements, which were partly included in the surveys on own-work and moonlighting in construction.

3. CAUSES OF THE HIDDEN ECONOMY

3.1. Preconditions for the existence of the hidden economy

The similarity of the 'plausible' estimates of the hidden economy, and in particular the similarity of the estimates of its industry and occupational structure in several countries, are a good guide for the understanding of the cause of the hidden activities.

The main reason to participate in hidden economic activities is the desire of people to increase real income (22). To increase income, people con engage in both legal and illegal activities in the hidden economy. In the following paragraphs, only the legal activities in the hidden economy (i.e. undeclared legal production) will be discussed (23).

The level of activities in the 'hidden economy' depends, like the level of other 'official' activities, on demand for their output. Demand for both is a function of disposable household income, of income distribution, and, also, of price differences between identical goods and services offered both by the official and hidden economies. The possibility to engage in hidden activities is, however, limited by their feasibility.

The feasibility of 'off-books' business depends on institutional constraints. The most important constraint is the size of the firm. Small firms and firms providing personal services can more easily hide a larger share of output than large firms. Other constraints can be administrative procedures or checking practices used by the tax authorities.

The feasibility of moonlighting depends on (i) technical simplicity and (ii) relative productivity. Moonlighters can carry out only technically simple operations. A brief look at any classification of economic activities (e.g. at the 1968 UN International Standard Industrial Classification) reveals, that most goods and services produced in a modern economy cannot be made by moonlighters. Modern production technology is complicated and requires expensive equipment. The economic profitability of a technically feasible operation depends on the relative productivity of the moonlighter, which must not be significantly lower than productivity of an employee of a firm selling the same good or service in the official economy.

Once these conditions are fulfilled, taxes, other (mainly social security) charges, enterprise overhead costs, distribution cost (i.e. trade and transportation margins) and profits decide the consumer's choice between the official and the hidden economy. In off-books business, tax evasion (i.e. evasion of the commodity or value added tax and lowering of taxed profits) is the sole source of hidden income. This is usually shared between the firm and the customer. Decisions on moonlighting are decided not only by taxes and social security charges, but also by overhead and distribution costs and by enterprise profits. Moonlighters save most of these costs. Their net wages are therefore lower than the gross wage costs accounted by the firms. (And can even be slightly higher then the net wages in their main occupations). Their productivity, however, must be not much lower than the productivity of a firm; only a small productivity difference allows them to keep the price of the hidden output below the market price of a similar good or service.

Most studies on the hidden economy overplay the role of taxes. True, tax evasion is the most important motivation to hide economic activities. But taxes can be evaded in the hidden economy only if the institutional and technological conditions are fulfilled. This can be demonstrated by two examples.

In Austria a person buying a personal motor car has to pay the value added tax, the rate of which is 32 percent. The tax rate on gasoline is around 100 percent. Car service and repair is subject to 20 percent valued added tax. But moonlighters are not able to produce a cheap new car. It is not possible to evade the value added tax by 'off-books' purchase, because the car can be registered only if the bill is presented. No gasoline station can sell cheap 'tax-free' gasoline. But car service and repair, having the lowest value added tax rate, are often executed 'off-books' or by moonlighters. Many repair firms are small. Most service and repair work is simple, and the productivity of moonlighters is not much lower than that of the employees of car service firms.

Surveys on the hidden and informal economy in the construction of family houses in Austria (Neubauer, 1984) have shown that moonlighters and houseowners frequently work on the basement and on the walls (with a share over 60 percent), but are less likely to construct the roof or to install heating, water, sewage and electricity systems (share are between 13 to 26 percent). The role of technical simplicity is obvious.

The institutional and technological constraints cause the hidden economy to be limited to a relatively narrow segment of the economy. In this segment, hidden activities give strong and unfair competition to firms producing for the official market. Increases in taxation cannot change much the basic preconditions of the existence of the hidden economy. It can expand only within a narrow space, constrained by technological and institutional circumstances. Entry into the hidden economy is not free for every occupation or every economic activity.

3.2. Specific causes of the hidden economy

Hidden activities can have also industry-specific causes. A good example is family house construction in rural areas. In Austria many future houseowners do not have enough money (24) to buy a turn-key house. Conditions for obtaining mortages (Bausparkredit) were not bad in the past, but deteriorated slightly in the inflationary seventies. The housing needs· of less rich people in the countryside are solved by a mix of the official and of the hidden economy. Application for building permits are 'official', they are signed by a firm; the name of the firm has also to be visible on the construction site. Small local construction firms know well that the housebuilders are short of money.
They help them to obtain building permits, and they have in any case a share in the project. Simple construction operations are executed by housebuilders, their relatives, neighbours and moonlighters, i.e. in a mix of informal and hidden activities. Moonlighters are sometimes employees of the construction firm, working 'privately' over the weekend. More complicated operations are done by the firm. At the end the housebuilders get (often after many years) (25) houses of good quality for a price they can afford to pay; construction firms make business, their employees (and other moolighters) have additional income. Even public authorities may gain. Families without adequate housing in towns are provided subsidized public housing. Its costs to public authorities may be higher then the tax losses due to the mixed 'official-hidden' family house construction in the countryside (26).
'Hidden' hairdressing is carried out by women, (employed or not) who visit customers at home. The advantages are lower prices and time saving for the customer and tax-free income for the 'moonlighter'. These 'moonlighters', however, have special skills, for which they were trained as apprentices. This kind of moonlighting can exist only if hairdressing firms train a surplus of skilled personnel.
Another cause can be better working conditions. Moonlighters feel independent and decide freely the disposition of their time. Customers may prefer personal contact and the direct cooperation with moonlighters to impersonal relations with firms. Women working at home have flexible working hours, more time to take care of the house and for the children and avoid time losses due to commuting.
The hidden economy can be also stimulated by unemployment.

44

Austria, having a relatively low unemployment rate, is not a good place for the assessment of the impact of the labour market situation on the hidden economy. Moreover, unemployment in Austria is concentrated in a few regions. Moonlighting can hardly flourish in places hit by recession, where the demand is generally weak.

Large number of foreign workers can also be a cause of the hidden economy (de Grazia, 1980). If they lose jobs and, consequently, working permits, or if they are smuggled illegally into the country, they can work only clandestinely. But the participation of foreigners in the hidden economy can also have structural reasons. Construction firms, strongly hit by the recession, employ many foreigners. In Austria clandestine work by foreigners is under normal conditions not significant. But at the height of the political crisis in Poland, many Polish citizens (who at that time did not need an entry visa), came to Austria and watched what happened in their country. To live, some of them worked clandestinely. These not-yet refugees probably did not cause a significant increase in the size of the hidden economy in Austria, but for a short time reduced work opportunities of other moonlighters.

Cheap foreign labour force can also indirectly stimulate clandestine employment. New industrial countries have a competitive advantage in cheap, labour intensive textile, clothing, shoe or leather products. Industrial countries respond to their competition by protectionistic measures, industry restructuring and, sometimes also, by clandestine employment (27).

4. CONSEQUENCES OF THE HIDDEN ECONOMY

The hidden economy influences tax revenues, revenues of the social security and health insurance systems, level of economic welfare and structure of output.

4.1. Public revenue losses

A shift of an activity from the official into the hidden economy instantly reduces public revenues. Off-books business is accompanied by an evasion of the commodity, turnover or value added tax and reduces the taxable profit of the firm. Moonlighting is an evasion of value added tax and of personal income tax. Taxes are also lost indirectly: firms selling on the official market pay corporate taxes which have high marginal rates. Should moonlighters pay tax (28) on the income they earned clandestinely, their marginal tax rates would be lower.

Tax evasion and 'hidden' increases in the level of economic activities caused by the hidden economy raise the disposable income of the population (29). A smaller part of this increase is probably saved, a larger part spent on goods and services, partly abroad, partly in the country. Additional purchases on the domestic market reduce tax losses caused by the hidden economy. (Actual tax revenues from purchases on the official market include also taxes on purchases for which money earned in the hidden economy was spent).

In Austria, the volume of the value added on the hidden economy in 1982 (corresponding to the 3.5 percent share estimated by Franz for 1976), was probably around 40 billion AS. Lehner (1984) estimated the instant hypothetical gross loss in public revenues to be equal roughly to 18 billion AS. This additional disposable income of the population was, however, largely spent on goods and services in Austria. This spending gave additional tax revenue of roughly 5 billion AS, thus reducing the tax loss to about 13 billion AS.

The hidden and official economies are not separated by an iron curtain. The tax effects of the hidden economy can therefore be (albeit a bit cynically) also interpreted in a Keynesian framework. The gross tax loss could be labeled as an involuntary 'expenditure' by the government. It stimulates the economy, raises welfare and brings tax revenues, which partly repay the 'stimulating expenditure'.

Additional income from the hidden economy is not equally distributed. Most moonlighters (not only workers, but also housewives, pensioners, students, foreigners) have low incomes, and most firms which engage in the off-books business are small. But it has not yet been shown empirically how far the hidden economy reduces income inequalities.

4.2. Other consequences

The few positive welfare effects of the hidden economy are outweighed by indisputable negative effects. Clandestine workers and moonlighters are not protected by social and health insurance. Evening work and over weekends does not improve their health. In Austria, the number of total hours worked by moonlighters in family house construction was estimated to be at about 40 million hours a year (Franz, 1984; Neubauer, 1984). Were the moonlighters employees of construction firms only, this would mean that they work on average an additional 50 days a year. But they come from other professions too, and the number of additional working days per capita during a year is probably lower than fifty (Skolka, Stermann, 1984). Hours worked by moonlighters have been estimated in other countries to be roughly at the same level, ranging between 9 and 18 hours, in Italy around 21 hours per week (de Grazia, 1980). (This revealed willingness to work longer is overlooked in the current discussion about the reduction of the duration of the working week).

The 'hidden economy' has strong reallocative effects. It reduces the demand for goods and services sold on the 'official' market by firms from branches with strong moonlighting or 'off-books' business. Additional disposable income from activities in the hidden economy creates additional household expenditure. Its composition differs from the composition of the 'official' demand lost due to the hidden activities. The losers due to the reallocation are firms from the branches where the hidden economy is concentrated. The winners are distributed over the whole economy in proportions which correspond to income elasticities of demand of those earning income in the hidden economy.

The shifts in the structure of marketed output due to the hidden economy cause also a reallocation of inputs and of production factors, and, in particular, of employment (30).

5. THE HIDDEN ECONOMY AND ECONOMIC POLICY

Discussion about the hidden economy was initiated years ago by the statement that statistical 'illusions' about economic growth, inflation and unemployment (due to the hidden economy) caused mistaken economic policies in the United States (Gutmann, 1979). After five years it is time to look again at these accusations. In 1984 the US statistics reported high economic growth, low inflation and declining unemployment. Are these data again statistical illusions? Not at all. The good shape of the US economy in 1984 was an indisputable fact. The illusion was the myth, created in 1979 with huge publicity, that the hidden economy is large and growing.

Nevertheless hidden economy amounting to about 5 percent of gross domestic product cannot be totally ignored. In Austria the 'Social Partners' established in 1984 a Working Group, the task of which is to study the hidden economy, its size, the grounds for its existence and tendencies in its development. The Group has to prepare recommendations for economic policy. Similar measures were taken in 1980 in France (31), in 1981 in the United Kingdom (32) and in Portugal (33), and soon after in the Netherlands (34).

Economic policy could undertake both short and long-term measures against hidden economy. A conventional short-term recommendation is more control and supervision. But most people have some sympathies for the hidden economy (35) and would probably not cooperate in its suppression (36). In particular the chances for success in combating moonlighting, in which a large number of people marginally participate (37), are not bright. Other proposals recommend the legalization (38) of some forms of moonlighting (which are illegal from the point of view of laws regulating entrepreneurship). Help could also bring simplification of income tax reports and a lump-sum taxation of small firms.

The aim of the long-term measures should be to weaken the preconditions for the hidden economy. One way could be changes in taxation. The contemporary tax systems in industrial countries levy a large share of tax revenues and all social security charges on personal income. Taxes and charges weigh more heavily on labour intensive activities, which have low productivity, use simple technology, are executed by small firms and thus belong to the segment of the economy exposed to hidden activities. Certain proposals for changes in taxation (Frank, 1983) and in collection of social security contribution (39) which would shift the tax burden away from personal income, were published recently. Their main aim is not suppression of the hidden economy, but once realized, they could have such an effect too (40).

Technological innovations (41) could also help. Industries in rich countries, which have to compete with labour intensive products from new industrial countries, are advised to turn to new products and to use new technologies. Competition by moonlighters has features similar to the competition from the developing countries. Wherever possible, modern technology should be the response to the hidden economy.

Should the improvement in economic situation of industrial countries, which began in 1983, continue for a few years, interest in the hidden economy would most likely decline. The share in GDP of the hidden economy was probably not smaller in the fifties and sixties than at present - at least there is no solid proof that the hidden economy increased significantly in the seventies (42). In the past, business did not mind if moonlighters took care of minor and less profitable operations in an overheated economic climate, and governments had balanced budgets. In the recession, business became more sensitive to the unfair competition of the hidden economy, and governments tried to close any loophole through which they were losing revenues.

NOTES

(*) The paper is based mainly on the research project (sponsored by the 'Jubiläumsfonds' of the National Bank of Austria) on the 'parallel' economy in Austria (Skolka, 1984). Empirical investigations carried out in other countries are also considered.

(1) Gutmann (1979) said that in the United States: (1) the actual economy is larger than the measured economy. (2) The growth rate of the actual economy is greater than that of the measured economy. (3) The official unemployment rate is clearly overstated. (4) Savings ratios, consumption ratios, saving functions and consumption functions are generally biased. These statistical 'illusions' result in 'mistaken policies'. Gutmann repeated his view in October 1983 at the Bielefeld Conference in Germany (Gutmann, 1985).

(2) A part of the Italian 'economia sommersa' is the consequence of the weakness of public administration. A good example is inaccuracies of Italian data about construction of family houses. It is ridiculous to assume that a house can be hidden. Many family houses in Italy are built without building permits, once finished, used without liveability permits and not recorded in official statistics (Del Boca, Forte, 1982). This error (or omission) should not be counted as the hidden economy.

(3) Two examples: In the United States in 1976 the undeclared legal production amounted to 2.2 percent GDP, out of which 1.5 percent was included in the national accounts. Illegal production amounted to further 1.5

percent and employee theft to 0.5 percent of the GDP. The hidden economy in the United States may have been about 4.2 percent of GDP, of which already 1.4 percent was included in the 'measured' GDP, which therefore understates 'total' GDP by less than 3 percent. (Blades, 1982). The undeclared legal production in Austria amounted in 1976 to 27.2 billion AS, but 2.2 billion AS (in the construction of family houses) were included in the national accounts (Franz, 1984).

(4) See also K. Macafee (1980): "The inclusion of crime within the national accounts definition of the hidden economy is problematical and ... estimates of value arising from crime should await better data". Estimates of crime in the United States were published by Simon, Witte (1982). Blades (1985) inserted them into a national accounting framework. In May 1984, the OECD Meeting of National Accounts Experts discussed the inclusion of certain illegal activities in national accounts (Quirino, 1984).

(5) The productive unpaid work differs from leisure by the criterion of the 'third person', proposed by Reid (1934): "If an activity is of such character that it might be delegated to a paid worker, then that activity shall be deemed productive". (Quoted from Goldschmidt-Clermont, 1982). See also Hawrylyshyn (1979).

(6) Neubauer (1984) evaluated several surveys on construction of family houses in Austria. The share of the work of the house-owners and moonlighters in the value added in family house construction was between 30-40 percent. Of this share, roughly two fifths were contributed by house owners and three fifths by moonlighters. Their exact separation was not possible.

(7) This is one the causes why married women prevail in the clandestine labour force. Most of them can use the health insurance of their husbands.

(8) Sethuraman (1981) defines the informal sector as follows: "It consists of small-scale units engaged in the production and distribution of goods and services with the primary objective of generating employment and incomes to their participants notwithstanding the constraints of capital, both physical and human, and know-how". In the early stages of industrialization the situation in the present rich countries was similar: ... "the surplus population of England, which keeps body and soul together by begging, stealing, street-sweeping, collecting manure, pushing hand carts, driving donkeys, peddling or performing occasional jobs. In every great town a multitude of such people may be found. It is astonishing in what devices this 'surplus population' takes refuge" (Engels, 1920).

(9) Katsenelinboigen (1978) distinguished among the semi-legal 'gray' economy and the illegal 'brown' and 'black' economies in the USSR. (A good example of colourfulness of terminology).

(10) There is rich literature on this topic. See e.g. Duchéne (1981), Grossman (1977), Kemény (1982), Dallago

(1984), Brus, Laski (1985) and many other studies. See also the contributions to the Trento Conference.

(11) See Gabor (1982), Kertesi, Sziraczki (1984), Cichy (1984) and Szita (1984).

(12) Two examples of fancy data were given for Belgium by Pestieu (1985): "I have been discussing figures which are based on well-defined methods. Besides these, there are numbers which are sometimes quoted under alleged scientific sponsorship - the name of a respectable organization, a scientific journal reference - whereas the slightest scrutiny shows they lack any foundation. Needless to say these numbers tend to be large and striking. In that respect, I would like to cite as examples of what surely happens in other countries two numbers which are quoted more often than those reported above as measuring the size of the Belgium hidden economy: 18 percent of the GNP and 7 percent of the total working force (300,000 unrecorded full-time jobs). Tracing the source of these two figures is quite typical of the sort of interplay in which the media, international organizations and academics are involved. In an excellent survey published in French and in English, Frey and Pommerehne (1981, 1982) quote the percentage 18.9 percent as measuring the size of the Belgian underground economy in 1970. They attribute it to Frank (1977) who was just estimating the size of personal income tax evasion. As this survey has been widely diffused, the quite high number of 18,9 percent is often cited. The second example is still more astonishing. In mid-August 1983, a large number of European newspapers echoed a press release from the ILO yielding allegedly new estimates of the irregular labor force. The figure quoted for Belgium was 300,000 jobs; that is, 7 percent of the working population. (See, e.g. Le Soir 18, 1983). Where does that figure come from? Does it result from a new study lead by the ILO as implied by the media? Not at all. In fact, this figure can be found in an earlier book by De Grazia (1983) who cites it quite incidentally and has found it in a Belgian newspaper (La Libre Belgique of 12, 1979). Going back to this issue, one just finds that this figure is given by a minister in an interview and does not come from any published source. Ironically, some people who remembered that 1979 interview were surprised by the relative stability of the Belgian irregular labor force over the last four years". In Austria in 1982 and 1983 several newspapers referred to an '1982 OECD study' with an 'OECD estimate' of the size of the hidden economy in Austria of 8.6 percent of GDP. Such an OECD study and such an OECD estimate do not exist at all, but this invented 'OECD figure' found its way even to the Austrian parliament.

(13) "Die bisher vorliegenden Schätzergebnisse sind äusserst kontrovers. Die höchsten Angaben stammen in der Regel von Wirtschaftspraktikern. Die Wissenschaft liefert durchwegs hohe, jedoch auch widersprüchliche Resultate.

Die Vertreter der amtlichen Statistik schätzen demgegenüber die Schattenwirtschaft in allen OECD-Ländern sowohl vom Niveau als auch von der Expansion her als nicht sehr bedeutend. Die Ansicht scheint berechtigt, dass die Schattenwirtschaft gegenwärtig für grösser gehalten wird, als sie tatsächlich ist. Hohe Schätzwerte können auch die Folge eines gesteigerten Problembewusstseins und einer - unzulässigen - Verallgemeinerung spektakulären Einzelfälle sein". (Buttler, 1984).

(14) One empirical survey for the United States casts doubts on the validity of this assumption: "In our study it appears that the use of check or cash for payment is determined pretty much by the same factors that determine their respective use in formal economy transactions, namely the size of the transaction and the confidence the vendor has that the check is good". (Smith, 1985).

(15) Buttler (1984) summarized published results of the application of the monetary approach in several countries. The size of the hidden economy, in terms of GDP percentages, looks as follows: United States: 3.4 - 33.0; Australia: 10.0; Canada: 2.5-21.8; Italy: 9.6-30.1; Spain: 22.9; Sweden: 6.9-17.2; Norway: 6.4-16.0; United Kingdom: 7.2-16.2; Germany: 2.0-27.0.

(16) The ratio of the hidden economy to the official GNP in India was estimated with the monetary method to have increased within eleven years only (i.e. between 1967/8 and 1978/9) from 9.5 to 48.8 percent (Gupta, Gupta, 1981).

(17) The findings for Austria can be compared with those for the United Kingdom: "The Bank of England consider that the recent increases in the circulation of higher denomination notes are consistent with the public's tendency to economise on the number of notes they carry. The number of notes in circulation varies inversely with the average denomination. Concrete instances of the increasing use of notes of higher denomination in quite open transactions are the agreements between employers and trade unions to include £10 notes in wage packets. Even so the circulation of higher denomination notes would have needed to have risen faster than it did for the average denomination to have kept pace with inflation. The problems surrounding the interpretation of movements in the amount and type of cash in circulation suggest that this cannot be a reliable method of measuring the hidden economy". (Macafee, 1980).

(18) The regression coefficient of the tax variable was significant only for C/M1. The difference between equations including and equations not including the tax explanatory variable were marginal in the case of C/M2 and C/M3, the regression coefficients of the tax variable were not significant. The regression coefficients of the tax variable were 1.108 for C/M1 (t=5.82), 0.385 for C/M2 (t=1.74) and -0.507 for C/M3 (t=1.81). the shift from positive to negative values supports the hypothesis that portfolio changes influence the cash-

money ratios more than taxes, which are supposed to provoke the hidden economy (Moonslechner, 1984).

(19) Doubts about simple monetary methods were expressed by Tanzi (1982). Criticism can be also found in other articles, e.g. by Smith (1981) or Cassel (1982). Denison (1982) could not find changes in US labour supply which would be compatible with Feige's estimates of the expansion of the hidden economy, McDonald (1984) has also found no impact of the hidden economy on the employment data.

(20) Similar information can be found in Dilnot, Morris (1981).

(21) See recent Austrian estimates of the value of the use of private cars by Puwein (1984).

(22) See also Klatzmann (1979): "La principale raison d'être du travail noir est d'ordre économique: l'un des partenaires améliore ses ressources, l'autre réduit ses dépenses. Deux causes économiques jouent un role prépondérant: l'insuffisance de la rémuneration du travail; le poids des charges fiscales et sociales". This was, inter alia, confirmed by a survey carried out by the University of Turin in 1978. Workers' principal reasons for moonlighting were, first and foremost, the need for extra income; secondly, the desire for work allowing fuller use or improvement of their professional qualifications; finally, the desire for independence in their work (Carcano, 1978; quoted by de Grazia, 1980).

(23) The discussion of the conditions for the existence of the hidden economy follows similar lines to the discussion of the conditions for the existence of the informal economy by Skolka (1976).

(24) The survey of the building industry have shown that the share of own work and work of moonlighters in the construction of family houses in Austria is lower in the western part of the country with higher per capita income than in the eastern part with lower per capita income (Neubauer, 1984).

(25) 40 percent of family houses built in Austria get the liveability permit later than four years after the issue of the construction permit. (Neubauer, 1984).

(26) See also the paper by Jessen et al. presented at the 1984 Trento Conference. In rural areas around Oldenburg in northern Germany "hardly any of the shipyard workers got a house of his own without contributing his own work and substantially mobilising all resources; holidays, shift work and overtime are often adjusted to the demands made by the informal work as to time and money". "This form of illicit work is a traditional and integral part of household production. Without possibilities of this kind many larger projects of informal work would never be started".

(27) In Italy, clandestine employment was called "an evil acting as a brake on the reconversion of industry that is indispensable if Italy is to have more in common with Europe than with south-east Asia". (Cacace, 1979,

quoted by de Grazia, 1980). A similar view was voiced
in France by Amselle (1981): "Le Tiers Monde jusqu'au
coeur de l'Europe".

(28) This is not a fantasy. The author was informed that at
least in one district of Austria. "Finanzamter" (the
Internal Revenue Service) know some moonlighters and
ask them to pay income taxes.

(29) The argument follows that of Peacock, Shaw (1982).

(30) "Die wachsende Schattenwirtschaft könnte Arbeitsplätze
in der übrigen Wirtschaft vernichten, die Arbeitslosig-
keit vergrössern und auf die Löhne drücken, anderer-
seits weckt die Schattenwirtschaft die zusätzliche
Nachfrage, lässt neue Märkte entstehen und fördert
generell die Wachstumsdynamik der Wirtschaft. Die be-
liebte Hochrechnung des Umfangs der Schattenwirtschaft
auf verlorengehende und folglich potentiell verfügbare
Arbeitsplätze ist jedenfalls unzulässig" (Cassel, Caspers, 1984).

(31) See Stoleru (1980) and Fédération Nationale du Bàti-
ment (1979).

(32) Two reports submitted to the British Parliament in 1981
included a special section on the "black economy", with
particular reference to moonlighting and tax evasion
resulting from it (quoted from de Grazia, 1984).

(33) In Portugal in May 1981 the Government set up a working party to look into the problems posed by home work
(quoted from de Grazia, 1984).

(34) In the Netherlands, an interministerial working party
has recently been appointed to prepare new measures for
combating clandestine employment (quoted from de Grazia, 1984).

(35) Isachsen, Strøm (1985) quote surveys on the hidden
labour market in Norway. To the question "Do you think
people in general accept that income from moonlighting
is not reported? "76 percent in 1980 and 80 percent in
1983 answered "yes". A similar question posed in Austria in a poll organized by the "Dr. Fessel + GfK
Institut got around sixty percent positive anwers.

(36) Klatzmann (1979) reports about the outcome of such
measures in France in 1977: "au cours d'opérations
"coups de poing", 11.000 vérifications avaient été
effectuées par la gendarmerie et les services du travail dans 41 departements. Bilan: 644 poursuites et ...
11 condamnations".

(37) The total number of economically active people in
Austria is at present over 3,200,000, the total number
of people engaged in moonlighting was estimated in two
independent studies to be 350,000 and 470,000 persons,
respectively.

(38) The French documents (Stoleru, 1980) include such
proposals. A similar recommendation can be found in
Buttler (1984), and, also, in Archambault and Greffe
(1984), in the "Présentation" of a collection of essays.

(39) The Austrian minister of social affairs Dallinger
recently proposed to levy social security charges not

only on personal income, but also on the value added of enterprises.

(40) Loebel (1976) proposed replacing the wage and corporate taxes by an aggregate sale tax: "It should be of the utmost importance to make it clear that it is the consumer who pays for all the bills of the nation". Geldens (1984) recommended: "It would be wise to stop imposing income taxes on Europeans and Americans who receive only average incomes. Income taxes should probably start only at three times average income. The tax revenue lost should be replaced by taxing non-regenerable raw materials (e.g. fossil fuels, iron ore, bauxite, certain types of rare timber), and later by increasing Vat. The advantages of such a system are obvious, but implications are mindboggling. The advantages would be a refocusing of technology on reducing raw material and energy content rather than labour content. Potatoes rather than petrochemicals could become a raw material of semi-synthetic fibres. Tax avoidance and the administration of taxes would be significantly reduced, individual incentives would be enhanced (the incremental effort to work would not be taxed so disproportionately), personal after-tax income would increase by 25 percent to 50 percent, but inflation should increase by less". Huber (1984) writes: "Exactly the last bearable tax psychologically, the tax on personal income, is still the cornerstone of public finance. ... We are living in a time in which machines produce more and manpower relatively less and in which only the minority of people belong to the "active" population, who work ever shorter working hours during an ever shorter working life. Under these conditions a well - functioning system of redistribution can no longer be based on personal income from labour, at least not in the first place".

(41) The construction of most family houses in the United States is the quick assembling of prefabricated parts. It is highly productive, and moonlighters have little chance to be competitive. Their opportunities are in house repairs and additions. Use of the American technology of family house construction in Europe could reduce the hidden economy and own-work in family house construction.

(42) An interesting comment was made at the October 1983 Bielefeld conference by Contini: "The average size of the establishments where production takes place (measured by the number of employees) is rapidly falling ... smaller size of establishments and firms seems to have become preferable ..." Such development could enlarge the scope for the hidden economy. (Contini, "A Macro-Economic Framework for the Irregular Economy").

REFERENCES

AMSELLE, J.-L., 'Economie souterraine, économie sans mystère, (part 1)', Futuribles 2000, no. 40, January 1981, pp. 55-62.

ARCHAMBAULT, E., GREFFE, X. (eds), Les économies non officielles, Editions La Découverte, Paris 1984.

BLADES, D.W., 'The Hidden Economy', OECD Economic Outlook, Occasional Studies, no. 2, 1982, pp. 28-45.

BLADES, D.W., 'Crimes: What Should Be Recorded in the National Accounts, and What Difference Would it Make?', in Gaertner, W., Wenig, A. (eds), The Economics of the Shadow Economy, Springer, Heidelberg 1985, pp. 45-58.

BOCA DEL, D., FORTE, F., 'Recent Empirical Survey and Theoretical Interpretation of the Parallel Economy in Italy', in Tanzi V. (ed) The Underground Economy in the United States and Abroad, Lexington Books, Lexington 1982, pp. 184-198.

BROESTERHUIZEN, G.A.A.M., 'The Unobserved Economy and the National Accounts in the Netherlands: A Sensitivity Analysis', in Gaertner, W., Wenig., A. (eds) The Economics of the Shadow Economy, Springer, Heidelberg 1985, pp. 105-126.

BRUS, W., LASKI, K., 'Repressed Inflation and Second Economy Under Central Planning', in Gaertner, W., Wenig, A. (eds), The Economics of the Shadow Economy, Springer, Heidelberg 1985, pp. 377-391.

BUTTLER, G., Schattenwirtschaft - Grenzen der Erfassbarkeit, Deutscher Instituts-Verlag, Koln 1984.

CACACE, N., 'Ma attenti a Terzo Mondo', L'Espresso, 29 July 1979, p. 95.

CARCANO, M., 'Doppio lavoro: come e perché', Conquiste del Lavoro, 18-25 December 1978.

CARSON, C.S., 'The Underground Economy: An Introduction', Survey of Current Business, Part I: No. 5, 1984, pp. 21-37; Part. II: no. 7, 1984, pp. 106-117.

CASSEL, D., 'Schattenwirtschaft - eine Wachstumsbranche?', List-Forum, no. 6, 1982, pp. 343-363.

CASSEL, D., CASPERS, A., 'Was ist die Schattenwirtschaft', Wirtschaftswissenschaftliches Studium, no. 1, 1984.

CICHY, E.U., Parallelwirtschaft und Wirtschaftsreform: Das unorthodoxe Experiment der Ungarischen Volksrepublik, Universitat Duisburg, 1984.

CONTINI, B., A Macro-Economic Framework for the Irregular Economy, Conference on the Shadow Economy, University of Bielefeld, 1983.

DALLAGO, B., The Underground Economy in the West and East: A Comparative Approach, Seminar on the Unofficial Economy, University of Trento, 1984.

DENISON, E.F., 'Is US Growth Understated Because of the Underground Economy? Employment Ratios Suggest Not', The Review of Income and Wealth, no. 1, 1982, pp. 1-16.

DILNOT, A., MORRIS, C.N., 'What Do We Know about the Black Economy?', Fiscal Studies, no. 1, 1981, pp. 58-73.

DUCHÉNE, G., 'L'analyse de la seconde économie', Travail et monnaie en systéme socialist, Economica, Paris 1981.

ENGELS, F., Conditions of the Working Class in England in 1844, London 1920.

EUCKEN, W., 'On the Theory of Centrally Administered Economy: An Analysis of the German Experiment', Economica, no. 58 and 59, 1948; reprinted in Bornstein, M. (ed), Comparative Economic Systems; Models and Cases, R.D. Irwin, Homewood 1965, pp. 157-195.

FEDERATION NATIONALE DU BATIMENT, Rapport sur les moyens à mettre en oevre pour lutter contre le travail clandestin, Fevrier, Paris 1979.

FEIGE, E.L., 'How Big is the Irregular Economy?', Challenge, Nov.-Dec. 1979, pp. 5-13.

FRANK, M., La fraude fiscale en Belgique, Institut de Sociologie, Bruxelles 1977.

FRANK, M., 'Towards the Adoption of a Progressive Personal Expenditure Tax? A General Outlook', in Public Finance, no. 2, 1983, pp. 185-201.

FRANZ, A., 'Schätzungen der hidden economy in Oesterreich auf der Basis offizieller Statistiken', in Skolka, J. (ed) Die andere Wirtschaft: Schwarzarbeit und Do-it-yourself in Oesterreich, Signum, Vienna 1984, pp. 83-99.

FRANZ, A., 'Quantifizierung der Schattenwirtschaft und amtliche Statistik', Quartalshefte der Girozentrale, no. 4, 1984, no. 1, 1985.

GÁBOR, I.R., 'The Second (Secondary) Economy', Acta Economica, no. 3-4, 1979, pp. 291-311.

GÁBOR, I.R., The Major Domains of the Second Economy in Hungary, Manuscript, July, 1982.

GAERTNER, W., WENIG, A., (eds), The Economics of the Shadow Economy, Springer, Heidelberg 1985.

GELDENS, H., 'Towards Fuller Employment: We Have Been Here Before', The Economist, 28 July 1984, pp. 17-20.

GOLDSCHMIDT-CLERMONT, L., Unpaid Work in the Household, International Labour Office, Geneva 1982.

GRAZIA DE, R., 'Clandestine Employment: A Problem of our Times', International Labour Review, no. 5, 1980, pp. 549-563.

GRAZIA DE, R., Clandestine Employment: The Situation in the Industrialized Market Economy Countries, International Labour Office, Geneva 1984.

GROSSMAN, G., 'Notes for a Theory of the Command Economy', Soviet Studies, no. 2, 1963, pp. 101-123; reprinted in Bornstein, M. (ed), Comparative Economic Systems: Models and Cases, R.D. Irwin, Homewood 1965, pp. 135-156.

GROSMANN, G., 'The Second Economy of the USSR', Problems of Communism, Sept.-Oct. 1977, pp. 25-40.

GUTMANN, P.M., 'Statistical Illusions, Mistaken Policies', Challenge, Nov.-Dec. 1979, pp. 14-17.

GUTMANN, P.M., 'The Subterranean Economy, Redux', in Gaertner, W., Wenig, A. (eds), The Economics of the Shadow Economy, Springer, Heidelberg 1985, pp. 2-18.

GUPTA, P., GUPTA, S., Estimates of the Unreported Economy in India, Kiel Working Papers, no. 130, Kiel Institute of World Economics, Kiel 1981.

HAWRYLYSHYN, A., 'Towards a Definition of Non-Market Activities', The Review of Income and Wealth, no. 1, 1979, pp.

79-96.

HUBER, H., 'Public Help and Self Help', Futures, no. 2, 1984, pp. 139-147.

ISACHSEN, A., STRØM, S., 'The Size and the Growth of the Hidden Economy in Norway', The Review of Income and Wealth, no. 1, 1985, pp. 21-38.

JESSEN, J., SIEBEL, W., SIEBEL-REBELL, C., WALTHER, U.-J., WEYRATHER, I., The Informal Work of Industrial Workers, Seminar on The Unofficial Economy, University of Trento, 1984.

KATSENELINBOIGEN, A., Soviet Economic Planning, Sharpe, White Plains 1978.

KEMÉNY, I., 'The Unregistered Economy in Hungary', Soviet Studies, no. 3, 1982, pp. 349-366.

KERTESI, G., SZIRACZKI, G., 'The Second Economy and Workers Behavior on the Labour Market in Hungary', Economia & Lavoro, no. 1, 1984, pp. 119-127.

KLATZMANN, J., 'Le travail noir', Futuribles 2000, no. 26, 1979, pp. 43-57.

KORNAI, J., Economics of Shortage, North Holland, Amsterdam-New York 1980.

LANGFELDT, E., Die Schattenwirtschaft in der Bundesrepublik Deutschland, J.C.B. Mohr, Tübingen 1983.

LEHNER, G., 'Schattenwirtschaft und der öffentliche Sektor', in Skolka, J. (ed), Die andere Wirtschaft: Schwarzarbeit und Do-it-yourself in Oesterreich, Signum, Vienna 1984, pp. 121-129.

LEONTIEF, W., 'Theoretical Assumptions and Nonobserved Facts', The American Economic Review, March 1971, pp. 1-7.

LOEBL, E., Humanomics, Random House, New York 1976.

MACAFEE, K., 'A Glimpse of the Hidden Economy in the National Accounts', CSO Economic Trends, no. 316, Feb. 1980, pp. 81-87.

McDONALD, R.J., 'The Underground Economy and BLS Statistical Data', Monthly Labor Review, January 1984, pp. 4-18.

MOOSLECHNER, P., 'Der monetare Ansatz zur parallelen Wirtschaft', Wirtschaftspolitische Blatter, no. 4, 1983, pp. 121-132.

MOOSLECHNER, P., 'Der monetäre Ansatz zur Schattenwirtschaft', in Skolka, J. (ed), Die andere Wirtschaft: Schwarzarbeit und Do-it-yourself in Oesterreich, Signum, Vienna 1984, pp. 101-119.

NEUBAUER, H., 'Schwarzarbeit und Eigenleistungen in der oesterreichischen Bauwirtschafts' in Skolka, J. (ed), Die andere Wirtschaft: Schwararbeit und Do-it-yourself in Oesterreich, Signum, Vienna 1984, pp. 131-160.

OESTERREICHISCHES STATISTISCHES ZENTRALAMT, Oesterreichs Volkseinkommen 1981, Oesterreichisches Statistisches Zentralamt, Vienna 1982.

PEACOCK, A., SHAW, G.K., 'Tax Evasion and Tax Revenue Loss', Public Finance, no. 2, 1982, pp. 269-278.

PESTIEAU, P., 'Belgium's Irregular Economy, Measurement and Implications', in Gaertner, W., Wenig, A. (eds), The Economics of the Shadow Economy, Springer, Heidelberg 1985, pp. 114-160.

POMMEREHNE, W.W., FREY, B.S., 'Les modes d'évaluation de

l'économie occulte. Différents approaches et quelques résults', Futuribles December 1981, pp. 3-32.

PORTELA, J.T., ARANGO, C.V., La Economia Irregular, Generalitat de Catalunya, Barcelona 1983.

PUWEIN, W., 'Parallele Wirtschaft im Verkehr', in Skolka, J. (ed), Die andere Wirtschaft: Schwarzarbeit und Eigenleistungen in Oesterreich, Signum, Vienna 1984, pp. 165-178.

QUIRINO, P., Illegal Activities in the National Accounts, Meeting of National Accounts Experts (23-25 May 1984), (mimeographed Consultant Report), OECD, Paris 1984.

REID, M., Economics of Household Production, John Wiley and Sons, New York 1934.

RENOOY, P.H., De schemerzone, Ministry of Social Affairs and Labour, Den Haag 1984.

ROSE, R., Getting by in the Three Economies: The Resources of the Official, Unofficial and Domestic Economies, University of Strathclyde, 1983.

SAUVY, A., Le travail noir & L'économie de demain, Calmann-Lévy, Paris 1984.

SCHUMACHER, E.F., Small is Beautiful: Economics as if People Mattered, Harper and Row, New York 1975.

SETHURAMAN, S.V. (ed), The Urban Informal Sector in Developing Countries, International Labour Office, Geneva 1981.

SIMON, C.P., WITTE, A.D., Beating the System. The Underground Economy, Auburn House, Boston, Mass. 1982.

SKOLKA, J.V., 'Long-Term Effects of Unbalanced Productivity Growth: On the Way to a Self-Service Society', in Solari, L., Pasquier, J.-N. (eds), Private and Enlarged Consumption: Essays in Methodology and Empirical Analysis, North-Holland, Amsterdam 1976, pp. 297-304.

SKOLKA, J. (ed), Die andere Wirtschaft: Schwarzarbeit und Do-it-yourself in Oesterreich, Signum, Vienna 1984.

SKOLKA, J., 'The Parallel Economy in Austria', in Gaertner, W., Wening, A. (eds) The Economics of the Shadow Economy, Springer, Heidelberg 1985, pp. 60-75.

SKOLKA, J., STERMANN, W., 'Die Schattenwirtschaft', Europäische Rundschau, no. 4, 1984, pp. 29-43.

SMITH, A., A Review of the Informal Economy in the European Community, European Community, Brussels, July 1981.

SMITH, J.D., 'Market Motives in the Informal Economy', in Gaertner, G., Wenig, A. (eds), The Economics of the Shadow Economy, Springer, Heidelberg 1985, pp. 161-177.

STORELU, L., Le travail illégal, Assemblé Permanente des Chambres de Commerce et d'Industrie, Paris, Fevrier 1980.

SUVIRANTA, A. et al., Housework Study, (Parts I-X), Ministry of Social Affairs and Health, Helsinki 1980-1982.

SZITA, E., New Forms of Small Economic Organization in Hungary and the Second Economy, Seminar on The Unofficial Economy, University of Trento, 1984.

TANZI, V., 'Underground Economy and Tax Evasion in the United States: Estimates and Implications', Quarterly Review: Banca Nazionale del Lavoro, no. 4, 1980, pp. 428-453.

TANZI, V. (ed), The Underground Economy in the United States and Abroad, Lexington Books, Lexington 1982.

TANZI, V.. 'A Second (and More Sceptical) Look at the Underground Economy in the United States', in Tanzi, V. (ed). The Underground Economy in the United States and Abroad, Lexington Books, Lexington 1982.

TANZI, V., 'The Underground Economy in the United States: Annual Estimates, 1930-1980', IMF Staff Papers, no. 2, 1983, pp. 283-305.

UNITED NATIONS, International Standard Industrial Classification of All Industrial Activities, Rev. 2, United Nations, New York 1968.

WECK-HANNEMANN, H., FREY, B.S., 'Measuring the Shadow Economy: The Case of Switzerland', in Gaertner, W., Wenig, A. (eds), The Economics of the Shadow Economy, Springer, Heidelberg 1985, pp. 76-104.

The nature and extent of unrecorded activity: a survey concentrating on recent US research

ANN D. WITTE

1. INTRODUCTION

You have all read accounts in recent years of a large and growing informal, subterranean or underground economy in various if not all developed economies. The more sensational accounts suggest that this economy was the most dynamic sector in many developed western countries during the 1970s and may have accounted for as much as one quarter of all economic activity in such countries as the U.S. and Italy in the late 1970s (Feige, 1979, 1980; Del Boca and Forte, 1982; Contini, 1982, 1984). Concern with this phenomenon has been widespread with the popular press, the financial press, congressional committees, executive branch agencies and the academic community all expressing interest.

There has now been a rather substantial amount of research on the underground economy. However this work reaches quite varying conclusions and is difficult to assess for at least two reasons. First, the work is of highly varying quality and makes use of statistics and techniques which even the sophisticated non-expert may find difficult to evaluate. Second, the existence of a large and growing underground economy has been used to support varying political positions and, thus, some research has been influenced by a desire to buttress a given political position rather than by a search for knowledge. For example in the U.S. and Great Britain conservatives have suggested that the growth of the underground economy supports the need to cut government interference in the free market, reduce taxes and reduce social insurance payments. By way of contrast in Italy the left has seen the existence of a large and growing underground economy as a sign of the decline and corruption of the capitalist system.

In this chapter, I will survey recent US research on the nature and extent of unrecorded activity. Specifically, in the next section, I use current US research to discern what types of activities are unrecorded, who carries these activities out and in what type of organizations they occur. In section III, I describe recent research by US Internal Revenue Service (IRS) that estimates the amount of income that is not properly recorded on tax returns. Making adjustments, I use this research to discern the amount of unrecorded activity and trends in this type of activity in the U.S. In the final section of the paper, I draw conclusions concerning the research conducted to date and make suggestions for future research.

2. WHAT TYPES OF PRODUCTION ARE UNRECORDED?

By definition, unrecorded economic activity can only exist if some entity is attempting to measure, regulate or tax this activity. In developed western economies the entities attempting to record general economic activity are various governmental entities with the central government being the most important and comprehensive but by no means the only entity attempting to do this. For the purposes of this section and the next two, I will define unrecorded activity as consisting of economically productive activity (i.e., activities which produce value) which is not properly and directly recorded in official measures of output and income. In the US these official measures include GNP and are derived from the US National Income and Product Accounts (NIPA) which are described in the material that follows. There are two major things to note about this definition. First, the definition includes only economic production in the underground economy. By economic production I mean activity carried out for economic as opposed to social or familial purposes. Thus, exchange in-kind for gain (i.e. barter) falls within my definition of the underground economy, but lending between neighbors or within the family does not (1). Second, the definition implies that the central government's ability to directly measure economic activity is the essence of a modern "formal" economy. Thus unrecorded activity is defined by the central government's inability to directly measure productive activity.
  As we have defined unrecorded activity it is a phenomenon which only exists when a governmental organization tries unsuccessfully to directly measure economic activity. Attempts to provide comprehensive estimates of economic activity are largely a twentieth century phenomenon. For example, in the United States attempts to measure all income and output in the nation began in the 1920s (2). Thus, we would not be at all surprised if unrecorded activity had been of concern at least for the last thirty to forty years in developed economies.
  Actually there have been two periods of interest in unrecorded activity in the developed economies. The first was of limited length and was concerned with unrecorded activity caused by the high tax rates, rationing and other government regulations during World War II and immediately thereafter in Canada and the US (Cagan, 1958; Macesich, 1962). The second began in the mid 1970s and is still very much with us. During this second period interest was not limited to North America, but occurred in most Western European countries as well.
  The fact that unrecorded economic activity has received extensive attention in a large number of developed western economies recently is an interesting phenomenon. I believe that in order to understand this phenomenon it is necessary

to think carefully about the nature of economic activity in developed western economies and about government attempts to record and measure this activity.

2.1. Unrecorded production of legal goods and services

Consider first economic activities which produce goods and services deemed to be legal. Here it is necessary to distinguish between production which takes place in large, generally formally incorporated entities (e.g. the Exxons, IBMs, etc. and their smaller, but still large, brethren) and that which takes place in smaller firms and by individuals who are self-employed. While some large productive enterprises undoubtedly misappropriate and misclassify items, keep double sets of books, and attempt to avoid social insurance payments and regulation, it does not appear that most large productive enterprises do this. Rather these entities with their large departments of accountants and lawyers attempt to take advantage of all legal means of reducing the cost of regulation and taxes (e.g., they practice tax avoidance). The visibility alone of these enterprises and their desire to maintain a good public image for sales, government contract, and antitrust purposes, among other things, encourages attempts to honestly and fully comply with government requests and regulations (3). Further, economies of scale in paperwork allow them to comply with governmental requests and requirements relatively more cheaply than smaller enterprises (4).

Unrecorded production of legal goods and services takes place mainly in small corporations, unincorporated enterprises, and partnerships. Self-employed individuals, whether working full or part-time also produce much that is not properly recorded by national statisticians.

Consider the US evidence. The Internal Revenue Service estimated voluntary compliance rates (income reported divided by an IRS estimate of the income that should have been reported) in 1981 of 70.2 percent for small enterprises filing corporate returns, 78.7 percent for the self-employed in non-agricultural enterprises and small enterprises not filing corporate returns, 88.3 percent for farmers filing individual returns and 20.7 percent for informal supplier income. These rates are markedly lower than the 1981 voluntary compliance rates for large corporations (i.e., corporations with assets of $1 million or more) of 90.6 percent and for wage and salary income of 93.9 percent. Unreported taxable incomes generated in small enterprises and by the self-employed are estimated to have been $90 billion in 1981 compared with only approximately $10 billion of unreported taxable income generated by large corporations. See US Department of the Treasury (1983) and the next section for details concerning the way in which the figures discussed in this paragraph were generated.

From the above, which is the best aggregate data currently available, it is clear that unrecorded productive activity occurs predominantly, but not exclusively, in small enterprises (5). To gain a better understanding of the type of unrecorded production in these small enterprises, we will rely predominantly on two aggregate US studies. One of informal suppliers by researchers at the University of Michigan's Survey Research Center (SRC) (Smith, 1982 and US Department of the Treasury, 1983, Appendix D) and one of production not reflected in US GNP statistics conducted by researchers at the Bureau of Economic Analysis (Parker, 1983). However, we will also use insights from a number of other special studies which have used surveys or ethnographic techniques to study particular types of unrecorded production. See, for example Dow 1977, Ferman, Berndt and Selo 1978, Del Boca and Forte 1982, Contini 1982, Hansson 1982.

The study by researchers at the Bureau of Economic Analysis (BEA) covers the broadest range of productive activities and, thus, probably most accurately reflects the overall nature of unrecorded productive activity in the US. In order to evaluate the BEA study it is necessary to have some understanding of the US National Income and Product Accounts (NIPA). These accounts are used to determine GNP, and other aggregate statistics designed to show the production, distribution and use of output. Comparison of NIPA statistics over time provides measures of economic growth, and recessions are defined by falls in output as reflected in the NIPA. Thus, NIPA statistics have major effects on macroeconomic policy and the course of the US economy.

The US NIPA are carefully constructed by BEA which uses a wide range of sources (censuses, surveys, administrative records, tax records, etc.) and attempts to correct for nonreporting in these sources where there is a reasonable basis for doing so (6). NIPA statisticians seek to obtain multiple estimates of as many statistics as possible in order to improve the accuracy of their various estimates. (Jaszi and Carson 1979 for a detailed description of the US NIPA). Thus, NIPA statistics undoubtedly reflect a larger proportion of productive activity than most other government information (e.g. tax return data). Adjusting for failures to record economic activity does not, I believe, shift this activity from the unrecorded to recorded sector. However, it does mean that the NIPA statistics are probably less affected by this type of activity than most other government statistics.

In their continual attempt to improve the NIPA, researchers at BEA recently undertook a study designed to estimate the amount of economic activity not recorded in the NIPA, even after current adjustments for underrecording. (See Parker 1983, 1984 for details). They began by carefully considering the sources and methods used to estimate each entry in the NIPA. One method of measuring production in the NIPA is summing all final purchases of goods and services, and it is the line items used in this method that we will use here. The BEA measures final purchases by using governmental budgetary material (for final purchases by governments), international trade statistics (for net final purchases by foreigners), regulatory agency reports (for final purchases of regulated business) and statistical surveys and trade sources (for purchases by nonregulated businesses and consumers). After carefully considering these and other sources of data BEA researchers concluded that their estimation methods only omitted significant amounts of final purchases for consumers. Considering the other final purchase categories (gross private domestic investment, net exports of goods and services and government purchases of goods and services), it appears that there may be one additional area where final purchases are understated: residential structures (part of gross private domestic investment). The BEA report contains a discussion of figures for residential construction and concludes that Census Bureau adjustments for underreporting are adequate and that although such activity is undoubtedly understated in many government statistics (e.g., taxable income) that it is not understated in the US NIPA accounts. However, whether reflected in NIPA or not this activity is still not directly recorded, and, thus, by the definition used in this chapter, is part of unrecorded activity.

The BEA report indicates that there are understatements of consumer purchases in the following areas: food and tobacco; clothing, accessories, and jewelry; personal care; household operations; certain types of medical care; legal services; funeral and burial services; gasoline and oil, auto repairs and other auto-related expenses; taxicabs; recreation; and hotel and motels. Thus, based on the BEA report it appears that the unrecorded activity of small enterprises and the self-employed occurs mainly in the area of services (i.e., personal household and automobile care, medical and legal services, recreation and tourism). The production of some goods (e.g., household remodeling and repairs, food and tobacco, clothing, jewelry and accessories, gasoline, oil and automotive parts) is also not completely recorded.

The study by researchers at SRC is much narrower than the BEA study since it deals only with purchases by consumers from informal suppliers. However, the survey upon which the SRC survey was based was nationally representative and carefully done. This study provides us with a check on BEA estimates of the type of production which is not recorded. In addition it provides information on the type of people working in unrecorded activity and the areas of the country where this type of activity may occur most frequently.

Researchers at SRC began by conducting focused group discussions with four sets of families: (1) families with incomes greater than $20,000 per year living in Detroit, (2) families with incomes less than $20,000 living in Detroit, (3) families living in small towns and rural areas of Michigan and, (4) families living in small towns and rural areas of Arizona. The discussions with these families were designed to learn how families perceived and identified informal suppliers in order to allow careful and accurate wording of survey questions. The focused group discussions revealed that those interviewed had a well-developed sense that there are vendors who work off the books and on the side, and a general belief that such suppliers are evading their tax obligations. Within Michigan the focus group discussions seemed to indicate that lower income urban families and families living outside urban areas make most use of informal suppliers. This evidence in consistent with other evidence (Dow, 1977; Ferman, Berndt and Selo, 1978; Simon and Witte, 1982; US Department of the Treasury, 1979, 1983) that seems to indicate that unrecorded activity is most likely to occur in lower middle class and lower class urban areas, and in nonurban areas.

Based on the focus group discussion SRC developed a series of questions concerning purchases from informal suppliers which were added to SRC's monthly Survey of Consumer Attitudes. Informal supplier questions were asked in September, November and December, 1981 with approximately 700 households being interviewed in each of these months. Households were selected randomly on the basis of the last four digits of their telephone numbers, after stratification by area code and central office number. It is known that selection by telephone number excludes the approximately 6 or 7 percent of the part of the population that do not live in quarters with telephones. This population tends to be disproportionately poor and black, and presumably makes greater than average use of informal suppliers. Thus, the SRC results are open to some, although I do not believe great, bias for this reason.

Note that SRC's survey results only reflect household purchases from suppliers perceived to be irregular. It will not reflect purchases of businesses from informal suppliers or purchases of either households or business from apparently regular suppliers who are not properly recording their productive activities. SRC's survey responses should be less subject to intentional falsification than surveys which attempt to deal with informal suppliers directly since purchasers have far fewer reasons to hide informal supplier activity.

The SRC study estimates that informal suppliers had $42 billion worth of sales to consumers and $25 billion worth of net income from these sales in 1981. Table 1 contains the value of consumer purchases from informal suppliers of various types of goods. The first thing to note is that most purchases are concentrated in the same areas that the BEA recognizes as having recording problems: personal, household and automobile care; food; home repairs and additions; and fuel. Thus, our two sources of evidence paint a similar picture of the areas in which unrecorded production is most prevalent.

The picture of reported economic activity that we have obtained to this point can be summarized as follows. It is mainly small enterprises, partnerships and the self-employed that produce output that is not properly recorded. The unrecorded output of these producers consists mainly of services, but the production of some type of goods (e.g., food, fuel, household repairs and remodeling, clothing and jewelry) is unrecorded as well.

The SRC survey asked purchasers questions concerning the occupational status of informal vendors. Unsurprisingly, purchasers often did not know the occupational status of

66

vendors (i.e., for approximately 50 percent of the dollar value of purchases). When they did, the vendor usually had a regular job (55 percent of the value of purchases). Vendors without regular jobs were most frequently friends or rela-

Table 1

Value of Consumer Purchases From Informal Vendors
By Types of Goods and Services, 1981
(amounts in millions of dollars)

Goods and Services	Amount
Home Repair and Additions	$12,245
Food	9,003
Child Care	4,955
Domestic Service	3,882
Auto Repair	2,810
Sidewalk Vendor Goods	1,782
Flea Market Goods	1,698
Lawn Maintenance	1,447
Lessons	933
Fuel	749
Appliance Repair	744
Adult Care	442
Cosmetic Service	411
Sewing and Related Services	392
Catering	300
	$41,793

Source: Smith (1982, p. 8).

tives (19 percent of purchases), retired (7 percent of purchases), working off-the-book full time (5 percent of purchases) or unemployed (3 percent of purchases). Recalling that the SRC survey covers only consumer purchases from informal vendors, and that BEA and IRS work indicates that activity also occurs in small enterprises, in partnerships and among the self employed, it appears clear that part time work is the rule for unrecorded production. Much labor for unrecorded production comes from those likely to be receiving social insurance payments (i.e., the retired and unemployed). (See also Ferman, Berndt and Selo, 1978). Full time employment in unrecorded activity apparently occurs mainly for informal suppliers and illegal aliens (7).

2.2. Production of illegal goods and services

Thus far we have only dealt with the unrecorded production of goods and services which are in and of themselves legal. However, a rather substantial amount of unrecorded production involves goods and services that have been declared illegal. The quantity and types of such production depends critically on the laws of the particular country. For comparability to the material on legal goods and services present in the previous section, we will consider the US situation. There are two broad types of illegal activity in the US: (1) production of illegal goods and services and (2) illegal transfers of assets. Under our definition only the production of illegal goods and services is part of unrecorded economic activity since illegal transfers (e.g., robberies, embezzlements, fraud) do not create value (they merely transfer it from one person to another).

The major goods and services produced illegally in the United States are: (1) certain types of drugs (mainly heroin, cocaine and marijuana), (2) prostitution, and (3) gambling. The most comprehensive information that we have on these types of activities come from two recent studies (Simon and Witte, 1982; and Carlson, 1983).

As we shall see in the next section, by far the largest type of illegal activity involves the illegal production and distribution of heroin, cocaine and marijuana. Unfortunately for the sake of brevity the production, distribution, and consumption of each of these drugs has unique aspects and, thus, requires some discussion.

Heroin is produced from opium which is derived from the opium poppy. This plant is grown extensively only in a limited part of the world (e.g., southeast Asia, Iran, Pakistan and Mexico), and most heroin is imported into the US. Given the often great distances and the relatively sophisticated production process, it is not too surprising that US production and distribution tends to be controlled by large, oligopolistic firms. It appears that these oligopolies operate in one or at most a few large cities. The rather limited geographic spread of these illegal organizations may be due to the need to establish distribution chains with contacts with a relatively small, heavy user population. Current estimates indicate that the vast majority of heroin consumed (estimated more than 80 percent) is consumed by daily consumers (i.e., addicts). Recent evidence seems to indicate that the heroin-using population has been rather stable during the 1970s and has aged (see Carlson, 1983).

The peak of heroin consumption appears to have occurred in the late 1960s. The income of US citizens from heroin production and distribution is estimated to have increased at an average annual rate of 12 percent between 1973 and 1979. It appears that the heroin industry was not stagnant during the 1970s, but it was not nearly as dynamic as the cocaine or marijuana industries.

Cocaine, like heroin, is produced in few areas of the world, mainly in western South America. Consumption of cocaine has grown rapidly in recent years. Incomes of US citizens from cocaine sales are estimated to have increased more than eightfold between 1973 and 1981 (US Department of the Treasury, 1983). Cocaine use is much more common (25 percent of young adults surveyed in the late 1970s admitted to having taken the drug at least once) than heroin use and is more frequent than heroin use among wealthier members of US society. Cocaine sales within the US appear to be less well organized and less hierarchically organized than heroin sales. Cocaine use has grown most rapidly among young adults (i.e. those 18 to 25 years of age).

In contrast to heroin and cocaine, marijuana is grown in many parts of the world, including the US. The widespread production of marijuana and limited processing needed for use has meant that there are a number of producers and distributors. Like cocaine use, use of marijuana has grown rapidly. Incomes from marijuana sales increased almost sevenfold between 1973 and 1981 (US Department of the Treasury, 1983). By 1979, a total of 68 percent of young adults said that they had used marijuana at least once and 35 percent admitted to having used it during the last month according to a nationally representative survey of drug use carried out by the National Institute of Drug Abuse.

Gambling and prostitution did not grow rapidly during the 1970's and, as one will see in the next section, were not major contributors to unrecorded activity. Thus, we will not discuss the nature of these activities.

3. HOW MUCH UNRECORDED ACTIVITY IS THERE?

In the previous section, I have attempted to describe the nature of the most important and most rapidly growing types of unrecorded production. In this section, I will seek to discern the relative magnitudes of various types of unrecorded activities. This, of course, requires sector by sector estimates of the various types of illegal activity. As far as we are aware, only Simon and Witte (1982) and the IRS have attempted to make such estimates in the US (US Department of the Treasury, 1979 and 1983). The Internal Revenue Service has developed the most thorough and complete estimates and, thus, I will use these estimates in this section.

One cannot use information from the recent IRS report (US Department of the Treasury, 1983) without adjustment to understand the nature and extent of unrecorded activity as we have defined it because the IRS report contains estimates of unreported taxable income not unrecorded production. These two concepts are quite different. The generally accepted method of measuring productive activity is that used in the NIPA. The US NIPA measure productive activity in two distinct ways: (1) as the sum of final expenditures and (2) as the sum of factor incomes (i.e., incomes received by the factors used in production: natural resources, labor and capital). The two methods produce identical measures of output theoretically but in practice there is a slight discrepancy between the two, called the statistical discrepancy. In section II, I have discussed the final expenditure approach to estimating productive activity. In this section, I will use the factor payments approach since the IRS report estimates incomes not final expenditures.

IRS estimates of income that is not properly reported for tax purposes differ from the concept of unrecorded factor incomes that I will use in this section. First, many transfer payments which are not factor incomes are taxable (e.g., capital gains, alimony). I exclude unreported income from transfer payments from consideration. Second, some income that is not reported for tax purposes is properly recorded by firms when they respond to regulatory agency and statistical survey requests. I do not feel that this income should properly be considered a part of unrecorded economic activity. Unfortunately I can think of no useful way of sorting out unreported production from unreported income which is estimated in the IRS report. Thus, I will use IRS results to estimate unrecorded factor incomes. The reader is warned that this probably serves to overstate wage and salary, interest and dividend income received as a result of unrecorded production. Third, the concept of factor income and taxable income differ conceptually. What income is taxable depends on the particular tax law applicable when the income is received. For NIPA purposes factor income is the value of sales minus the value of all purchase of intermediate products used to produce the goods sold (i.e., value added). Table 2 contains estimates of factor incomes and overstated business expenses that were not properly reported to the IRS.

The first thing to note in Table 2 is that IRS estimates of unreported income show a dramatic increase between 1973 and 1981, from approximately $100 billion to $280 billion. These estimates suggest that unrecorded activity was large and growing rapidly during the 1970s. Comparing these estimates with National Income (i.e., recorded total factor payments) it also appears that the share of unrecorded activity in total production increased during the 1970s, although not dramatically.

Before proceeding further it is wise to carefully evaluate the methods that the IRS used to obtain its estimates. The IRS used a wide range of different sources to obtain estimates of various types of unreported incomes and we will only describe the major sources here.

3.1. Estimates of unreported income earned in legal activities

The single most important source of information for the IRS estimates was the Tax Compliance Measurement Program (TCMP). IRS used TCMP data to obtain estimates of unreported income for individuals and small corporations that file tax returns. Every three years IRS's researchers select a stratified random sample of approximately 50,000 individual tax returns to be intensively audited. TCMP audits are conducted only by experienced examiners and these examiners consider every line item on the tax return. IRS used the line item

70

differences between auditor and taxpayer results to estimate
unreported income and overstated expenses. Relatively few
TCMP auditor recommendations are overturned on appeal and,
thus, it appears that TCMP results are the best direct
information that we are likely to have for a large number of
returns.

In preparing the 1983 report, IRS researchers used TCMP
results for 1965, 1969, 1973 and 1976 (1979 TCMP results
were not yet available). To obtain estimates for 1979 and
1981, IRS made straight line projections of voluntary
reporting percentages (VRPs) obtained from the 1965, 1969,
1973 and 1976 TCMPs to estimate VRPs for 1979 and 1981.
Estimates of unreported income and overstated expenses for
1979 and 1981 were then obtained by using information on
returns actually filed in 1979 and 1981 (8) and the projec-
ted VRPs. This method of obtaining information for 1979 and
1981 means that estimates for these years, and more importantly the trends that they represent, are largely a projection of the past. They may well not reflect the actual
trends in unreported activity during the late 1970s and
early 1980s.

The IRS has long realized that even the very thorough TCMP
audits cannot detect all unreported income. To try to discern the extent to which TCMP auditors could detect income,
the IRS carried out a special study in 1977. Researchers
collected all information documents (e.g. forms 1099 and W-
2) for approximately 12,000 of the 50,000 1976 TCMP returns.
They used the information documents to discern the proportion of total income of various types that auditors were
able to uncover. Using mainly this information they multiplied all TCMP estimates of unreported income by 3.5 to
obtain estimates of the unreported income of filers used in
the 1983 report. This method assumes that auditors uncovered
only one dollar of every $3.50 that was not reported.
Needless to say, this procedure is open to question.

Estimates of unreported income for individuals who did not
file a tax return were obtained by using data files for 1972
and 1977 which contained individual information from the IRS
master file (this file contains tax return information), the
Census Bureau's Current Population Survey (CPS) and the
administrative records of the Social Security Administration
(SSA). The CPS, which is used to measure labor force statistics (e.g., the unemployment rate), is a monthly survey of
living quarters in the US. Living quarters included in the
survey are selected randomly and about 60,000 individuals
living in these quarters are interviewed each month. Questions concerning labor market status, occupation and income
are asked. Respondents are assured, and indeed have, anonymity. The first interview is carried out in person with
subsequent interviews being conducted by telephone.

Records in the three files were matched on the basis of
social security numbers. The resulting file is called the
Exact Match File. Individuals with SSA or CPS records indicating receipt of income, but no IRS file were potential
nonfilers. (It should be noted that IRS did not receive any
information that would directly identify these individuals.

Table 2

IRS Estimates of Unreported Factor Income and
Overstated Expenses
(in $ millions)

Legal Source Incomes	1973	1976	1981
Individuals			
Wages and Salaries	$33,304	$46,274	$94,581 (1)
Dividends	1,920	3,638	8,747 (1)
Interest	4,440	6,763	20,479 (1)
Small non-farm enterprises	23,906	32,565	58,400 (1)
Farm proprietors	5,742	4,542	9,547 (1)
Informal supplier incomes	10,346 (2)	12,721 (2)	17,080
Rents	1,335	2,390	3,049 (1)
Royalties	312	1,088	2,770
Estate and trust income	487	695	1,330 (1)
Overstated business expenses	5,250 (5)	8,500 (5)	16,179
Corporations (3, 4)	6,912-9,368	8,833-11,947	11,968-16,407
Taxable income of tax exempt organizations (3)	68-113	152-253	218-363
Fiduciaries (3)	82-137	84-140	216-360
Illegal Source Incomes			
Illegal Drugs	5,100	7,400	23,400
(estimated standard error)	(2,200)	(3,000)	(8,500)
Illegal gambling	1,600	2,200	3,400
(estimated standard error)	(520)	(2,670)	(n.a.)
Female prostitution	2,600	3,800	7,400
(estimated standard error)	(2,400)	(3,500)	(6,800)
TOTAL UNRECORDED INCOME	103,404-105,960	141,623-144,916	278,764-285,492

(1) These are projections based on 1976 TCMP results.
(2) These figures are based on the 1981 SRC results and the relation-
     ship between the reported and nonreported income of informal
     suppliers. IRS assumed that the proportion of informal supplier
     income reported to IRS was the same in 1973 and 1976 as it was in
     1981.
(3) The IRS does not provide estimates of unreported income for corpo-
     rations, the tax exempt organizations and fiduciaries. I have
     estimated these incomes from IRS tax gap estimates by assuming tax
     rates of 0.4 and 0.5 for large corporations and tax rates of 0.3
     to 0.5 for other organizations.
(4) The tax gap for small corporations was estimated using TCMP data
     for 1969, 1973, and 1978. Only the 1978 TCMP study included
     returns with no balance sheet.
(5) These numbers were not available in the IRS report and were cal-
     culated from IRS estimates of the tax gap by assuming that the
     same average tax rate existed in 1973 and 1976 as 1981.

Source: US Department of the Treasury, 1983.

Anonymity was maintained). The income levels and other relevant information for these individuals were checked to see if they indeed should have filed a tax return.

The average Adjusted Gross Income (AGI) of non-filers as identified by the 1972 Exact Match File was $6,826 while the average AGI of nonfilers in the 1977 file was $12,026. This suggests an extraordinary growth in the number of wealthier individuals who do not file a return.

Note that the numbers presented in Table 2 which combine filer and nonfiler information are for 1973, 1976 and 1981, and that Exact Match Files were only available for 1972 and 1977. IRS obtained nonfiler income estimates for the years used in the report by assuming that the rate of growth in income revealed in the 1972 and 1977 Exact Match Files occurred evenly over the period. For the 1979 and 1981 estimates, the IRS assumed that this rate of growth moderated. Again I am left with the conclusion that the information in the IRS report for 1973 and 1976 is the most reliable.

The IRS believes that neither TCMP nor the Exact Match File captures all of the unreported income earned by informal suppliers, illegal aliens or in illegal activities. Thus, they commissioned special studies to estimate the unreported incomes earned in these types of activities. The special study of the unreported income of informal suppliers is described in some detail in the previous section. Recall that SRC's estimate of informal supplier income was for 1981. IRS's unreported income estimates for informal suppliers for other years were obtained by extrapolations based on trends in net non-farm proprietors income from the NIPA. Thus for informal supplier income our most reliable data are for 1981.

To estimate illegal alien income not reflected in the TCMP and Exact Match data bases IRS began by surveying existing estimates of the size of the illegal alien population. It concluded that there were between 3.5 and 6 million illegal aliens in the US in 1979. It next estimated, using social science research, that between 65 and 90 percent of illegal aliens were employed. To obtain earnings for these individuals IRS estimated the occupational structure for this population using Immigration and Naturalization Service (INS) and General Accounting Office (GAO) work. Wages for illegal aliens in each occupation were estimated using INS information. Interestingly it appears that over 50 percent of illegal aliens have taxes withheld and, thus, are not working in unrecorded activity.

3.2. Estimates of unreported income earned in illegal activities

To estimate incomes earned in illegal endeavors, IRS commissioned a detailed study of illegal activity by Abt Associates (Carlson, 1983; Weisberg and Goldstein, 1983). Recall from the previous section that under the definition of unrecorded activity used in this chapter, I am only concerned with illegal activities that produce goods and

73

services not with illegal transfers. IRS was interested in the income from illegal transfers, which is taxable, as well.

The structure of illegal production is complex and output is difficult to measure. To measure the production of illegal goods and services researchers at Abt and the IRS considered for each illegal activity two different approaches: (1) the direct measurement of net output (the production approach) or (2) the measurement of final sales (the consumption approach). In order to estimate the output of the drug and gambling industries researchers at Abt and the IRS used the results of nationally representative sample surveys to estimate the final consumption of the illegal product. To estimate the output of the prostitution industry the production approach was used. Since the methodologies used are complex, I will only describe the way in which the output of the drug industry was measured. Recall that this is the most important illegal industry.

Estimates of drug use have been made using both consumption and production-based approaches. Consumption-based approaches rely on estimates of the user population while production based estimates rely on acreage estimates. Most researchers who have considered the two approaches to estimation believe that consumption based approaches provide more reliable estimates. (For example, see Simon and Witte, 1982, and Carlson, 1983). As a result, I will discuss only consumption based estimates here. The interested reader is referred to the above references for a discussion of production based estimates.

There are a number of possible ways of estimating the size of the drug using population: (1) sample surveys, (2) arrest information, (3) treatment program information, and (4) incidence of drug related diseases (e.g., drug overdoses, hepatitis). All of these sources of information are subject to biases (e.g., surveys are subject to both response and nonresponse biases, arrests and treatment program admissions are determined jointly by agency and drug user actions, diseases related to drug use are generally as much a function of dealer and user experience and market conditions as the size of the consumer population). Those who have assessed these alternative sources of information have generally concluded that the very careful surveys of users conducted by the National Institute of Drug Abuse (NIDA) provide the most reliable estimates of the user population. For example, see Simon and Witte, 1982 and Carlson, 1983.

NIDA sponsors a national household survey every two years which asks over seven thousand people about their previous experience and present use of various types of illegal drugs. In order to lower the number of inaccurate responses, respondents to the NIDA survey are asked to mark their answers on cards which they seal and drop into mailboxes. Hochhauser (1979) has reviewed a number of studies which attempt to measure the nature of the biases in drug surveys. He concludes: (1) reporting of current use is more consistent than recall of past behavior, which tends to underestimate the recency and frequency of use; (2) some respon-

dents, particularly young people, fabricate use; and (3)
individuals who consent to respond are different both socially and demographically from those who do not respond.
Approximately 14 to 20 percent of the individuals selected
for the NIDA survey are not interviewed; however, only about
half of those not interviewed refused to participate.

The sampling units in the NIDA survey are individuals over
12 years of age who live in households. The use of this
sampling frame probably means that NIDA results do not paint
a completely accurate picture of drug use since it excludes
all individuals living in group quarters (e.g., military
barracks, college dormitories) and casual housing (e.g.,
hotels, "abandoned" buildings). Due to this limitation of
the sampling frame NIDA results probably underestimate drug
use. Carlson (1983) provides confidence bands for NIDA estimates when using Nida results. He further warns that NIDA
surveys may underrepresent heavy users. As a result, he uses
a National Narcotics Intelligence Consumer Committee (NNICC)
estimate of the number of heroin addicts which attempt to
adjust for some NIDA biases. Precisely what adjustments are
made is unclear and hence this number should be treated with
even more caution than other drug user information.

In order to estimate the value of drugs consumed (final
purchases under the NIPA terminology) in any year, it is
necessary to multiply the number of consumers by their
average consumption to obtain the quantity of drugs consumed. The number that results is multiplied by average
price to obtain the value of drugs sold in the US.
Researchers at Abt/IRS made estimates of average daily dosage by user type and drug, using a variety of sources including medical evidence of effective dosage, informant
reports of drug user practices, and information from law
enforcement agencies. These researchers report that their
estimates of dosage is "somewhat conjectural" (Carlson,
1983, p. 15). My own evaluation is that they should be seen
as informed conjecture. Drug prices used in the Abt/IRS
study are the average price paid by agents of the Drug
Enforcement Administration (DEA). Since DEA makes frequent
and continual purchases these prices are likely to be accurate.

Before one can obtain an estimate of the output of the
drug industry in the US, three further adjustments are
necessary: (1) for drugs sold at retail rather than
wholesale price, (2) for payments to foreign suppliers, and
(3) for purchase of domestic inputs. When all these adjustments are made it appears that the drug industry is an
important and rapidly growing sector of unreported production. Estimated taxable income from the US illegal drug
industry is estimated to have increased from $5.1 billion in
1973 to $23.4 billion in 1981, a more than four fold in-
crease. Sales of the so-called recreational drugs (cocaine
and marijuana) appear to have increased far more rapidly
than did heroin sales during this period. However, it appears that even the drug industry produced a relatively
small proportion of total unrecorded output, an estimated 8
percent.

As noted earlier the prostitution and gambling industries are quite small and relatively stagnant. Gambling is estimated to have produced only an estimated 1 percent of total unreported income and prostitution less than 3 percent. It should be noted that estimates for both of these sectors are subject to substantial errors (note estimated standard errors reported in Table 2) and that the estimates are quite controversial. See Carlson (1983) for details.

3.3. The structure of unrecorded activity

The information in Table 2 paints an interesting picture of the structure of unrecorded activity. Much unrecorded activity results in the receipt of wage and salary income; however, as noted previously, the estimate of the quantity of wages and salaries generated by unrecorded activity in Table 2 probably overstates the importance of this type of income.

The unreported wages and salaries of those who filed tax returns (20 percent of the total) consisted mainly of under-reported tip income and payments to agricultural and domestic workers. Nonfiler wages and salaries form the major part (80 percent) of IRS estimates of unreported wages and salaries. It appears that between 60 and 70 percent of the nonfilers had taxes withheld and thus were working in recorded rather than unrecorded activity.

The above discussion, when combined with the data in Table 2 and other information, seems to indicate that the majority of unrecorded productive activity in the US occurs in small enterprises (small corporations, sole proprietorship and informal suppliers). The owners and organizers of these types of enterprises received more than 30 percent of the total unreported income recorded in Table 2 and probably were responsible for an even larger proportion of unrecorded activity.

Illegal incomes account for slightly more than ten percent of all incomes recorded in Table 2. While it seems likely that illegal production accounts for a greater proportion than this (perhaps 20 percent) it seems clear that most unrecorded activity in the US involves the production of perfectly legal goods and services.

4. CONCLUSIONS AND SUGGESTIONS FOR FUTURE RESEARCH

I began this paper by noting the widespread interest in unrecorded economic activity and by repeating some of the more sensational claims regarding this type of activity. The review of existing research contained in Sections II and III provides a basis for assessing those claims. I conclude that neither the most reliable aggregate information available (the 1983 IRS report) nor a careful assessment of the methodologies used by those making sensational claims provide support for those claims. The conclusions that one can draw on the basis of the best information currently available are: (1) unrecorded activity was approximately 10 percent as large as recorded GNP in 1976/1977, and (2) unrecorded activity grew at an average annual rate slightly (1 to 2 percent) greater than recorded GNP during the 1970s.

I believe that what is currently most needed if we are to better understand unrecorded activity is carefully developed conceptual approaches to the issue at both the micro and macro level. I have made some suggestions as to a possible direction for this research at the macro level in Witte (1984). At the micro level, researchers need to carefully develop models for various types of unrecorded activity (e.g., informal suppliers, unrecorded production of small enterprises, illegal aliens, various types of illegal activities).

I am convinced that carefully conducted empirical studies can eventually provide us with a better understanding of the various types of unrecorded activity. This increased understanding will allow us to improve our estimates of the amount of various types of unrecorded activities. The kind of research needed is of various types ranging from ethnographic studies (see Klockars, 1974, for an example) to careful and detailed analyses of existing statistical series and data collection methods. Both types of work are currently underway in the US. Work on statistical series and data collection methods are being carried out by a number of administrative and statistical agencies: e.g., in the US the Bureau of the Census (US Department of Commerce, 1983a, 1983b); the Bureau of Labour Statistics (US Bureau of Labor Statistics, 1983); and the Bureau of Economic Analysis (Parker, 1983, 1984; Carson, 1984). The work of the statistical and administrative agencies needs to be encouraged and carefully coordinated. In addition, research by external researchers on new data collection methodologies, and estimates of bias in collected data (particularly response bias) would be very useful.

I would like to discuss one final question: what should one reasonably want and expect from research on unrecorded activity? I think that one should reasonably want a set of national accounts and other aggregate statistics (e.g., labor force statistics) that more clearly reflect the nature and type of productive activity in a country. One should never expect to have exact estimates of unrecorded activity. However, I believe that it is possible to have better estimates of this type of activity than we currently have. It would be useful to present for many statistical series (e.g., GNP, labor market statistics) the amount of activity actually directly recorded, and the best estimates of activity which is not recorded. Many of our current statistical series use various types of adjustment for underrecording but these estimates are not currently cumulated and presented as an estimate of unrecorded activity. I suggest that this be done. For example, I believe that, to the degree possible, the national income and product accounts should be broken into three sectors: (1) legal economic activity directly reflected in statistical series, (2) estimates of the unrecorded production of legal goods and services and (3) estimates of the production of illegal goods and services.

The breakdown of the national income and product accounts in this way could allow the national income accountants to estimate the level of accuracy in their estimates for each sector. Further, comparison of levels and rates of growth of the various sectors could provide valuable information about structural change. Under the tripartite system of statistical reporting, researchers would be more adequately warned about possible errors and limitations in aggregate statistical data and would be better informed about both cyclical and secular trends in various types of economic activity. In addition, cross-national comparisons would be improved, since differences in such things as laws and the level of regulation and taxation would not serve to alter GNP estimates which report information for all the three of the quite different types of economic activity listed above.

I also suggest that researchers think more carefully about the way in which families and individuals satisfy their needs and wants. Studies which recognize the full spectrum of institutions for satisfying these needs - the social to the formal economy - are more likely to understand the nature of adjustments to both secular and cyclical change. This type of research requires for background detailed studies of the way in which the less well-known of basic institutions, those in the illegal and informal sector, operate.

NOTES

(*)   Department of Economics, Wellesley College, Wellesley, MA 02181
      Ann Dryden Witte is visiting professor of Economics at Wellesley College and Professor of Economics at the University of North Carolina at Chapel Hill. A large number of individuals have provided valuable comments on earlier drafts. I would particularly like to thank Al Blumstein, Bruno Dallago, Berj Kanadjian, Frank Malenga, Norval Morris, Tom Thompson, Michael Tonry and Jim Wilson. The research assistance of Brad Smith greatly aided in making revisions of earlier drafts. The first draft of this paper was written while I was a resident scholar at the Rockefeller Foundation's Study and Conference Center in Bellagio, Italy. The graceful atmosphere of the Center and the beauty of its setting helped to make this paper better than it otherwise would have been. The second draft of the paper was completed while I was a Fulbright Lecturer at the Federal University of Ceara in Fortaleza, Brazil. My experience in the northeast of Brazil gave me a new appreciation of the roles and functions of unrecorded economic activity. The weaknesses of the paper are due to the author's own limitations.
(1)   Some authors, particularly sociologists and anthropologists, define the economy to include noneconomic actity such as do-it-yourself activities, housework and aid between neighbors. For example, see Dow (1977); Henry

(1978); and Mars (1982). We define our concern more narrowly for two basic reasons. First, we believe that the essence of the underground economy lies in the relationship between the government and economic activity. An underground economy can only exist if there is a formal economy. In developed western countries the formal economy is defined, measured, regulated and taxed by the government. Thus far, governments have not generally extended their powers as widely into social and family relations as they have into economic relationships. For example, governments do not generally seek to tax or measure noneconomic exchanges with the family (e.g., childcare, household chores, transfer payments within the household) although they may try to regulate certain types of family activities (e.g., violence within the family). Second, the major policy concerns associated with unrecorded activity relate to the economic portion of that activity. Those desiring to understand the many ways in which human needs and wants are fulfilled may well be advised to adopt a broader definition, and economic and noneconomic activities.

(2) The first official national income statistics for the US were published in 1926 by the Federal Trade Commission. The Bureau of Economic Analysis, which is still responsible for national income statistics, was not established until the 1930s. See Henry (1983) for a discussion.

(3) In the US very large corporations are audited continuously by the Internal Revenue Service (IRS) and other large corporations are audited on a three year cycle. See US Department of the Treasury, 1983, p. 241.

(4) There has been limited work on the way in which administrative costs associated with governmentally required record keeping change with size, but both casual intuition and some existing work suggest that economies of scale are likely to be large. See, for example, Oldman and Woods' (1983) discussion of a recent UK study that suggests that the costs of complying with the British value added tax are substantial and relatively much higher for smaller firms.

(5) Information for countries other than the US is less extensive, but leads to a similar conclusion. See, for example, Del Boca and Forte (1982), Contini (1982) and Hansson (1982).

(6) For example, when researchers at BEA use IRS tax data they correct for underreporting of taxable income by using IRS estimates of underreporting of taxable income which are obtained by thorough audit of a random sample of tax returns.

(7) See Dow (1977) for a colorful portrait of informal suppliers. We have not discussed illegal aliens, but the interested reader can find extensive material in Simon and Witte (1982) and US Department of the Treasury (1983, Appendix E). It appears that more than half of the illegal alien population in the US (estimated

54.4 percent) had federal income tax withheld and, thus, their production is very likely to be recorded. Illegal aliens work predominantly in agriculture, light industry (e.g., textiles, food processing), services and construction. This distribution seems to support the BEA's contentions concerning areas where production is most often not recorded.

(8) This is not strictly correct. IRS used information on a random sample of filed returns (Statistics of Income (SOI) program data). As SOI data were not available for 1981, IRS had to project filed returns as well as VRPs for this year.

REFERENCES

CAGAN, P., The Demand for Currency Relative to Total Money Supply, Occasional Paper 62, National Bureau of Economic Research, Inc., New York 1958.

CARLSON, K., Unreported Taxable Income from Selected Illegal Activities, vol. I, Consensual Crimes, Abt Associates, Cambridge, Mass. 1983.

CARSON, C., 'The Underground Economy: An Introduction', Survey of Current Business, May, 1984.

CONTINI, B., 'The Second Economy of Italy' in Tanzi, V., (ed) The Underground Economy in the United States and Abroad, Lexington Books, Lexington, Mass. 1982.

CONTINI, B., 'Italy's Unobserved Economy: A Survey of Recent Contributions', in Feige, E. (ed), The Unobserved Economy, Cambridge University Press, Cambridge 1984.

DEL BOCA, D. and F. FORTE, 'Recent Empirical Survey and Theoretical Interpretations of the Parallel Economy in Italy', in Tanzi, V., (ed), The Underground Economy in the US and Abroad, Lexington Books, Lexington, Mass. 1982.

DOW, L.M., jr., 'High Weeds in Detroit: The Irregular Economy Among a Network of Appalachian Migrants', Urban Anthropology, no. 6, 1977.

FEIGE, E. L., 'How Big is the Irregular Economy?', Challenge, November/December, 1979.

FEIGE, E.L., A New Perspective on Macroeconomic Phenomena: The Theory and Measurement of the Unobserved Sector of the United States Economy: Causes, Consequences and Implications, Unpublished paper, University of Wisconsin, Madison, Wisconsin 1980.

FERMAN, L.A., BERNDT, E. and SELO, E., Analysis of the Irregular Economy: Cash Flows in the Informal Sector, report to the Bureau of Employment and Training, Michigan Department of Labor, 1978.

HANSSON, I., 'The Underground Economy in a High Tax Country: The Case of Sweden', in Tanzi, V., (ed), The Underground Economy ·in US and Abroad, Lexington Books, Lexington, Mass. 1982.

HENRY, J.S., 'Non-Compliance with US Tax Law - Evidence of Size, Growth and Composition', in Sawicki, P., (ed), Income Tax Compliance Research, American Bar Association, Washington DC 1983.

HENRY, S., The Hidden Economy: The Context and Control of Borderline Crime, Martin Robertson, Oxford 1978.

HOCHHAUSER, M., 'Bias in Drug Survey Research', International Journal of Addictions, no. 14, 1979.

JASZI, G. and CARSON, C.S., 'The National Income and Product Accounts of the United States: An Overview', Survey of Current Business, no. 59, 1979.

KLOCKERS, C.B., The Professional Fence, The Free Press, New York, 1984.

MACESICH, G., 'Demand for Currency and Inflation in Canada', Southern Economic Journal, no. 29, 1962.

MARS, G., Cheats at Work: An Anthropology of Workplace Crime, George Allen and Unwin, London 1982.

OLDMAN, O. and WOODS, 'Would a Value Added Tax Relieve Tax Compliance Problems?' in Sawicki, P., (ed), Income Tax Compliance Research, American Bar Association, Washington DC, 1983.

PARKER, R., Bias in NIA and Other Economic Data, Paper prepared for Wharton Quarterly Model Meeting and Seminar, Washington DC, 10 February 1983.

PARKER, R., 'Improved Adjustments for Misreporting of Tax Return Information Used to Estimate the National Income and Product Accounts', Survey of Current Business, June, 1984.

PORTER, R. and THURMAN S., The Currency Ratio and the Underground Economy, Working paper, Board of Governors, Federal Reserve System, Washington DC 1979.

SIMON, C.P. and WITTE A.D., Beating the System: The Underground Economy, Auburn House, Boston, Mass., 1982.

SMITH, J.D., The Measurement of Selected Income Flows in Informal Markets, Report prepared for Internal Revenue Service on Contract No. TIR81-28, April 1982.

US Bureau of Labor Statistics, Report of the BLS Task Force on the Underground Economy, Report, Office of Research and Evaluation, Washington DC 1983.

US Department of Commerce, Bureau of the Census, Minutes of the Meeting of the Census Advisory Committee of the American Economic Association, 22 April 1983a.

US Department of Commerce, Bureau of the Census, Underground Economy: Agenda Item B, meeting of the Census Advisory Committee of the American Economic Association, 22 April 1983b.

US Department of the Treasury, Internal Revenue Service, Estimates of Income Unreported on Individual Income Tax Returns, Department of the Treasury, Publication 1104, Washington DC 1979.

US Department of the Treasury, Internal Revenue Service, Income Tax Compliance Research: Estimates for 1973-1981, Department of the Treasury, Washington DC 1983.

WEISBERG, H. and GOLDSTEIN N., Unreported Taxable Incomes from Selected Illegal Activities, Vol. II, Predatory Crimes, Abt Associates, Cambridge, Mass. 1983.

WITTE, A.D., Unrecorded Economic Activity: A Survey and Some Suggestions, Working paper, Department of Economics, University of North Carolina, Chapel Hill 1984.

The anatomy of the underground economy

EDGAR FEIGE

1. INTRODUCTION

When physicists conjecture the existence of a heretofore unobserved particle or energy force whose presence would challenge some current interpretations of natural laws, such claims are rightfully met with both excitement and skepticism. The excitement is engendered by the possibility that observed anomalies might be reconciled within a broader conceptual framework. The skepticism is motivated by the lack ·of precision which characterizes most novel rudimentary ideas and by the absence of reliable empirical observations for verification.

Economists have responded in like manner to the challenges generated by the 'unobserved income hypothesis' (UIH). During the past five years, a growing amount of professional attention has been focused on the conjecture that there exists a significant and growing 'underground economy' that has eluded the observational domain of professional economists. If that conjecture is correct, it requires a rewriting of recent economic history in order to correct the biases introduced into our key economic indicators. Hopefully, such modification of the economic 'facts' will help to resolve some of the macroeconomic anomalies of the 1970's wich are acknowledged to have thrown our profession into a state of crisis. The hypothesis, furthermore, encourages a thoroughgoing reexamination of theories entertained to explain such key issues as the decline in economic growth rates, high levels of unemployment, the productivity slowdown and growing government deficits (2).

At its core, the UIH challenges the veracity of the fundamental data base that macroeconomics relies on for the formulation of theories and tests of prevailing hypotheses. It is therefore not surprising that the issue of the 'underground economy' has provoked considerable academic controversy and a strong reaction from the traditional custodians of the economic information system. Governmental agencies responsible for the production of national income accounts, census information, labor market indicators and tax records have been challenged to reexamine and appropriately revise the basic statistics upon which policy makers and academics rely.

Those of us who have been troubled by the malaise which has characterized our discipline during the past decade, have embraced the notion that the existence of a growing 'underground economy' might shed new light on the current controversies in macroeconomics and public finance (3). In our enthusiasm to pursue a new line of thinking, we have perhaps both overstated the promise of the idea and placed too much confidence in the valiant, albeit rudimentary, efforts to measure the 'underground economy'. The skeptics have rightly pressed for a more precise definition of the phenomenon and a more rigorous derivation of its conjectural implications. Most prominently, they have challenged the methods proposed for its measurement.

Concern with the implications of the 'underground economy' has raised a new set of questions for investigation:

(1) How are we to define the 'underground economy' and how can we measure its size and growth?

(2) How will a growing 'underground economy' affect traditional measures of economic growth, prices, unemployment, productivity, and budget deficits?

(3) What are the causes of a growing 'underground economy' and what are its implications for stabilization policies, economic efficiency, the distribution of income, taxation and expenditure policy and general economic welfare?

Now that the ideas of 'underground economists' have permeated the consciousness of the academies and governmental agencies, their usefulness and truth value is being more seriously investigated. Sufficient time and energy has been expended by both enthusiasts and critics alike, to warrant a fresh assessment of the state of the art. This paper addresses two issues which are prerequisites to such an assessment. The first is to explicate a more precise taxonomic framework for describing the phenomenon in question. The second is a more technical examination of some of the empirical measures which have been proposed to measure the size and growth of the 'underground economy'.

Unfortunately, the term 'underground' has been used by different investigators to mean quite different things. These unresolved questions of definition introduce considerable confusion in the literature. Theoretical and empirical research require a finer set of conceptual distinctions to clarify both the differences and the interconnections among the variety of descriptive terms presently employed by 'underground economists'. To this end, I wish to put forward a taxonomic framework which differentiates economic, fiscal, and social concepts of income. The first section of this paper elaborates these income concepts and establishes their interrelationships.

The second section discusses the empirical counterparts to the conceptual definitions developed in section I, and reviews some of the recent contributions of government agencies in the United States to estimating the size and growth of the 'underground economy'. Extensive efforts have been undertaken by the Internal Revenue Service (IRS) to measure the degree of non-compliance with existing tax codes. These

84

results, in turn, have led the Bureau of Economic Analysis (BEA) to undertake significant revisions in the U.S. National Income and Product Accounts (NIPA). These new results are of considerable importance since they go well beyond earlier government admissions of data base deficiencies and represent the first steps in the process of historical revision. Although there are still significant differences between conceptually comparable estimates of the 'underground economy', these recent government findings lend greater scientific credence to the proposition that the 'underground economy' is a vital area of investigation whose full fruits have yet to be harvested.

The third section utilizes both the IRS findings and the transaction method results to estimate 'tax gaps', namely, the shortfall in tax revenues which results from non-compliance with the tax codes. The tax gap estimates in turn enable us to estimate the 'full compliance deficit' for the years 1979 and 1980.

The final section contains a summary and conclusions.

1. ALTERNATIVE CONCEPTS OF 'INCOME' AND THEIR RELEVANCE TO ECONOMIC INQUIRY

The burgeoning literature produced by 'underground economists' has generated a plethora of vague and evocative terms (underground, subterranean, informal, hidden, parallel, black, clandestine, second, etc.) which have served to confuse rather than to clarify the important substantive issues raised by the discovery that potentially significant segments of economic activity may be imperfectly accounted for in the conventional data bases forming the very foundation of empirical inquiry in economics.

Alternative measures of the size of the 'underground economy' have revealed a wide range of estimates of its magnitude. These apparent inconsistencies suggest not only the difficulty of attempting to estimate a phenomenon whose raison d'être is to defy detection, but more importantly, the fact that the different measures are incommensurable since they are estimates of different conceptual entities. To date, little effort has been devoted to the elaboration of useful conceptual distinctions of different notions of 'underground income' and to the reconciliation of diverse empirical measures. What is required is a taxonomic framework that discriminates among different aspects of the phenomenon and provides empirical links between the various theoretical constructs and their real-world counterparts. One of the key ambiguities which plagues the literature on the underground economy is the repeated confusion between economic and fiscal concepts of income. All too often, the underrecording of income in the National Income and Product Accounts (NIPA) has been erroneously identified with the issue of tax evasion.

85

1.1. Total economic income

Macroeconomic theory defines income as the maximum amount of consumption which can be undertaken in a given period without altering the stock of wealth. In principle, this broad notion of total economic income makes no distinction between market and non-market consumption. Conceptually, consumption of goods and services includes all items which have positive market or shadow prices due to their relative scarcity. In practice, however, empirical measures of economic income are limited to the consumption of legally produced market goods and services (produced by labor, capital and property) supplied by residents of a given country during a specified time period. The conventional macroeconomic accounting practices which are embodied in the National Income and Product Accounts (NIPA) thus necessarily sacrifice conceptual completeness in order to reduce the cost and error of quantification. If we define recorded income as that component of total economic income which is empirically captured in the NIPA statistics, then unrecorded income can be seen to consist of:

1) income produced in economic activities socially deemed 'illegal'
2) income produced in non-market (bartered) legal activities
3) income produced in legal market activities (monetary) which, for various reasons, escape NIPA measurement.

A simple taxonomic framework for Total Economic Income and its components is displayed in Table 1.

In principle, total economic income includes all income produced in both the market and the nonmarket sector. Precisely what determines the boundary (AB) between these two sectors is one of the major substantive issues of micro labor economics with its emphasis on labor force participation rates. Development economics, is largely concerned with the macro determinants of the boundary, and the rapidity with which it shifts up over time. Empirical estimates (4) suggest that the nonmarket sector (primarily household production) ranges between 32 percent and 60 percent of the market economy. Some authors have referred to the output of the nonmarket sector as the 'informal economy' (5) whereas others have used the same term to describe market activities (6).

Both market and nonmarket income-producing activities can be further classified according to the societies' social conventions as embodied in legal statutes which distinguish between legal and illegal activities. Social income, as distinct from economic or fiscal income, identifies those income-producing activities which are regarded as illegal under criminal law. Illegal income-producing activities are presently excluded from United States NIPA, whereas the UN-OECD System of National Accounts (7) makes no distinction between legal and illegal activities. In the United States, the boundary displayed in Table 1 as CD is established solely by social convention.

Table 1

Taxonomic Framework for Economic Income

Theoretical Construct	Market Classification	Legal Status Activity	Reporting Status	NIPA Component
		Illegal Activity — C___D	Unrecorded Income — E___F	Monetary Unobserved Sector — G___H
	Market Income — A___B	Legal Activity — A___B	Recorded Income — A___B	Estimated Gross National Product
Total Economic Income			Imputed Income — E___F	
	Non-market Income	Legal Activity — C___D	Unrecorded Income — E___F	Non-monetary Unobserved Sector — G___H
		Illegal Activity		

What is germane to the issue of the 'underground economy' as it relates to <u>economic income</u> is the question of what is and what is not <u>recorded</u> in NIPA. As displayed in Table 1, <u>recorded income</u> (8) includes most legal market income as well as minor imputations for particular components of legal nonmarket income (9). <u>Unrecorded income</u> thus includes illegal market and nonmarket activities. In addition, unrecorded income includes legal market income that unwittingly escapes NIPA detection (the upper CD - EF boundary in Table 1) as well as legal nonmarket income (the lower CD - EF boundary) which is conventionally excluded from NIPA accounts due to the difficulties engendered in measuring the size of this component.

Unrecorded 'illegal' income arises from the production and distribution of goods and services which are regarded as illegal by social convention. In the United States, such goods include drugs and pornographic materials; services include prostitution and value added in loan-sharking. In practice, such illegal activities are excluded from the accounts, except to the extent that some illegally produced income might be 'laundered' into data sources underlying NIPA.

The final component of total economic income is unrecorded legal market income. Legally produced income can escape measurement in NIPA's as a result of deficiencies in NIPA estimation procedures and underlying data sources.

1.2. Fiscal income

<u>Fiscal Income</u> is defined by legislative tax status which identify those sources of 'income' which are to be included in the nation's tax base. On the one hand, fiscal income is a broader concept than total economic income since it includes realizations of appreciated asset values in addition to income earned from currently produced goods and services. On the other hand, it is a narrower concept, since economic income includes categories of income which are explicitly excluded by the fiscal code. Most nonmarket household production is excluded from fiscal income although it is legitimately considered to be part of total economic income. It is also the case that fiscal income may exclude items which are specifically imputed in NIPA's (10).

The components of fiscal income are determined by fiscal legislation rather than by the economic criterion of current production of scarce goods and services. As displayed in Table 2, a nation's potential income tax base (including total economic income and capital gains realizations) is legally subdivided into taxable and untaxed income. In the US, taxable income includes income earned from illegal activities.

The IJ lines in Table 2 define the tax avoidance boundary, insofar as individuals have legal discretion to shift their activities between taxed and untaxed sectors. Taxable income, from both legal and illegal activities, is further subdivided into reported and unreported income components.

Table 2

Taxonomic Framework for Fiscal Income (Personal Income Taxes)

Potential Tax Base	Legal Classification	Reporting Status	Effective Tax Base	NIPA Relationship
	Untaxed Income I___J	Legally Non reported Income I___J	Avoidance I___J	
		Unreported Income K___L	Evasion M___N	O___P
Total Economic Income	Taxable Income	Reported Income L	Adjusted Gross Income M___N	Personal Income O___P
===
Capital Gains and Other Gains		Unreported Income K___L	Evasion M___N	
		Legally Non reported Income I___J	Avoidance I___J	
	Untaxed Income I___J			

89

Shifts from the reported taxable income sector into the unreported taxable income sector (crossing the KL line) constitute one form of tax evasion, namely underreporting of legal and illegal source taxable income. A second source of tax evasion arises from the overreporting of deductible adjustments to income. Fraudulent overstatement of these adjustments to income is strict tax evasion. On the other hand, tax-induced expenditures on goods or services which constitute allowable deductions are a legitimate form of tax avoidance. The fragility of this distinction has led to the introduction of yet another neologism, 'avoision', to describibe questionable practices which raise adjustments to total reported income.

The effective tax base (before deductions) for the Federal personal income tax is known as Adjusted Gross Income (AGI). AGI is the sum of all taxable income sources which have been reported on tax returns, minus adjustments to income. 'Underground income', in the fiscal context, is simply 'unreported income', measured as the difference between the income that should have been reported had the fiscal code been adhered to, and the income actually reported (the areas, IJKL in Table 2).

From the foregoing discussion, it is evident, that 'unreported fiscal income' in not synonymous with 'tax evasion', since tax evasion also includes overstated tax deductions. Moreover, 'unreported fiscal income' is a totally different concept than 'unrecorded economic income'. The former represents an empirical understatement of total taxable income, whereas the latter reflects an underestimation of total economic income.

2. EMPIRICAL ESTIMATES OF UNRECORDED AND UNREPORTED INCOME

The task of identifying and correcting data source and estimation deficiencies in tax data and NIPA accounts is a technically complex and demanding undertaking. For the academic economist, the task is all the more difficult, because of the absence of a comprehensive description of current sources and methods used to construct the accounts. In the United States, thirty years have passed since the last publication of a comprehensive description of the sources and methods employed to construct the nation's most vital economic information base. In many nations, such a compendium of sources and methods is totally lacking. Despite the technical explanations which have accompanied the spate of revisions in NIPA estimates, the foundations of our fundamental economic information system remain in relative obscurity.

One of the most significant contributions of the early academic research on the underground economy has been to stimulate governmental agencies to reexamine their methods of estimation in order to take greater account of data source deficiencies, and to devote more resources to their overdue efforts to document current accounting practices. Major revisions of NIPA's are now being undertaken to reflect new information on the extent of tax evasion which has recently been documented by the Internal Revenue Service in the United States. The extent and implications of other forms of underreporting in non tax related underlying data sources have still to be examined.

If one ignores for the moment the conventional exclusion from NIPA of non market, non-monetary income produced in the household, then it can be shown that unrecorded economic income and unreported fiscal income share an empirical relationship, due largely to the fact that national income accountants are forced to rely on tax data as a major source of information for the construction of NIPA. Since fiscal data sources are essential for the construction of NIPA, we first turn our attention to the measurement of Adjusted Gross Income (AGI).

AGI is the total income subject to Federal individual income taxes less certain adjustments such as employee business expenses, moving expenses and alimony payments. Taxed income, is the difference between AGI and various itemized and standard deductions currently permitted under US tax codes. Ignoring for the moment overstatement of standard and itemized deductions, the extent of the understatement of AGI represents the major source of the erosion of the tax base due to tax evasion. The term 'underground economy' when applied to the concept of fiscal income refers to the underreporting of income which is legally reportable for tax purposes. This concept is of critical importance to policy issues in public finance. To the extent that AGI constitutes the empirical basis for the determination of the effective personal income tax base for the United States, underreporting of AGI has direct implications for revenue losses due to the fiscal 'underground economy', and concomitant implications for the size of observed government deficits (11).

The extent of the understatement of Personal Income (PI), on the other hand, reflects the 'underground economy' when economic income is the focus of attention (12). I shall refer to the understatement of NIPA income measures as 'unrecorded income', and to the understatement of fiscal income measures as 'unreported income'. If 'unrecorded income' is large and changing over time, official NIPA statistics will give a misleading impression of the size and growth rates of total economic activity.

The empirical relationship between unreported income and unrecorded income, depends in considerable measure on the relationship between AGI and PI. (See Table 2) The Bureau of Economic Analysis (BEA) has prepared a reconciliation of PI and AGI for the period 1947-1981, which permits a comparison of the AGI figures reported by the Internal Revenue Service (AGI-IRS) with an estimate of AGI based on NIPA statistics (AGI-BEA). The reconciliation is achieved by estimating those components of PI which are not included in the AGI concept as well as those components of AGI which are not included in PI. By subtracting the former and adding the latter to measured PI, it is possible to derive BEA's estimate of AGI.

91

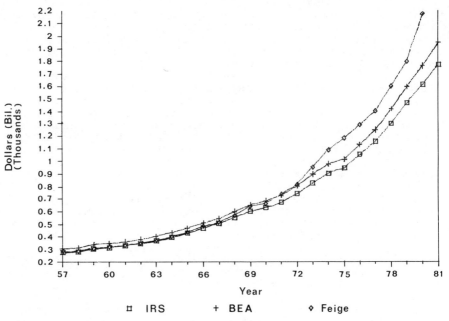

Figure 1: Estimates of adjusted gross income

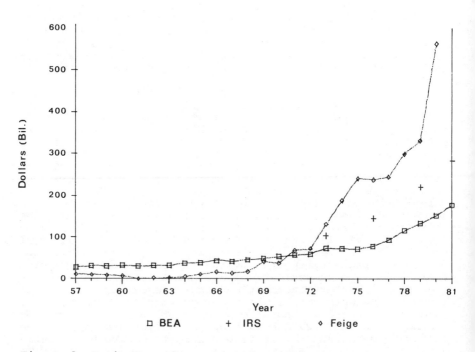

Figure 2: Estimates of unreported taxable income

Figure 1 displays three measures of AGI. The lower curve (IRS) displays the AGI as reported to the IRS. The middle curve (BEA) displays the BEA estimate of AGI based on the method described above, and the upper curve displays an estimate of AGI based on Feige's transaction method (13).

The vertical distance between BEA's estimate of AGI and the IRS reported AGI represents one measure of non-compliance with fiscal codes. This measure is commonly known as the AGI gap. The vertical distance between the transactions estimate of AGI and the IRS AGI represents a conceptually comparable estimate of non-compliance based on the transactions method. Figure 2 presents these two estimates of unreported fiscal income along with a new set of estimates of unreported fiscal income provided by the IRS.

Table 3 presents the values of the alternative estimates of unreported fiscal income for selected years. Column (1) displays the BEA estimates of the AGI gap; column (2) shows the IRS estimates of total unreported income and the final column represents the transactions method estimate of unreported income.

Table 3

Alternative estimates of unreported fiscal income
in billion of dollars

Year	(1) BEA-AGI Gap	(2) IRS-Unreported Income	(3) Feige-Unreported Income
1973	74.3	103.2	130.6
1976	78.2	144.9	237.4
1979	132.6	220.3	330.7
1980	142.0	252.1*	563.5
1981	176.9	283.9	NA

(*) Interpolation from 1979 and 1981 estimates.

As is discussed below, it must be noted that both the BEA estimates and the IRS estimates for the year 1979 and thereafter are 'projections' based on data for 1973 and 1976. For the latter years, no new information is incorporated in the projections. Thus if one is to compare trend growth in unreported incomes based on the different methods the only valid comparison is for the years 1973-1976. For these years, the BEA estimate suggest an average annual growth in unreported income of only 1.8 percent, whereas the IRS and transactions methods produce growth rates of 13.5 percent and 27.3 percent respectively. For the latter years, the transactions method estimates are the only estimates based on new data and these suggest that unrecorded income grew at an average annual rate of 34.3 percent between 1976 and 1980. Had the IRS 'projections' been based on the growth rates implied by the transactions method, rather than on the growth rates that prevailed in the early 1970's, their estimate of unreported income for 1980 would have been $ 343.9 billion rather than the $252.1 reported in Table 3.

In light of the differences in magnitude between these estimates, and the ambiguities concerning their interpretation, it is necessary to review their derivation in greater detail and to further examine their conceptual congruence.

2.1. Bureau of Economic Analysis Estimates of Non-Compliance

The first approximate (14) estimate of non-compliance is the difference between BEA's estimate of AGI and the actual AGI reported to the IRS (the AGI gap). According to the original BEA description of this series, the 'AGI gap can be taken as evidence of non-compliance with the tax code with the following caveats' (15):

1) The AGI gap overstates actual non compliance because it is based on personal income estimates which already include some adjustments for misreporting on tax returns as well as the income earned by individuals whose income is so low that they are not required to file tax returns.
2) The AGI gap understates actual non compliance because no estimate is made for under reporting of capital gains income or illegal income.
3) The gap is affected by errors in the reconciliation items, errors in other source data used to estimate personal income and sampling errors in AGI.

In a recently published article on the Underground Economy (16) the BEA reiterates the foregoing caveats, but now characterizes the AGI gap as a 'misunderstood estimate', claiming:

"Although it has been referred to as a measure of the underground economy because it is viewed as isolating the major part of underground income that is not reported on income tax returns, the AGI gap is not such a measure" (17).

How then are we to interpret the BEA's estimate of the AGI gap? The AGI gap can be considered a conceptually appropriate estimate of non-compliance (underreporting of AGI) once allowances are made for the overstatements and understatements listed as items (1) and (2) above. Its empirical accuracy, on the other hand, depends critically upon the degree to which personal income is itself adequately measured and the degree to which the reconciliation items are accurately measured.

With respect to the possible overstatements suggested by item (1) above, we know that in 1977, BEA adjusted personal income upward by $11.5 billion to allow for what they then thought was misreporting from tax information (18). In addition, the gap would be overstated to the degree that personal income estimates include income earned by individuals

94

who were not required to file tax returns. The IRS has estimated that, in 1976, the amount of unreported income of non-filers on which no tax was due amounted to $21.6 billion and in 1979 the estimate was placed at $32.7 billion (19). Linear extrapolation between these years suggests a figure of $27.1 for 1977. Thus, these sources together suggest that the AGI gap was overstated by some $38.6 billion.

The items leading to an understatement of the AGI gap include estimates of underreporting of capital gains and unreported illegal source income, neither of which is included in PI nor accounted for in the standard reconciliation items. On the basis of new IRS data (20), unreported capital gains for 1977 were approximately $13.1 billion and illegal sector income amounted to approximately $19.6 billion. Ignoring for the moment any illegal sector income which had been laundered into personal income, the net effects of the forgoing conceptual adjustments would be an overstatement of BEA's estimate of non-compliance of approximately $6 billion for 1977, or about 0.5 percent of reported AGI.

Having corrected for these conceptual departures from an appropriate non-compliance measure, any remaining flaws in the BEA estimate of non-compliance will be the result of errors in the reconciliation items and the extent to which personal income itself is underestimated due to its exclusion of unrecorded economic income. The direction and nature of errors in reconciliation items is unknown but given the magnitudes of these items, even small percentage errors could significantly reduce the accuracy of the BEA's non-compliance measure.

2.2. Internal Revenue Service estimates of unreported income

In 1979, the IRS publicly admitted that unreported fiscal income had attained significant proportions (21). It revealed that underreported legal source income amounted to $74.9 billion in 1976 (22). Four years later (23), the IRS revised its original estimate to $131.5 billion, almost double the initial figure.

The updated study, moreover, estimated that by 1981, total unreported income had reached $284 billion, an amount approaching 75 percent of the entire GNP of the United Kingdom. For that year, the number of non-filers was estimated to have exceeded 6.2 million individuals with a total income in excess of $115 billion. Unreported legal source income for filers of tax returns was estimated to be $133.8 billion and an additional $34 billion of unreported income was attributed to the illegal sector.

The IRS characterized the method employed to obtain its estimates as a 'direct' approach, but even a casual perusal of their complex studies reveals that their methodology is anything but 'direct'. Indeed, the vast number of assumptions incorporated in their procedures makes an evaluation of their overall results extremely difficult. Several particular aspects of the IRS findings do however deserve special attention.

As will be developed below, there are strong reasons to

believe that even these significantly higher estimates still are contaminated with downward biases. These result, ironically, from the very 'indirectness' of their approach, one that requires literally hundreds of assumptions. Many of these assumptions are candidly discussed and justified, but at critical junctures in the research, subjective decisions are made which exert a highly conservative bias to their final estimates.

Earlier estimates of unreported income were based entirely on the IRS Taxpayer Compliance Measurement Program (TCMP) which involved intensive audits of some 50,000 tax returns included in a stratified sample. Aside from the importance of TCMP reports for determining the unreported income on tax returns, these same reports formed the basis for upward revisions of NIPA accounts in order to adjust the accounts for the inherent downward bias in tax-related source data. The virtual doubling of the earlier IRS estimate of unreported income was not based on new TCMP data, but rather was the result of an internal audit of the IRS's own auditing procedures. This audit produced the remarkable finding that the intensive TCMP audits found only 22 percent of unreported wage, salary, interest and dividend income for which separate information returns had been filed with the IRS. Thus, for these categories with relatively high information reporting coverage, the ratio of total covered unreported income to detected unreported income ranged from 4.25 to 5.0. Other categories revealed higher multipliers and of course lower information return coverage. In light of these findings, the IRS proceeded to estimate the total unreported income for filers by multiplying detected unreported income from the audit by a factor of only 3.5. Had a multiplier of 5.0 been used instead, the 1981 estimate of legal source unreported income of filers alone would have been raised by almost $ 95 billion dollars. Similar conservative judgements affected the estimates of non-filers' unreported incomes. Having estimated the number of non-filers using a complex matching procedure between Social Security data, survey data and individual IRS tax records (24), the incomes of non-filers were estimated by assuming that individuals fully reported their incomes in the household survey. It is well known that the non-response rate on these income questions is very high, and that tax evaders are likely to be highly represented in the non-response categories. Moreover, to the extent that tax evaders are among the respondent group, it seems implausible to assume that they will correctly report the incomes which they have hidden from the tax authorities to survey interviewers. The report admits that:

"a suspicion lingers that people may be inclined to be more reticent about the incomes they earn 'on the side' than their earnings from other sources. To the extent such incomes were not reported during the household surveys ... the estimates ... are downward biased and understate the true amount of nonfilers incomes" (IRS, 1983, p. 75).

If one accepts, for the moment, the point estimates of the IRS for 1973 and 1976 (the only years for which complete data were available), it is still necessary to examine the time trends of non-compliance. The IRS study indicates that:

"trends in noncompliance with tax laws may be at least as significant as the amount and pattern of noncompliance existing at any given time ... The estimates prepared for this report represent the most comprehensive attempt made to date by IRS to assess trends in noncompliance with US tax law" (25).

The estimates presented for 1979 and 1981 form the basis for the IRS's concern over the growth in unreported income (see Figure 2 and Table 3), yet they are not based on any additional data collected for those years. According to the IRS report, "these estimates show the approximate levels noncompliance would have reached by 1979 and 1981 had past trends in these variables continued" (p. 7). A closer examination of the IRS projections for the latter years reveals that the agency actually chose to ignore 'past trends' which suggested that "adjusted gross income (AGI) per non-filer ... had increased at an extraordinary pace, from $6,826 in 1972 to $12,036 in 1977" (p. 83). Rather than incorporate these findings into its projections for latter years, the IRS simply ignored its own data with the rationale:

"This surprising situation led to speculation that perhaps the unusual growth of non-filer incomes was at least in part due to limitations of the estimation method used, rather than any fundamental change in the types of persons electing not to file individual income tax returns. Until further data are developed on the non-filer problem, therefore, it seemed more prudent to consider part of the unusual increase in average non-filers incomes between 1972 and 1977 to be suspect. Consequently, while the growth of non-filers income from 1973 to 1976 was assumed to have proceeded at the estimated rate of growth from 1972 to 1977, this rapid pace was moderated in deriving projections for 1979 and 1981" (p. 83).

One justification for focusing on so called 'direct' methods was that the resulting estimates could be "decomposed into separate elements that must be individually analysed for effective monitoring of compliance with the tax laws" (p. 42). As a means of providing a 'validity check' on its own estimates, the IRS turned to BEA data which itself is deeply based in tax related sources. According to the report:

"It was important, therefore, to compare these estimates with alternative measures based on data from sources external to the IRS. In order to have a valid comparison, however, the alternative measures could not be conjectural or based on financial ratios not sufficiently stable to yield reliable estimates of unrepor-

ted income .... The only external source of data that
came close to yielding the needed yardsticks with which
to evaluate the non-compliance estimates prepared for
this report was found at the BEA" (p. 135).

The results of the 'validity check' are characterized as
follows:

"It is noteworthy, that often, but not always, the
discrepancy in the BEA-IRS reconciliation tables shows
substantial confirmation of the IRS income gap estimates" (p. 152).

On closer scrutiny, these reconciliation tables reveal that
although overall discrepancies might be characterized as
bearing out 'substantial confirmation', this result depends
entirely on the fortuitous offsetting of major discrepancies
in individual items.
As displayed in Table 4, the BEA estimate of unreported
wages and salaries is approximately half of the IRS estimate, whereas its unreported interest figure (26) is more than
2.5 times the IRS estimate (p. 137).
In light of the foregoing examples, it is difficult to
escape several key conclusions regarding the IRS results:

1) The novelty of the new IRS study stems from its acknow-
ledgement that earlier estimates of non-compliance based
directly on intensive audit findings represented gross
underestimates of unreported incomes, since the audit
procedures uncovered less than 25 percent of the unreported income which could be independently documented by
information returns.

Table 4

Percentage discrepancies between BEA and IRS
estimates of unreported income components
1 9 7 9

Income Source	Percent Discrepancy*
Wages and Salaries	- 51.90
Farm Propietor Income	35.78
Nonfarm Proprietor and	
Partnership	8.19
Interest	173.39
Dividends	128.57
Rents and Royalties	134.62
Pensions	15.87
Other Income	- 9.33
TOTAL	3.40

(*) The percent discrepancy is calculated as
(BEA - IRS) / IRS x 100.

2) Even the new estimates of unreported income are likely to be gross underestimates because a lower multiplier was used for adjustment than was suggested by the IRS's own findings. Similarly, unreported incomes of non-filers are based on survey data which take no account of self selection biases among both respondents and non-respondents.

3) The IRS estimates of the trends in non-compliance are not based on any new information beyond 1976. Moreover, the projections estimated for 1979 and 1981 ignore information which was available to the IRS on non-filer incomes. Incorporating this information would have raised estimated non-compliance in subsequent periods.

4) An examination of separate sources of non-compliance reveals major discrepancies between the IRS findings and existing BEA estimates.

Although the IRS study candidly admits these inadequacies in its methods, it continues to assert, rather than demonstrate, that:

"Despite their limitations, direct methods of estimation relying on survey data and administrative records are believed to be superior to the indirect methods others have used" (p. 26).

The above-mentioned limitations of the IRS approach are of considerable importance, since it is the IRS estimates of unreported income which provide the basis for the current revisions of the NIPA accounts. A recently released report (27) reveals that the BEA has now incorporated an improved adjustment for tax source misreporting in 1977 amounting to $81.5 billion for charges against GNP and $69.3 billion dollar improved adjustment for Personal Income. To the extent that the IRS estimates are too low, similarly, the BEA adjustments for unrecorded income will be too low. Moreover, the BEA plans to extrapolate its tax source misreporting adjustments for the post-1977 period on the basis of the assumption that the proportion of unreported income remains constant. In light of the foregoing discussion, such a procedure will understate unrecorded income for all subsequent years because the proportions used for extrapolation will be based on an underestimate of unreported income. Moreover, the procedure will take no account of the growth in the proportion of unreported incomes revealed by both the IRS estimates and the transaction estimates.

3. THE CONSEQUENCES OF UNREPORTED INCOME ESTIMATES FOR BUDGET DEFICITS

In many Western economies, budget deficits have risen to unprecedented heights, stimulating demands for higher taxes and substantial cutbacks in social programs. In the United

States, the annual budget deficit averaged $0.5 billion in the decade of the 1950's, $5.7 billion in the 1960's, $30.2 billion in the 1970's, and $109 billion in the early 1980's. Estimated US budget deficits for the mid 1980's are in excess of $200 billion. This growth of government deficits has stimulated considerable controversy concerning the measurement, interpretation and implications of sizable deficits. These issues are intimately connected with the growth of unreported fiscal income.

The introduction of Keynesian economics, with its emphasis on the consequences of fiscal policy for macroeconomic activity, focused attention on the impact of government budgets on economic fluctuations. By 1947, it was acknowledged that the actual government surplus or deficit was a poor indicator of the thrust of discretionary fiscal policy, since the actual budget reflected both the automatic responses of revenues and expenditures to cyclical fluctuations in the economy and discretionary changes in fiscal policy (28). In order to develop a more refined measure of discretionary fiscal policy, free of cyclical influences on the budget, the question was posed, "What would be the size of the government budget if the economy were at full employment?". The answer to this question was the development of the 'full employment' or 'cyclically adjusted' budget, which reflected the 'structural' or discretionary component of the budget (29). Partitioning the actual budget into its cyclical and structural components remains a complex problem of measurement (30) but there is no longer any controversy about the importance of making this conceptual distinction.

The apparent growth of the 'underground economy' raises a new and potentially equally significant issue, namely, "What would be the size of the government budget if there were full compliance with tax regulations and social expenditure programs?". The answer to this counterfactual question is provided by the concept of the 'full compliance' budget (31).

Given estimates of unreported taxable income, it is possible to construct rough estimates of the 'tax gap', namely, the loss of tax revenue due to underreporting of taxable income. One of the most useful aspects of the recent IRS report is its attempt to construct estimates of the 'tax gap'. The IRS report calculates separate components of the tax gap based on their estimates of unreported income as well as from audit data on overstated business expenses and deductions. Since the report yields separate estimates of unreported income of filers and non-filers, it uses different average marginal tax rates to access the tax losses implied for different income source category. To the extent that the separate income source categories are misspecified (See Table 4) the tax losses will also be in error (32). Table 5 presents estimates of the tax gap for the years 1979 and 1980 derived from the IRS report, and roughly comparable estimates of the tax gap based on the transaction method estimates of unreported income.

Table 5

Alternative estimates of tax gaps and
the full compliance deficit
in billions of dollars

1979-1980

Tax Gap Source	IRS-79(1)	TRANS-79	IRS-80(2)	TRANS-80
Unreported Legal Income				
Filer	38.4	60.2	52.2	108.6
Non-Filer	2.0	3.1	2.9	5.3
Illegal	6.3	6.3	7.7	7.7
Corporate Gap	6.4	6.4	6.3	6.3
Business Expenses	4.7	4.7	5.5	5.5
Overstated Deductions	5.0	5.0	5.8	5.8
Net error	0.5	0.5	0.5	0.5
Remittance Gap	5.3	5.3	6.1	6.1
Total Tax Gap	68.6	91.5	87.0	145.8
Actual Deficit	- 14.8	- 14.8	- 61.2	- 61.2
F.C. Deficit	+ 53.8	+ 76.7	+ 25.8	+ 84.6

(1) From Internal Tax Compliance Research.

(2) Estimates based on linear interpolations for 1979 and 1981.

Although the transaction method only produces estimates of total unreported income, the component estimates from the IRS study can be used to decompose total unreported income into unreported illegal income, and filer and non-filer unreported income (33). By applying the same tax rates used by the IRS, it is possible to make a comparison between the IRS tax gap estimates and those estimated from the transactions methods. For 1979, the transaction methods yields a tax gap that is $22.5 billion above that estimated by the IRS. For 1980, the difference amounts to $58.8 billion (34).

Table 5 also displays the corresponding values of the 'full compliance deficit' (F.C.) assuming that social fraud is zero. The substantial budget deficit of 1980 would have become a sizable surplus, had there been full compliance with the tax code. These results suggest that a tax reform which lowers rates, simplifies the tax code and reestablishes the perception that there are no free riders in tax matters, may be the most hopeful solution for the massive deficits which currently threaten the stability of economies throughout the world.

4. SUMMARY AND CONCLUSIONS

In order to gain a clearer perspective on the measurement and implications of the growth in the 'underground economy', an essential first step is the development of an appropriate taxonomic framework which clarifies the distinction between various concepts of 'underground' activity. When the primary concern is the measurement of economic activity, total eco-nomic income is the appropriate concept, and its conponents, recorded and unrecorded income, reflect the differences between conventional measures and those which properly ac-count for the effects of the growth of the 'underground economy'. When the primary concern is with the public finan-ce implications of the underground economy, the appropriate concept is fiscal income and its components, reported and unreported income. Recorded economic income is empirically reflected in measures of personal income, whereas reported fiscal income is reflected in measures of adjusted gross income, and these two different concepts can be empirically reconciled on the basis of available data sources. Estimates of unrecorded income reflect the extent to which current national income accounting procedures are defective in their omission of an important segment of economic activity, whereas estimates of unreported income are required in order to correctly assess the implications of non-compliance with existing fiscal legislation.

Although there remains considerable controversy about the size and growth of both unrecorded and unreported incomes, governmental agencies in the United States have responded to the issues raised by academic researchers and have conducted their own major research projects to determine the extent and significance of underground activities. These new fin-dings reveal that both unrecorded and unreported incomes are much greater than had previously thought to have been the case, and they confirm the primary assertions of earlier studies that the underground economy has exhibited considerable growth during the 1970's and 1980's.

The spectacular growth of government deficits, and the controversy surrounding their macroeconomic consequences, stimulates the need to extend the insights of 'underground economics' to the domain of federal budget analysis. The concept of the <u>full compliance</u> deficit enables us to distinguish between structural, cyclical and noncompliance budget components, and leads to a new perspective on the intended and unintended consequences of discretionary fiscal policy. Further research is required to determine the cyclical patterns of unrecorded and unreported incomes so that current measures of the high employment budget can be appropriately modified in order to eliminate biases introduced by the fluctuations in the underground economy.

Given the magnitude of current estimates of the tax gap and the additional non-compliance component of social fraud, it appears that political concerns about the size of deficits might well be directed toward the study of major fiscal reform programs aimed at the reestablishment of voluntary high levels of compliance with fiscal regulations. Higher tax rates and reduced social expenditures appear on the surface to be the most expeditious manner of reducing deficits. However, the unintended consequence of such policies is to stimulate further underground activity, thus thwarting efforts to reduce deficits. The alternative policy prescription is to simplify the tax system in order to make it both more comprehensible and equitable, and to reduce marginal tax rates with base broadening, in order to reduce economic incentives for non-compliance. Only when tax laws are perceived as being equitable and universally administered are we likely to see a reversal of the trends toward greater noncompliance.

NOTES

(1) The author gratefully acknowledges research support from the Alfred P. Sloan Foundation.
(2) See Feige (1980), Feige and McGee (1985).
(3) Feige (1984).
(4) Murphy (1981).
(5) Skolka (1981).
(6) Smith, Moyer and Trzcinski (1982).
(7) UN (1953).
(8) Recorded income can be measured with different degrees of 'grossness', thus giving rise to distinctions between GNP and NNP. Estimates of national income are derived from NNP by subtracting indirect tax and nontax liabilities, business transfer payments, and the statistical discrepancy, and by adding subsidies less the current surplus of government enterprises. Finally, personal income is derived from national income by subtracting corporate profits with inventory valuation and capital consumption adjustments, net interest,

contributions for social insurance, and wage accruals less disbursements, and by adding government transfer payments to persons, personal interest income, personal dividend income, and business transfer payments.

(9) The Bureau of Economic Analysis makes imputations for food produced and consumed on farms and also includes imputations for non-monetary transactions such as rent for owner-occupied housing.

(10) An example would be food grown and consumed on a farm which is excluded from fiscal income under US tax law, but is considered to be a segment of total economic income for which NIPA imputations are undertaken.

(11) Feige (1985).

(12) Personal Income represents one of the major components in the construction of the broader measure of economic activity, namely GNP. We focus our discussion on personal income, because it is, to date, the only NIPA concept for which it is possible to derive a direct empirical relationship to empirical measures of fiscal income, eg. AGI.

(13) The IRS and BEA measures are reported in the Survey of Current Business, November 1981 and July 1982. The transactions method estimates of AGI are based on the relationship between adjusted total transactions and reported AGI. The transactions method is described in Feige (1980).

(14) The estimate is approximate due to some conceptual departures from a pure non-compliance measure and due to various errors in both the reconciliation items and errors in other source data used to estimate personal income.

(15) See BEA (1981).

(16) Carson (1984).

(17) It is not surprising that the BEA would disavow the AGI gap as a measure of the 'underground economy' since it characterizes the underground economy as: "economic activities - or income from those activities - that elude, wholly or partly, a tax or other reporting requirement. As the focus moves to measurement, such a characterization is not specific enough to be useful". (See Carson, (1984), p. 24).

(18) Parker (1984).

(19) See IRS (1983), pp. 78-79.

(20) Derived from IRS (1983), p. 9 and p. 39 with linear interpolation between benchmark years.

(21) IRS (1979).

(22) These initial findings were criticized as containing serious downward biases. See Feige (1980).

(23) IRS (1983).

(24) In describing its efforts to identify non-filers using match techniques between different data sources, the report indicates "such indirect means of identifying potential non-filers were necessary because the IRS does not maintain lists of individuals who do not file tax returns." IRS (1983) (p. 71)

(25) IRS (1983), p. 7.

(26) The IRS states that "Care has also been taken to state all of the assumptions, together with enough background figures to permit the interested reader to make alternative estimates using the same data but with different assumptions" (p. 1). However, once the interested reader delves more deeply into the report, he encounters some difficulty in assessing the reliability of the reported results. For example, in discussing the unreported income reconciliations, the report states, "some of the BEA estimates are based on indirect procedures that raise questions about their potential use in estimating non-compliance. To cite an extreme example, 63 data sources were required to prepare estimates of the unexplained portion of the gap between BEA and IRS data for personal interest income" IRS (1983), (p. 136).
(27) Parker (1984).
(28) CED (1947).
(29) SCB (1980), (1982).
(30) De Leeuw and Holloway (1983).
(31) Feige (1985).
(32) The IRS applied an overall average marginal tax rate of 39% to its estimate of unreported income for filers, and an effective overall average tax rate of 2.3% on total unreported income of non-filers for its 1981 estimate.
(33) The IRS estimate of illegal source income was subtracted from total unreported income, and the residual 'legal' component was then allocated between filer and non-filer unreported income on the basis of the proportions estimated in the IRS report.
(34) When the tax gap is estimated by simply applying Barro's estimate of the average effective marginal tax rate to total unreported income, the differences between the IRS tax gap and the transaction method tax gap becomes $27.3 billion for 1979 and $82.0 billion for 1980. See Feige (1985).

REFERENCES

BEA, Survey of Current Business, November 1981.
CARSON, C., 'The Underground Economy: An Introduction', Survey of Current Business, July 1984.
CED, Taxes and the Budget: A Program for Prosperity in a Free Economy, Committee for Economic Development, New York 1947.
DE LEEUW, F., HOLLOWAY, T., Measuring and Analyzing the Cyclically Adjusted Federal Budget, Federal Reserve Bank of Boston Conference on the Economics of Large Government Deficits, October 1983.
FEIGE, E.L., A New Perspective on Macroeconomic Phenomena: The Theory and Measurement of the Unobserved Sector of the United States - Causes, Consequences and Implications. presented at the 1980 Meetings of the American Economics Association, 1980.
FEIGE, E.L., 'Macroeconomics and the Unobserved Economy', in

Block, W., Walker, M. (eds), <u>Taxation: An International Perspective</u>, The Fraser Institute, 1984.

FEIGE, E.L., 'The Meaning of the Underground Economy and the Full Compliance Deficit', in Wenig, A., Gaertner, W., (eds) <u>The Economics of the Shadow Economy</u>, Springer, Heidelberg 1985.

FEIGE, E.L., McGEE, R.T., 'Policy Illusion, Macroeconomic Instability and the Unobserved Economy', in <u>The Unobserved Economy</u>, Cambridge University Press, 1985.

IRS, <u>Estimates of Income Unreported on Individual Income Tax Returns</u>, Internal Revenue Service: Publication 1104, September 1979.

MURPHY, M., <u>Comparative Estimates of the Value of Household Work in the United States</u>, Seventeenth General Conference of the International Association for Research in Income and Wealth, August 1981.

PARKER, R., 'Improved Adjustments for Misreporting of Tax Return Information Used to Estimate the National Income and Product Accounts', 1977, <u>Survey of Current Business</u>, June 1984.

SKOLKA, J., <u>The Parallel Economy in Austria</u>, presented at the Bielefeld Conference on the Shadow Economy, October 1983.

SMITH, J., MOYER, T., TRZCINSKI, F., <u>The Measurement of Selected Income Flows in Informal Markets</u>, prepared for the Internal Revenue Service, December 1982.

SCB, 'The High Employment Budget: New Estimates, 1955-80', <u>Survey of Current Business</u>, November 1980.

SCB, 'The High Employment Budget and Potential Output', <u>Survey of Current Business</u>, November 1982.

UN, <u>A System of National Accounts and Supporting Tables</u>, Studies in Method no. 2, United Nations, New York 1953.

Unofficial economy and the meaning of labour: toward a theoretical hypothesis

FEDELE RUGGERI

1. PREMISE

A word of caution is first needed since the range of the subject under consideration is such that the brief remarks contained herein are of necessity inadequate to the task at hand, especially if one is convinced that we are dealing with a subject of such importance as to be representative - in one way or another - of the general nature of social dynamic. Nonetheless, when a matter of such consequence is considered in relation to the emergence of processes of rapid transformation, it seems convenient to try to gather together whatever fragmentary data we have and to attempt a summing up. However provisional the results may be, at least they may be expected to stimulate further investigation.

It must be specified that herein the term <u>labor</u> is taken to signify that part of human experience relating to the <u>productive activities necessary to materially sustain life</u>, even though we are aware that such a definition may seem overly generic, and that in and of itself much remains to be detailed (1).

2. SOME PROBLEMS

A meaningful compendium of the matters just touched on is afforded by the debate over the centrality or noncentrality of the work experience with respect to human existence and that part of the culture concerned with the labor movement (2).

On the one hand, for a long time this experience has been held to be capable of designating a certain situation internal to social relations and at the same time of expressing instances and values lived as root motives of the actions of both single individuals and aggregations. Thus the workers, defined as such by their relationship with the material production of wealth, have been considered to be the special object of social domination and exploitation <u>and</u> the principal repositories of the possibility of the emancipation and reshaping of the social order (3).

On the other hand, it has been pointed out that not only does actual physical labor nowadays engage an ever-diminishing share of the population, itself in a phase of de-acceleration, but also how that very work experience as concretely manifested can only with difficulty be looked on as a full realization of human experience. This observation calls to mind the fact that the percentage of the population officially employed - especially in the primary and secondary sectors - has been decreasing, while the reduction of working hours - from the standpoint of both the number of hours in the work day and over the entire span of a working life - has had the effect of placing greater stress on other aspects of human existence. Moreover, it has been observed that in those contexts where the ascendancy of work of an industrial type has provided an opportunity for social mobility, previous forms of social identity - both individual and collective - have been lost, without the creation of meaningful substitutes.

Thus one might come to affirm that the work experience no longer provides the central criterion in the formation of individual and social identities. Rather, the coordinates of such processes may be determined along other lines, such as - to offer a few examples - those defined by old age, the female gender or youth. Features then come to the fore which have the common characteristic of representing social relations in terms of a central/peripheral sense of otherness - that is, of exclusion or, otherwise with respect to 'strong' focal points of the formation and distribution of socially relevant resources, rather than in terms of polarization with respect to a given social structure as was the case in the relationship between capitalist/entrepreneur and working class - a connotation, therefore, more essential, and in a certain sense existential, with a possibility of mediation either lesser or completely absent.

Significantly, a substantial coincidence would appear evident in the above situation and that found in the theses of the '50s and '60s concerning the identification with the middle class of the more skilled and better rewarded members of the working class: work per se would not cause the formation of a collective identity, nor would it inform related behavior, but would merely represent a criterion of income distribution, and not the main one at that, if one only stops to consider the role of the state with its expenditures in terms of welfare and social security.

Here questions arise which, if squarely faced, can help in detailing the causes of these vexed issues and offer an opportunity to arrive at a more profound understanding of the meaning and nature of presence in the labor force.

Given that over the years the weight assigned to the importance of labor in the existence of man has been a mixed affair - or, at a minimum, has been less than crystal clear - we are forced into a consideration of why in the last couple of hundred years work was deemed a fundamental moral principle and a decisive criterion with respect to social integration (4). Certainly, one can locate a root cause in the Protestant Ethic, strengthened and articulated as it spread - one might say taking on a lay aspect - in the 'spirit of capitalism' (5); the question remains, however, as to why and in what sense the work was first assigned a central role in the individual and social experience, and why later such a role was negated.

Taking for granted, at least for the moment, the 'loss of centrality', we must ask ourselves: Does the work referent still play an appreciable role (and if so, which) in the understanding of social change, or rather at this point is it scarsely significant in this sense, even marginal?

And consequently, what indications do we have, what hints emerge in an effort to track down the 'functional equivalents' of such change and of the related strategies of the actors?

The range of problems thus emerging turns out to be particularly complex; included herein are problems of substance and of method - how to define labor and social change, for example. The program of study research suggested cannot but be ample, and therefore far beyond the scope of the present contribution; nonetheless, such are the considerations the theme demands and such, therefore, are the questions that must be addressed.

It may be helpful to note that there is a differentiation of the ambits of reference, which become increasingly well-defined as our treatment of them progresses. Proceeding by successive degrees of abstraction, the first level to be taken up is that of the specific sites and methods of the work experience per se. That is, here we must take into account the physical changes, so to speak, which affect the same, in order to understand how its contours are thereby altered, and to gain from this some indication of the changes in meaning involved. This reference obviously regards the factory system without, however, neglecting changes that have taken place at the white collar level which have made the office environment ever less clearly distinguishable from the factory work place, and likewise the burgeoning instances of 'decentralized production', of the unofficial or para-official economy and of 'work at home', which have led to the coining of the expression 'fabbrica diffusa' - literally, diffuse (spread out) factory. For this reason it is probably more useful to bear in mind such strategic variables as technological and organizational change which characterize and animate these work places, rather than merely the specific work environment - a factory of greater or lesser size, say, and/or an office with given structures and mechanisms.

The second level relates to the formation and manifestation of subjectivity. Given that work activity is one of the variables - structuralizing, to a degree - of such processes, we can hardly fail to analyze the perception/behavior/ projection process of the workers, linking such to their methods, by focusing on whatever emerges empirically. Thus a study of subjectivity with reference to work would seem opportune, which study would at once be capable of taking into account any possible coincidence between objective characters and subjective dynamics, and to make evident the problems of 'meaning' that characterize the work experience.

The third level concerns social relations. However marginal the role of work activity may become from the standpoint of various types of socially useful mechanisms for the production and distribution of resources, we cannot neglect to question ourselves about the connections that form between such activity and the salient features of social relations, at least until such a time when it is taken for granted that the articulation of that activity is socially irrelevant with respect to the determination of the subjects, to its fulfilment and to the conditions and characteristics of its realization. In other words, even though conditions have changed, it remains necessary to go back and research the connections and interactions between the authority/power mechanisms of a society and the modalities of accomplishing such activity.

While still keeping in mind the provisional nature of the undertaking stated at the outset, it would seem useful to proceed along these lines, referring in particular - in the following paragraph - to the contribution of such scholars as Pahl and Miles (6) for the purpose of recalling more efficaciously the characteristics of the problem under examination and then - in the paragraph following that - advancing some reflections useful for their comprehension.

3. REDEFINITION OF WORK ACTIVITY OR THE END OF WORK?

The thematic area in which Miles's contribution is located is that concerning the relationship between occupation and the introduction of technologies whose purpose is to inform the individual elements of the work process, with references both to the quantitative aspects (employment trends and distribution by occupational sector) and to the qualitative aspects (changes regarding the content and modality of job performance), as well as the character of the productive system with reference to the reciprocal relation among the classic sectors: primary (agricultural and extractive), secondary (manufacturing) and tertiary (service), while at the same time keeping in mind the possibility that these sectors alone may prove inadequate when one takes into account the 'nebulous' quality of those activities which do not show up in surveys of the official economy, but which nonetheless definitely involve the production and consumption of necessary goods and services (p. 1).

With respect to employment trends, prospects appear substantially negative; results emerging from data up to 1975 are confirmed by the characteristics of the most recent technological developments - "new technologies are being introduced more for the purpose of rationalization than of expansion" (p. 13) - and the growth of the service industry (whatever the various articulations and differentiations internal to it) is insufficient to replace jobs lost in the other two sectors.

As regards the quality of the work performed (the second point) Miles's treatment is less certain. Thus, after a careful evaluation of the literature in general and of the work of Braverman (7) in particular, he ends up affirming that the new technologies per se are incapable of producing

110

any consequences, but rather that "it is their use, and the social relation under which they are designed" (p. 15) which causes the changes in question.

Clearly, to avoid banality, here one must study the mechanisms that condition the use of technological innovations (at bottom their very appearance on the scene) with reference to both the factory system and to relations to the marketplace. In the first instance, change regarding the quality of labor must undergo close analysis; however, this point appears secondary with respect to the problem at hand, so that for the time being it seems sufficient to refer the observations made in the latest study by Manacorda (8). In the second instance, the effects of technological innovation must be analyzed thoroughly examining the previous reference to the contractation of employment ("more for the purpose of rationalization than of expansion"); in particular transformations in the service sector must be studied to evaluate whether such transformations indicate a process of change in the role played in the actual production of goods.

To this end Pahl's contribution may prove most helpful in that he deals with the problem of the unofficial economy with respect to the changes which characterize labor. The thesis advanced is that the expression 'unofficial economy' is incorrect. In fact, in the overwhelming majority of the activities thus labeled the classic economic parameters are valid; moreover, even in those cases where they do not strictly apply, the logic of the marketplace still seems to influence, at least metaphorically, the expectations and evaluations of the various situations (pp. 2-3).

Can the opposite then be maintained - that "the logic of the formal economy is expanding into the calculations of everyday life?"

It would seem more suitable to maintain that processes varied in nature are present which, taken together, produce a rather composite picture.

We may suppose then - in highly schematic fashion - that on the one hand (a) a tendency is underway of economic marginalization of the sectors producing goods and services, while on the other hand (b) the ambit of applicability of values proper to the marketplace is undergoing expansion.

In the first case, certain forms of production, necessary though they are for survival, tend to exit from the logic of the marketplace; this is what occurs in many forms of activity (in agriculture, in maintenance and technical assistance) in general more or less directly related to the reproduction of the labor force, which no longer tend to be part of the dynamic of the investment/ profit of capital, but rather to occur in the area of social relations of a non-mercantile type, practically without a market-determined price; this can probably be affirmed even though such exit derives from the very way the logic of the capitalistic system develops, and even if in a certain sense the marketplace and its mechanisms are still present in the background as parameters of evaluation of whatever transpires.

In the second case, instead, an actual expansion of the model itself is evinced, so that new activities and ambits

111

come into being.

Here as well it appears necessary to distinguish between:

I) those areas where it becomes possible to invest in a
capitalistic sense with an aim of profit - such as
occurs in scientific research, in the elaboration and
transmission of knowledge, in certain technical assistance and maintenance services;

II) that area where the reference to the marketplace is
only indirect, metaphorical, taking place through a
sort of transposition of the operative criteria - for
example, the calculation of the remuneration for work
done in private non-profit organizations such as labor
unions and political parties. In the first case we are
in the presence of a dynamic of a strictly economic
nature, in which portions of previously untouched reality are now subject to capitalistic production and/or
use in the interest of gain; the second case, instead,
while certainly indicating an expansion of the market
model, with assigning of a price to the activity performed, takes place for the most part through an affirmation of a process of 'cultural' and ideological homo-
genization.

In this situation as well a distinction can be made - and
it is probably useful to make it - between two radically
different categories, each capable of providing an explanation of the phenomenon in question; we refer, on the one
hand, to (a) the circumstance in which an activity is reduced to the level of merchandise, for which a price is
assigned, so that it may be acquired as a service rendered
by one person to another, which process can be spoken of as
merchandising; on the other hand (b) to the fact that a
whole series of activities - political and union activity in
particular, but health and welfare as well - are financially
rewarded in one way or another, all of which would seem to
indicate that social development has come to couch in specific terms the dealing with its problems, with the implicit
possibility of technical specialization, which therefore
allows us to speak of socialization (9).

To reason thusly about the relation between the official
and unofficial economy allows the bringing together of diverse phenomena which, however, taken together represent a
certain way of achieving an adjustment of social relations
and their attendant tensions: the matter of whether we are
dealing with an expansion of the unofficial economy or of
the official economy becomes secondary; what becomes decisive instead for an understanding of the difference between
the various phenomena present and the diverse forms of work
activity associated with them is to find a system capable of
explaining the relationship that links them and that causes
the passage from one to the next.

In this respect it seems necessary to refer to that which
the author calls social relations of work or social relationships, for the reason that, in his opinion, and in ours
as well, material activity itself changes meaning as the

social relationship changes (pp. 4-5, and p. 19): "in all these descriptions of a given task being done, the type of work determined by the pattern of social relationships in which it is embedded".

To refer to such social relations requires defining them in narrow and unequivocal fashion, since otherwise we are left with a sort of residual area variables, but which still does not allow critical comprehension of observed phenomena. One has the impression that by 'social relations' we end up meaning interpersonal relations and their relative warp and woof of expectation/ gratification, with respect to which authority/power relations, natural conditions and even economic characteristics cannot but represent an external framework, decisive in defining the field action, but irrelevant to, and not subject to, conditioning by the fabric of the actions and reactions of the actors. Certainly in this way one may distinguish one work activity from another (the act of cleaning for a cleaning agency, to help a friend, for personal satisfaction, out of personal necessity, because imposed by family obligations, by virtue of the authority vested in the head of a family), but we have no sociologically systematic criterion for defining a single activity as distinct from the rest: what is revealed is a series of separate pictures depicting the social dynamics, but without the availability of a definition of labor and of an interpretive criterion of the changes in progress.

Certainly the consequent proposal of indicating the multiplication of phenomena of work activity outside the wage-system with the term 'new mixes of work' has the advantage, with respect to the proposal relative to the enlargement of the area of the unofficial economy, of underlining the presence of a process capable of explaining the modalities by which new equilibria are produced within households. But this route fails to track down elements useful in reaching a definition of the work activity performed within the household unit. In point of fact the undertaking becomes nearly impossible because whatever such activity is concretely would come to depend on the various work situations which charcterize it. Not for nothing Pahl himself feels the need to point out, with respect to how concrete modalities and work loads are determined, that a problem to be solved "is how the relative ranking of different degrees of necessity is to be determined and by whom" (p. 18).

In this regard Pahl's reference to the character of 'task oriented' as a way of defining work activity says nothing, per se, about the social dynamics in progress. Such reference, to be socially significant, cannot merely coincide with the experience of individual satisfaction derived from the service one has rendered, nor with the fact that some activities are autonomously determined, but must come to grips with the social significance that characterizes them. In other words, from the standpoint of the actor to prepare a meal for oneself, to make oneself a tool, to fix up a house are all task-oriented activities, but to say the same from the standpoint of the social dynamics (one may say, with a degree of approximation, from the standpoint of the social division of labor) it is necessary to verify the social significance of that activity.

It may be useful to specify that by no means do we mean to hypothesize the existence in some more or less remote past of a situation in which the determination of work activity was autonomous and rich in individual and social significance - a situation finished off by industrialization and the coming of modern society characterized by complexity and integration; instead, we believe that the dialectic betweem these two poles of the work situation - self-directed/ other-directed, rich/poor in meaning both to oneself and to society - reappears in different social conditions in the form of connotations peculiar to each, in the guise of a discrete element of internal tension. Any comparison between different historical moments that fails to take into account this mechanism of the re-proposal of the terms of a certain dialectic not only fails to respect the specificity of each historical context, but also fails to respect the very aspirations and views of those involved.

4. SOME POSSIBILITIES FOR FURTHER RESEARCH

With the forgoing observations we now set aside the suggestion of the two contributors cited to enter into the matter of an independent proposal regarding the theme under consideration. In doing so it is helpful to recall in summary certain references of an empirical nature in order to delineate what seem to be emerged features of the current stage of history.

First of all we note a decrease in the amount of labor employed in the production of material goods. However, associated with this we find - leaving aside a consideration of the effects on compensation - an increase in wage-earning employees occupied in the production of services in a broad sense (the role of the government worker) and a diffuse, though inorganic and not readily subject to analysis, situation of mobilization and of self-employment directed to production of goods and services useful for survival.

Further emerging from studies on organization and on technological development is the lesser importance of technical control (the classic paradigm of the 'one best way') and of the greater importance of functional co-ordination, of organization based on objectives to be reached, as being more transparent, less burdensome and more efficacious vehicles of social control.

Finally, taking off from the aforementioned traits, social production seems to be directed to an ever-lessening degree toward objects necessary for physical survival, and to an ever-increasing degree toward the production and control of society in and of itself. We are referring first of all to the production of knowledge, to transmission of the same with the necessary support systems, to communication systems, as well as to the processes involved in the production of services, among which figures education - all elements which appear to an ever-lesser extent to be external and

114

instrumental, and to an ever-greater extent to be strategic mechanisms in the characterization of social equilibria. In particular this reference regards scientific research, communication systems, educational systems, social policies; from this standpoint previously existing services, such as those dealing with public order and public health, are redefined.

The three aspects just mentioned seem to be extremely integrated among themselves - almost different ways of looking at the same reality, both as to point of view and to complexity of reference.

In a more circumscribed way it is of interest here to consider what derives from this with respect to the character and role of work experience.

Proceeding from the first aspect to the third we find a rarefication of the features of said experience: in the first case the experience is clearly focused and the more evident changes can be measured; in the second the reference is indirect, more relative to the modalities of its management than to its contents and to the weight of its presence; in the third it does not even come into play in an explicit way, while the lens is centered on the new or renewed emergence of the production and control of society. This different vantage point should not mislead us, however, in that even in the third case there is 'work to be done' - that is, the phenomena mentioned are concretely present in things that need doing; it is the very diversity of vantage point that allows discussion to develop about <u>labor</u> with reference to the contents that characterize it and to the social significance proper to it.

What can be said about these three different instances with regard to the theme proposed is that work activity seems to wane in terms of concreteness and materiality, manifesting itself rather as <u>process</u>.

Certainly from the standpoint of the individual actor this still consists of concrete things to be done; it still is measurable in terms of expenditure of energy, of application, of knowledge on the hand, and on the other of remuneration and gratification. But from the standpoint of the organization that provides the job (ranging from the factory to the office, from the educational system to the health care system, from the research industry to the communications industry) it is virtually no longer a closed aggregate of skills (the welder or lathe operator, but also the teacher or social worker), but rather the constant in a social process of comprehension/transformation/control of whatever reality is present. Thus the paying of wages - with reference to the first aspect; functional coordination and organization based on goals - the second; and the burgeoning of the tertiary sector - the third - represent a dynamic of social participation/integration where the logic of the relationship between the worker and his work loses its distinguishing characteristics vis-a-vis the natural order to become ever more readily identifiable as social process in the production of society (10).

Can it then be said that such transformation renders

marginal the reference to _labor_ as one of the significant sites for the understanding of society and its characteristics? What we have gleaned thus far authorizes, if anything, the opposing view, while radically underlining the poverty of the conceptual tools at our disposal - a poverty which may _per se_ account for the current tendency to de-emphasize the importance of the work experience in social analysis and practice.

As a consequence of this last observation another point needs underscoring. If it is true that serious thought about _labor_ is still central - perhaps even more so than in the past - it is likewise true that to reflect on labor no longer merely entails working out considerations and obser-vations on the work experience as such, but rather means focusing on the social relations and dynamic that characte-rize the same.

With respect to the details we felt obliged to clarify, the loose definition of work activity we used at the begin-ning does not seem incorrect. As a matter of fact, the reference to _necessity_ on the one hand, and to _finalization of the production of the material conditions of social existence_ on the other hand, takes into account:

1) the obligatory rather than gratuitious nature of work performed both as concerns the individual, who is bound by social ties, and as concerns society, since it is the sum of all work performed that allows society to keep functioning;

2) its constituting of one of the fundamental elements in the structuring of society: the reference to _material condi-tions_ is at once a way of avoiding the classic distinction between cultural attributes and natural prerequisites and to underline the concrete, objective character proper to the same;

3) the specifically social nature of such existence in the sense that it can be distinguished from all other forms of existence by strategic prevalence of social functions; in the latter the former are re-amalgamated and redefined.

However, such a definition - although not incorrect - does not _per se_ provide an explanation of the tensions which mark the work experience, causing important modifications both in working conditions and in social relations; yet it is precisely in this direction that we must move if we want to utilize _labor_ as an indicator for the study of social relations. That is, it is necessary to single out those elements which provide an explanation of the changes being registered through a consideration of the causal processes; from the latter - no matter how broad and complex - we can expect to come to grasp the logic (or various logics) of detectable changes. More precisely, the definition used up until now is one that focuses on the _essential_ nature of work activity, but which is not capable of taking in the specific modalities, much less the peculiar characteristics, through which the various social forms become concrete. Moreover, such a definition fails to take into account the specifics of the work place. On the contrary, the former are necessary and meaningful references for an effective utilization of that notion in social analysis, while the latter represent empirical instances with respect to which we must definitively solve the matter of the congruence of such a notion. Obviously we are dealing with a process of the reduction of an abstraction, necessary in order to achieve a controlled approach on both the theoretical and empirical level.

A first step in this direction, however modest it may seem, is represented in the reasoning about works (_lavori_) rather than work. By this we mean not a mere substitution of the plurality of the concrete instances for the singleness in the conceptual reference, but rather the assuming of a hypothesis according to which, above and beyond the various manifestations of the works experience, we may find diverse types of linkage between that activity and social reality; and that diversity is a sign of the tensions present, an indicator of the changes in progress and/or of the complexity of the social order.

A second step is represented in considering the social ambience where work activity takes place as the structuralization of the polarization between the _logic of the social system_ and the _logic of the actor_. In other words, each individual work activity as well as all work activities taken together, correspond in their concrete manifestations to the instances, possibilities and reciprocal challenges that these two referents express. This hypothesis corresponds to the emphasized, variously formulated references found in the literature to the motivations/strategies of both individuals and groups. Moreover, it corresponds to what was intended in the preceding definition using the expression _necessity_, right at the point where we dwelt upon the reciprocal links between the individual and the social order. Lastly, it can probably be stated that within it we have at our disposal a dialectical principle (the reference to challenge and polarization) capable of accounting for the articulation of the various situations and, relatively, for the act of their coming into being.

Certainly, we are still at a high level of abstraction; the reference to the _social system_ needs to be further articulated distinguishing, for example, between the modalities of general organizations and of decision-making, and between the social relations of production; likewise, the reference to _individual_ necessarily cannot be rendered articulate without taking into consideration the contexts in which such strategy takes shape and action is made manifest. However, in the framework of the present study, rather than pursuing these leads it would seem more useful to underscore the presence of another type of articulation. That is, we maintain that the references to _actor_ and _social system_ can be further specified underlining in both cases a second type of polarization relative to the difference between _structural characteristics_, which define their 'morphological' identity, and the _processes relative to the demand/response for meaning_. A clarification is needed.

Normally we are prone to associate the first (_structure_)

117

with the social system and the second (_meaning_) with the actors. This sort of approach does not, however, take into account the fact that the social system expresses _objective-ly_, precisely in the articulation of its structures, a certain way of _conceiving_ its existence and its possibilities of development - a way which differs from one structure to the next (_vide_, for example, how different the organization may be in a government office, in a factory and in a voluntary association) and that internal to a given structure are evident certain purposes which in some measure trascend it (_vide_, for example, the whole thematic concerning preservation/change in the objectives of a given organizational structure). The end result in this case is that we do not succeed in grasping the whole warp and woof of tensions and the relative alternatives which are nonetheless part of every situation, thus being left with a flat, partial - however meaningful - picture, making it impossible for us to understand the potentialities (variability) likewise present. Analogously, to consider the _actor_ as the seat where the processes of awareness manifest themselves means undervaluing the role of all those factors, both internal and external, which actualize his capacity to perceive, to take cognizance of and to respond to such stimuli as affect him (from the functioning of the personality to the economic, organizational and cultural characteristics of his environment). Even more, it indicates a radical incapacity to grasp the importance of the processes of groups formation (ranging from diffuse social movements with a modest degree of formal organization to those associations which are more consciously and rigidly organized). The result is an incomprehension and a hiding of that whole complex of tensions which in fact animate the processes by which the actor reaches an understanding of himself and his environment and makes a judgment about them - processes which confer upon the reality in question its highly problematic nature.

A further advantage of the proposal advanced is offered by the fact that the second type of polarization allows the representation, in a certain sense, of the system/actor relation as a relationship between distinct levels of mediation among diverse modalities (structure/meaning) and not as radical incommunicability among totally antithetical terms; the advantages here is that we can thus succeed in pinpointing and explaining all the mutual adjustments, the exchanges, in a word, the continuity that somehow takes place among them, all of which situations otherwise can only be understood as extemporaneous accommodations, devoid of systematic meaning.

If we wish to represent graphically what has been said, we can think of a pair of Cartesian axes which serve as a point of orientation for the comprehension of social reality and its various instances, and in particular to provide a framework for the way in which the various work situations are located with respect to the social dynamics, which are expressed in those polarizations, as in the following illustration:

118

```
I                    **│ structure                    II



*
─────────────────────────┼──────────────────────────────────
sense                    │                  structure



III                      │sense                          IV
```

(the two axes represent the different levels of realization
of the actor (*) and of the social system(**); no direction (+,-) has been indicated in order to avoid the
impression of having surreptitiously introduced value
judgements about the different possible solutions; the
hypothesis advanced is that the work situation can be
traced, obviously with different meanings for both actor
and system, in each of the four quadrants)

   The reference to work activity then comes to result
from the outcome of the crisscrossing <u>challenges</u> between
system and actor and from the exigencies of construction/
modification of the structures and demand/response of sense.
   We have attempted here to work out a series of observations concerning the cognitive importance of the graphic
representation proposed with respect to the relation between
the various geometrical areas it is composed of (for example, the quadrants) and such notions as <u>production</u>, <u>repro-
duction</u>, <u>social integration</u> and <u>collective and individual
identity</u>, and of the implications of a formal nature that
are made evident (for example, an open or closed field,
significance and mode of measuring the coordinates). The
necessity of thoroughly researching the suitability of proposing such a representation counsels caution, and suggests
the need for a profound consideration of the substantive
aspects of its adequacy, with respect to which these notes
were intended as nothing more than a stimulus and provoca-
tion.
   Referring back to our previous remarks about the oppor-
tuneness of thinking in terms of <u>works</u> rather than of <u>work</u>,
if anything it can be noted that an empirical study of work
activity cannot but take into account a triple order of

references.

What becomes immediately plain is the precise and detailed analysis of the concrete ways in which that activity is carried out, with special attention paid to organizational solutions, technologies and specific contents of the operative intervention required and performed. Obviously, this does not involve listing and describing the so-called 'neutral' technical characteristics: the employment of notions such as manual/intellectual work, repetitive/creative work, other/self-directed work is not in and of itself to be discounted as self-evident, requiring instead the formulation of interpretative hypotheses having reference to the modes and terms of the social dialectic stressed above.

A second direction of study is relative to the historical/social situation. In this case the importance of the social dialectic comes into direct focus, but that should not fool us since here as well the conceptual systemization is not at all taken for granted. Thus, for example, the distinction between work performed with production as the end, and work performed with reproduction as the end, is not at all definitive and obvious.

A third, but no less important, reference can be none other than the relation between work activity and the warp and woof of significance and meaning of the individual who performs such activity. In this case as well, the reference to one of the two extremes of the polarization outlined above does not mean that the solution of the problems of method present is taken for granted. This does not mean merely registering the statements of the individuals observed, but rather reconstructing the cognitive and motivational routes which orient their strategies and behavior toward work, consciously soliciting them in this perspective.

These three general references may in turn constitute the guiding structure of a typology of work-related phenomena: a sort of synoptic picture capable of descriptively summing up the various existing situations. Concerning this picture, it is necessary to study in depth the connection between the Cartesian representation proposed above: from the outset it can be said that we have to keep coming back to it in order to construct the interpretative hypotheses which will then make possible the proposition of a typology of work-related phenomena. A like solution is still overly general.

At this juncture, even though we are aware of the scant resolution and exactitude of the foregoing, it becomes useful to go back to the issues raised at the beginning of these notes in order to complete the discourse with respect to our premises, even though such discourse is anything but complete with respect to the problems raised by the topic.

The first question we posed was what was the basis for the central role which labor appeared to occupy for a certain historical period (from the beginning of the Industrial Revolution almost up to the present time) and for what reason such centrality faded away or, alternatively, how it was transformed. The reference to social relations which we have attempted to specify has allowed us to avoid losing our way in a listing of the various manifestations of work activity and instead to lead us back to the criterion of the altered role of _labor_ and to the warp and woof of those relationships and their relative transformations. Thus, the centrality of labor turns out to be based on the connection between the various forms of work activity and the production/reproduction of those same social relationships, while its disappearance pertains to certain concrete forms of activity, and not to other forms already existing or coming into existence. In this way we have been forced into a more variable use of the notion of _labor_ which, even though remaining an activity _necessary_ to the _reproduction of society_, witnesses the transformation of its concrete referents (from the work of the family unit of pre-industrial societies to industrial manufacture managed by the entrepreneur/capitalist to salaried work, even though the denotations used in this circumstance need both additional study and more careful definition).

The answer to the first question permits a delineation of the answers to the other two. In fact, we can state that, defining _labor_ as resulting from the challenge between system and actor within the relation between diversely oriented exigencies of the construction/modification of the structures and of the demand/response for meaning, a study of the same cannot but be a particularly useful indicator for the social order and its transformations. Certainly, _labor_ at this point loses its empirical connotations of a specific activity, in that it acquires new (or renewed) connotations as the criteria of _necessity_ and _finalizations_ to which we have referred are progressively modified. We are not, however, dealing with functional equivalents, but rather with an arriving at the salient points of the autonomous factors of the process of determination of societal equilibria on the part of other elements present in social relations, and that in correspondence with the enrichment of the social dynamics and the multiplication of its strategic elements.

It is worthwhile to repeat in closing that we did not presume to resolve the issues raised, much less to reach all attainable cognitive results in our consideration of them, but rather, in more circumscribed fashion, to present what appear to be possibilities for further study.

NOTES

(1) Without any pretension of reducing such a matter to a footnote, in the interest of greater exactitude it would seem helpful to refer to Marcuse (1969), for its conscious attempt to go beyond a strictly economic approach and in particular for its references to the connotations relevant to this paper, even if such references are not always fully attentive and adequately circumstantiated.

(2) This is a topic which _per se_ deserves a separate study, since we can expect that in a situation of rapid and profound change, as seems to be the current case, such

will represent a significant indicator of the processes underway; a helpful exemplification here might be Accornero (1980).

(3) Adumbrated in what we have stated is the problem of the definition of <u>productive labor</u>, which is anything but obvious and to be taken for granted. To specify the connotations of such definition or even just the criteria of operability is a still-open question of theoretical and empirical research; it is opportune to note that such a line research would prove useful in a general study of the labor-related material herein introduced; for a treatise on the tensions internal to the definition of this concept cf. Mingione (1980).

(4) The history of social representation of work to a considerable extent has yet to be written; of its toilsome course and the antinomies that have characterized it we have a clear indication in the diversity of the expressions used to indicate the same; a significant contribution in this regard is Mondolfo (1982). Of particular concern here is to recall that beginning with the end of the 18th century, throughout the 19th century and for the greater part of the present century, the reference to work comes to be particularly insistent and is tied on the one hand to the problems of citizenship and individual rights, and on the other hand to the problems of overcoming indigence and maintaining public order.

(5) It seems useful and even crucial to call attention to those indications derived from Weber (1970), since they relate in one way or another to the causal nexuses and to temporal contingencies particularly close to the problems under discussion; to obtain an idea of the profundity of those roots it is worthwhile to recall the rule of the Benedictine Order: "Ora et labora".

(6) Miles (1981), Pahl (1981); The quotations reported with the page number refer to the mimeographed texts. It is necessary to cite the periodical <u>Inchiesta</u>, no. 59-60, 1983, entirely to cite the problem of the 'unofficial economy'. In it appears, among other things, Pahl (1983).

(7) Braverman (1978).

(8) Manacorda (1984).

(9) The use that we propose here of the expression <u>socialization</u> is not the usual one which indicates the processes of adaptation/recognition of the individual in reference to a given social context. In this way, in fact, the hypothesis posits a fundamental stability in the context in which the characteristics, and in particular the system of expectation/gratification of the individual are formed (or modified) vis-a-vis the said context. In the present case, instead, we want to directly focus on the characteristics proper to the context, and on the transformations therein realized. The first effect of this different perspective is that of problematizing the features of the context, which thus comes to be seen as a dialogical process (on this

point the intuitions and views of Habermas (1975), seem particularly rich) rather than as a matrix. The second effect, in some ways more important, is that of calling attention to the changes being recorded, to the increase in its range - almost of its bounds - and to the redefinition of its structure (on this point Touraine (1975) offers a wealth of stimuli and proposals.

(10) This change is worh underlining again because it is probably one of the most important observation - points for studying and explaining the transformations which the work experience is responsible for and the knowledge thereof. In fact, it can probably be said that it is just in the passage from the concrete and, often, material work object, in some way not immediately expressive of the social conditions of production, to an abstract and general work object (from the standpoint of the form of the work performance required) and more directly referred to the characteristics and to the transformations of society (from the standpoint of the determining of its content) that the fundamental elements of a different way of manifesting the social dialectic and a different manifestation of the contents and modalities of individual and collective identities are posited. It is meaningful in this regard to consider the development of the contribution of a scholar like A. Touraine, in that he shows himself to be just as sensitive and perspicacious in grasping the new developments that the social dynamic evidences as he reveals himself to be steadfast in the detection of work through its natural object. The reference to work and workers becomes fossilized, becoming at last marginal beyond every different affirmation, while the reference to the social dynamic and its protagonists (social movements) becomes indefinite and allusive. In this sense it may be useful to examine, from among Touraine's numerous works and in addition to the work already cited in Footnote 9, Touraine (1965).

REFERENCES

ACCORNERO, A., Il lavoro come ideologia, Il Mulino, Bologna 1980.
BRAVERMAN, H., Lavoro e capitale monopolistico, Einaudi, Turin 1978, (Labor and Monopoly Capital, Montly Review Press, New York 1974).
HABERMAS, J., La crisi di razionalità nel capitalismo maturo Laterza, Bari 1975, (Legitimationsprobleme im Speatkapitalismus, Suhrkamp Verlag, Frankfurt a.M. 1973).
MANACORDA, P., Lavoro e intelligenza nell'età microelettronica, Feltrinelli, Milan 1984.
MARCUSE, H., 'Sui fondamenti filosofici del concetto di lavoro nella scienza economica', in Cultura e società, Einaudi, Turin 1969, (Kultur und Gesellschaft, Suhrkamp Verlag, Frankfurt a.M. 1975).
MILES, J., Restructuring Employment ... and Work, paper

presented at the FAST Congress in Marseilles, Nov. 1981.

MINGIONE, E., Lavoro produttivo, lavoro improduttivo e classi sociali, Savelli, Milan 1980.

MONDOLFO, R., Polis, lavoro e tecnica, Feltrinelli, Milan 1982.

PAHL, R.E., From the Social Relations of Work to Household Work Strategies, paper presented at the FAST Congress in Marseilles, November 1981.

PAHL, R.E., 'Strategie del lavoro domestico ed economia informale', Inchiesta, no. 59-60, 1983.

TOURAINE, A., Sociologie de l'action, Edition du Seuil, Paris 1965.

TOURAINE, A., Produzione della società, Il Mulino, Bologna 1975, (Production de la societé, Edition du Seuil, Paris 1973).

WEBER, M., Etica protestante e spirito del capitalismo, Sansoni, Florence, 1977, (Die protestantische Ethik und der Geist des Kapitalismus, in Gesammelte Aufsätze zur Religionssoziologie, I.C.B. Mohr, Tübingen 1922).

PART II
UNOFFICIAL ECONOMY AND ECONOMIC SYSTEMS

The shadow economy and economic policy in East and West: a comparative system approach

DIETER CASSSEL, ULRICH CICHY

1. THE SHADOW ECONOMY - A PROBLEM FOR ECONOMIC POLICY?

Even though the so-called shadow economy stands for a well established phenomenon of considerable size, it has been neglected for a long time. Recently in capitalist market economies it is receiving more interest - not so much due to its mere existence, but as it has rapidly been growing throughout the '70s and early '80s (Feige, 1979, 1984; Weck-Hannemann, 1984; Kirchgassner, 1983; Langfeldt, 1984). It may be classified as a true 'growing industry' because its size is increasing both absolutely and in proportion to the formal sector of the Western market economies (Cassel, 1982). A similar pattern appears in the socialist planning economies of Eastern Europe (Wiles, 1981; Landau, 1984; Brezinski and Ros, 1984; Cichy, 1984). The global growth of the shadow economy seems to be related to political pitfalls in Eastern and Western industrialized countries during the recent decade:

- Major economic reforms in Eastern bloc countries have aimed at reducing the slack in the official economy and improving the efficiency of the planning system; however, shortages on the goods markets and suppressed inflation have not been eliminated, such that shadow activities continue to play an important valve function.
  If there are income losses in the official economy, economic subjects try to compensate for these shocks by increasing their activities in the shadow economy. The shadow sector is emerging as a flexible subsystem which contributes thereby to the absorption of planning failures, by serving as a resilient complement to the production of goods and services in the official economy.
- The severe economic crisis since the mid '70s in Western market economies indicates serious shortcomings of economic policy with respect to the diagnosis of slow growth, high inflation, and mass unemployment; increasing marginal tax rates and the pressure of the philosophy of the welfare state have reduced the individual's incentive to act in the official market system and have encouraged the immigration into the shadow economy.

This immigration can be classified as a system-indifferent phenomenon: with increasing structural rigidities in the

official sector of the economies, the importance and size of
the shadow sector is rising both in central planning systems
and in market economies. These findings are not surprising
as both sectors are subject to a common causation and rationale. The shadow economy and the official economy are simultaneously affected - mostly with opposite impact signs -
when the transaction conditions of the official economy are
changing. The intellectual discovery of a booming shadow
economy in recent years is therefore obviously related to
the crisis symptoms in Eastern and Western industrialized
countries.

Apparently, the development of the shadow economy is not
only related to symptom of economic crisis and corresponding
stabilization policies (Cassel, 1984a, 1984b); its growth
must be analyzed in the context of the economy's institutional framework ('Wirschaftsordnung') too. Consequently,
important questions for 'framework policies' ('Ordnungspolitik') arise that define the role of government and of private economic agents (Cassel, 1984c):

- How does the state define itself as a predominant factor
  in the economic process?
- Which incentives for shadow economic immigration result
  from the specific types of government interference?
- Which growth patterns of the shadow economy can be observed in different economic systems?
- Which consequences result from a growing shadow economy
  for the political system?

2. THE GROWING UNDERGROUND ECONOMY: CAUSES OF AND IMPACTS ON
   THE ALLOCATION OF LABOR

2.1. The economic role of the state in modern industrialized
     countries

Both in capitalist market economies and in socialist planning economies the state has a great impact upon the transaction conditions of the official economy. As the state
acts for collective interests it tries to realize a variety
of production goals. These range from welfare aims and the
set-up of growth and structural goals to internal and external security. Laws and directives are instruments to realize
interests directly, at the same time these regulations limit
the degree of freedom for individual private action. Furthermore, the state's procurements are important for those
goods that it intends to be subject to direct control.
Realizing this goal makes it necessary to steer the economy's allocation to a wide degree. Allocation via the government budget in Western market economies is made possible by
tax receipts and indebtment; thereby the state obtains the
funds to enter in the allocation process of goods and factor
markets. In socialist planning economies it is the command
system itself that gives the central authorities a direct
access to determine overall allocation.

However, the question arises whether this public allocation corresponds to the preferences of private households. The administration's own dynamic and unchecked self-interest of politicians may lead to misallocation. The process of administered allocation costs resources in itself that might have been devoted to different ends if the private sector had directly determined their allocation.

2.1.1. Government in the allocation process. Misallocation in socialist planning economies due to the dominant role of the state is quite obvious: waiting lists and queues reflect shortages ('thirst for goods'; Szeliga, 1977) and the corresponding cash balance inflation - i.e. the buildup of undesired money balances within the private sector - reveal that centralized factor allocation does not fully meet private households' preferences. While shortage can be understood as indicating misallocation in certain cases (stochastic influences - for example, bad harvests entail excess demands in particular markets) suppressed inflation signals that there is a general and sustaining imbalance between the national product (supply) and national income (demand). The cause of suppressed inflation is the insufficient coordination between money funds and consumption funds. The resulting inflation potential - the excess supply in the money market - is reflected only partly in a rising price index (increase of the price index, G_pI) since prices are generally government-fixed; the suppressed inflation is mainly reflected by the (undesired) rise of the cash balance coefficient k' (g_kI) (Cassel, 1985; see Table 1).

According to the theoretical concept of cash balance inflation, a rising cash balance coefficient indicates that government is increasingly allocating factor inputs in an inefficient manner and that labor obtains higher nominal wages buying less than before. What is the explanation for sustaining cash balance inflation? Planning with material balances leads - due to ambitious industrialization and armament projects - to disproportionate developments of department I and II in the sense of a failure to meet consumers' preferences. This imbalance and the bias in favor of collective goods leads to an excess demand for labor: The government-preferred sectors are awarded sufficient factor endowments by the central plan (generous wage and premia funds); the other sectors try to make up this bias by soft planning methods, especially by meeting planning goals with unplanned rises of the wage fund that are credited by the central banking system (Hartwig, Thieme, 1985).

The result of this 'struggle for income and resources' is a bias of the economic system towards a permanent excess demand for input factors, above all labor. This induces both the central authorities and the directors of firms to have a perfectly elastic demand for labor: "... it seems rational to continue bringing labour reserves into production as long as the wages paid for that labour power produce some new value, no matter how small it is" (Gabor, Galasi, 1981). Permanent excess demand in labor markets means that planned wage funds are overrun regularly. Therefore a permanent

Table 1
Inflation in selected countries, 1960-83

(average annual change of official consumer price indexes $g_P I$, of the cash balance coefficient $g_K I$ and of $g_P I + g_K I$ in per cent).

YEAR	GERMANY		WORLD	GERMAN DEMOCRATIC REPUBLIC			POLAND			ČSSR			USSR	BULGARIA	RUMANIA
	$g_P I$	$g_K I$	$g_P I$	$g_P I$	$g_K I$	$g_P I + g_K I$	$g_P I$	$g_K I$	$g_P I + g_K I$	$g_P I$	$g_K I$	$g_P I + g_K I$	$g_P I$	$g_P I$	$g_P I$
	1	2	3	4	5	6	7	8	9	10	11	12	13	14	15
1960	1.5	0.1	1.8	-1.2	14.0	12.8	1.8	17.2	19.0	-2.0	-	-	-0.7	-0.4	-2.2
1961	2.2	-0.2	1.8	0.2	4.1	4.3	0.8	7.2	8.0	-0.4	-	-	-0.7	0.4	-1.6
1962	3.0	1.1	2.5	0.2	7.8	8.0	2.5	10.3	12.8	1.1	-	-	1.4	3.5	-0.9
1963	2.9	-1.1	2.6	0.0	9.1	9.1	0.9	3.9	4.8	0.5	-	-	0.8	2.4	0.0
1964	1.8	0.5	2.4	-0.7	8.3	7.6	1.7	18.1	19.8	0.4	-	-	0.0	0.3	1.3
1965	3.8	0.5	3.0	0.5	9.2	9.7	0.8	5.3	6.1	1.2	-	-	-0.7	-0.5	0.4
1966	3.5	0.2	3.4	0.0	7.0	7.0	1.3	11.5	12.8	0.3	7.5	7.8	-0.7	-0.2	0.0
1967	1.7	-0.1	3.0	-0.1	6.6	6.5	1.5	·7.9	9.4	1.3	7.0	8.3	0.0	0.1	-0.4
1968	1.7	0.6	3.9	0.2	6.2	6.4	1.5	4.6	6.1	1.4	0.0	1.4	0.1	4.0	1.3
1969	1.9	0.2	4.7	-0.2	4.7	4.5	1.2	4.4	5.6	0.5	-4.3	-3.8	0.5	-0.1	1.0
1970	3.3	0.2	5.6	-0.1	3.3	3.2	1.1	2.1	3.2	1.7	11.4	13.1	-0.2	-0.4	0.1
1971	5.2	-1.0	5.2	0.3	2.2	2.5	0.0	6.7	6.7	-0.4	10.2	9.8	-0.1	0.0	0.8
1972	5.6	-0.2	4.6	-0.3	2.1	1.8	0.0	7.4	7.4	-0.4	9.3	8.9	-0.2	0.0	0.0
1973	7.0	0.1	7.6	-1.0	3.1	2.1	2.8	10.9	13.7	0.2	6.8	7.0	0.0	0.2	0.6
1974	7.0	-0.3	13.3	-0.4	1.0	0.6	7.1	10.2	17.3	0.5	1.6	2.1	-0.1	0.5	1.0
1975	6.0	-0.1	11.1	-0.5	3.0	2.5	3.0	2.3	5.3	0.5	4.7	5.2	-0.1	0.4	0.2
1976	4.3	0.2	8.3	0.0	1.9	1.9	4.4	-2.7	1.7	0.8	-	-	0.0	0.2	0.7
1977	3.7	-0.2	8.5	0.0	2.8	2.8	4.9	-1.8	3.1	1.3	-	-	0.3	0.4	0.5
1978	2.8	1.1	7.2	0.0	2.7	2.7	8.1	3.2	11.3	1.6	-	-	0.7	1.5	1.5
1979	4.1	0.3	9.1	0.2	1.7	1.9	7.0	4.2	11.2	3.9	-	-	1.3	4.6	1.0
1980	5.5	0.5	11.9	0.7	-1.8	-1.1	9.4	5.5	14.9	2.9	-	-	1.0	14.0	2.2
1981	5.9	0.2	9.9	0.2	0.4	0.6	21.2	9.2	30.4	0.8	-	-	0.9	0.5	1.8
1982	5.3	-0.3	7.5	0.0	3.1	3.1	100.8	-22.8	78.0	-	-	-	-	-	-
1983	3.3	-0.3	5.0	-	-	-	-	-	-	-	-	-	-	-	-
1960-80 [a]	3.7	0.1	5.7	-0.11	4.7	4.59	2.9	6.5	9.4	0.8	-	-	0.12	1.4	0.32
1960-80 [b]	3.59	-	-	1.21	-	-	4.97	-	-	2.79	-	-	2.30	4.05	2.74 (1970-80)

1 Consumer price index (cost of living for all private household).
2 Difference between the growth rates of the money stock M1 and of real GNP.
3 Weighted consumer price index for 21 Western industrialized countries: USA, Canada, Australia, Japan, New Zealand, Austria, Belgium, Denmark, Finland, France, Germany, Iceland, Ireland, Italy, Luxemburg, Netherland, Norway, Spain, Sweden, Swizerland, United Kingdom.
4, 7, 10, 13, 14 and 15: Retail price index for goods and services.
5, 8, 11 Ratio of cash plus private sector deposits to retail sales.
a Average annual change in per cent (geometric mean).
b Average annual change in per cent according to calculations of Pryor (1984), based on SNA figures (P : = nominal consumption/real consumption).

Source: Col. 1: Statistisches Bundesamt, Fachserie 17, Reihe 7 (current issues); col. 2: own calculations; col. 3 IMF, International Financial Statistics (current Issues); col. 4, 7, 10, 13, 14 and 15: Seurot (1983), p. 21 (until 1979); Kleps (1984), p. 183 (1980-81): col. 5 and 8: Hartwig (1983,1), p. 233; Staatliche Zentralverwaltung für Statistik, Statistische Jahrbücher der Deutschen Demokratischen Republik (current issues; GDR 1981-82; own calculations); Glowny Urzad Statystyczny, Rocznik Statystyczny (current issues; Poland 1981-82; own calculations); col. 11: Seurot (1983), p. 50; col. 6, 9, 12 and a: own calculations.

imbalance between money funds and consumption goods funds will be observed.

As regards the government's role in the allocation process in capitalist market economies, at first glance only investment ruins - due to subsidies - in farming, steel and shipbuilding etc. can be interpreted as misallocation. However, increasing tax resistance, e.g. in Denmark in the 1970s (Glistrup-movement), indicate that public goods supply is only partly recognized to be a desired equivalent for foregone private consumption. Rising tax burdens (see Fig. 1) are not anymore interpreted as sensible collective goods supply but as a pressure and burden for the private sector production. Individuals identify public goods supply less and less as desired (e.g. in the field of social security, infrastructure, armament expenditures); the state becomes a burden for many groups.

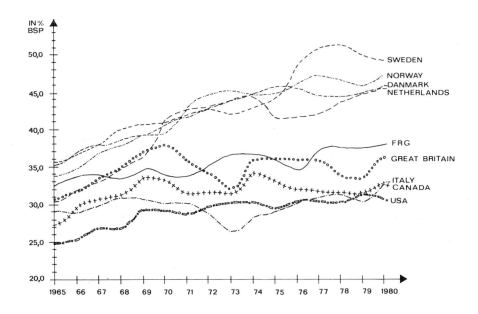

Fig. 1: Tax burden in Western industrialized countries

Source: B. Mettelsiefen, 1984.

2.1.2. Mechanisms of sectoral transformation. Tax burden and cash balance inflation, respectively, are system-specific symptoms for the system-indifferent phenomenon of state misallocation. They reflect the fact that the state forces the private sector to renounce part of its income claims in real terms; the state in turn does not supply the desired collective goods as a substitute. Cash balance inflation and rising tax burdens are the consequence.

The forced reduction of private income claims is an incentive for private households to reconsider their allocation decision for their time budget. While traditional microtheory perceives the alternative uses of working and leisure (Bender, 1977), the discussion over the shadow economy highlights the full range of alternatives and the associated transformation tendencies: private households shift a considerable part of their value-adding activities from the official into the unofficial economy (Cassel, 1982). Part of their time budget is devoted to the self-service economy, or they enter the underground economy. The growth of the self-service economy is explained by additional factors: the official work becomes less status-relevant (Noelle-Neumann, Strumpel, 1984), while 'self-determined work' enjoys a high social valuation (Huber, 1984); however, the growth of the underground economy is clearly related to the changes in the transaction conditions of the economy as the consequence of government interference (Schenk, Wass von Czege, 1983). Consequently, the increasing importance of the self-service economy is a secular phenomenon that is closely related to the transformation process of industrialized countries towards post-industrial societies (Gershuny, 1977, 1979).

Therefore, it stands only partly for a problem facing economic policy and may be neglected in the subsequent considerations. The growth of the underground economy as a policy-induced phenomenon cannot be neglected as it concerns the respective system's own logic in a fundamental sense; the ultimate reason for the underground economy lies in the attempt of private households to counter cash balance inflation-induced erosion of their income claims (Laski, 1983) or to increase real disposable income by circumventing tax payments (Gretschmann, Heinze, Mettelsielfen, 1984).

2.2. Capitalist market economies: the rising burden of taxes

The analysis of underground economic activity is based on the assumption of rational household behavior. Rational decisions mean here that households allocate working time between the official (white work) sector and the unofficial shadow economy (black work or moonlighting). The objective function is to maximize income by allocating the individual's time budget (Cassel, 1984a). The difference between the white wage rate WO (wage in the official economy) and the black wage rate WU (wage in the unofficial economy) provides the incentive to realize 'income arbitrage' (Cichy, 1984). The notation of the respective supply and demand curves in Fig. 2A is as follows:

LOS = labor officially supplied,
LOD = labor officially demanded in the white market
LUS = labor unofficially supplied
LUD = labor unofficially demanded for the black market.

- The demand for white work LOD is a negative function of the official gross wage rate (WO^g) and a positive function of the black wage rate (WU):

$$LOD = LOD (WO^g, WU).$$
$$-\qquad +$$

The higher the gap between the wage rates WO^g and WU, the greater the incentive to shift labor demand towards the underground economy.

Fig. 2A

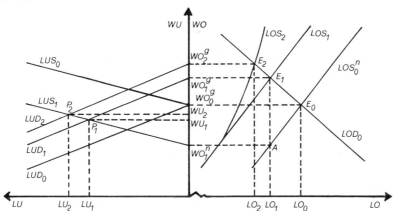

Fig. 2B

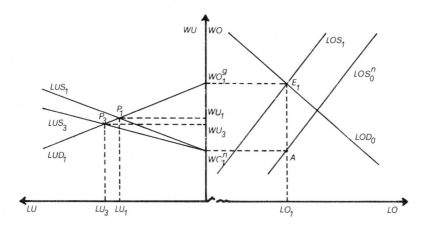

Figure 2: Official and unofficial labor market in capitalist market economies

133

- The optimizing behavior of households results in a labor supply for the official economy that depends positively on the real net wage rate in the white market (WO^n) and negatively on alternative income opportunities as represented by the wage rate in the unofficial economy (WU): as WO^g and WO^n differ by income and social security taxes T, one can express the labour supply function as

$$LOS = LOS\ (WO^n,\ WU,\ T)\ \text{or}\ LOS^n(WO^n,\ WU),\ \text{if}\ T = 0.$$
$$+\quad\ -\quad -\phantom{\text{or}\ LOS^n(}+\quad\ -$$

In the absence of taxes the official employment is given by LO_0 in Fig. 2A.

- The supply of black work LUS is a positive function of the underground economy wage rate WU which is in turn depending on a risk premium R (De Gijsel, 1984); moonlighters face a genuine rational behavior problem under risk (Mettelsiefen, 1984). In Western market economies moonlighters may have to pay a fine or they may be sentenced to jail in extreme cases; foreign workers face additionally the risk to lose their residence permit. There is also the risk of accidents which are not covered by public insurance schemes. Furthermore, the risk-free white net wage rate determines the labor supply in the underground economy: that wage rate is a lower boundary for the underground labor supply - apart from special cases, e.g. illegal aliens, workers would shift totally into the official economy at $WU = WO^n$.
Consequently, the supply of labor in the black market is determined by

$$LUS = LUS\ (WU,\ R,\ WO^n).$$
$$+\quad\ -\quad -$$

- The official gross wage rate is an upper boundary for the demand for black labor. If WU exceeds the official wage rate WO , the incentive for any underground labour demand would vanish:

$$LUD = LUD\ (WU,\ WO^g).$$
$$-\quad\ +$$

Fig. 2A shows our situation of departure, namely a coincidence of white and black wage rates as taxes are assumed to be zero. There is no underground economy, because all transactions take place at the going official wage rate WO_0 (point E_0). Introducing taxes, the price for white work is raised (AE_1) and adjustment behavior on the supply and the demand side occurs.
The demand for labour in the official economy is reduced (E_1 with $LO_0 > LO_1$), at the same time the demand in the underground economy is rising. The officially regulated working time is reduced in favor of untaxed unofficial overtime work or the employment of illegal aliens and registered unemployed (LUD_1 at P_1 with $WU_1 < WO_1^g$); households in

134

turn use this opportunity of price differentiation in labour markets ($WO_1^n < WU_1$).

They shift part of their working potential into the unofficial economy: either the unemployed enter the unofficial economy or the officially employed with flexible office hours take advantage of this by earning an extra income in the shadow economy by reducing their effective working hours in the formal economy. On the other hand, labor productivity will drop as part of the official working time is devoted to preparing or performing black work (Stein, 1985; Gretschmann, Mettelsiefen, 1984). Furthermore, there will be a substitution of leisure by black work: LUS_1. The underground economy is characterized by the size of LU_1.

As regards the growth of the underground economy this expansion depends mainly on two factors:

- the income tax rate structure; a linear structure as it is assumed in the derivation of LOS_1 leads not only to a stronger reduction of official employment than LOS_2 ($LO_0 > LO_1 > LO_2$), but increases the potential price range (E_2 with $WO_2^g > WO_1^g$) in the unofficial economy, too. Because of LUD_2 the underground economy is growing (LU_2 at P_2);
- the degree of risk for the unofficial labor supply; e.g., a reduced supplier risk (R) due to loosening controls or lower fines means a growth impulse for the underground economy in the sense of establishing LUS_3. The more elastic labor supply leads to a drop of the black wage rate ($WU_1 > WU_3$) and to a rise of unofficial employment ($LU_3 > LU_1$ at P_3; see Fig. 2B).

Summarizing, the conclusion is to be drawn that risk considerations have only a secondary impact upon the relative expansion of the underground economy whose basic growth is related to the growing tax burden in the official economy (Weck-Hannemann, 1984). Growing income taxes and social security taxes in a capitalist market economy lead to the dismissal of workers as those raise ceteris paribus the price of labor relative to that of real capital. At the same time the relative wage structure between the official and the unofficial economy is changing. Similar effects are associated with government regulations or excessive wage claims that try to anticipate the inflation process. These factors worsen the supply-side conditions both in labor and in goods markets thus providing increasing incentives for immigration into the unofficial economy.

2.3. Socialist planning economies: suppressed inflation and shortages in goods markets

The development of the underground economy in Eastern Europe can basically be explained in similar terms as for Western market economies, namely by the government's goal to interfere with state production and allocation plans in the determination of market income, where the price for labor does not reflect any more its true value-adding capacity: in

the socialist planning economy the purchasing power reduction caused by cash balance inflation (and the underlying
allocation disproportions) indicates a transfer of real
resources to the state; monetized nominal income claims
cannot fully be redeemed by the private sector. However,
purchasing power erosion and increasing shortages provide
incentives for private households to become active in the
underground economy (Dallago, 1984). Shadow economic value-
added rise (Thieme, 1985) along the following mechanisms
(Fig. 3A):

Fig. 3A

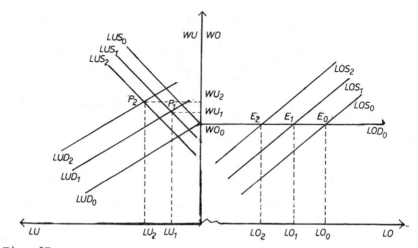

Fig. 3B

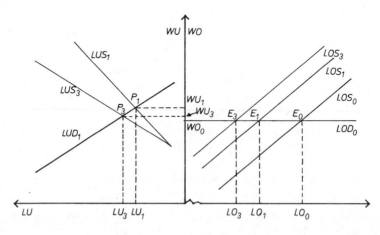

Figure 3: Official and unofficial labor market in socialist
planning economies.

- The demand for white labor (LOD) is - contrary to the capitalist economy's crucial relation between wage rate and marginal product - determined by the system-inherent excess demand (I) for labor. This means that any available worker is integrated into the production process as long as this leads to an increment of output. The wage rate is predetermined by the centrally allocated wage funds:

$$LOD = LOD \ (WO, \ I).$$
$$\quad\quad\quad\quad - \quad +$$

The lack of profitability considerations in employment policies and the elastic credit-and-money supply system (soft budget constraints; Kornai, 1980; Haffner, 1985) lead to a perfectly elastic labor demand (LOD).
- The white labor supply (LOS) depends on the perceived white wage rate WO and the black wage rate WU; taxation of incomes plays a minor role: only the income of some private 'entrepreneurs' - craftsmen, shopkeepers and farmers - are taxed significantly (H. Brezinski, 1985). As households are not subject to money illusion in the long run and as they take into account purchasing power value of money incomes for their labor supply decisions, the rate of cash balance inflation (g_k) is another parameter of the official labor supply:

$$LOS = LOS \ (WO, \ g_k, \ WU)$$
$$\quad\quad\quad\quad + \quad - \quad -$$

- The supply of black work (LUS) has a bottom price limit, namely the official wage rate (WO); the more WU exceeds WO, the greater the incentive to work in the unofficial economy. There is no unambiguous upper boundary wage rate as no wedge with respect to official wage rates (typically observed in capitalist countries) exists. But risk factors (R) play a crucial role. As prosecution and penalties are rather tough - individuals face even the risk of the death penalty (Bryson, 1984) - the LUS-curve is less elastic than in capitalist market economies:

$$LUS = LUS \ (WU, \ R, \ WO, \ g_k).$$
$$\quad\quad\quad\quad\quad + \quad - \quad - \quad +$$

- The black market demand (LUD) is determined by the black wage rate (WU) and the degree of shortage in official goods markets. A rise of the degree of shortage in consumption goods markets stands for a higher rate of cash balance inflation (g) and to a rising labour demand in unofficial labour markets:

$$LUD = LUD \ (WU, \ g_k).$$
$$\quad\quad\quad\quad\quad - \quad +$$

Fig. 3A shows at first a situation E_0 without any cash balance inflation. Official employment is LO_0 and there is no unofficial employment. With suppressed inflation there

are incentives for households to shift part of their potential labor supply into the underground economy: in the short
run, rising cash balance inflation is considered to reflect
increasing shortage in goods markets and private households
increase consequently their demand for goods in the underground economy, leading to LUD_1. This demand shift towards
the underground economy causes black wage rates to exceed
white wage rates; this means an opportunity for income
arbitrage (LUS_1). The new equilibrium is P_1 with employment
LU_1. The rise of black labor supply is explained by the substitution of leisure time on the one hand and by 'stealing'
official labor time (Brezinski, 1985): wage differentials
constitute an incentive for individuals to deliberate 'withholding of performance (Gábor, 1979); absenteeism and 'leisure on the job' are increasing. In the long run, cash balance inflation is fully recognized by individuals: forced
savings mean a further incentive to withholding performance
(Seidenstecher, 1982; Thieme, 1985; Stein, 1985). The first
equilibrium is therefore at E_1 with $LO_0 > LO_1$.

As a consequence of reduced working performance in the
official economy there is a widening gap between the amount
of goods produced and the size of the wage funds. This
results in another inflationary impulse, irrespective of an
initially congruent plan by the government authorities. At
first, unofficial labor demand increases (LUD_2), then unofficial labor supply (LUS_2). The new black market equilibrium
point is P_2 with $LU_2 > LU_1$, while the new white market
equilibrium - reflecting the shift of supply and demand to
the shadow economy - is given by E_2 with $LO_1 > LO_2$. Under a
rise of withholding working performance the further growth
of the shadow economy is predetermined.

The growth of the underground economy depends mainly upon
two factors:

- the cash balance inflation rate and the degree of shortage in goods markets, respectively;
- the degree of risk: a reduction of risk leads to a rising
  black labour supply (LUS_3 at LU_3; see Fig. 3B).

However, similar to the case of market economies, risk
considerations play only a secondary catalytic role for the
growth of the shadow economy, where the basic force is the
system-specific cash balance inflation. This particular
inflation type is not a transitory phenomenon but the necessary consequence of a system that has no consistent accounting framework and fixed prices for the overall economy with
due consideration of relative scarcity of goods and production factors. Generally, worsening demand conditions in consumption goods markets result in a potentially destabilizing
growth of the underground economy.

4. IMPLICATIONS FOR ECONOMIC POLICY

The existence of the shadow economy is a system-indifferent phenomenon, but as regards the typical growth pat-

terns, system-specific differences can be observed. In capitalist market economies discretionary tax rises lead to a limited and cyclical growth of the underground economy. The basic mechanisms of socialist planning economies constitute persistent impulses and incentives for the growth of the underground economy. These characteristics must be recognized if we are to give an adequate assessment of the problems economic policy is facing. Here, the most important criterion is the impact on the stability of the politico-economic system: Does the underground economy absorb or reinforce disturbances, shifts and shocks, of the official economy?

4.1. Capitalist market economies: underground economy as a stabilizing factor

In capitalist market economies the relative price mechanism seems generally capable to serve successfully as an incentive and control device ensuring that allocation reflects households' preferences. A rise of the public sector size and the corresponding increase of the tax rates do not undermine the consistency of the economy's accounting framework: the price mechanism still works, although the changing weights of the white and the black economy can entail a loss of economic efficiency. Changing tax rates alter the relative price of black and white work and consequently the intersectoral allocation of labor. Depending on the effective tax and regulation burden the structure of the economy is characterized by a specific mix of activities in the official and in the unofficial sector: as the two sectors of the economy show a balancing interdependence - i.e. the shadow economy is booming when the official economy is stagnating (and vice versa) - the overall economy may be characterized by structural transformation, but by overall equilibrium, too.

The stabilizing characteristics of the shadow economy can be summarized as follows (Cassel, 1984a):

- Economic lubricant: the underground economy serves as a flexibility reserve since activities can be shifted between the official and the unofficial economy. Being free of public or private regulations and using the price mechanism the shadow economy offers a flexible supply potential, namely, both across products, time and space. The underground economy has a considerable shock-absorbing potential with respect to political or economic shifts and shocks. Its buffer function is the more important, the more inflexible the structures of the official economy are. With respect to the overall economy shadow, economic activities have an economic lubricant function.
- Social mollifier: with strains in the labor market, private households shift, both on the labor supply and the goods demand side, to the shadow economy. Consequently, the social costs of stabilization policy - e.g. in phases of disinflation policies - are not as heavily felt as in the absence of an underground economy; therefore the political resistance against an anti-inflation policy is

less pronounced, thus increasing the chance of finally reestablishing price level stability. Hence, the underground economy mollifies the struggle for income in recession periods and serves as a flank protection in the field of incomes policies.
- Built-in stabilizer: besides the above-mentioned two passive functions (political stabilization, additional opportunities for employment and production), the shadow economy might have an active function, too, since unofficial incomes are partly used to buy products from the official sector (Peacock, Shaw, 1982). E.g. every unemployed who earns - additionally to unemployment benefits - income in the underground economy is likely to spend part of the income increment in the official economy; most activities in the shadow economy require certain crude products from the official economy. A growing underground economy will thus have positive spillover effects into the official sector, too.

Apart from certain illegal activities that undermine basic social standards, e.g. dealing drugs etc., economic policy should tolerate the underground economy to a certain degree. The necessity to fight the unofficial economy arises only when its growth is very high as compared to that of the official sector: when politico-economic key factors, such as unemployment and inflation rates, are fundamentally affected and distorted, the political information and control problem become serious.

An economic policy that attempts to roll back the growing underground economy could choose the strategy to change the transaction conditions of the informal sector: e.g. by increasing controls and prosecution measures or by raising penalty costs (see Fig. 2B). However, this would mean to cure the symptom, but not to fight the underlying failure of economic policy in the official sector. The example of tax burden effects has made clear that growth impulses for the underground economy are ultimately due to worsening transaction conditions in the official economy. Obviously, fighting the underground economy is unnecessary if the official economy has a sound economic policy; consequently, economic systems that are characterized by tax rates on the downward-sloping segment of the Laffer curve should cut tax rates drastically, thereby reducing the counterproductive incentives for immigration into the shadow economy.

4.2. Socialist planning economies: underground economy as a destabilizing factor

For socialist planning economies, planning with material balances is the dominant trait of the system. Monetary planning has a mere supporting role. The system of centrally administered prices does not have the function of a flexible indicator system for relative scarcity. Therefore monetary impulses that result e.g. from disproportions between consumption goods funds and money funds do not translate into changing factor allocations via relative price movements or into inflation by free-rising goods prices. The decisive effect is suppressed inflation in the form of cash balance inflation. The lack of consistency in the economy's accounting framework means, however, that private households can meet the inefficiency in government allocation by expanding their activities in the unofficial sector. This results in an intersectoral transformation, where the shadow economy is growing and contributing to the economy's imbalances.

What is the significance of the unofficial economy? As in capitalist market economies, it seems to be an economic lubricant and social mollifier. On the one hand, the shadow economy compensates for shortages in the official economy (O'Hearn, 1980; Katsenelinboigen, 1977). On the other hand the underground economy lifts the tolerance margin of individuals with respect to economic policies. Especially the case of Hungary has shown that the unofficial economy serves as a buffer for political mismanagement and reforms (Hegedüs, 1984; Szita, 1984). The underground economy has no unambiguous function as a built-in stabilizer: a growing unofficial economy provides incentives to divert working potential and other resources from the official economy, thereby aggravating shortages and cash balance inflation in the official sector. This in turn stimulates a further growth of the unofficial economy. However, a continuous growth of the shadow economy reduces the stability of the overall economy since the inconsistencies of the central planning process for the official economy become more obvious, more accentuated; it becomes increasingly difficult to establish a consistent macroeconomic planning and accounting framework.

Because of the danger of an increased destabilization of the overall system, socialist planning economies are characterized by the necessity to fight the underground economy - contrary to the case of market economies. If such a counter-strategy simply aimed at the unofficial economy by worsening its transaction conditions (e.g. by increasing risks, see Fig. 3 B), political costs would be high: the overall supply of goods would shrink, but the real causes of the problem would not be addressed. As in capitalist economies, solving the problem requires restoring the efficiency of the official economy. Those changes are necessary that guarantee the congruence of production goals with consumers' preferences and minimize discrepancies between goods and money funds; the reforms could range from a change of the production structure in favor of consumption goods (reduction of public consumption) to a strategy of monetary restraint or even a currency reform (Hartwig, 1982). Generally, introducing more market elements seems to be a success-promising policy.

5. THE GROWING SHADOW ECONOMY: A CHALLENGE FOR ECONOMIC POLICY

Summarizing, we find that the growth of the shadow economy is a major problem for economic policy. This statement needs some qualifications: the growth of the self-service economy reflects a secular trend of industrialized societies and can therefore be classified as a minor problem; however, the underground economy and its transformation tendencies constitute a challenge for economic policy. It has been argued that a growing underground economy can be explained by the interference of government; the state as a predominant factor of the economic process has increased its impact on the allocation process, and in the socialist planning economies it has created conditions in the official economy that leave only the underground economy as a means of shock absorption. There is a challenge for economic policy in order to reform the institutional framework in a way that economic efficiency is restored and that basic incentive mechanisms govern the allocation of production factors (Ordnungspolitik).

For the socialist planning economies there is a basic necessity to introduce market mechanisms in goods and factor markets. Especially as regards the labor market, government should make it impossible that inefficient production - an output increase 'at any price' - occurs. Revealing actual relative scarcities by using free prices and market mechanisms would be·helpful; at the same time this would show the conflict between planners' and consumers' preferences. As long as these reforms do not take place, the unofficial economy will persist and grow in a potentially destabilizing manner: the underground economy is a surrogate - spontaneously emerging from private action - for required changes in the economy's institutional framework (Grossman, 1977; Haffner, 1985a).

In capitalist market economies, fundamental changes of the economic framework are not necessary if the underground economy problem is to be solved. We have identified policy failures and problems on the supply side of the economy as the underlying cause of shadow economic growth; taxes and regulations reduce the adjustment possibilities of economic subjects both in the labor market and in the goods markets. However, the recent renaissance of institutional economics indicates which type of remedy for increasing economic efficiency is necessary. Theory and application of supply-side economic policies show that government interference is generally reduced and that tax reforms and restored labor market flexibility can rejuvenate the incentive mechanisms and economic structures of the system; deregulation, reducing the tax burden and encouraging timely adjustment across sectors, subsystems and regions can effectively improve the politico-economic performance via the supply-side (Welfens, 1985). Finally, the shadow economy phenomenon remains on the research agenda for comparative economics for a long time, as many issues have not been settled yet, and as the intellectual discovery of an informal sector is stimulating research in this field in many ways.

NOTES

* We gratefully acknowledge comments by Paul J.J. Welfens, University of Duisburg, FRG.

REFERENCES

BENDER, D., 'Angebot des Haushalts I: Arbeitsangebot', in
Albers, W. et al. Handwörterbuch der Wirtschaftswissen
schaft, Mohr, Stuttgart 1977.
BRYSON, P. The Consumer under Socialist Planning. The East
German Case, Praeger, New York 1984.
BREZINSKI, H., ROS, C., The Development of the Second Econo-
my in Hungary. Arbeitspapier des Fachbereichs Wirtschafts
wissenschaft der Universität-Gesamthochschule-Paderborn,
Paderborn 1984.
BREZINSKI, H., 'The Second Economy in the Soviet Union and
its Implications for Economic Policy', in Gaertner, W.,
Wenig, A., (eds), The Economics of the Shadow Econo-
my, Springer, Berlin 1985.
CASSEL, D., 'Schattenwirtschaft - eine Wachstumsbranche',
List-Forum, no. 6, 1982.
CASSEL, D., 'The Growing Shadow Economy: Implications for
Stabilization Policy', Intereconomics, no. 5, 1984a.
CASSEL, D., 'Stabilitätspolitik und Schattenwirtschaft', in
Schäfer W. (ed), Schattenökonomie. Theoretische Grund-
lagen und Wirtschaftspolitische Konsequenzen, Vandenhoeck & Ruprecht, Göttingen 1984b.
CASSEL, D., 'Wirtschaftspolitik in alternativen Wirtschaftssystemen: Begriffe, Konzepte, Methoden', in Cassel, D.
(ed), Wirtschaftspolitik im Systemvergleich. Konzeption
und Praxis der Wirtschaftspolitik in kapitalistischen und
sozialistischen Wirtschaftssystemen, Vahlen, Munchen
1984c.
CASSEL, D., 'Inflation und Inflationswirkungen in soziali-
tinschen Planwirtschaften', in Thieme H.J. (ed), Geldtheorie. Probleme und Effekte monetärer Steuerung in
unterschiedlichen Wirtschaftssystemen, Nomos, Baden-Baden 1985.
CICHY, E.U., Parallelwirtschaft und Wirtschaftsreform: Das
unorthodoxe Experiment der Ungarischen Volksrepublik,
Diskussionsbeiträge des Fachbereichs Wirtschaftswissen-
schaft der Universität-Gesamthochschule-Duisburg, no. 69,
Duisburg 1984.
DALLAGO, B., The Underground Economy in the West and the
East: a Comparative Approach, paper presented to the
International Conference on "The Unofficial Economy.
Consequences and Politics in East and West", Trento 1984
(Cf. this volume).
DE GIJSEL, P., 'Ökonomische Theorie des Schwarzarbeitsange-
bots und der Mehrfachbeschäftigung', in Gretschmann, K.,
Heinze, R.G., Mettelsiefen, B., (eds), Schattenwirt-
schaft. Wirtschafts-und sozialwissenschaftliche Aspekte,
internationale Erfahrungen, Vandenhoeck & Ruprecht, Göt-
tingen 1984.
FEIGE, E.L., The Anatomy of the Underground Economy, paper
presented to the International Conference on "The Unofficial Economy. Consequences and Politics in East and
West", Trento 1984 (Cf. this volume).
GÁBOR, I.R., 'The Second (secondary) Economy: Earning Activity and Regrouping of Income outside the Socially Orga-

nized Production and d.Distribution', _Acta Oeconomica_, nos. 3-4, 1979.

GÁBOR, I.R., GALASI P., 'The labour market in Hungary since 1968', in Hare, P.G., Radice, H.K., Swain, N. (eds), _Hungary: A Decade of Economic Reform_, Allen & Unwin, London 1981.

GALASI, P., 'Schattenwirtschaft, Staat und Beschäftigung in den sozialistischen Ländern Osteuropas - eine ordnungs-politische Betrachtung', in Gretschmann, K., Heinze, R.G. Mettelsiefen, B. (eds), _Schattenwirtschaft. Wirtschafts- und sozialwissenschaftliche Aspekte, internationale Erfahrungen_, Vandenhoeck & Ruprecht, Göttingen 1984.

GERSHUNY, J.I., 'Post-Industrial Society. The Myth of the Service Economy', _Futures_, April 1977.

GERSHUNY, J.I., 'The Informal Economy - its Role in Post-Industrial Society', _Futures_, February 1979.

GLOWNY URZAD STATYSTYCZNY (current issues), _Rocznik Statys-tyczny_, Warsaw.

GRETSCHMANN, K., METTELSIEFEN, B., 'Die Schattenwirtschaft-sdebatte - eine Retrospektive', in Gretschmann K., Hein-ze, R.G., Mettelsiefen, B. (eds), _Schattenwirtschaft. Wirtschafts- und sozialwissenschaftliche Aspekte, Inter-nationale Erfahrungen_, Vandenhoeck & Ruprecht, Göttingen 1984.

GRETSCHMANN, K., HEINZE, R.G., METTELSIEFEN, B., 'Vorbe-merkungen der Herausgeber' on GALASI, P., in Gretschmann, K., Heinze, R.G., Mettelsiefen B. (eds), _Schattenwirts-chaft. Wirtschafts- und sozialwissenschaftliche Aspekte, internationale Erfahrungen_, Vandenhoeck & Ruprecht, Göt-tingen 1984.

GROSSMAN, G., 'The Second Economy in the USSR', _Problems of Communism_, Sept.-Oct. 1977.

HAFFNER, F., 'Wirtschaftsformen in Osteuropa: Effizienzstei-gerung oder Sackgasse', _DIW-Wochenbericht_, no. 8, 1985a.

HAFFNER, F., 'Monetäre Zentralplanung und Volkswirtschafts-planung', in Thieme H.J. (ed), _Geldtheorie. Probleme und Effekte monetärer Steuerung in unterschiedlichen Wirtschaftsystemen_, Nomos, Baden-Baden 1985b.

HARTWIG, K.-H., 'Output- und Beschäftigungswirkungen einkom-mens- und währungspolitischer Massnahmen in sozialisti-schen Planwirtschaften: Ein rationierungstheoretischer Ansatz', in _Zeitschrift fur Wirtschafts- und Sozialwis-senschaften_, no. 4, 1982.

HARTWIG, K.-H., _Monetäre Steuerungsprobleme in sozialisti-schen Planwirtschaften_, noch underöffentlichte Habilita-tionsschrift, Bochum 1983.

HARTWIG, K.-H., THIEME, H.J., 'Determinanten des Geld- und Kreditangebots in sozialistischen Planwirtschaften', in Thieme, H.J., (ed) _Geldtheorie. Probleme und Effekte mo-netärer· Steuerung in unterschiedlichen Wirtschaftssy-stemen_, Nomos, Baden-Baden 1985.

HEGEDÜS, A., _The Consequences and Perspectives of the Expan-sion of the Second Economy in Eastern Europe Countries_, paper prepared for the International Conference on "The Unofficial Economy. Consequences and Politics in East and West", Trento 1984 (Cf. this volume).

144

HUBER, J., Die zwei Gesichter der Arbeit. Ungenutzte Moglichkeiten der Dualwirtschaft, Fischer, Frankfurt 1984.
IMF (current issues), International Financial Statistics, Washington, D. C.
KATSENELINBOIGEN, A., 'Coloured Markets in the Soviet Union', Soviet Studies, no. 1, 1977.
KIRCHGÄSSNER, G., 'Size and Development of the West German Shadow Economy 1955-1980', Zeitschrift fur die gesamte Staatswissenschaft, 1983.
KLEPS, K.-H., Staatliche Preispolitik. Theorie und Realität in Markt- und Planwirtschaften, Vahlen, München 1984.
KORNAI, J., Economics of Shortage, vols. A and B, North Holland, Amsterdam, 1980.
LANDAU, Z., Selected Problems of Unofficial Economy in Poland, paper presented to the International Conference on "The Unofficial Economy. Consequences and Politics in East and West", Trento 1984 (Cf. this volume).
LANGFELDT, E., Die Schattenwirtschaft in der Bundesrepublik Deutschland, Mohr, Tübingen 1984.
LASKI, K., '"Second Economy" in sozialistischen Ländern und Inflationserscheinungen', in Hedtkamp, G. (ed), Beiträge zum Problem der Schattenwirtschaft. Schriften des Vereins für Socialpolitik, NF 132, Duncker & Humblot, Berlin 1983.
METTELSIEFEN, B., 'Besteuerung und Schattenwirtschaft', in Gretschmann K., Heinze, R.G., Mettelsiefen, B. (eds), Schattenwirtschaft. Wirtschafts- und sozialwissenschaftliche Aspekte, internationale Erfahrungen, Vandenhoeck & Ruprecht, Gottingen 1984.
NOELLE-NEUMANN, E., STRÜMPEL, G., Macht Arbeit krank? Macht Arbeit glücklich? Eine aktuelle Kontroverse, Piper, Munchen 1984.
O'HEARN, D., 'The Consumer Second Economy: Size and Effects', Soviet Studies, no. 2, 1980.
PEACOCK, A., SHAW, G.K., 'Tax evasion and Revenue Loss, Public Finance, no. 2, 1982.
PRYOR, F.L., 'A Quantitative Study of the Structure and Behavior of Consumption and Prices in Different Economic Systems', in Bohnet, A. (ed), Preise im Sozialismus. Kontinuität im Wandel. Teil II: Zur Theorie und Praxis gesamtwirtschaftlicher Preissysteme, Dunker & Humblot, Berlin 1984.
SCHENK, K.-E., WASS VON CZEGE, A., 'Second Economy und Wirtschaftsordnung - Ein systemübergreifender, transaktionsökonomischer Erklärungsansatz', in Hedtkamp, G. (ed), Beiträge zum Problem der Schattenwirtschaft. Schriften des Vereins für Socialpolitik, NF 132, Dunker & Humblot, Berlin 1983.
SEIDENSTECHER, G., 'Machen Ersparnisse arbeitsscheu? Zur Entwicklung des Sparens in der Sowjetunion', Osteuropa-Wirtschaft, no. 4, 1982.
SEUROT, F., Inflation et emploi dans les pays socialistes, Presses universitaires de France, Paris 1983.
STEIN, B., 'Subterranean Labor Markets: A Conceptual Analysis', in Gärtner, W., Wenig, A., (eds), The Economics of the Shadow Economy, Springer, Berlin 1985.

STAATLICHE ZENTRALVERWALTUNG FÜR STATISTIK (current issues), Statistische Jahrbücher der Deutschen Demokratischen Republik, Berlin.

STATISTISCHES BUNDESAMT (current issues), Fachserie 17, Kohlhammer, Stuttgart.

SZITA, É., 'New Types of Enterprises and Organizational Forms in the Hungarian Economy', paper presented to the International Conference on "The Unofficial Economy. Consequences and Politics in the West and East", Trento 1984 (Cf. this volume).

SZELIGA, Z., 'Polen in den Jahren 1971-1980', in Ajnenkiel, A., et al., Polen, Interpress, Warsaw 1977.

THIEME, H.J., 'Produktions- und Beschäftigungseffekte monetärer Impulse in sozialistischen Planwirtschaften', in Thieme, H.J. (ed), Geldtheorie. Probleme und Effecte monetärer Steuerung in unterschiedlichen Wirtschaftssystemen, Nomos, Baden-Baden 1985.

WECK-HANNEMANN, H., '"Weiche Modellierung" der Schattenwirtschaft - Ein internationaler Vergleich', in Gretschmann, K., Heinze, R.G., Mettelsiefen, B. (eds), Schattenwirtschaft, Wirtschafts-und sozialwissenschafliche Aspekte, internationale Erfahrungen, Vandenhoeck & Ruprecht, Göttingen 1984.

WELFENS, P., Theorie und Praxis angebotsorientierter Stabilitätspolitik, Nomos, Baden-Baden 1985.

WILES, P., Die Parallelwirtschaft. Eine Einschätzung des systemwidrigen Verhaltens (SWV) im Bereich der Wirtschaft unter besonderer Berücksichtigung der UdSSR. Sonderveröffentlichung des Bundesinstituts für ostwissenschaftliche und internationale Studien, Köln 1981.

The underground economy in the West and the East: a comparative approach

BRUNO DALLAGO

1. INTRODUCTION

An irregular (unofficial) increase in the supply of goods and services (here termed the underground economy) is present in Soviet and in capitalistic-type economies. Similar characteristics manifest themselves in both economic systems. In general, underground production is present in labor-intensive and less standardized activities, where economies of scale are irrelevant and technology permits the splitting-up of the production process into smaller units. Goods and services produced underground are legal and are also produced in the regular economy. They belong to the irregular economy because of the way they are obtained. Generally, the producing enterprise or part of its production is underground (i.e. does not officially exist). Often this happens when operation of a certain type of enterprise is prohibited by law. Underground economy is strictly interwoven with other irregular activities. In many instances, they are different components of the same economic process (e.g. underground production and corruption or tax evasion). The aspect of production will be the focus of this paper.

2. BASIC FEATURES OF THE UNDERGROUND ECONOMY

2.1. In the <u>Soviet-type economic system</u> there are two major components which together form the so-called underground entrepreneurial sector: underground private enterprises and underground private activities (Gábor and Galasi, 1981; Grossman, 1977; Katsenelinboigen, 1977; Simis, 1982).

Underground private enterprises are real enterprises run by private owners and entrepreneurs; these enterprises hire workers in order to gain a profit. They are - and will remain - underground because this type of enterprise is prohibited by law or because an underground existence is more profitable. Underground private enterprises generally supply consumption goods and personal services because of their simpler and less risky marketability. Less frequent is the case of the supply of production goods and services, also to socialist enterprises. The vast range of production items includes: garments, footwear, household articles, houses, home-brew alcohol, and various services (car and home repair, sewing and tailoring of garments, transportation of persons and goods, and the like).

Underground private activities, on the other hand, reach large dimensions and are not independent, but are in symbiosis with a socialist enterprise. The latter unofficially produces goods and services; and inputs are paid for by private persons, owners of the products and services supplied.

Another example of this symbiosis between regular and irregular activities is typified by socialist enterprises managed and run as virtually private enterprises. Here, production takes place according to plan but yields a higher quantity. Surplus remains underground, is sold on the irregular market; and revenue is taken by organizers of the underground activity. It is evident that without widespread corruption, this type of mechanism could not function.

2.2. In the capitalistic-type economic system, private activity has few limits and underground economy is confined to relatively few sectors. Among the most typical are: acts of illegality, such as illegal construction, production of alcohol, transportation of goods and persons, and the illegal or irregular supply of professional services (e.g. dental technicians working as dentists); acts of forgery, such as forgery of documents, banknotes, records and paintings; and underground production induced by other underground activities (like the production of speed-boats for smugglers) (Feige, 1979; Gutman, 1977; Simon, Witte, 1982).

There are also many examples of underground production of goods and components in the manufacturing industry, such as in the garment, footwear, and car industries. In the capitalistic-type economic system there exist independent underground activities as well as activities vertically integrated with regular enterprises (Brusco, 1973; Cantelli, 1980; Contini, 1979; Saba, 1980).

3. CAUSES

Activities are said to be underground because they break the law, escape regulation, or transgress social agreements. Either they are prohibited (such as private enterprises in certain sectors of Soviet-type economies) or are performed underground in order to circumvent prohibitions, limitations, and controls. The existence of these activities is explained by the institutional structure of the economic system.

3.1. In the Soviet-type economic system, underground activities are all-pervasive. They seem to be prosperous mainly because there is a wide demand for goods and services not satisfied by the regular economy, and because underground activities grant the organizers considerable rewards. The institutional organization of the economy causes shortage in the regular economy, thereby fostering demand for goods and services supplied by underground activities (Kornai, 1980).

There exist three major groups of goods. The first group consists of goods and services utilized by enterprises. When enterprises have no inner constraints against input demand increase (as in the Soviet-type economic system), only an administrative policy is effective. In such circumstances, input shortage is unavoidable, creating ample room for irregular activity. However, owing to technological factors and control and repression activity, underground economy is confined mostly to irregular exchange of production goods and services among socialist enterprises and much less to underground production.

A second group is made up of consumption goods and services utilized by consumers (families) and the private sector of the economy. Both consumers and the private sector have hard inner constraints against demand increase. Here shortage can be regulated and controlled also by monetary policy. Underground activity permits an increase in both income and consumption. This group of goods constitutes the main area of underground production; controls are difficult and production technology is often simple.

Goods and services utilized by enterprises on the one hand and families and the private sector on the other make up the third group. This is a very wide category and the most difficult to control through economic policy. In fact, there is an imbalance between socialist enterprises and families, of which only the latter have an inner constraint against demand increase. For this reason, economic policy alone produces a displacement effect to the disadvantage of families. Utilization of policy instruments in order to limit demand will be effective on the consumers' side but will have little effect on discouraging enterprise demand. The consequence for aggregate demand may be negligible. In fact, a relative strengthening of enterprise position may develop, inducing enterprises to increase their demand even further. In doing so, they may be indirectly aided by a central policy aimed at increasing production in order to increase consumption. As a result, economic policy may be a good means of controlling consumer demand; but only administrative policy can effectively control enterprise demand. This displacement effect, which forms the basis for the incapability of the traditional Soviet-type economy to rapidly increase consumption, further stimulates the demand for underground production by families.

The pervasiveness of shortage creates ample space for the underground economy. On the one hand, shortage means that demand is higher than supply and that people and enterprises have a purchasing power (both monetary and non-monetary) higher than that necessary to buy or obtain all the available (regular) goods and services. Goods and services in shortage or goods and services of better quality can be procured from the underground economy. On the other hand, the underground economy provides the possibility of increasing individual incomes.

3.2. In a capitalistic-type economy, causes of unofficial economy differ radically from those described above. An enterprise (with inner constraint to gain a profit) will try to control its input demand and diminish costs in order to increase profit rate or decrease prices, to gain a higher market share, keep the previous one, or simply in order to survive. The underground economy may provide a powerful means of reaching one or more of these targets without decreasing input utilization. This, however, depends on four major factors: technology, the structure of costs, the role of regulation, and flexibility.

The underground economy may be utilized in industries where production consists of many stages, which can be decentralized or performed with different technology (Contini 1979, 1981). Underground production has no role in industries characterized by a continuous production process (like the chemical and metallurgical industries).

One of the major motivations for utilizing the underground economy is the possibility of diminishing costs. In particular, underground activities evade taxes, social contributions and sometimes monopoly prices (e.g. in state monopoly products, like cigarettes and alcohol). For this reason, underground economy is found particularly in labor-intensive productions and is most useful for those industries in which at least one stage of production is labor intensive or may be replaced by a cheaper, labor intensive technology. In an oligopolistic market, when costs decrease there is a tendency to keep the previous price level, thus raising the profit rate (Sraffa, 1926; Sylos Labini, 1984). Underground activities, when vertically integrated with regular activities, may give rise to a higher rate of profit for regular enterprises.

Regulation is introduced to protect society or individual groups from the harmful consequences of firms pursuing microeconomic gain (e.g., pollution and other forms of environmental destruction, product adulteration, and the like). However, for individual market producers, regulation may increase costs and decrease flexibility and adaptability to changing market conditions. Regulation may also create a shortage of certain goods (e.g. regulation of building land). The underground economy allows producers to avoid regulation and may result in an increased supply of goods (e.g. illegal constructions on protected land).

Finally, the underground economy may increase the flexibility of input utilization (mainly labor), preserving managerial control over the enterprise's inner life (e.g. avoiding trade-union controls). An enterprise, operating in a growing industry, can decide not to expand its productive capacity and decentralize a part of its production. This prevents its production structure from growing rigid and social problems and internal control within the enterprise from growing stronger (e.g. a stronger trade-union organization) (Gaetani-D'Aragona, 1979, 1981).

3.3. The situation of consumers in both economic systems is more alike than that of enterprises. In both economic systems, consumers have inner constraints against demand increase. However, the macroeconomic situation of consumption is different. In a capitalistic-type economy, where demand is often low relative to potential supply and there is no relevant displacement effect from consumer to enterprise demand, consumers demand underground production mainly because of lower price level. In a Soviet-type economy, owing to shortage, consumers demand underground products mainly because of their better quality or simply because they are the only available products, even if their price is higher.

3.4. The situation in the labor market in a capitalistic-type economy is often characterized by unemployment of primary workers and by a supply of labor by marginal workers (women, students, retired people, immigrants). Marginal workers are willing to supply labor in the underground economy because of flexibility of working time, lack of alternatives in the regular economy, and the fact that the net wage is often higher than in the regular economy (due to evasion of taxes and social contributions). Underground economy also offers primary workers the opportunity to increase income through moonlighting. Demand for underground labor is fostered by a low gross wage level, caused by tax evasion, evasion of social contributions, and higher flexibility (Gallino, 1982; Barsotti and Potestà, 1983).

In a Soviet-type economy, full employment prevails. People supply labor in the underground market to increase their income (net wage rates being generally much higher than in the regular economy) and to obtain personal satisfaction. The latter is true mainly for underground entrepreneurs and craftsmen. Underground labor demand is generally high because it is the only type that underground enterprises can utilize. Underground labor demand is determined, therefore, by institutional and structural factors (Gábor and Galasi 1981).

4. THE UNDERGROUND MARKET OF CONSUMPTION GOODS AND PRODUCTION INPUTS

4.1. Depending on the intensity of shortage in the regular market and differences in quality and price level between the two markets, consumers in a Soviet-type economy take advantage of the underground market of consumption goods and services. This is determined by their income and capability to pay with acceptable payment means, the situation in the market of substitutes and alternative goods, and the willingness of people to substitute the good in shortage. The latter derives from the degree of indispensability of the good or service in question.

Supply depends on four main factors:

- the possibility of the underground producer to find production inputs;
- the efficiency of repression and, alternatively, of corruption;
- the possibility of buyers to offer acceptable payment means (in a situation of high inflation or excess of

purchasing power, the country's official currency may
be replaced by convertible currencies or goods such as
alcohol, cigarettes, or imported goods.);
-    the possibility of the producer to spend the revenue
obtained or to gain particular satisfaction from underground performance.

4.2. In a capitalistic-type economy, underground producers
have to compete with regular producers to create demand.
Given certain disadvantages of an underground market (such
as lower confidence of consumers, difficulties of location
and smaller dimensions), underground producers can be
successful only if they are more competitive than regular
ones - either in price, quality, time necessary to obtain
goods or services, or regulation. Where shortage is the
cause of going underground, the situation may be similar to
that of a Soviet-type economy (as in the case of building
land or the underground market of personal papers and certi-
ficates).
In the labor market of a Soviet-type economy, there is no
unemployment. As a consequence, working time in the underground economy is supplementary to and not substitutive of
regular working time. Therefore, labor supply is entirely
made up of the moonlighting of primary workers and of labor
by marginal workers who do not accept a regular job. Labor
supply in the underground economy, with absenteeism in the
regular one, is also widespread.
Underground labor demand in both economic systems depends
on the level of underground activity; that is, on the level
of demand for goods and services produced underground (given
the efficiency of repression and corruption). However, in a
Soviet-type economy, costs are secondary to enterprises, in
contrast to capitalistic-type economies where the difference
between wages in the regular and underground economy is an
important one.
In a capitalistic-type economy, a large part of the underground labor supply depends on the existence of unemployment. In many instances (unemployed people, illegal aliens,
marginal workers), underground employment may be the only
way to get a job.
In any case, the underground economy offers flexible jobs
and permits tax evasion, paying a net wage sometimes higher
than the regular one. In fact, net and gross wages coincide
or are very close to each other.
The underground labor market has a dual structure composed
of strong and weak workers. The underground economy offers
strong workers the opportunity to increase personal income.
They supply labor, depending on the net wage level. This
group is made of primary workers with a job in the regular
economy, often with a qualification for which there is an
overall shortage. On the other hand, there exists a group of
weak workers, for whom the underground economy offers the
only possibility of getting a job and for whom the net wage
rate is not the only determinant. The weakest group is
clearly that of illegal aliens (Lewis, 1979; North, Houstoun, 1976; Reubens, 1978; Weintraub, Ross, 1980, 1982).

Between these two groups of workers, there are many others whose families already have an income, however modest, and for whom the underground economy offers the only or most favourable opportunity to increase personal or family income (unemployed people gaining unemployment benefits, retired people enjoying a pension, housewives and students who enjoy social security thanks to their family position) (CENSIS, 1976; Gallino, 1982; Il Mondo, 1982).

As a consequence, in a capitalistic-type economy, underground labor supply supplements as well as substitutes for the regular labor supply. Morever, the underground market is characterized by heterogeneity, which overlaps that existing in the regular market.

4.3. In a Soviet-type economy, demand and supply of capital are basically seen in physical terms, because of the inexistence of a regular financial market. On the one side, it is very hard for an underground entrepreneur to find investment goods in the regular market. Even if this were possible, a private individual buying investment goods would raise suspicions. For these reasons, an underground entreprenuer is able to obtain investment goods mainly through a regular enterprise, either with its cooperation or by stealing from it (Grossman, 1977; Simis, 1982).

On the other side, the underground supply of financial capital is limited. Underground entrepreneurs often initiate their activity, utilizing personal savings or the savings of relatives and friends. However, a large share of this money is spent on corruption.

The underground market of investment goods is rather active and relatively widespread. Goods and services exchanged are:

- stolen goods and services. investment goods needed by an underground entrepreneur are stolen from a regular enterprise, often by its employees. The same refers to services: regularly employed workers perform a service for an underground enterprise (e.g. transportation), during regular working time and with the use of regular enterprise assets;
- goods and services irregularly obtained from a regular enterprise, through an illegal agreement with its managers. This form involves widespread corruption of control and repression bodies;
- use of goods and services of and within a regular enterprise during or after regular working time. This form is widespread when the underground activity is in symbiosis with the regular activity;
- goods and services bought on the regular market. This possibility is limited;
- goods and services exchanged on the underground market;
- goods built or transformed by the promoter of the underground activity. This category is basically comprised of tools and small machines for underground craftsmen.

Given the efficiency of repression and, alternatively, of

corruption, shortage determines the level of production, and therefore the underground demand for investment goods and services. The effect of repression varies according to the type enforced. Successful repression may cause a decrease in demand and in underground activity in general only if it is continuous and seen as permanent. In this case, corruption loses its effectiveness. However, even successful repression, seen as temporary and discontinuous, is likely to foster demand (in order to replace confiscated goods) and increase corruption. Due to shortage in Soviet-type economies, monetary factors (the price of investment goods and services, the interest rate on borrowed capital) are not very effective. As to supply, two main causes can be isolated.

Supply and investment decisions are explained by the drive to gain a higher personal income (through profit and rent). Psychological and social factors (personal satisfaction, prestige) are also important. However, supply of investment goods, services, and monetary capital may have passive motivations. Reinvestment in underground activities is dictated by a lack of alternatives, in particular when underground entrepreneurs and capitalists are unable to consume their underground income, mainly because of the fear of exposure.

At this point, a question is legitimate: why should people try to increase their personal income in a shortage economy? Shortage should eliminate every incentive to gain a higher income, because spending is limited. However, shortage at both macro- and microeconomic levels does not mean that individual consumers are unable to spend additional income.

There are four possible adjustments to a shortage situation in which the underground economy plays a role. One widespread form of adjustment is 'queueing up': the buyer is unable to find in the regular market the good or service he is looking for and waits for his turn in a queue. If he has additional income from underground activity, he is able to 'shorten' or 'jump over' the queue and immediately obtain the good or service by offering a reward (tip, bribe, present) to the allocator (worker, seller, bureaucrat).

Another adjustment is forced substitution: the buyer is unable to find the needed good or service in the regular market and is forced to buy a substitute of lower quality or at a higher price. Additional income from underground activity permits him to buy a substitute of higher quality (and higher price) or allows him to offer the allocator a reward, thereby persuading the allocator to find the needed good or service.

A third possible adjustment is forced saving. Although forced saving (in the traditional sense of unspendable money due to absolute shortage) does not play a role, saving in order to later buy an expensive good or service (a house, a long pleasure journey) certainly exists. In this case, additional underground income is helpful.

Finally, the buyer can turn directly to the underground market for goods and services in shortage in the regular market or for a higher quality (although generally at a higher price).

4.4. In a <u>capitalistic economy</u>, the underground capital market is similar to the regular one. Because private capital flow and utilization is almost unconstrained, there is no such thing as lack of investment alternatives. On the contrary, a private capitalist will balance various alternatives open to him, including the possibility of investment in the underground economy, when this becomes more profitable. To make a decision, he has to base his calculation on three important elements.

One element is determined by direct costs, i.e. those costs to be paid directly by the capitalist; in the irregular economy, these costs are lower due to lower gross wage rates and tax evasion. However, taxes and social contributions which burden regular enterprises may be momentarily reduced or paid for by the government, decreasing the comparative advantage of going underground. Also, underground enterprises have higher costs than regular ones: costs of hiding their activity; difficulties of access to the regular market; the danger of growing beyond a certain dimension. Therefore, economies of scale cannot play a relevant role, and technical progress may be slower due to organizational difficulties. Sometimes underground enterprises have to pay bribes; the risk of being caught may make it more difficult to find financial capital and input. In short, the cost of avoiding regulation and control may be high in time, bribes, risk, and uncertainty.

A second element consists of labor productivity and flexibility. Due to the absence of trade-unions and flexibility in hiring and dimissing workers, labor productivity (including labor intensity) and flexibility in the productive structure of underground enterprises may be higher than in regular enterprises. However, labor mobility may be too high and out of entrepreneurial control. Moreover, the underground economy often cannot survive alone and has to enter into a symbiotic relationship with a regular enterprise (usually larger), losing its independence.

Lastly, final market prices of underground products play a role in underground entrepreneurial calculation. As already seen, underground market prices are generally lower than in the regular economy, and may be a disincentive to investment.

Taking these elements into account, the entrepreneur can get an idea of the underground profit rate, probably higher in many fields than the regular one. However, he must also consider the efficiency of repression, which adds risk and additional cost to underground economic activity. When an entrepreneur has decided to invest in an underground activity and financial capital is available, ther are no particular problems in finding investment goods, apart from the possibility of control by authorities.

The case of capital coming from irregular activities (drug production and trade, illegal gambling, and the like), is different. In this case, the underground economy offers a good opportunity to 'launder' illegal money by investing it in the production of regular goods. From here, it is easier to invest this money in the regular economy. This is impor-

tant for the Mafia, for instance (Arlacchi, 1982). Given the
overall demand of goods and services, the technology, and
the situation in the labor market, capital in a capitalistic-type economy flows from the underground to the regular
economy and _vice versa_ with few obstacles, according to
differences between regular and underground profit rates and
the risk coming from repression activity.

5. ADVANTAGES AND DISADVANTAGES OF UNDERGROUND ACTIVITIES

5.1. Underground enterprises in _Soviet-type economies_ have
both advantages and disadvantages in comparison to regular
enterprises. Diffusion of the underground economy depends on
their balance.
   One major field of analysis is _input procurement_. Because
of the non-existence of a regular free market of capital and
investment goods and services, underground enterprises are
clearly at a disadvantage. Input procurement is a permanent
worry for them and may expose them to detection. Shortage
worsens the situation. The same applies to regular enterprises. In the labor market, there are no particular disadvantages to underground enterprises; they are generally able
to obtain the labor they need because they can pay higher
wages than regular enterprises.
   From the point of view of costs, instead, the situation of
underground enterprises seems unproblematic. Material inputs
are often obtained for a low price or for free, with only
bribe or reward to the supplier. However, an underground
enterprise has additional costs of hiding and protecting the
underground activity. These range from material and human
costs of performing the activity in hidden places or by
night, to costs for bribes and those costs incurred by the
impossibility of utilizing the regular trade system. Finally
to be taken into account are the monetary, material and
human costs in case of detection. As to wages, underground
enterprises have no particular advantages. On the contrary,
they generally pay higher wages, and evasion of taxes and
social contributions lends only a modest advantage.
   The comparison of advantages and disadvantages on a cost
basis has little significance in a Soviet-type economy,
where regular enterprises remain insensitive to costs and a
pervasive shortage exists. Therefore, it can be supposed
that underground enterprises would exist and flourish even
with much higher costs and prices than regular enterprises.
Due to shortage, both underground and regular enterprises
have no serious problems selling products. However, underground enterprises must care about quality in order to sell
goods and services supplied by regular enterprises. On the
other hand, shortage makes demand relatively price-inelastic
and this allows for higher selling prices.
   The main advantage of underground enterprises lies in the
flexibility, participation and interest of the collective.
Due to institutional and organizational factors, there is a
close connection between the economic outcome of the enterprise and personal income of its participants. Psychological

and social motivations of workers, entrepreneurs and capitalists promote higher efficiency and productivity. However, these same motivations in difficult times may cause abandonment of the enterprises. The threat of difficulties of economic origin may provide a powerful incentive towards entrepreneurial performance, higher organization and productive flexibility.

5.2. In a capitalistic-type economy advantages and disadvantanges are quite different due to the different situation in both regular and underground enterprises. A fundamental difference lies in the fact that both regular and underground enterprises are cost-sensitive. There are no particular differences between the two enterprise types as far as input procurement is concerned. Both procurement difficulties and prices are approximately the same. However, underground enterprises can easily evade taxes, both in input and output, as well as social and other contributions (e.g. costs for being granted a license or a permit to produce and sell). Very often, underground production is decentralized, taking place in workers' homes. In this case, a part of the fixed costs is saved by the underground enterprise.

Evasion increases the risk of detection and compels underground enterprises to defend themselves by hiding the activity (both physically and economically) and by bribing public officials in charge of the repression of underground activities. This increases costs and decreases the possibility of spending profits and rents gained from underground. Moreover, the relative advantage over regular enterprises in the field of taxes and contributions may be diminished by governmental policy which decreases these burdens in certain economic sectors.

As to flexibility, the advantage to underground enterprises is clear. Flexibility is increased by avoidance of regulation and management of labor. Trade unions do not exist in underground enterprises and it is generally easy to hire and dismiss workers. However, due to their irregular existence, underground enterprises face other previously mentioned costs.

Concerning final demand, underground enterprises have no particular advantages or disadvantages over regular ones. They must compete with each other in the same market for a generally limited demand or vertically integrate with regular enterprises.

Overall, in a capitalistic-type economy, underground enterprises have very soft social and political constraints, since they are relatively similar to regular enterprises. Their survival amd growth depend strictly on economic factors. They require a higher profit rate and a looser organization than do regular enterprises in order to compensate for the disadvantages of an underground existence. For this reason, they develop only in labor-intensive industries where economies of scale are irrelevant and technology permits subdivision of the production process.

In Soviet-type economies, underground enterprises have very soft constraints on the production side. Shortage assures an almost endless market for their supply and excludes any room for competition with regular enterprises. However, they have multiple social and political constraints. There is a considerable difference between underground and regular enterprises and for this reason underground enterprises are easily detectable. They spend more energy and resources on hiding their activity and on bribery. The main advantage they have compared to regular enterprises lies in the participation and interest of the employee collective which gives rise to a higher quality of production, with final (consumer) prices generally higher.

6. THE RELATIONSHIP BETWEEN REGULAR AND UNDERGROUND ENTERPRISES

Relationships between regular and underground enterprises are manifold, depending on such factors as the dimension of enterprises, the sector of activity, and the overall situation of the economy. However, common features may be found in the two economic systems.

6.1. In a Soviet-type economy the situation is asymmetric on the two sides of the economic process, production and input procurement. Due to shortage, regular and underground enterprises do not compete in sales with each other, because the market can absorb their production. At most, if the quality of underground production is higher, consumers may become discontented with regular enterprises; but this may be compensated for by price differentials.
Shortage also exists on the input side. Government authorities directly allocate regular input to regular enterprises and only irregularly produced inputs are available to underground enterprises, though in modest quantity since underground enterprises almost exclusively produce consumption goods and services. For this reason, hard competition develops in the input market between regular and underground enterprises. Due to lack of a true market for investment goods and services, underground economies try to obtain part of the inputs allocated to regular enterprises or to utilize both, when possible. Underground enterprises are parasitic on regular enterprises, increasing input shortage. However, regular enterprises can ask the central allocator for a greater quantity of inputs, and generally obtain them. This is less true for labor, where supply comes from moonlighters and marginal workers, who, supposedly, are not willing to offer labor to regular enterprises. However, absenteeism is a widespread phenomenon that matches underground labor supply.

6.2. In a capitalistic-type economy, regular and underground enterprises compete in a similar way for inputs, the only major difference in their position being in the regular financial market where underground enterprises have difficulties of access. In the output market, it is necessary to take into account the role of underground enterprises.

If underground enterprises produce goods and services equal to those of regular enterprises, hard competition may develop where there is limited demand. in this case, the result depends on the difference in costs and on economic policy. As already surmised, underground enterprises enjoy lower unit costs. Regular enterprises may react, accelerating technical progress; but, where underground enterprises can, they may expel regular enterprises from the market, when government does not help regular enterprises by diminishing taxes and social contributions.

When underground enterprises produce goods and services that enter the regular production process as inputs, the situation is quite different. Here mutually advantageous vertical integration may develop. A widespread phenomenon is that of a regular enterprise decentralizing a stage of its production process to an underground enterprise, sometimes created by itself. In this case, the regular economy can take advantage of the lower costs that characterize underground enterprises, since the regular economy can control the underground economy by controlling its output market. A regular enterprise vertically integrated with an underground enterprise presumably has lower unit production costs or enjoys a higher profit rate and may expand its market share without having to invest in new technology. Here, underground enterprises may help competition with completely regular enterprises.

In an oligopolistic market, vertical integration may substitute a higher price in order to increase profit; or, in the case of price decrease, may permit the survival of less efficient enterprises without the reorganization of production process. This form of vertical integration may also serve as a substitute for capital export to countries where labor cost is lower. In this way it can facilitate exports.

7. SOME MACROECONOMIC CONSEQUENCES

Underground economy can have quantitative and qualitative macroeconomic consequences. Considering the former, because underground enterprises produce goods and services, the overall (regular + underground) national income is higher than regular income alone. At the same time, the existence of underground enterprises modifies the working and structure of the overall economic system. Particularly relevant are distributive effects.

Consequences of quantity and quality represent two different sides of the same phenomenon, which conveniently bear separate analysis. Once again, the situation is quite different in the two economic systems.

7.1. In the Soviet-type economic system, underground enterprises distort economic information and calculation. Through irregular appropriation of regular inputs, underground enterprises are able to charge a great part of their costs to regular enterprises. This gives regular enterprises the

opportunity to demand more inputs from the central allocator. Consequently, governmental bodies possess distorted
information about characteristics and working of the economy.

Wrong information leads to wrong decisions. Planning and
economic policies are less efficient; the government has to
increase allocation of state budget resources to enterprises
and, therefore, will also increase centralized enterprise
revenue; administrative intervention is fostered, and economic reforms are impeded.

The situation in the labor market is also distorted, as a
consequence of the fact that underground enterprises operate
in a shortage economy with full employment of workers willing to offer labor to the regular economy. On one hand,
there is an intensification of labor shortage in the economy, due to demand coming from underground enterprises. Increased shortage is experienced by regular enterprises
through increased absenteeism of primary workers. Moreover,
moonlighters are probably tired and their productivity decreased. All this may have negative social (e.g. in family
relations) and health consequences. On the other hand, underground enterprises help diminish labor slack existing in
regular enterprises ('unemployment behind the doors') when
workers are utilized in underground sections of regular
enterprises (underground enterprises in symbiosis with regular enterprises). As a consequence, there is an increase in
working time actually supplied to the overall economy (regular + underground). Employment increase is much lower and is
limited to marginal workers willing to work only in the
underground market.

Assuming that underground enterprises exclusively produce
consumption goods and services (a supposition close to reality), the demand for investment goods and services as well
as the supply of consumption goods and services are increased. Because of the way in which material inputs are obtained, a net income is also generated - equal to the aggregate
price of goods and services produced, net of the aggregate
price of material inputs - that approximates gross income.
Income is distributed to underground workers, entrepreneurs,
and capitalists, but not to the state, which contributes a
large part of the inputs. Income is spent almost exclusively
in the market of consumption goods and services (both regular and underground). Shortage in this market is attenuated,
therefore, only as far as a portion of underground income is
saved: e.g. because no luxury goods are disposable or because underground entrepreneurs fear detection is made easier
by luxury consumption. The same result is reached if underground income is partially utilized to buy imported goods,
which may be accomplished through the underground market (as
in the black market of convertible currency).

It is seen, therefore, that underground activities increase shortage in the market of investment goods and services and only slightly attenuate shortage in the market of
consumption goods and services. This refers, however, to
overall shortage. The intensity of shortage (the relation of
shortage in money or physical terms to overall supply) is

lower, if underground production is taken into account. This means that actual consumption of goods and services is higher than the official one. However, this also means that underground economy is not, in itself, a solution to the problem of shortage, which can only be eliminated by a comprehensive reform of the economic system.

7.2. Suppose that in a capitalistic-type economy, underground enterprises exclusively produce consumption goods and services as well as the supply of consumption goods and services. In a situation of unemployment and excess capacity, an increased demand for investment goods and services stimulates production through a multiplicative effect. The opposite is true in the market of consumption goods and services. In a situation where no new technological solutions exist, if regular and underground enterprises supply the same goods and services (or close substitutes) and if underground enterprises sell for lower prices (due to lower costs), regular enterprises can be displaced from the market, since the overall increase of consumption demand is lower than the increase in overall supply of consumption goods and services. In fact, a part of the underground income is spent in the (regular) market of investment goods and services, and another part saved. An overall positive effect will result only if cheaper underground products are exported. As a consequence, regular enterprises tend to concentrate more on the production of investment goods and services and less on the production of consumption goods and services than in the absence of underground enterprises. Therefore, underground activities have an expansive effect on the regular production of investment goods and services and a recessive effect on the regular production of consumption goods and services.

When underground enterprises are vertically integrated with regular enterprises, there is a displacement effect against regular enterprises not integrated with underground enterprises; and integrated regular enterprises can decrease prices and/or increase profits. This impedes the introduction of new technology, because competition is based on cost evasion (taxes and the like) and not on productivity increase.

Overall, if the existence of the underground economy is accounted for, production, national income, and standard of living are higher. Moreover, a dual price level may develop, in particular where the role of autonomous workers is relevant: a higher level for regular activities (generally for the public sector and large private enterprises) and a lower level for goods and services supplied to individual consumers and small enterprises (if an underground agreement is accepted that leads to tax evasion for the supplier). Finally, technical progress may be slowed down, because a simpler and less expensive solution, such as going underground, is available.

Quite different is the situation of government. By definition, underground activities evade taxes and social contributions, but utilize goods and services offered by the government. As a consequence, the underground economy increases the state budget deficit and is a direct cause of the increase in taxation and social contributions burdening regular activities. As far as taxation has a depressive effect on economic activity, underground economy is a cause, not just the consequence.

In the labor market, on the one side, the underground economy increases labor market flexibility, because irregular activities are utilized to weaken the workers' position. On the other side, as a consequence of an underground demand for labor, workers (as a group and as individuals) are in a stronger position; danger of true unemployment is less pressing (probably other family members have jobs). Given this stronger position, workers, as a group and as individuals, are less ready to accept a wage decrease in order to keep their regular jobs in a time of crisis. Regular wages then become more rigid.

Policy consequences are also relevant. Mistaken and insufficient information leads to wrong decisions; and policies (in particular, demand control policies) lose effectiveness (Feige 1979). The existence of an underground economy has a relevant role in causing present economic problems and it impairs the ability of economic policy to solve them.

NOTES

(*) Parts of this research have been supported by a grant from the Consiglio Nazionale delle Ricerche (CNR 85.01150.10) and by a grant from the Ministero della Pubblica Istruzione for a research project on "Formal and real decentralization in Soviet-type economies". The author would like to thank, in particular, Prof. Gregory Grossman of the University of California at Berkeley for the valuable help and hospitality received while the author was a guest of the Department of Economics at Berkeley, and the Russian and East European Center of the University of Illinois at Urbana-Champaign. The author, of course, bears all responsibility for the final product and its content.

REFERENCES

ARLACCHI, P., La mafia imprenditrice, Il Mulino, Bologna 1983.

BARSOTTI, O., POTESTA', L. (eds), Segmentazione del mercato del lavoro e doppia occupazione, Il Mulino, Bologna 1983.

BRUSCO, S., 'Prime note per uno studio del lavoro a domicilio', Inchiesta, April-June 1979, pp. 33-49.

CANTELLI, P., L'economia sommersa, Editori Riuniti, Roma 1980.

CENSIS, L'occupazione occulta, Roma 1980.

CONTINI, B., Lo sviluppo di un'economia parallela, Edizioni di Comunità, Milano 1979.

CONTINI, B., The Anatomy of the Irregular Economy, mimeo.,

162

January 1981, pp. 26.

FEIGE, E.L., 'How Big is the Irregular Economy?', Challenge, November-December 1979, pp. 5-13.

GÁBOR, I.R., GALASI, P., 'A "második" gazdaság' (The 'Second' Economy), KJK, Budapest 1981.

GAETANI-D'ARAGONA, G., 'I sommersi', Nord e Sud, no. 7, 1979, pp. 26-46.

GAETANI-D'ARAGONA, G., 'The Hidden Economy: Concealed Labor Markets in Italy', Rivista Internazionale di Scienze Economiche e Commerciali, no. 3, 1981, pp. 270-289.

GALLINO, L., (ed), Occupati e bioccupati, Il Mulino, Bologna 1982.

GROSSMAN, G., 'The 'Second Economy' of the USSR', Problems of Communism, September-October 1977, pp. 25-40.

GUTMANN, P.M., 'The Subterranean Economy', Financial Analysis Journal, November-December 1977, pp. 26-28.

KATSENELINBOIGEN, A., 'Coloured Markets in the Soviet Union', Soviet Studies, January 1977, pp. 62-85.

KORNAI, J., A hiany, KJK, Budapest 1980 (English transl.: Economics of Shortage, North Holland, Amsterdam 1980).

IL MONDO, 'I bioccupati', Il Mondo, September 13, 1982.

LEWIS, S.G., Slave Trade Today: American Exploitation of Illegal Aliens, Beacon Press, Boston 1979.

NORTH, D.S., HOUSTOUN, M.F., The Characteristics and Role of Illegal Aliens in the U.S. Labor Market: An Exploratory Study, Linton and Co., Washington D.C. 1976.

REUBENS, E.P., 'Aliens, Jobs, and Immigration Policy', The Public Interest, no. 51, Spring 1978, pp. 113-134.

SABA, A., L'industria sommersa e il nuovo modello di sviluppo, Marsilio, Venezia 1980.

SIMIS, K.M., USSR: The Corrupt Society: The Secret World of Soviet Capitalism, Simon and Schuster, New York 1982.

SIMON, C.P., WITTE, A.D., Beating the System. The Underground Economy, Auburn House Publishing Company, Boston, Mass. 1982.

SRAFFA, R., 'The Laws of Return under Competitive Conditions', The Economic Journal, December 1926.

SYLOS LABINI, P., Le forze dello sviluppo e del declino, Laterza, Bari 1984.

WEINTRAUB, S., ROSS, S.R., The Illegal Alien from Mexico. Policy Choices for an Intractable Issue, The University of Texas, Austin 1980.

WEINTRAUB, S., ROSS, S.R., 'Temporary' Alien Workers in the United States. Designing Policy from Fact and Opinion, Westview Press, Boulder, Co. 1982.

The role of unofficial economy in North African countries

ZBIGNIEW DOBOSIEWICZ

1. GENERAL REMARKS CONCERNING UNOFFICIAL SECTORS OF ECONOMY IN NORTH AFRICA

It must be admitted that any serious examination of unofficial economy in North African countries is bound to run into trouble. It is hardly surprising since the existing statistical data are far from complete and basic research is effectively lacking. Compared with North African statistical yearbooks, Polish or Italian publications of this type are an unmatched ideal of perfection. All the same, unofficial economy occupies an important position in North African countries and plays a by far greater role there than in most industrialized states (1).

In the present paper I shall try to present some results of research on unofficial sectors of economy based chiefly on field studies conducted in Egypt and Algeria and, to a lesser extent, in Tunisia and Morocco in the last eight years. Regrettably, I did not manage to cover Libya in my research nor did I find any reliable statistical data concerning Libya. That is why my considerations take no account of that country.

By unofficial sectors of economy I mean, in the North African context, a mix of dozens of various sectors diverse in importance but knit together by their unofficial character. Among the persons employed in unofficial sectors of economy we include every person exercising professions or occupations not conforming to the official regulations in force. In many professions, e.g. off-hand sellers, solicitation of the legal status is actually impossible because taxes and social security payments should exceed real income (with some exceptions, e.g. persons selling merchandises from smuggling and in Algeria resellers of scarce items bought in state warehouses, who can not legalise their situation for obvious reasons). We consider as taking part in unofficial sector mainly the following persons:
a) employees and owners of enterprises which are not officially registered, i.e., persons formally illegally employed (2);
b) permanent and seasonal unregistered (3) employees in legal enterprises;
c) persons employed in various unregistered systems of cottage industry;
d) persons actually doing work other than formally regi-

165

stered (for example, employees of workshops registered as shops);

e) unregistered persons doing permanent or seasonal work as street vendors or other street business (among others, shoe-shine boys, porters);

f) criminals and their associates (for example, persons deriving their main profit from dealing in smuggled goods) and persons exercising illegal professions (e.g. unregistered prostitutes).

Unofficial sectors of economy usually play a less prominent role in rural areas, with the exception of the villages surrounding either such big cities as Cairo, Machalla-al-Kubra, Tunis, Algiers, Oran, Casablanca, or some other towns of special character such as Kairouan, Tlemcen, Maghnia. Another exception are villages situated in some special region such as Western Kabylie or Rif (4). At the same time unofficial economy flourishes in urban areas.

One could ask a number of questions concerning the role played by unofficial economy, but the most important among them would inevitably be the following: how do unofficial sectors of economy influence employment, production, distribution, services and the income structure of the population? We will concentrate our attention on the first two.

2. THE ROLE OF UNOFFICIAL SECTORS OF ECONOMY IN THE FIELD OF EMPLOYMENT

The specificity of the impact of unofficial sectors of economy on employment is directly connected with the social changes that have occurred in North African countries in the past 20 to 30 years. Crucial among them is a rapid growth of towns caused, on the one hand, by mass migrations from rural areas, and very high and sustained natural growth of urban population on the other.

In the whole region, at least 400,000 persons moved to towns annually, setting in motion the process of transformation of North African communities from basically rural (in the period before World War II) to urban. About the year 1988 the majority of the population in the region will be living in towns, while in 1984 urban population accounted for 45 percent of the total population of Morocco and, respectively, 47 percent for Egypt, 58 percent for Algeria and, 53 percent for Tunisia.

The process of urban migration has been discussed in numerous analyses whose authors emphasize, along with its positive effects also its drawbacks, particularly for farm production. They point to the fact that the migration process has for some 20 years been developing at a too fast pace to which the towns and the urban economy have not as yet accommodated. Urban growth has by far outstripped the development of 'official' productive forces and services. Ultimately, the gap between the 'officially' employed part of the urban population and those looking for a job has been ever widening in North Africa - not unlike, for that matter, the situation in other Third World areas.

At present nearly one-third of males in North African towns (i.e. on a regional scale; the situation is different for individual towns) fail to find an 'official' job. Under the circumstances, they are compelled to take up 'unofficial' jobs as unregistered workers and, not infrequently, on a part-time basis. This was not necessary several dozen years ago. Then the newcomers to towns and their families could rely on the well-known family solidarity or rural comradeship in finding lodgings and accommodation with some distant relation or former dwellers of the same village. However, various sociological studies have confirmed a gradual erosion of family solidarity, which has by now shrunk to such forms as personal (and financial) participation in ceremonies and special occasions such as weddings, in some cases circumcisions, funerals, etc. and in the long run each family has to secure for itself its own source of income. Neither has this process been reversed by the developing Moslem integrist movements whose leaders strongly denounce the decline of traditional social and familiar ties. At any rate, persons without an 'official' job were forced to take up any jobs even such that were against their ambitions and expectations, for example, street sales usually bringing very little profit.

Observations prove that only in some cases is work in unofficial economy justified by a drive to easy life and big money (5); quite often work in unofficial sectors of economy is hard and unprofitable. From my observations in Cairo and Aswan I may conclude that unregistered employees in private business usually work 10 to 11 hours a day and have a 6-day working week. They work about 9 hours daily in Algeria and Tunisia but it still amounts to a working-time rate far in excess of that for those officially registered in state-run sectors of economy. The work of street vendors, which has no specific working hours and which is seemingly untaxed, still takes over 10 hours daily irrespective of the weather. Small wonder then that state-sponsored big industrial projects significantly contribute to a rapid drop of employment in unofficial sectors of economy which can be seen e.g., in Safi (Morocco), Annaba, Tizi-Ouzou, Setif in Algeria or Aswan in Egypt.

It is not possible to determine the exact number of people living off 'unofficial' sectors of economy in North Africa. However, some approximate figure could be ventured on the basis of official statistical data. In doing so we must skip the term 'economically active population', which does not cover students and non-career soldiers, in favour of a more convenient instrument for our analysis, i.e. the category of potentially economically active urban male population. This category includes (in North Africa) men aged 18 to 65 but leaves out students, conscripts, and the disabled.

The 1980 estimates put the number of potentially economically active males in towns at 1,800,000 for Algeria, 1,850,000 for Morocco, 700,000 for Tunisia, and 3,500,000 for Egypt. Official employment figures for urban males over 18 stood, according to the estimates for the same year, at 1,100,000 for Algeria, 1,030,000 for Morocco, 560,000 for

Tunisia, and 2,800,000 for Egypt (6). These data do not include the rural population employed in towns. A comparison of respective figures gives us the volume of urban males without a 'formal' job. They total an estimated 690,000 for Algeria, 820,000 for Morocco, 140,000 for Tunisia, and 700,000 for Egypt (7). For an overwhelming majority of them the chief source of income is seasonal or permanent work in unofficial sectors of economy. In order to illustrate the magnitude of these figures let me give for comparison the number of people officially employed in manufacturing industry and in handicrafts: in 1980 the figure was 270,000 for Algeria, 1,600,000 for Egypt, and 130,000 for Tunisia. We must not forget the age structure in North Africa where children under 15 make up over 40.0 percent of the population (46.0 percent for Algeria and Morocco). In effect one bread-winner has to keep more persons than in Europe.

The estimated number of the population living off unofficial sectors of economy does not include one important element, i.e. children and adolescents below 18 years of age. In the majority of economic branches the employment of persons under 18 is considered illegal (except for Egypt where juvenile labour regulations are very complex) (8). Exactly for the same reason workers under 18, very numerous in reality, are not officially registered in Algeria, Tunisia and Morocco.

All in all, minors included, the number of males employed in unofficial sectors of economy in North Africa could be estimated very cautiously at 2,800,000, which accounts for 30.0 percent of all men employed outside agriculture, and about 40.0 percent of urban working males. At the same time, as was mentioned elsewhere, the role of unofficial economy in rural areas in negligible.

The above data seem to indicate that unofficial sectors of economy are a very important factor in male employment in towns. However, its significance will be diminishing. The historical significance of unofficial sectors of economy in the countries of North Africa consists in that they enable a substantial portion of the population to survive until a time when, after the migration to towns slows down and the development of productive forces permits the employment of the potential surplus of the labour force in modern industry, administration and services.

So far I have omitted in my analysis the complexities connected with the question of women employment. Owing to the domination of Islam, women came to be associated with the home as their only work-place, in spite of old tradition-enshrined customs widespread in North Africa. Even among university women-graduates, a significant percentage never take up any professional work. According to official data, only 7.0 percent of women in Egypt and Algeria, 8.0 percent in Morocco, and 19.0 percent of women in Tunisia have an officially registered job.

On the basis of observations carried out in North Africa, it could be said that a majority of illegal production enterprises did not employ women at all. This also concerns a large part of illegal textile workshops. There are more formally registered women to be found in the services (ex-hairdressers) and the number of women in trade (until recently very small) is also growing, in particular older women working as street vendors. Young unmarried women often find employment in their homes in totally illegal cottage industry. For example, they do the washing, combing, carding and spinning of wool, manufacture clothes for women and children, make trimmings and embellishments or weave carpets. In most cases the goods are produced on concrete commission, and therefore the daily work-time varies (from 3 to 14 hours a day) depending on the volume of commission, but usually women remain jobless for a good part of the year. In Tlemcen (Algeria) only about 6,000 out of 28,000 women over 15 years of age were employed in cottage industry, quite often working less than one hundred days in a year - according to unofficial estimates by former director of the Crafts Department, Mr. Chalaby Hadj Djillali. Similar figures could be found in the surveys of the Moroccan town of Sale, and slightly bigger numbers are given for Aksjut in Egypt (but there Copts form part of the population).

Female labour in cottage industry is in most cases (except for Tunis, Algiers, Tizi-Ouzou) very low-paid. It is often hazardous to health; production of carpets has earned itself a particularly bad reputation in North Africa because it causes lung diseases. Socially important as a source of employment for thousands of women and as a supplementary income for the poorest households, cottage industry yields limited productive results; various estimates for individual plants only (a regrettable fact) indicate that the value added per one working woman is very small indeed.

3. THE ROLE OF UNOFFICIAL SECTORS OF ECONOMY IN THE FIELD OF
   PRODUCTION

While playing a tremendous role in employment, unofficial sectors of economy offer a disproportionately small production. Partially it could be explained by the structure of employment - both in legal and unofficial sectors of economy the part of employed working in productive sectors is only minor (9).

Quick actual development of employment makes it nevertheless interesting to compare the labour effectiveness in both sectors. We could easily prove that, if we present labour effectiveness in those sectors in the form of the value of final product per one worker, it would amount to far less than in officially registered fields (10) where these indicators are by no means high. The picture seems to change when we consider surplus production per one worker. Here, in spite of considerable differences in technical equipment, the value added in unofficial sectors is on a par with state-run industries, while in many small illegal workshops it is even higher than in exemplary state factories (11).

What is the share of unofficial sectors of economy in production in North Africa? It is different in various branches:

1) it is practically non-existent in one very important field in all the countries discussed here, namely, in mining industry;
2) it is very insignificant in agriculture (locally, of some importance is only the illegal growth of plants like indian hemp-cannabis);
3) it is little in the production of big industrial plants: a good number of those plants employ numerous unregistered workers (12) but predominantly outside production lines;
4) it is big in small-scale industry: in all North African countries considered here, a substantial part and in some cases even a majority of the employees, are not officially registered;
5) it is positively dominating in the crafts and in enterprises based on cottage industry system.

Although the overall volume of production in unregistered enterprises or ones registered as non-productive could not be determined, nevertheless one might look to individual businesses for clues as to how big this production might be. There are several thousand such 'illegal' establishments with the number of employees varying from 2 to 20. The one that I happened to examine was located near a well-known bazaar Khan-el-Khalili. It manufactured tin buckets. The actual production goes on right in the street in front of a small room (about 7 sq. meters) where all the necessary tools and materials are kept. Two 3-men shifts are supervised by the proprietor. Despite primitive man-powered appliances about 130 buckets are produced daily, which gives about 3,200 buckets a month; the value of added production per one worker more than doubles that achieved in 1980 in Egypt's largest steel-mill in Helwan.

A nearby tombac and brass jewellery workshop, registered as a souvenir shop offers another example. Two obsolete machine tools and various hand tools are used by a team of nine persons aged 12 to 22 and sporadically joined by their boss, to produce bands, rings, necklaces and metal embellishments fitted on pieces of furniture. The value of added production per one worker is three times that of the Helwan steel-mill.

And yet another example: a workshop or, to be more precise, a textile factory in North-Western Cairo registered as a warehouse. It has about 40 workers, chiefly youngsters, working 11-hour shifts. The added value of production per one worker in rough figures is very low and is about five times less than the state industry average.

Let us now look for examples in Algeria. A good illustration here is the production of shoe craftsmanship. In 1983, there were 210 shoemakers in Tlemcen and the surrounding province. About one-third of them have one or two apprentices. Each shoemaker is allowed to make, apart from mending shoes, 150 pairs of shoes a month from state-guaranteed leather supplies. But since shoes made in Tlemcen are no longer sewn but glued and given the fact that shoemaking is much more profitable than repairs, nearly 55 shoemakers in Tlemcen are making 350 to 700 pairs of shoes (depending on whether they work alone or with helpers) each month for a greater part of the year. The whole production is commissioned by middle-men who supply the shoes to shops (13). Each pair of shoes brings the manufacturer about 70 dinars, while the retail price stands at 120 dinars and the material costs about 30 dinars. Theoretically this gives nearly 12,000 dinars in monthly added production per one shoemaker. The real value is however somewhat smaller; for example during Ramadan (religious feasting) and in July and August (high temperatures) production drops by over one third and quite often work is held up due to lack of material. All in all, an average monthly added production per one shoemaker is closer to 6 or 8 thousand dinars (14).

An overwhelming number of industrial plants and workshops in Algeria employ male workers. There are, however, two exceptions, namely, the privately-owned food processing plants where women find seasonal occupation and illegal textile workshops in Algeria where women find permanent employment. There are over a hundred food processing plants where production becomes particularly large during some parts of the year (processing of olives, tomatoes, paprika and oranges). An increasing number of small (3-5 workers) establishments hire seasonally several or even several dozen workers, chiefly women. It goes without saying that seasonal work force is not officially registered and a substantial part of the profits is never reported to the tax collector. The character of this type of production rendered impossible any precise calculation of the value of added production; it appears to me it is very low and if the whole venture turns any profit at all it is solely a matter of extremely low wages of seasonal workers.

Let us now return to textile factories. There are close to one hundred textile factories in Algiers. Contrary to the food processing plants, their added production is usually very high. Employing two to several dozen workers, some of these illegal enterprises are officially registered as shops or warehouses. Others, according to the official Algerian weekly Algerie-Actualite (15), are not registered at all. Typically, large apartments partitioned into small rooms accommodate 5-6 women with sewing machines and knitting machines (16). As a rule copies of French models (blouses, dresses, sweaters, underwear), and Egyptian fashion (nightgowns, 'traditional' wear) are imitated not infrequently with labels of foreign firms attached to them to suggest their origin. They fetch very high prices, therefore the added product per one worker is high, too. This situation persists owing to nearly non-existent legal imports of textiles on the one hand, and unattractive home products on the other.

The problem looks entirely different in Morocco, Tunisia or Egypt. Big textile factories there turn out fairly high quality goods that suit the tastes of the local customer. Under the circumstances, poorly equipped illegal workshops as well as those employing unregistered labour focus their business activity on production of the cheapest goods inferior in quality (for example, haiks, burnouses, djelabiyahs). It is similar with shoe-manufacture: small unregistered workshops produce various kinds of cheap sandals and traditional footwear for a large part of the local population. As concerns Morocco and Egypt, part of the supply comes from several villages specializing in artisanal production for generations.

The situation is not much different in the manufacture of furniture. More expensive furniture is made in official workshops and in the growing number of factories. Cheaper furniture pieces for less well-off customers, including simple beds, sofas, tables, stools, occasional tables, etc., are made either in unregistered enterprises or those registered as furniture magazines, market huckster's stands or simply by people who make simple pieces of furniture anywhere near the souks or as a side-occupation in enterprises producing completely different things (17). The quality of this production is low, but the products are relatively cheap.

Important as it is in textile, shoe or furniture production, the role of unofficial economy is decidedly more modest in food processing industry (18). This is connected with a long-established system of state subsidies. In an indirect manner it strengthens state control of food processing production, of course except seasonal food production from non-subsidized products. Equally meagre is the unofficial production of machines and appliances even simple ones, such as writing utensils, dyes and varnishes (thanks to tax reductions, many producers made their businesses legal in recent years).

I have mentioned elsewhere that extensive research on production aspects of unofficial economy in North African countries has yet to be carried out. In private conversations with higher officials in Revenue Offices in Algeria, who wanted their names to remain undisclosed, they estimated this production at 30-40 percent of the value of non-oil-related Gross National Product (GNP); this means 15.0 to 20.0 percent of total material product (19). Similar figures may be quoted with respect to Morocco and Egypt, while they should be smaller for Tunisia in view of a relatively correct activity of revenue offices and state administration.

In conclusion, it could be said that viewed from a perspective of social welfare, unofficial sectors of economy offer very bad conditions: work is hard and dangerous to health and inadequately paid; there is no social welfare system (20).

From the point of view of production gains, however, those economic sectors play an important role, given the overall weakness of national industries. They offer cheap production for the poor, or to be more precise, to the majority of the population who cannot afford more expensive goods. Most probably this is the main reason why the state tolerates so many illegal enterprises. Unofficial sectors of economy also prove to be advantageous for the foreign trade balance, as at least a part of unofficial production is clearly anti-import-oriented. In these conditions it seems that North African countries will in the future seek a partial legalization (legitimisation) of these sectors of unofficial economy which on the whole make a positive contribution to the development of their national economies.

NOTES

(1) We could make the same comparison concerning 'unregistered economy' (an expression covering a much larger part of national economy).

(2) Frequently such enterprises are well-known and their business activity is, for various reasons, tolerated by the authorities.

(3) By registration I mean here obligatory registration of an employee with the Labour Inspection Office (in Egypt - Employment Office) and connected there with social security payments and income tax.

(4) In Kabylie a growing portion of the population have full-time or part-time jobs in unregistered services and handicrafts while in Rif drug production is growing in importance.

(5) This may serve as a partial explanation of migration to some centres of smuggling business, i.e., to Maghnia on Algerian-Moroccan border or Tetuan near duty-free Ceuta.

(6) Calculations on the basis of official statistical yearbooks from Morocco, Algeria, Tunisia and Egypt.

(7) Only a fraction of those without an "official" job register themselves as jobless. According to UN (1984), p. 83, the unemployment figures were as follows: 457,000 (Egypt, 1978), 66,000 (Tunisia, 1980), 19,000 (Morocco, 1979).

(8) According to ILO, (1983), p. 38, in 1980 in Egypt 842,000 boys and 260,000 girls under 15 years were employed; the official statistical data quoted by ILO for the three other countries in the same region reported no employment of minors.

(9) Industry and workshops 'officially' employ in a majority of North African towns from 1 to 6 percent of the total population.

(10) The factor that hikes up the volume of final production in big industrial plants of North Africa is a very high share of imported semi-finished products; production in many plants is limited to the assembly of imported parts.

(11) It is not possible to give accurate data for unofficial trade and services turnover per one worker; it appears that (although there are many persons who can boast a high turnover value, i.e., derived from trafficking in smuggled goods) national averages are several times lower than those for legal trade and services.

(12) This also concerns numerous big state-owned factories where a part of their employees are on short-term contracts renewed at regular intervals; these workers do not have social security benefits, while their unsettled legal position makes it impossible to join in the ever more frequent strikes in state-run industries.

(13) Some shoemakers sell shoes in their own shops.
(14) The net income of shoemakers is much lower because we must take into account the rent for the house, taxes, workers' wages and other expenditures.
(15) Afredj (1980).
(16) This concerns in particular several dozen small establishments operating in the Casbah town-quarter.
(17) In some cases a peculiar brand of cottage industry system is employed. For example, an owner of a big furniture shop in Tlemcen buys wood, processes it in his unregistered workshop, gives the components of furniture to a local auto repair workshop to be varnished and then these components are put together in private homes. Illegally produced furniture is sold in his perfectly legal shop.
(18) This remark does not concern an important part of meat processing by butchers, which the economists usually include in the sphere of services.
(19) According to DS (1984), oil production accounted for nearly 50.0 percent of the value of Algeria's material output.
(20) The victims of accidents on the job usually receive substantial compensation but only out of a sense of moral duty on the part of the proprietors who are predominantly religious men. No compensation is paid, however, to those suffering from occupational diseases.

REFERENCES

AFREDJ, R., 'Trop d'ateliers clandestins', Algérie-Actualité, December 25, 1980, pp. 14-15.
DS, L'Algérie en quelques chiffres, 1983, Direction des Statistiques, Alger 1984.
ILO, Yearbook of Labour Statistics, 1980, Geneva 1983, p. 38.
UN, Demographical Yearbook 1982, New York 1984, p. 83.

Selected problems of unofficial economy in Poland

ZBIGNIEW LANDAU

The existence in Poland of a well developed unofficial economy is widely known both by the public opinion and by the country's leadership. However, no thorough studies have been started on the range and socio-economic effects of this phenomenon. The unofficial economy still remains a domain of analyses by lawyers, prosecutors and courts. Legal analyses and studies of economic delinquency cannot nevertheless suffice to explore the problem.

The lack of any studies on the unofficial economy in Poland makes my position as a reporter very difficult. In some cases, I will have to confine myself to proposing hypotheses which cannot be verified. Some conclusions may be thought more intuitive than substantially grounded. The only comfort can be found in the fact that all studies on the unofficial economy can hardly be exemplified or verified by means of statistical evidence.

Some spheres of unofficial economy seem to be common in all countries no matter what their socio-economic system or political situation is. These include tax offences, smuggling or violation of currency restrictions wherever they are in force. Other spheres of unofficial economy result from the nature of the economic system. In capitalist states there does not exist a whole sphere of activity connected with the private sector's distrust in stability of system, financial and legal regulations. Thus, if authorities allow a wider spread of private economic activity, it is usually aimed at maximum gains in the shortest possible time without regard to the future or legality. On the other hand, in the socialist countries there are no problems connected with legal limits of competition between private producers or their associations.

The range of unofficial economy is changing. It is mainly due to legislation which specifies what activities are legal and which are not. A simple change of law may shift certain activities from the realm of lawfulness to the sphere of delinquency and vice versa. This may be illustrated by many examples from the postwar economic history of Poland. For instance prohibition of private meat trade immediately extended the range of unofficial economy since this regulation was not and is not respected. A private producer sells meat from illegal slaughter through an illegal middleman to an illegal customer. Another example: a ban on alcohol sales before 1 o'clock p.m., introduced in the 1980s, immediately

175

led to the creation of a network of places where vodka was offered all around the clock but at much higher prices. Such regulations could only widen the range of the unofficial economy.

The admission of possession of foreign exchange deposits by Polish citizens in home banks acted in an opposite direction. It decreased an illegal transfer of foreign exchange from Poland to capitalist banks. Similar examples may be found in all branches of the national economy.

The second most important factor influencing the range of unofficial economy consists of economic decisions made by the central authorities and concerning plan targets and prices. This is perhaps most apparent in the case of prices. In the socialist countries most prices are fixed centrally and oblige the whole trade apparatus (only recently this system has been modified in Poland). Therefore if a price is relatively too low as compared with other goods, it may come to buying up and reselling at speculative prices. Sometimes it is just the opposite - too high prices (e.g. vodka in recent times) may lead to illegal production (secret distilleries). Of a similar nature are decisions which missed the optimum supply of individual commodities. If the planned supply is too low, the article becomes subject to speculation. In such cases only an increase of production may bring the market perturbations to an end and confine unofficial economic activities.

Thus, the third factor may be described as the market situation. The better it is and the more available the demanded goods and services are, the lesser the unofficial economy is. This refers also to the supply of private producers (handicraft, small-scale industry or private agriculture) with the necessary raw materials. If there are no limitations, the producers can buy them legally. But all market shortages lead to the necessity to seek illegal sources of supply. The higher the shortage of demanded raw materials, the wider the unofficial supply is. Producers usually do not want to limit production of goods or services for which they have an absorptive market.

Sometimes the supply of private workshops comes from the state-owned or co-operative enterprises in which a part of production finds its way to private hands and not to the market or other state-owned enterprises as a result of bribery or theft or using one's 'backstairs' influence. Even the relations between socialized enterprises tend, under the disequilibrium on the supply market, to show signs of an economic pathology. Despite plan targets and agreements between enterprises which determine the size and time of delivery, actual shipments are sometimes due to additional services of the receivers for the suppliers. These are not monetary benefits but various facilities. For example workers of the supplier enterprise may receive some places in the holiday centre of the receiver enterprise, or the supplier enterprise may be given a special assistance in its attempts to get additional supplies of raw materials or machinery etc.

Deterioration of the market situation leads to a series of

pathological effects in trade. Private trade turns towards speculation. But even the socialized sector of trade is not entirely free from additional pressure. Above all, some dishonest sellers do not sell the articles in short supply in shops but place them on the black market at higher prices. Sometimes such articles go to the seller's acquaintances with a hope they would return the service. The latter phenomenon may be illustrated with a seller's remark to her colleague: "Today we've got such a lot of merchandise that we even sold some in the shop".

The fourth source of unofficial economy is the relationship between the planning and management centre and individual state-owned enterprises. This relationship is subject to the existing management system. Within the directive and rationing system the economic anomalies are bigger than under an indirect (or parameter) influence of the management centre on enterprises. In the directive and rationing system there is a strong fight between the centre and the enterprises. The former tries to impose maximum targets at minimum investments, floating assets or wages, the latter endeavour to be given the least possible targets and maximum means of their realization. Sometimes they resort to presenting a false image of their capacities and economic situation. Enterprises usually fear to accept tasks reaching their maximum capacity since they desire to exceed the planned targets, which is connected with considerable extra earnings of the factory's management and workers. The factory management tries therefore to show the centre only a part of their capacity, so that they can increase production and exceed plans for a number of subsequent years. This gives them additional earnings but the dishonesty makes it impossible to maximize production within a short time. The fight between the centre and the enterprises does not refer to the plan targets only. Its mechanism, including all the important questions of production, is generally focussed on the size of output. Though these phenomena do not belong to the unofficial economy they are very close to it.

The four above-mentioned factors, which are conducive to the unofficial economy, seem to be of a primary significance, but perhaps some more could be specified. It should be however pointed out that most of them do not result from the maintenance in Poland of a relatively wide margin of private economic life, and those economists who seek a major reason for economic pathology and unofficial economy in this field are mistaken.

At present, the range of the unofficial economy in Poland is wider than in other periods of her post-war development. This seems to be a result of two important phenomena. Firstly, Poland has been in a state of crisis for a few years. Falling industrial production leads to disorganization of factory and market supply. The pressure to raise nominal wages is not accompanied by a growth of labour productivity, while the deficit of the state budget and credit plan have brought about a serious inflation. The economic blockade of Poland by some capitalist countries makes it more difficult to overcome the crisis since it checks Polish exports and new credits. Considerable problems are also due to a large indebtedness of Poland and to costs of service of foreign debts.

Under these circumstances, in order to prevent a collapse of the market of foodstuffs and necessities, rationing of some articles was introduced. Their list is decreasing and at present it includes sugar, flour, cereals, butter, margarine, chocolate for children and meat. Rations of some articles (e.g. meat) sometimes do not suffice, which leads to illegal speculative operations. The latter refer also, even to a higher extent, to certain durables (cars, washing machines, refrigerators etc.) or, rather less, to other consumer goods (e.g. petrol). In the latter case, in 1984 corrupt practices were recorded in about 1/3 of filling stations in Poland.

Difficulties resulting from the crisis are accompanied in Poland by problems due to the theoretically far-reaching system reform. The previous directive and rationing system is modified by means of quasi-market solutions, the central planning being maintained. At present the new system is only being created and includes some elements from the old one, or solutions adopted temporarily as a result of the crisis difficulties and the socio-political tensions involved. Within the new system, enterprises were given a certain amount of liberty but were obliged to self-finance their activity. Thus enterprises can determine the size of production, its structure, some prices, distribution of profits as well as the size of employment, wages etc. The mechanism was aimed at introducing a sort of competition which was to make enterprises optimize production, decrease costs, introduce new products and so on. In practice, however, most enterprises made use of the market shortages to raise prices in order to maintain profits without increasing output, diminishing costs of production or optimizing employment. As a result, the whole economy is pretty disordered, which naturally stimulates unofficial economy. In trade it causes speculation, while in production the private sector flourishes (including small foreign firms allowed to function in Poland). The increasing output of private firms is largely based on leakage of raw materials from the socialized industrial and trade enterprises. In some cases, private producers buy raw materials abroad but have to illegally purchase and transfer foreign exchange outside Poland. Sometimes they collide with tax authorities as a result of underestimation of the turnover and profits. In this connection they have to conceal the actual size of employment, which leads to violation of the labour legislation.

Evaluation of the situation in Poland is very difficult. Unofficial economy outside agriculture stimulates the market supply but it disorganizes the socialized sector which prevails in the national economy. It is not only the problem of illegal interception of supplies or foreign exchange turnover but also of attracting more experienced or skilled workers who are better paid by the private firms.

The effects of this situation are not confined to the economic life but also influence social relations. Unofficial economy substantially changes the national income distribution. On the one hand it makes rich a limited group of people, on the other hand it decreases real earnings of all those who partly satisfy their needs thanks to speculation. Anyway, this seems to be the price of the present crisis in Poland and of the attempts to reform the economic system. It may be expected that along with stabilization of the Polish economy and introduction of the system reform, the range of the unofficial economy will gradually diminish to the range which seems common for all countries.

New types of entrepreneurial and organizational forms in the Hungarian economy

ÉVA SZITA

At the end of the seventies, the slowdown and then stagnation in the rise of the standard of living, as well as the lively interest shown by economists, writers and journalists in the 'second economy', brought the work done after official working hours, and the important problem of the income derived therefrom, to the attention of bureaucracy and the political leadership. The official view rejected the term 'second economy', and tried instead to react to these phenomena, which had existed for a long time and had continued to spread, by using the term 'auxiliary economy'. The direction and main purpose of the reaction was, on the one hand, to stimulate, and on the other, to draw under the control of legal regulation such activities and incomes which existed also independently of the intentions of the central planners. The most efficient measure was the government's 'package deal', which - from the beginning of 1982 - made the legal structuring of such activities possible by the legal constitution of numerous new entrepreneurial and organizational forms.

The establishment of organizations of a new type aimed at the bringing about of a system consisting of medium and small plants and small enterprises; these would be able to fill in the 'gaps' in production left by large enterprises and to solve tasks profitably, the carrying out of which were barely economical or uneconomical for large production units. At the same time, in order to raise the standard of supply of the general public and to improve the quality of services, the modernization of organizations expressly carrying out service activities also became timely. In this way, by mitigating shortages of various kinds in the most diverse areas (from communal services to the shortage of manpower in big companies) disturbances in the economy could be moderated and living conditions could be improved. Endeavours aimed at the transformation of the structure of industry were accompanied by the objective that the new small organizations should create new employment opportunities and thereby help to solve employment difficulties that might occur in respect of particular sections of society or in some areas of the country. Expectations were also expressed that some of the assets or saved income would flow back into production.

The interest of the enterprise sphere was also very strong. The unfavourable world economic situation, the more

181

rigorous terms of financial regulation, the desire to hold on to skilled manpower, and central restrictions tying up the wage system, stimulated the management of firms and cooperatives to establish and to support new forms within enterprises.

It had been a cause of earlier tension among those working in industry (state or cooperative) that farming on household plots offered opportunities - granted that they involved additional work - to obtain a legal additional income. In areas outside agriculture such opportunities were hit and miss; they did not really pay in their legal forms, or were illegal. Thus an interest on the part of members of the work force was also present (or at least could be expected).

The new types of economic organizations are the following:

A. Units functioning as legal entities

1. Small enterprises: these are established by the transfer of state-owned means and their manager is appointed by the authorities. Their establishment is justified if they employ a smaller number of people than companies operating in the same range of activity, or they dispose of fewer fixed assets, or the nature of the activity makes the functioning of small enterprises possible and desirable (in the case of services). Their organizational autonomy - owing to their strong dependence on the state administration - is limited.

2. Subsidiary enterprises may be established by existing companies. They obtain their capital from the parent company which also exercises employer's rights over management and the work force. The dependence is very strong: the founding company guarantees the debts of the subsidiary; at the same time the founding company - to the extent laid down in the articles of association - shares in the profits of the subsidiary.

3. Small cooperatives: these may be established on the initiative of private persons or by seceding from some large organization. They may carry out productive and/or servicing activities by obeying simpler administrative rules than those that apply to large cooperatives. Their membership may be between 15 and 100 persons. In addition to full-time members, people doing accessory or part-time work, college and university students, or retired persons may also be members of small cooperatives.

B. Organizations tied to legal entities

4. The enterprise business work partnership is not a legal entity, as the bulk of resources necessary for its operation is made available by the founder. It may have between 2 and 30 members and, with the exception of commerce, it may be established for any activity which does not infringe a state monopoly. Its membership may consist exclusively of the

workers and retired workers of a given economic unit who are responsible for debts only to the extent of the income earned by them. (Their contribution to assets is so minute that it may be considered symbolic). Beyond this, the founding company is responsible for all debts.

5. Industrial and service cooperative groups: these dispose of certain autonomy and economic independence. They correspond to the enterprise business work partnership in the cooperative sector. They may be established primarily to perform services and produce goods for the general public, but they may also act as a supplier to the cooperative (the host organization) or other companies as well. At least five persons are needed to found one. Any adult (over 15 years of age) may be a member of a cooperative group, and - doing work after working hours - also a member of the cooperative whithin which the group functions. The group may also have employees.

6. Agricultural groups: these are established by private persons, but their activity must be tied to some economic organization. (The organizational and legal antecedents of this form have been proved viable for a long time in non-collectivized private farming). The rules referring to them are in general identical with those that apply to industrial and service cooperative groups.

7. Contractual operation: this is an operational form which relies on a contract between the company and the entrepreneur. In the contract the entrepreneur commits himself to achieve a certain income within a determined period and to pay a fee proportionate to it, while the company transfers to him for use - for this period - the production capacity needed for operation. Any private person may operate under contract who has the necessary trade qualifications for the type of work.

8. Lump-sum accounting system: this may be established in respect of industrial and agricultural cooperatives which employ a maximum of 15 persons and may engage either in industrial production or services. The lump-sum accounting system substitutes in essence for contractual operation in the case of production cooperatives; it is a self-accounting unit (profit centre) which can only employ persons who are members or employees of the cooperative.

9. Leasing: according to the new rules, the economic organizations may lease small industrial and service units - mainly those suitable for satisfying the requirements of the general public - to artisans, other private persons, or to economic working groups of private persons (see the following point in the list).

C. Organizations established by private persons

10. Economic working groups of private persons: these are organizations established by private persons functioning on the basis of a contract of association. They may have full-time or part-time members. Their membership may vary between 2 and 30 persons. They manage the means which are owned (used) in common and have been contributed by the members, and may engage in any activity, outside commerce, which does not infringe on a state monopoly.

11. Civil law associations: this is not a new form, as the legal framework for it existed already before 1982, but it has been revived by the 'package deal' of 1982. They are mainly associations of professional people; no permission is necessary from an employer for its foundation (it may be established by private persons); the number of members is unlimited; it does not require the investment of capital or the contribution of major assets. However the tax paid (40 percent company tax) is very high, and for this reason a considerable proportion of the civil law associations has been transformed into an economic working group in the past two years (type 10) or a small cooperative (type 3).

Of the forms listed, only the last two (10,11), can be said to have a private nature, although - from the aspect of initiative and financial responsibility - the small coopera-tives (3) and the agricultural groups (6) show similar characteristics. All other forms are linked to the existing state and cooperative sector, using their resources. Their establishment depends on the initiative or approval of the official sector, and mostly also enjoys the financial pro-tection of the latter.

These organizational forms can be called enterprises to a limited extent only: they mostly do not own capital, and their responsibility is not proportionate to the paid up capital. In fact only the civil law association (11), the economic working group of private persons (10) and the small cooperative (3) are enterprises; lump-sum accounting (8) and contractual operation (7) may be considered enterprises to a limited degree, as in them, although the 'entrepreneur' is not the owner of capital, his financial responsibility and risk considerably exceed the expected income. But these forms are not open to everybody.

As the list shows, the majority of the new forms opens up opportunities for private and collective economic enter-prises in productive and service activities. The new commer-cial organizations (retailing and catering) may be consi-dered an antecedent: there contractual operation (7) has been possible since 1980. The private operation of small shops, coffee shops, restaurants and snack-bars is perhaps the most spectacular phenomenon of the new processes wel-comed - or cursed - as 'entrepreneurial socialism', since these activities are carried out in full view, in the street. In 1982 the contractual form covered 1,700, and in 1983 already approximately three thousand small shops, of

which two thirds are food stores, 12 percent of the shop
units of the food retail trade, approximately 9 percent of
the entire retail trade network, function in a contractual
form.

A further growth is likely since this arrangement has
visibly been successful. A shopkeeper interested in increasing his turnover is compelled to carry a broader range of
goods and to acquaint himself with, and meet, the demands of
his customers. Dynamism has even been more spectacular in
catering where, in 1982, 4,200 and, in 1983, already 6,100
units were operated under contractual arrangements. About 42
percent of public catering establishments (their total is
14,000, in addition to which there are 4,400 cafeterias and
snack-bars at work places) are managed by an entrepreneur
under contract. Since the contractor for a shop or restau-
rant needs trade qualifications, the majority of persons
working in these were earlier the - less well-paid and less
well-motivated - employees of state and cooperative retail
shops and catering establishments. In catering fluctuations
are higher; the desire to become rich quick often leads to
business failure following an unrealistic raising of prices.
At the same time the effect of driving up prices lasts, and
consequently in the area of these services the new contractual forms undoubtedly contribute to inflation. At the same
time private retailing activities - shops, etc. in private
ownership - also boomed in the past two years. In the last
resort, however, the new forms mean that the general public
is better supplied with a greater variety of goods. They are
at the same time also schools of trade and trading morality.

In essence, all new organizational forms have proved to be
viable, and the dynamism of their growth is imposing. The
question is rather which forms stand out, and how long
growth will last, since it is easy to grow from nil.

There were 23 (type 1) small enterprises and 145 small
cooperatives (type 3) in 1982, 204 and 255 in 1983 respectively. Their combined number reaching 570 by mid-1984. The
subsidiary enterprises (type 2) function mostly in a small
enterprise form; these two forms are likely to merge. The
number of persons employed has risen in 18 months from 6200
in 1982 to over 35.000.

There were 2.775 enterprise business work partnerships
(type 6) at the end of 1982, 7,500 eight months later, and
9,200 at the end of 1983. According to the most recent data
(mid-1984) their number at present exceeds 14,000. This is
unequivocally the most rapidly spreading and most popular
form. I shall revert to the reasons for this later and
discuss the problems arising in the operation of these
partnerships. In 1982 29,000, at the end of 1983 98.000
persons worked in them. At present they employ approximately
145-150,000 persons.

The number of cooperative groups of a similar construction
(type 5) was 477 at the end of 1982, 1,243 at the end of
1983, and is at present approximately 1,800. It is characteristic of their growth that the number of persons working in
them has doubled by the second half of 1983 (from 21,000 to
41,000). At present they employ 58-60.000 persons. One quar-

ter of their members work for them full time, three quarters outside their official working hours, doing extra work; 40 percent of these groups operate in agricultural organizations.

There were 2,341 <u>economic working groups of private persons</u> (type 10) at the end of 1982, and their number approximately doubled one year later. More than 6,400 functioned in mid-1984. The number of persons working in them rose from 11,000 (1982) to 24,000 (end of 1983), and to 32,000 according to the latest figures.

The majority of the other forms - not listed here - operate in the already mentioned commercial activities. Among them the contractual retail shops and catering establishments (their combined number was approximately 9,000 at the end of 1983) and the productive and service sections working under a system of <u>lump-sum accounting</u> (type 9) (approximately 4,000 units) may be considered of importance.

One can measure the size of activities of the most important types listed above by their income. This is not proportionate to their numbers. The small enterprises employing 19,000 persons enjoyed, in 1983, an income of 5000 million forints; the enterprise business work partnerships, in which five times as many people - true, outside normal working hours - had the same income. The small cooperatives - with 10,000 persons - registered a total income of 3,600 million forints, the cooperative groups (the majority worked part-time here too!) - with 42,000 persons - 4,200 million forints. Exact figures are not available about the turnover of the economic working groups established by private persons.

As far as the nature of their activities is concerned, the small enterprises and enterprise business work partnerships carry out owerwhelmingly industrial services (in the case of the latter productive services and job work for the host organization). The production of industrial goods represents the largest weight in the income of small cooperatives while building industrial activity dominates in the cooperative groups. Contrary to expectations, the share of services to the general public is insignificant in the income of these four forms; the weight of services performed for the general public is worthy of notice (around one third) only in the turnover of small enterprises.

At the same time the spectacular dynamism is also somewhat misleading. The existence of the new organizational forms and the demand for the amendment of their regulation figure with relatively great weight in Hungarian economic journals and in the daily press and the media. It is not surprising that the journalistic echo abroad is also strong, and mostly friendly and encouraging. However, for the purpose of a proper appraisal by economists - both in Hungary and abroad - it is desirable to put aside the surprise and joy felt over the novelty, and of course the fears and anxieties as well. In the past two years Hungary has not been transformed into a 'country of entrepreneurs'. The combined income of the above-mentioned four types of new organization accounts for only 0.8 percent of GNP. Including the performance of the other types which is more difficult to record, we can

still not reckon with a higher order of magnitude than 1-2
percent of GNP.
   Only 4-5 percent of the active population of the country
takes part in economic organizations of the new type. According to a public opinion poll in 1981, at least one person
did additional work to complement income in 54 per cent of
Hungarian households; at that time two thirds of active
earners derived some income from the second economy. A
survey carried out two years later found such activity (and
income) already for 75 percent of the employed. True, this
also includes agricultural earners, of whom approximately 90
percent participated in the second economy. But the ratio of
participation of the industrial workers (active and retired)
was also high (70 percent and 40-45 percent respectively).
When looking at these figures, it must be taken into consideration that complementary income derived from agricultural
activity can be identified in the case of 40 percent of
Hungarian households (although the extent of this is of
course highly scattered). All this shows that the 4.5 percent affected by the new forms is an extremely low figure.
Consequently, one cannot explain the <u>spreading</u> of participation in the second economy (which is undoubtedly continuous) by the appearance of the new organizational forms,
and it cannot be claimed either that these small organizations have successfully <u>legalized and integrated</u> semi-legal
and unlawful participation in the second economy. The latter
continues to occur mostly in agricultural production (i.e.
in forms which were already integrated earlier), and in the
old semi-legal and illegal ways.
   The value, and at least the character, of the novelty, is
also relativized and neutralized by the fact that some of
the new organizational forms are in essence but elements of
organizational restructuring <u>with the socialist sector</u>. For
instance, the growth in the number of <u>small enterprises</u> is
partly caused by centrally decided breaking up of some large
nation-wide firms. (The earlier had twenty county - regional
- sub-units, which were still pretty big company units which
could be sub-divided further). Some of the <u>small coopera-
tives</u>, - legally satisfying the criteria of enterprises -
came about by the decree simply obliging cooperatives employing fewer than one hundred workers (members) to transform
themselves into small cooperatives. In these cases of course
only the sign-board changed. It is characteristic of the
economic position of these two forms that the <u>average wages</u>
paid by small enterprises are lower than the average wages
in socialist industry, and in the small cooperatives they
exceed the latter by only 1 percent.
   True, compared to the entire industrial-service cooperative sector, the wages position of the last-mentioned
small organizations is more favourable, and the proportion
of legal additional income has also risen in them. But all
in all, those working in these two forms do not find themselves in a better income position, or it is only marginally
better than they enjoyed earlier, and their relative position on the manpower market has remained practically unchanged.

Besides, these two types of organization were characterized in 1983 by job mobility of approximately one fifth of
the total numbers employed, which was high compared to the
national average. In other words, the small enterprises and
small cooperatives can hardly be considered attempts at the
integration of the 'second economy' or the stimulation of
the spirit of enterprise. They may rather be called the
forerunners of the reform process in management which was
decided on in the spring of 1984. Right now, however, an
ideological kinship only can be observed, rather than an
organic and organizational interconnection between these two
organizational novelties of the Hungarian economy (the stimulation of independent enterprises and the reform of management by the state).

The economic working groups have undoubtedly proved to be
the most important and most popular forms of private enterprise. In respect of their activity, these may be divided
into three groups of an approximately identical size: groups
engaged in professional services, groups engaged in other
services of a mixed nature, and groups engaged in industrial
activity. Three-quarters of their members are only part-
timers, i.e. they have kept their jobs in the socialist
sector. Among these organizations, those of an industrial
nature best meet the expectation that, thanks to them, a
flexible, fast complementary sector should appear in the
productive sphere of the Hungarian economy. In respect of
their social or professional composition, these are either
associations of highly qualified professional men and women
(graduate engineers), or of tradesmen or workmen possessing
special skills. It is a joint characteristic of their activities that the majority of their members have not abandoned
their earlier jobs; they are not in the position to own
means of production of any size, nor do they desire to do
so. They usually react with some caution and uncertainty to
their combined - and individual - new economic position. At
the same time, this is the form where the possibility exists
to make use of a certain accumulated private capital in
production, and sometimes this happens.

The ambiguity of the organizational 'package deal' of 1982
is undoubtedly reflected by the most wide-spread type, the
enterprise business work partnership (type 4) and their cooperative 'kindred organizations', the cooperative groups
(type 5). These forms operate mostly in the manufacturing
and building industries. Such small organizations have been
formed in approximately one fifth of the economic organizations. Within industry nearly one half of these partnerships
work in the engineering sector. Their number is relatively
high also in the metallurgy and the chemical industry. In
light industry the organization of these forms started relatively late. Large companies exist where more than one
hundred work partnerships have been formed, and in some
cases approximately 10 percent of all employees are members.
But in the majority of companies fewer than ten enterprise
business work partnerships were established. The average
number of the members of enterprise business work partnerships is 10-11, and that of industrial cooperative groups

33. (The average membership number of the economic working groups mentioned above is 5).

The majority of the enterprise business work partnerships do industrial work, approximately one fifth are engaged in building, and the same number offer professional services. The enterprise business work partnerships functioning in the building industry mostly use equipment leased from their company and generally work weekends for outside customers. Enterprise business work partnerships offering professional services were mostly formed in research and design (R and D) institutes and also work for outside customers.

The situation is entirely different as far as enterprise business work partnerships and cooperative groups which do industrial work are concerned. Here the companies and cooperatives initiated the establishment of the small organizations to complement their own activities and cope with shortages of capacity and manpower, as well as to substitute for outside suppliers. According to data which are at the moment only approximate, three-quarters of the enterprise business work partnerships and cooperative groups do work exclusively for their own company, a further 20 percent mostly for the host company, and here and there for outside customers. Only approximately 5 percent work exclusively for outside customers. In the case of industrial companies, approximately one half of the industrial enterprise business work partnerships operate in the main process of production, i.e. in the carrying out of planned company programmes. These make up, in essence, for missing manpower. Approximately one half of the industrial enterprise business work partnerships are active in areas serving production, while 10 percent provide professional services. The enterprise business work partnerships doing industrial activity do much to help avoid bottlenecks in enterprise operation: they moderate the shortages and internal tensions. There are cases where the small organization was formed for the performance of a particular job; after it was completed the partnership was dissolved. The operation of the enterprise business work partnerships is often periodical, adjusting to company needs.

All this makes it obvious that the enterprise business work partnerships do not function according to the original ideas. Their main job is not the improvement of the approvisioning of the general public or the creation of a supply basis which had been lacking. There were expectations that the enterprise business work partnerships would mainly be formed at companies which have unused capacities or underemployed workers, and where the utilization of the capacities to do work for others is a sort of common interest, but this did not eventuate. On the contrary, the sectors and companies up against the greatest manpower shortages most urged the establishment of the internal small organizations. The enterprise business work partnerships have many advantages for the host company, which can also be expressed by the proposition that it is primarily the existing enterprise organizational system which profits from their activity. It is able to buy the 'free' time of the workers; it is able to

pay - and thus tie to itself more strongly - the most skilled manpower. And it can do all this by avoiding central
income policy restrictions on the raising of wages, substituting for missing manpower, and is thus able to carry out
its production programme (which may otherwise be uneconomical, and was perhaps forced on it from the outside, or is
simply outsize).

In the last resort, the system of the enterprise business
work partnerships does not renew and change but conserves
the organizational structure of industry. And this is not
all. It usually remains hidden at the back of the benefits
listed: that the surplus work done by the enterprise business work partnership does not only make up for shortages of
capacity but also for shortcomings in internal work organization and sales policy. These are certainly not features of
the socialist economy which are worth preserving.

The enterprise business work partnerships would of course
not spread if powerful labour interests were not also present. The central limitation on wage rises is first of all
unfavourable to the work force. The growth in official
incomes does not keep up with accelerated inflation. This is
why more and more people wish to join in the unofficial
second economy. If the additional work necessary can be
described as legal, it is obvious that many would wish to
choose this form. According to experience, the most frequent
type of the industrial enterprise business work partnership
or cooperative group member is a skilled worker who has been
working for a company for a long time. What he undertakes is
in fact no more than overtime work, which he has done before
too, and which he would anyway be compelled to do sooner or
later. The members of the partnerships and groups do their
work outside working hours and on days off. It may happen
that they use their paid holidays for the same purpose. The
hours worked in small organizations within the enterprises
differ and depend partly on the order of magnitude and
urgengy of the business in hand. It frequently happens that
the company or cooperative sets the number of hours that may
be performed by one person per month. In several cases this
may be as many as 90-100 working hours per month and per
head. (Official average full-time working hours amount to
184). The members of the enterprise business work partne-
ships exploit this time much better than official working
hours. The loss in production owing to disorganization is
minimal, the members work in a disciplined way, demanding
the right conditions for performance, and actively participate in organizing their work. The organizational and preparatory work often encroaches also on official working hours.

What the member of the enterprise business work partnership or of the cooperative group receives is considerably
higher income. Partnership members earn on the average 1.5-
1.7 times as much as their non-member colleagues. The proportions are similar in cooperative groups. Full-time members of cooperative groups also earn more by one half as
much as the industrial average wage. Since the work done in
the small organization is on the average about one third of
official working hours, it is obvious that the hourly rates

that can be earned in the enterprise business work partner-ships is much higher than those that can be obtained in the official working hours, exceeding the latter 2.0-2.4 fold. This is more than the company would be able to pay its workers as official overtime pay; (the amount of the latter being maximized, the majority of the work partnership mem-bers would not do the same work for ordinary overtime pay. At the same time, this is probably less than what the compa-ny would have to pay if it were to entrust an outside con-tractor with the job done by the enterprise business work partnership. In other words, the payment of the higher wages is good business for the host organization as well.

Legalized, well-paid extra work of course also has effects which go beyond the changes in total income and total wor-king hours. I mentioned the better, more disciplined utili-zation of working hours, the spontaneous improvement of the organization of work. The changes which occur in the bar-gaining and power relations within the company are at least as important. Although domination by the company management remains, collective worker interests acquire a better bar-gaining position in the discussion around the contracts to be concluded with the host organisations. Their organisation provides a certain protection and strength, in contrast to bargaining in the recent past where a joint position taken by workers could be described as a violation of labour discipline or perhaps even as a wild cat strike. The manage-ment is forced to reckon with these new power relations.

As may be seen, in the exchange, on the one side there are the long additional working hours, and higher incomes, which are supplemented by the spontaneous demand for the better organization of work and the learning of new forms of social bargaining. The other side, the company management gets rid of some central restrictions, ties manpower to the company, and is at the same time able to carry out its production programme. But on the national level these latter advantages do not necessarily add up: the internal small enterprise conserves the established errors of factory work organiza-tion, while the appearance is created that <u>internal reserves</u> are mobilized in this structure. The truth is that these are mostly <u>extensive</u> reserves (longer working hours), and the results are only to a smaller extent the success of rationa-lization. Although it is clear that the <u>same</u> can also be achieved more rationally, this only has importance inasmuch as the two contracting parties are interested. In addition, their common interest helps the survival of companies and sectors which produce uneconomically; the slow phasing out of which is desirable. In some cases production programmes carried out thanks to a common interest and the exertion of great excess physical and mental energy do not make sense.

What the system of the new small organizations changes and mobilizes is, then, extremely contradictory. The mobili-zation of the entrepreneurial spirit and private capital is only partly involved. Vacillating confidence and caution permit only small steps in this area - although it is true that they at least may get started. Part of the new organi-zational forms is in fact but a cautious experiment in the organizational reform of the official sector. The most frequent and most popular forms, small organizations established within the companies, become integrated in the official organizational system - even if in a rather involved way - and carry in themselves also the characteristic drawbacks of every compromise of this kind. Hidden abilities come to light but always in the service of rational objectives. The mobilized virtues include also some tough constraints and some ambiguous conventions: selfexploiting excess work, the demand for a strong tie to the employer and centuries-old traditions in Hungary. It is not surprising that these are able to assist technical and intellectual modernization in an ambiguous way only. As far as the social value of the compromise is concerned, the successes of the Hungarian social contract are obvious, and the appearance of the small organizations described here may also be considered part of this series of contracts. The analysis of their functioning brings us perhaps nearer to understanding why we - who participate in, and profit from, this compromise - look at our social contracts being renewed from time to time with more anxiety and ambivalence than do sympathetic foreign observers of the Hungarian situation.

REFERENCES

BÁNHÁZI, M., 'Az iparban és az épitøiparban müködö vállalati gazdasági munkaközösségeknél és szövetkezeti szakcsoportoknál végzett vizsgálat tapasztalatai Magyarországon. (Hungarian Experiences with Enterprise Business Partnerships and Cooperative Groups in Industry and the construction Industry). Iparpolitikai Tájékoztató, no. 9, 1983, pp. 23-30.

GÁBOR, R.I., GALASI, P., Második gazdaság' (The Second Economy), Közgazdasági és Jogi Könyvkiadó, Budapest 1981.

GÁBOR, R.I., 'Második gazdaság' (The Second Economy), Valóság, no. 1, 1979.

HETHY, L., 'A második gazdaság - a gazdaság és a társadalom' (Second Economy - Economy and Society), Társadalmi Szemle, no. 11, 1980.

HETHY, L., 'Második gazdaság, kisvállalkozás és gazdaságirányitas' (Second Economy, Small Enterprises, and the Guidance of Economic Life), Társadalomkutatás, no. 1, 1983.

LAKATOS, J., 'Uj tipusu ipari gazdasági szervezetek', (New Forms of Economic Organizations), Ipargazdaság, no. 2, 1984, pp. 31-35.

LAKY, T., 'Mitoszok és valosag - kisvallalkozasok Magyarorszagon' (Myths and Reality - Small Enterprises in Hungary), Valosag, no. 1, 1984, pp. 1-17.

LUKÁCS, E., 'Kisszervezetek 1983-ban' (Small Organisations in 1983), Területi Statisztika, vol. XXXIV, no. 5, 1984, pp. 575-590.

MEDGYESSY, P., 'Small-Scale Enterprise in Hungary', Marketing in Hungary, no. 3, 1983, pp. 15-20.

TARDOS, R., 'Magatartástipusok a családi gazdálkodásban' (Different Types of Behaviours in the Household Economy),

Közgazdasági Szemle, no. 1, 1983.

STARK, D., 'The Micro-Politics of the Firm and the Macro-Politics of Reform: New Forms of Work-Place Bargaining in Hungarian Enterprises', paper presented at the Eighth Annual Political Economy of the World-System Conference on "States Markets in the World-System", Brown University, April 1984, pp. 1-42.

'Az uj vállalkozási formák tapasztalatai a fővárosban' (Experiences of New Enterpreneurial Forms in the Capital City), Munkaügyi szemle, vol. 27, no. 4, 1983, pp. 1-6.

'VGM Külkereskedelmi vállalatnál?' (Enterprise Business Partnership Organizations in Foreign Trade Enterprises?) Külgazdaság, no. 10, 1983, pp. 73-77.

PART III
ORGANIZATIONAL
FORMS

Case studies in second economy production and transportation in Soviet Georgia

GERALD MARS, YOCHANAN ALTMAN

INTRODUCTION

In this paper we offer examples and analyses of case studies from second economy production and transportation in Soviet Georgia. We have examined in considerable detail the illicit workings of three factories and the means by which their managements facilitated the transport of raw material inputs into their plants and transported their final products to retail outlets. Here we focus attention on one factory manufacturing biscuits, situated in a small town in Georgia. In our second paper, we discuss the affairs of four stores which differ in size, type and location. Our data refers primarily to the mid 1970s.

We chose to look at the second economy of Soviet Georgia because it is generally recognized that this republic demonstrates an extraordinary economic ebullience (1). On measures such as the number of private cars per capita, for instance, it leads all Soviet Republics (Kipnis, 1978), while Wiles notes that "it is obvious to the eye of any traveller that Georgians are considerably richer than the population of RSFSR" (Wiles, 1980). Such commentators have been unanimous that this ebullience is linked to a parallel effervescence in Georgia's second economy, which Soviet watchers have, again, continually affirmed as being particularly dominant compared to those of other Soviet Republics (Grossman, 1977, 1983; Kaiser, 1976; Smith, 1976; Wiles, 1980). Our concern, therefore, was to examine the social and cultural bases underlying the operation of this second economy and, particularly through the use of case studies, to note how it articulates with the formal economy. The social and cultural bases were discussed more fully in an earlier paper (Mars and Altman, 1983).

Our principal source of data was derived from a community of 5,000 expatriate Georgian Jews who had moved from Soviet Georgia in the early and mid 1970s and who had settled in one area of Israel (2). Research was basically anthropological in that it involved two years of patient participant observation amongst the Israeli community based in the town of Ashkelon. In addition, data was obtained by a visit to Soviet Georgia, by library research, by monitoring the Soviet and Georgian press, and by cross-referencing the data obtained from Israel with Georgian sources in London.

Reconstructive research has several well-accepted precedents in the anthropological tradition (particularly notable is the Columbia University Research in Contemporary Cultures 1947-1953: Mead, Metraux, 1953) as well as on the Soviet scene (the Harvard Project on the Soviet Social System of the early 1950s, e.g., Bauer et al, 1964). The present study used traditional anthropological tools and anthropological concepts, particularly the idea of understanding economic behaviour from the point of view of a people's value system and within a given cultural milieu. The size of our sample allowed us to cross-check data received from several sources and from different levels of the same organizations.

A more detailed account of methodology is given elsewhere (Altman, 1983). We would, however, like to emphasize here one main point - the selectivity of our sample: our subjects being both emigrants and Jews. This potential threat of bias, however, has been dealt with successfully before (Bauer et al., 1964) and in our particular case did not prove a major handicap. Georgian Jews were exceptionally well integrated in the larger society and in any case, with the exception of their exclusion from the topmost post, were well represented in formal as well as informal economic activities (Altamn, Mars, 1984). Furthermore, in the period covered by this study - the 1960s and 1970s - there was neither "a Jewish economy" nor "a Jewish second economy" in Georgia. Yet, while in some sectors - notably agriculture and the higher economic levels - Jews were largely underepresented, in others - particularly trade and handicrafts - they were deeply involved (3). This allowed us to base our accounts on a richly comparative data bank and enabled rigorous cross-checking of information.

The criteria governing the choice of case studies were particularly concerned with de-emphasizing any Jewish peculiarities and seeking the more general outlines. Close association with gentiles was considered a necessary demand in the choice of informants.

Soviet Georgia is an 'honour and shame' type society, such as is found around the Mediterranean (Peristiany, 1966). While Georgians trace descent on both sides, Georgian families stress the male line and within it an emphasis on agnates - on the solidarity and mutual obligations of brothers. Women are important in Georgian society but primarily as the articulation points between groups of males and as the ensurers of male descent. Whereas the honour of men is achieved by the characteristic macho qualities of assertion, dominance and competition, the honour of women is passive and associated mainly with sexual modesty. Both a man's and a woman's honour reflect on the wider honour of their family and therefore their menfolk, and to a lesser extent on that of their associates.

Honour and its corollary shame are constant preoccupations in Georgia. Within families, spheres of action are well defined, do not overlap and are non-competitive - everyone knows his place. Beyond the family, however, these limitations are reversed. Insecurity and instability in the perpetual ranking and re-ranking of personal relationships is the norm. An individual has therefore, constantly to prove himself as <u>Katzo</u> - a man. He is, in this respect, perpetually 'on show'. He has constantly to demonstrate his worthiness to public opinion in general and to his colleagues and peers in particular. This requires the extravagant use of goods and resources in display and consumption, which are judged as exhibitions of 'manliness'. One of the principal foci of such conspicuous consumption is in the almost frenetic feasting and drinking sessions that serve to extend linkages between males and are thus a principal method of extending personal support networks (Mars, Altman, 1986).

Appreciating these basic cultural features allows us also to appreciate and identify the underlying need for extra resources, as well as the mechanisms for their achievement through a developed parallel economy. To be a somebody, to be a man, to be <u>Katzo</u> - one has to display. But this is difficult if one depends only on one's official salary. This means taking risks. But taking risks is, in the very nature of this society, actually a clear macho virtue. 'Screwing the system' has therefore not only obvious economic bene-fits, but the very honour of a man demands it and the social environment supports it.

It is for these reasons, then, that in a familial, macho-based 'honour and shame' society, a centrally organized hierarchy such as the Soviet economic system has little chance of working as it is designed to work. Not only is there necessarily a fusion of work life and private life, but positions and relations at work form only one dimension, and not the most important one of an individual's total role set. Here nepotism is perceived as a moral duty, and inter-personal relations dominate decisions at the workplace. There is no room for abstraction; all relationships are personalised in such a culture, and formal organisational structures are bent, modified and adapted to serve personal and familial needs.

The mechanism through which such adaptation occurs and which permits Georgia's second economy to develop and thrive is quite naturally the social network binding indivi-duals and families together. In a highly personalised socie-ty, the body of people to whom a person can intimately relate, and through whom extend relations with others who might latently prove significant, becomes his major so-cial resource. We have shown elsewhere how the 'weight' and scope of a person's network are primary determinators of the type of occupation he may hope to enter (Mars, Altman, 1983).

This linkage through personal networks of the formal and relatively rigid organizational level of Georgian society and its informal and flexible second economy, raises pro-blems when we come to define corruption. Corruption viewed from without has a negative connotation; it is seen as damaging to the operation of a formal system. The problem arises when we realize that we are dealing not with deviance but with the norm, with a daily pattern of behaviour to be found in every corner of life. It has long been observed by anthropologists that a bribe, for instance, can be easily confused as a customary gift, since in many cultural systems this issue is genuinely ambiguous. In Georgia we have a similar confusion. If the expectations of Soviet law, labour regulations, or Communist morals are taken as the ideal standard, then the norm varies widely from this in Georgia and, further, the operation of this norm is regarded as laudatory.

2. THE BISCUIT FACTORY

2.1. Background

There has been little systematic work on the operation of Soviet factories and even less on their place within the Soviet second economy. The seminal work is Berliner's (1957) study of factories and their managements, derived from interviewing refugees as part of the Harvard Project on The Social Soviet System. He focused on the formal organization of production and his mention of second economy institutions was concentrated on the Tolkachi - the middlemen 'pushers' or 'fixers'. But they were concerned to use illicit means for legitimate ends - to ensure that production met the level demanded by the Plan - not to exceed it as we found to be the case in Georgia.

During our investigations we obtained information on three different factories, located in three different regions of Georgia. One, employing two hundred people, was in the food industry, one was a textile factory with about one thousand employees, while the third involved light metal manufacturing and employed under a hundred. For each of these we managed to obtain cross-checked information from different managerial levels within each factory, thus corroborating the amounts of their illicit production, the difficulties in obtaining raw materials, the problems involved in the products distribution and the range and extent of their necessary external involvements. In addition, we obtained considerable anecdotal data from a wide variety of informants who had different lower-level sub-managerial contact with a variety of different factories. Most of these people were shopkeepers and drivers who corroborated the major factory case data.

This data is now presented as a case study which concentrates particularly on information derived from the food industry. In addition, however, and where relevant, we introduce comparisons and distinctions that arise from the other two cases as well as from other informants. It will be appreciated that certain facts have been changed so that identification of particular events and locations will not be possible. In our opinion, this does not detract from the concrete evidence of the material nor from its validity as a vehicle for providing an understanding of how Second Economy production works.

The enterprise upon which we concentrate here is a medium-sized factory and employs several hundred staff. It produces biscuits and, in addition to the requirements of its formal plan, it illicitly and consistently produces extra biscuits

in the ratio of 4:10, that is - four 'informal' biscuits to
ten 'formal' ones. This illegal 40 percent is a rather safe
extra output. We show later how the approach of this management consistently emphasizes caution. We have, however, come
across factories where illicit production has been erratic
and where production has on occasion reached up to ten times
more than in this case - that is, where production has reached a level four times higher than the planned output. This
dimension of safety versus risk will be elaborated later.

2.2. Setting up the illicit enterprise

Illicit enterprises, like regular ones, have their rational
structures, respond to market forces and are bought and
sold, as has been noted by others (e.g. Simis, 1982). In the
biscuit factory case the business was inherited by 2 of the
3 partners from their fathers. The third, a qualified en-
gineer who was the production manager became so indispensable that he was offered a share equal to the others. Profits
were divided equally among the three.
   In the case of the textile factory, on the other hand, the
entreprise grew from a small-scale textile workshop employing four men. It grew not from the initiatives of distant
planners, but because of the enterprise and pressure of its
official director. This man expanded production to such an
extent that he was able to persuade the appropriate authorities to supply him with larger premises and more plant, and
to do so on three successive occasions as he outgrew capacity at each stage. He was able to expand because informal
capacity was growing faster than official capacity permitted, and it was his earnings from this source that were used
to bribe the appropriate formal authorities and obtain their
necessary sanction at each new level of expansion. In all,
this entrepreneur's capacity expanded in four stages: from a
staff of four, to forty, to several hundred, to almost a
thousand before he achieved his final site. What lay behind
his expansion was the prospect that he could offer greater
illicit profits to those who controlled the sources of
legitimate state capital.
   To return, however, to our biscuit factory: its three
partners shared all the responsibilities of their private
enterprise. Their individual responsibilities corresponded
to their formal roles which were the three top functions in
the legitimate, state-owned factory: these were the direc-
torship of the enterprise, its production management and its
stock warehouse control which included responsibility for
accounting. These positions and their incumbents personal
contributions will be more fully discussed later.

2.3. Circumventing the plan

An easy and relatively risk-free way to engage in illicit
production is to have a formal production target - the Plan
- which allows leeway for additional produce. The way to
obtain this is by seeking cooperation of the person(s)
responsible for setting the formal planning targets and by

influencing them to obtain as lenient a planned target as possible. There is nothing novel about this - as writers on the working of the Soviet economy have long ago observed (e.g. Berliner, 1957; Nove, 1976). But usually this is done to maintain the official production of a plant, while in second economy production its purpose is to reduce the level of official output in order to capture the spare capacity for illegal production. Fiddling of capacity in this way is then the first and simplest method of achieving illegal production. It provides an easily-achieved flexibility which allows machinery, people and time to be employed to produce more than the Plan requires - with the additional produce then able to be aimed at the lucrative private market.

There is another and similarly simple way in which the Plan setter - the official who sits in Tbilisi and to whom an annual pilgrimage is made, may be of assistance. This is for him to permit a further degree of flexibility by allow- ing for a higher level of waste in production process than would normally be strictly necessary. Such a high rate of waste will then leave spare raw materials to be used for illicit produce. Official connivance can only provide a relatively small surplus, however. To maximize illicit output depends on the illicit manipulation of the products' raw materials.

2.4. Maximizing illicit output

To produce more than the plan asks for on a regular basis requires first and foremost extra raw materials. These can be either obtained from outside the enterprise, or the firm's legitimate supplies can be 'milked' to provide a surplus for illicit production. Whatever measure is chosen, the decision on how to obtain raw materials is a factor which will have a major influence in shaping the structure and conduct of the illicit production/distribution process.

There are several alternatives and these are listed below:

2.4.1. Cheating on the quality. Let us return to the biscuit factory. Biscuits need the following ingredients: flour, sugar, eggs, fat, yeast, spices, preservatives, artificial colours and water. This is not a comprehensive list. In principle, as with other products, the list contains some components wich are almost free, others which are easy to obtain - like water or spices, and some which are relatively hard to obtain, or are costly, like sugar, eggs and flour. The simplest way to overcome 'hard to obtain' products, as in this instance, is to use less sugar or eggs than is required by the standard (and in the Soviet Union everything has a standard) or to use cheap substitutes for dear ones. However, these methods are also easily detectable to any thorough control - though perhaps not to the naive consumer. Since control methods are integral to the Soviet economic system, consequently there is always the possibility that the fraud might be discovered - which would necessitate a massive cover-up operation in order to keep the illicit enterprise going.

The likelihood of a sudden check applies not only to food. One informant who used to be a bricklayer in Georgia commented: "Well, food is only half the trouble; food is eventually eaten - but if you fiddle with bricks, they stay forever ... You always live haunted with the fear that one day the fiddle will be detected", And yet this method has some considerable advantages as the extra raw material is attainable and in constant flow from inside the plant - a benefit not easily ignored.

The biscuit factory entrepreneurs, however, refused to employ this the most common method, so that the volume of their illicit production necessarily remained limited. In all the cases we came across in which the level of illegal production was much higher than the legitimate, people had to adopt this alternative (or the next one, which is a variation only) in order to obtain a sufficiency of raw materials. The management of the biscuit factory, however, stuck firmly to required standards and for three good reasons:

a) as stated, they were able to avoid the risks involved in the operation of sudden and unplanned checks; as well as the danger of a long - term detection ("You never know in whose hands a packet of these biscuits might end up");

b) its products were thus able to achieve a good reputation and were able to sustain a demand for their illicit produce;

c) their high standard provided a basis of reputation on which they could count in times of need. "The rumour spread", said one informant, "that we are strictly straight. It was considered almost inappropriate to check on us". It also become a source of strength for other figures, who had some responsibility for the running of the formal as well as the informal) business. "The Mayor (who was on our payroll) was very proud when in other places he was welcomed with a handful of our products". Thus, by ignoring alternative A, the biscuit factory lost the opportunity of maximizing its output, but avoided considerable risks.

2.4.2. <u>Cheating on the quantity</u>. This alternative is a variation of alternative A. In the biscuit factory for example, it would mean the manufacture of its biscuits at say 9 grams instead of the compulsory 10 grams. In this way it would free a 10% extra supply of raw materials. This method is rather common in some industries where the raw material comprises such goods as metal, wood or cloth, in which it is difficult for the consumer to check the amount involved in manufacture. As one informant from the textile factory explained: "If you're making stockings, for instance, it's not easy, even for expert controllers, to determine a deviation from the standard. The standard itself allows flexibility - it has to - due to human error and machine variability". However, with foods that are sold in fixed quantities, a consumer may detect that he has received short-measure. This is where much of the danger lies - the weak point in the chain. No one can anticipate to whom the goods will be sold or the standing of those who will buy them. Planned safeguards are normally employed against 'traditional' overt dangers only: the police and the sources of regular control.

2.4.3. <u>Falsifying qualities</u>. While in alternatives A and B a manufacturer will attempt to sell a cheap product as if it were a perfect one, another alternative is to consciously sell a second rate good at the price set for a first rate one. This practice then encourages a manufacturer to make as many seconds as he possibly can. The surplus of raw materials then becomes his property and is available for further production. An informant gave the following account of how he acted as a distributor for production achieved by this method:

> "One day I went to Kharkov on a regular working trip and as usual I was looking for a business opportunity. So I went to a shoe factory, with which I'd already done some deals in the past. They were producing galoshi - a sort of rubber boot, much in demand in rural areas for use on muddy roads. I met my contact man there and he suggested to me that I should buy a whole series of galoshi which were really supposed to be 'disqualified goods'. Really, there was nothing wrong with them: they were all perfect Class A items - but this was the Levi. So I bought three railway wagons full of galoshi: small, large, medium; galoshi for women, for children, half-boots, full-boots, extra long boots - thousands of them. They were all stamped inside with 'Uzenyon brak', that is 'faulty product', which means they were supposed either to be destroyed or sold at a special few shops which specialize in such merchandize. I paid 30 Kopeks a pair, which went straight into my man's pocket, as the goods were officially declared as destroyed. I shipped them all back to Georgia where each pair fetched 2.08 rubles, after, of course, rubbing out the false statement. It took months to sell out the whole stock but it made a nice little deal.

The main disadvantage here, however, is that such a 'combination' has to be a one-off event. One cannot go on producing defects continuously, and it is consistent operation which marks successful illicit production. One can see that for illicit production to really succeed it needs to be continuous, and this in its turn needs the application and support of an extensive persoonal network. Such networks are expensive to maintain both in obtaining material and social contacts. This type of maintenance is only made worthwhile by a long and enduring commitment.

2.4.4. <u>Copying the existing product</u>. This alternative was the one adopted by the biscuit factory. It produces superfluous goods - more than the quota, but not excessively more, and it makes its illicit production indistinguishable from its formal production. In this way advantage is taken of existing machinery, the production process and the existing work force.

Because such illicit output is indistinguishable from legitimate output it is able to pass undetected at all points in its passage from production to the consumer. This is particularly important in its movement from the factory to the store. The presence of ubiquitous road patrols at all main intersections in Georgia, as elsewhere in the USSR, makes the transport of illicit goods a high risk aspect of illicit production. Once in the store, however, copied goods can readily pass as official goods.

The incentive for the retailer in stocking copied goods is obvious: he gets private produce, which is an exact copy of the state produce but at a cheaper price. In this particular case, it was sold to retailers at 15 percent less than the official price. This allows considerable profit without having to sell at an artificially high price.

This method, though safe, is difficult to expand upon, since it depends upon the same productive resources required for the Plan, only more so. And it also has problems - the constraints and difficulties will be examined in detail throughout the remainder of this paper.

Having made a choice among these possible alternatives, let us now examine in detail how the biscuit factory conducted its illicit operations.

2.5. Obtaining raw materials from retailers: 'the closed loop'

As we have seen, most methods of obtaining extra raw materials involve 'milking' supplies from formal production, thus reducing either the official products' quality or its quantity. Our entrepreneurs, however, decided not to follow this path. So how did they obtain their raw materials, and from where did they come? They created what can be thought of as a 'closed loop'.

"You buy them in the shop, like any ordinary customer", our informant explained. "Well not like an ordinary customer", he continued, "but basically what we needed were daily household goods: sugar, flour, eggs, fats and salt. So we had contacts with our four shops which we used to turn to for our regular supplies: of course we paid them more than the normal price. After all, the shopkeeper takes a risk in selling a large quantity to a sole customer. In urgent cases, though, like if we were expecting a possible control and we had just consumed a lot of official raw material for our private ends, we could always get the extra stocks from a bigger number of stores. If we were really desperate, though, we might even have to go to brokers who we knew had the knowhow about where to get the stuff we needed, but who would need paying extra. Some of the supplies we needed would be part-exchanged for ready-made biscuits we delivered to the same shops."

By operating a closed loop in this way, both producer and retailer become locked into a repetitive and balanced exchange. And because such exchange is normally limited to the parties directly involved, it necessarily reduces the need for other, more insecure, alliances. We were assured that, for these reasons, closed loops are a frequent feature of second economy production, especially by small and medium food producers.

2.6. The dangers of dependence on the outside

2.6.1. <u>Organizing illicit packing and labelling</u>. A frequent and universal hurdle that bedevils much black production is involved in obtaining ingredients which make up the final product but which are not made in the factory. In this particular case, these comprised the packaging and labels. Like raw materials, they too are supplied according to the official quantities designated in the Plan. Consequently, it was necessary to have contact with a printing workshop and with a packing paper manufacturer. Printing in particular offers a possibility of serious bottlenecks to illicit producers since controls on printing are extensive in the USSR, where even typewriters are licensed and photocopiers must be kept under lock and key. And labels themselves are a potent source of control since soviet labels have to show not just the name of the product but a mass of data showing details of origin, quality, batch and date of manufacture.

One of us visited a tea plant in Georgia which manufactures five different varieties of tea. They are supplied with five different boxes, five different labels, and five types of packing - each supplied by one manufacturer (fifteen manufacturers in all). The plant is penalized if they retain stock for more than one month.

Whatever the reasons for this practice it certainly serves as both a safeguard and control against illicit production. At the same time, however, it highlights the inbuilt paradox of the system. After all, collusion with only one of the fifteen suppliers allows at least some illicit dealings. Thus, the more control and sanctions a hierarchy imposes, the more power leaks from the centre to the periphery. In this case, the print shop chosen (presumably because of personal contact) was some 50 miles from the factory, which added the additional risk of transportation (on the risks inherent in using illegal transport, see below). Usually the print-run would be made only once or twice a year, to reduce the risks involved as well as to lower costs. But there was still the problem of storing these components. To store them in the factory's warehouse would be too dangerous. There could be no possible legal justification for holding large stocks, so different people - normally not directly connected with the private enterprise - would be used to store them on their premises, usually for short periods.

And yet to be dependent on an outside source for produce and supply is a major risk - there is always a danger of being detected, not through any fault of one's own but as a result of the exposure of a secondary manufacturer. The biscuit factory faced a real crisis on these grounds with one of its label suppliers.

2.6.2. The case of the deceptive nuts. It is for the reasons
that every effort is made to contain production of secondary
ingredients inside the enterprise. As Georgians say: "When
you are desperate - you always find a way out". The following case illustrates this:

> "Some of the biscuits needed a special nut on the top and
> our supplies of these were limited, according to the
> specified production Plan. This might seem a very tiny
> detail, but nevertheless it's a crucial one. You just
> can't complete some biscuits without the right nut. Now,
> where do you get them from? It happens to be that not
> only are they supplied from outside (the factory and
> locality), but they are imported from another republic.
> So we had no hope of obtaining extra nuts from the offi-
> cial source.
> At the beginning, then, and for two years, we used to cut
> down the full-sized nuts into halves, so that we doubled
> the available quantity. There were times when two girls
> used to sit the whole day long slicing these nuts and
> various explanations were produced to account for this:
> that some of the nuts came spoiled and the faulty bits
> had to be removed, and so on. But it looked as if this
> could not continue for long. So, we worked out a new
> substitute which we made ourselves out of local ingre-
> dients so that it could be produced in the factory and
> was cheaper. It looked and tasted the same. I was praised
> for that invention and so we switched to artificial
> nuts."

From discussions with informants we were assured that this
kind of inspired innovation and adaptation is almost routine in black production. It is indeed in this sector of the
economy that innovation and a fast adaptability are institutionalized. It is not surprising either that the 'formal'
economy benefits indirectly as well.

2.7. Obtaining manpower and machinery

The next question to be answered is <u>by whom</u> and <u>with what</u>
are the black products to be made? Normally we found it to
be with factories' existing manpower and with state-owned
machinery.
  In some industries, employees are not aware at all of the
fact that they are working for private ends. If a management
employs alternative A or B to obtain its extra materials,
only those involved in certain stages of the production need
to be involved in overt knowledge of the deception. In the
case of the biscuit factory, these were those involved in
preparing the dough and in operating the electrical machinery. The rest, the majority, of production line workers, the
packers, and the clerks, would not be involved. Here the
intelligence principle: 'the need to know', operates clearly. The fewer involved, the less likelihood that knowledge
might be misused. This kind of deception was usual practice
in most cases of black production that we discussed.

In the biscuit factory there was, however, a higher than usual chance of detection because of the necessarily regular movement of raw materials from other than officially expected sources, and this necessarily involved a wide extension of dangerous knowledge. The entrepreneurs were therefore cautious. They acted on the assumption that <u>all</u> their employees might have some idea about what was going on (even though this had never been discussed with them) and they remunerated all of them accordingly.

The time needed for black production normally causes further concern. In the biscuit factory this raised no major problem as the ratio of private to legal produce was rather modest: 4:10, and the annual contribution by the Plan fixer in Tbilisi was designed to leave room for additional produce without much difficulty. However, occasionally even here overtime and even weekend work was sometimes required.

In the other cases we know of, where the ratio of illicit produce was much higher, the people selected for regular overtime were carefully chosen - not only for their occupational merits but also on the bases of trust, loyalty and familial reference.

Black production necessarily involves the extra, and sometimes the excessive, use of machinery. In the biscuit factory, however, this too did not prove a major problem, possibly because no faults or premature amortization could be directly attributed to above-normal use. In other cases, however, two different methods were adopted to enable machinery to last longer. Firstly, machines were declared broken at more or less fixed intervals in order to establish a false norm for breakage wich took into account the factories' additional black production. Second, those spares which were worn out, as a direct outcome of excessive use, were either maintained or replacements were acquired privately - usually via official channels and for an adequate reward.

The biscuit factory's shop-floor workers would also, normally, receive a non-cash reward of extra produce.

"We didn't want to give them cash, because this is clearly an offence and why bother? ... Today we are are friends - tomorrow perhaps you go to the police and complain. So we preferred to give them gifts, like sugar, flour, butter or eggs - this is not too committing yet these are a real perk. They were perhaps not extremely happy with what they got, but they would make their calculations and see that they were still better off than most of their colleagues in other plants."

It should be noted that the 'payment' and consequently involvement of shop-floor workers is not usually necessary. Especially where the primary fiddle includes cheating on the quality or quantity, the shop-floor workers would have no idea of what the real quality or quantity should be. Although the biscuit factory employed a different method for obtaining raw materials, its employees did not necessarily know what was going on because the proportion of extra produce was rather modest. Their share in profits was therefore an extra safeguard, characteristic of the circumspect way the biscuit factory handled its illicit operation.

2.8. Fixing stock and book-keeping

A universal problem exists when two parallel production systems operate under the same roof, and especially when one is official and the other is black. This involves having to balance an account for all the elements of production used in both systems, and to keep a feasible and a reasonable ratio of final stock to raw materials. These accounting problems become crucial in the Soviet system because of the ever-present fear of a sudden control swoop. Control over production (under the responsibility of the Ministry of Trade) would come in the form of an audit carried out once or twice annually and the dates of these would usually be known beforehand. This kind of intelligence is one of the services expected of the regularly paid local officials and it therefore serves to defuse the danger inherent in such audits. As has been stated, however, the real dangers arise from sudden unplanned swoops. The aim then is to perpetually keep all elements in balance so that any sudden control will not find too much or too little produce in relation to the expected balance of raw materials and supplementary items such as packaging and labels.

This need for balance certainly affects both the production and the distribution of black goods. In the biscuit factory, since the management had decided on a policy of caution, the tendency was always to produce in small quantities only, and to do so on a continuous basis. Linked to this, and maintained rigorously as a matter of high priority, was the policy always to move all goods out of the factory to their designated customers as soon as possible. However, if there should arise an unexpected demand for black foods, then it would always be possible to take some from official production since the product was the same. When this happened, the balance between production, stock and book-keeping needed to be re-established and this usually meant acquiring the missing raw materials quickly.

Book-keeping in the 'second', informal biscuit factory was relatively simple and tended to be verbal and not written. For some time a second set of books had been kept on his own private premises by one of the partners, but this practice was subsequently abandoned. The close and daily relations between the partners allowed an efficient transfer of information and decisions were always able to be taken on the spot. This was also the case in the metal factory.

In more complex systems with a higher rate of illicit business, and especially when deliveries were not made on a strictly cash basis, some record of illicit book-keeping was essential. We found that typically these records were kept by a key figure in the enterprise, often the warehouse manager, who controlled the flow of stock and who in addition was normally responsible for formal accounting. This was the case in the textile factory.

3. ARRANGING FOR SALE DISTRIBUTION AND TRANSPORT

The distribution of illicit biscuits was normally limited to only four shops which were also taking official goods - thus allowing use of the normal channels of distribution. As the illicit output was rather modest, there was never any real problem of choice in assessing who was suitable as an approved outlet and who was not. But even with greater quantities to dispose of, we found in other industries that distribution was the easiest element to organize in the whole complex of the private enterprise. In an economy of scarcity consumer goods are easily disposed of.

An understanding of the role of transport is a key element in understanding second economy activity within the USSR. It determines, to a great extent, the effectiveness or otherwise of the illicit enterprise, and often the limits of its expansion.

The problems of delivering goods by road are identical, whether the movement is to the factory - in the form of raw materials - or from the factory - in the shape of finished products. Whether at the beginning or end of the process, however, transport is invariably a bottleneck for those involved in illicit production. The difficulties involved derive from the controls exercised by the police, who patrol all main roads and who are based at road intersections throughout the USSR. The typical way of dealing with police road patrols is to bribe them or those who control them. There are problems, however, that arise when one comes to bribe a road patrolman. Since the base level policeman is relatively junior and is likely to be frequently changed, this itself makes for uncertainty. Another problem is that only one 'straight' policeman on a route can jeopardize a whole undertaking.

Because factory managements find that their biggest transport problems come from road patrols, they naturally try to reduce their dependence on road transport. It has been suggested to us that one of the principal reasons Soviet factories so often reduce the quality of their goods by fiddling their constituents is because this method at least supplies them with raw materials and, in doing so, increases their independence from transport hazards.

3.1. Obtaining transport

The first question to consider is from where do managements obtain their transport? The supply of vehicles is strictly controlled and their allocation limited. Georgia, however, has the largest number of cars per capita in the Soviet Union (Kipnis, 1981) which is indeed an excellent indication of its primary position in the Second Economy.

The most common and the safest way to obtain access to transport is simply to employ official vehicles, whether in the formal service of the factory or of the retailer, and to use them only partially for the transport of illegal items. But transport requires not only vehicles, it also needs a driver and not <u>any</u> driver will do. In the biscuit factory, for instance, only one of the factory's two drivers could be trusted, though both were technically proficient. Normal driving skills, however, are not enough: as already descri- bed, a driver in the services of a private enterprise has also to be able to cope with emergencies (e.g. by being able to cope when stopped by road patrols) and to have sound social contacts (that can be activated, for instance, in emergencies). But the most desired characteristic of a dri- ver according to several of our accounts, is that he must, above all, be discreet - he must be trusted not to speak out abour what he sees.

One cannot, therefore, underestimate the importance of a driver where the job involves delivering illicit goods. Even if formally the responsibility for the content of a delivery is not his - as for instance when he is accompanied by the person in charge of the goods - he still has to account for the excess mileage which will often be involved. Because he is technically liable for only small offences, he therefore becomes a potential weak link in the private factory's chain of security. This is why drivers have to be carefully cho- sen, are well rewarded and possess a prestige well in excess of their formal social standing.

After the questions of vehicle and driver have been sati- sfactorily solved, any collection or delivery of illicit goods still has to take account of two further issues: documentation of the goods and road patrols.

3.2. Documentation of goods ('Faktura')

Any purchase of goods involves an accompanying documentation called a 'faktura', which serves the functions of a detailed log of quantities, prices, times and personal certification. The faktura is designed to specify the contents of a con- signment and to state responsibilities of job holders in relation to it. It is designed to minimize error and make discrepancies easy to detect. As a result, it identifies and makes vulnerable those who are involved in illicit produc- tion or distribution. Obviously, if one move extra cartons which are not accounted for in the faktura, or if the whole delivery is unofficial, then the people involved face some danger. To provide needed protection from the faktura, four typical methods are employed. These firstly depend on using dual records, second on the multiple use of records, third on the use of taxis, and finally what can be called 'opening the road'.

3.3. Dual records

A dual record involves the creation of a document with only temporary validity. Such a document describes the correct shipment that is in transit and it is produced at the appro- priate check points, for the departmental accounts and to the security staff at appropriate gates. The only difference between this document and a bona fide faktura is that these copies are not recorded until the safe return of the driver. Then, all dual documentation is destroyed and an alternative faktura can be prepared and, if considered necessary, be recorded in the books. It is this method that operates in the more sophisticated illicit factories such as textiles factories that have a large output to dispose of and who needed to transport it for distribution along routes at a distance from their power base. Dual records in these circumstances also allow some degree of control over a large and steady flow of illicit produce and permit the maintenance of some form of continuous (even if temporary) record-keeping.

3.4. The multiple use of records

In the biscuit factory, where illicit produce and shipment was not a matter of daily routine and where illicit output was relatively small, the method used was more primitive. The driver would first complete one legitimate delivery journey backed by true documentation. He would then rush back to the factory for a second, identical load, this time of illicit produce. He would still keep the same documents and so they served him twice. This was possible in the biscuit factory case for two reasons: firstly, the unofficial produce matched the official - it was identical in all respects; and second, distribution lines were short so that the time discrepancy between the first and second departures was minimal.

This type of deception is only possible when deliveries are relatively infrequent and when they take place within a relatively small radius of the factory. It reveals, however, a structural dilemma for small-scale business, in that expansion often appears to be limited by inability to distribute beyond a small constraining radius. As distributional distance increases, the hazard of involvement with ever more distant patrols, who exist increasingly beyond the scope of one's network, also increases. The management of the biscuit factory consciously decided to limit its operations to its local scene because it lacked both the social and economic resources to capture these more distant sources of state control.

The multiple use of documentation does not, however, end with the safe arrival of goods at the store. One shopkeeper explained:

"If, say, I get 100 units of lampshades from a factory, and this is official, on a faktura, then I will keep that faktura as a cover for any future unofficial transaction. But it's only useful if I can get the same product from the factory as a private venture. However, I'll never take more than 90 units unofficially. Then if it's necessary, I can always produce the true documentation and claim: 'You see, I sold ten items but unfortunately this stock is not in demand. I can't get rid of it'. In this way I can use one official faktura for months; all the

time privately ordering the same product again and again
but never to the full amount specified in the document.
It would look too suspicious not to have sold a single
item over a long period of time."

3.5. The alternative - taxis

Taxis have the advantage of not being normally suspected by
road patrols of serving as a means for illicit delivery.
They can, therefore, be used for goods which could not
possibly be covered by formal documentation - as for instance, where the illicit product differs widely from those the
factory is chartered to produce. For example, if a factory
that manufactures copper plates for industrial use only
unofficially switches to produce household items, such as
pipes for domestic supplies, saucepans, plates and ornaments
(Georgia is acclaimed for its copper artistic work), then
the factory cannot back its unofficial deliveries with any
relevant documentation. It would then use the taxi service
instead.
  For the taxi-driver this would prove a worthwhile collabo-
ration. According to our information, a moderate estimate of
illegal transport frequency for the average black market
taxi-driver is one trip a week, which would amount to some
30 percent of a driver's total weekly income. One informant,
a taxi-driver from a rural town, estimated that hardly 10
percent of the taxi-drivers he knew would not collaborate in
such illegal journeys. Agriculture proved to be an almost
unlimited source of income to taxi-drivers, since many of
the villagers who trade their produce in the market towns
lack any means of transport.

3.6. Opening the Road': taking advantage of the controls

Another method is of interest because it highlights one of
the fundamental weaknesses of the formal system of controls
and central planning. An informant explains:

  "One way of 'playing it safe' in getting both extra raw
  material for private produce and transport would be to
  speed production at the beginning of the year (on the
  month) thus exhausting the existing stock - providing
  materials would reach us in a steady flow, according to
  production targets. We would then ask official permission
  to withdraw additional raw materials from the central
  warehouse or perhaps from another similar factory, on
  account of the expected future supply. With this official
  permission, of course, will come official transport authority. Or we would announce a machinery failure which
  resulted in a line of faulty produce, again 'urgently'
  needing raw materials. We will then find a volunteer
  among our sister-plants who would agree to 'lend' us our
  needs; thus we would get not one, but two official permits which allowed us raw materials and the allocation of
  a vehicle, driver, petrol and adequate documentation to
  travel between two points: once to receive the materials,

and later to return them.

4. PARTNERSHIPS AND NETWORKS

One universal characteristic of factories producing for the second economy is the need for collaborative effort, i.e. for partnerships. This is a marked difference to the operation of stores. While the unofficial side of even a large super-store can be run by one person, we did not come across any factory (even those with only six employees including the managers) that ran without some sort of cooperative partnership. Partnerships are necessary because of the complex nature of illegal manufacturing, which, as has already been seen, involves not only the dual production, but also the dual organization of deliveries: raw materials into the factory and final products out of it. It would appear that the complexity necessary for illicit production means that no single person and no single personal support network is able to encompass all the necessary bonds to keep the operation going and to ensure the mobilization of support in times of crisis.

We now examine in some detail the functional relations among the three partners of the biscuit factory and assess the role of their personal support networks in establishing and maintaining their factory's informal organization.

The factory's General Manager, one of a large family of brothers, had the strongest personal support network (the method of assessing network strengths is given in Mars, Altman, 1983). It is not surprising that he held the most senior position in the factory, since his network was probably even stronger than the figures suggested as his father was general manager of another biscuit factory in a nearby region. The combination of a father (first-rate obligatory bond) in a powerful position in a similar plant goes a long way in asserting one's own standing.

The Stock/Warehouse Manager, who also acted as Accountant, had a weaker personal support network. However, he had a particular strength: three members of his family worked in middle positions (though in different capacities) at a nearby factory. Two of the three were dealing with stock control and book-keeping in the same area as himself.

The Production Manager's position is particularly interesting since he had a very weak family network. His father was dead at the time he entered the factory, and he had no brothers - that is, no first-rate bonds. He however had some unique contributions which helped him in taking up a share in the partnership, though not without a struggle. Initially, he had difficulty in entering the factory, but a lucky link with the Mayor obtained him a place and his exceptional abilities as a footballer ensured a wide range of contents. He was fortunate too in having a technical qualification where their possession was being insisted upon by the central authorities.

The Production Manager's exceptional qualifications - technical as well as social (he was the only Jewish footballer in the town's team) - meant that he had access to people and resources not usually approached by Jews. He was also renowned for his drinking capacity, so that for all these reasons he gradually come to adopt the role of the factory's 'foreign minister' in the words of a companion - it was he, for instance, who made contacts with officials, which, traditionally, would involve hard feasting in local restaurants.

It is important to note that while the core of a personal support network is based on familial bonds - its extension and indeed actualization - often depends upon the age-based peer group. The three partners were part of the same peer group, which helped to ease their personal relationships with each other. In addition, each of the three partners had some three to four close friends (altogether ten friends) who formed part of their overall total social support net-work. In a very real sense, therefore, the factory management, as an entity, had its own social support network.

Decision-making regarding illicit activities was highly informal. This was, firstly, because the three had a close relationship; secondly, because the level of illicit produce was relatively modest and, finally, because the production process was fairly continuous and both the sources of raw materials and the number of agents for the final product were few. Indeed, in this factory illicit production did not require frequent decisions: it had become largely routine.

Another reason for limited decision-making was because a degree of specialization existed among the partners. The Production Manager would deal with outside agencies, while the Stock Controller quite naturally took over the functions of stock balancer and book-keeper. The General Manager tended to deal with manpower and hence took responsibility also for extra remunerations. But in no way were these speciali-zations exclusive, and roles tended to overlap.

Apart from the three partners, who shared profits equally, the employee most closely involved in running the illicit enterprise was a foreman on the production line. He was a Gentile and he, of course, brought to the enterprise his own personal support network. He also contributed muscle to the coalition. He not only looked ugly and could be extremely frightening, but he also had a proven record of ability as an amateur boxer. Like the Production Manager, he too had climbed to his position by having the right qualities at the right time and place. In a particular crisis, to have muscle and a frightening visage were thought to be necessa-ry, and he had carried out the job as 'heavy' to perfection. Since then he had become closely associated with the facto-ry's illicit activities. Though he did not have a share in the partnership, he was frequently remunerated 'to keep him happy', as our informants put it.

5. THE FACTORY AS AN OPEN SYSTEM

All parties involved in planning the factory's formal opera-tions have a stake in its informal - that is, its illegal activities. The person responsible for setting the production targets, the local government official who licenses the plant, the head of the enterprise who has administrative responsibility for the factory and, last but not least, the shop-floor workers are all involved in both aspects of the factory's production.

The only difference between the working of the factory's formal and informal structures are a number of additional bodies: the police force - who are always involved in illegal activities and expect to be bought off - or else ... and the Komsomol - the Communist Youth Movement - whose members are used as guardians of morality. Factories have usefully been seen as open social and economic systems set within an overall environment with which they engage in interactions (e.g. Katz, Kahn, 1966). This simple conception applies just the same to illicit factories engaged in the wider system of second economy relationships.

As in any transaction, there are at least two parties to a deal. Not only have the factory managements a vested interest in obtaining the cooperation of the agencies which govern their operations, but the latter are likely to have corresponding interests as well. Sometimes, as the saying goes, 'the calf wants to suck and the cow wants to suckle', which only suggests that certain enterprises with potential spinoffs are prone to pressure from their surrounding environments. All my informants who held managerial positions agreed that pressure to operate illegally is just as likely to come from outside the enterprise as from within it. One manager explained:

"You cannot afford to be innocent. Different people expect you to pay them and if you don't they'll either see you're removed from your job - that is, if you don't take their advice and resign. Or they'll incriminate you. This last possibility isn't too difficult. Everyone makes a mistake from time to time, only in Georgia it's assumed that there are no genuine mistakes, and any incident - anything at all - can be used as a pretext against you. You either pay or you are out of business. It's as simple as that."

This kind of duress may come from any of the three bodies which have some sort of control over a factory: the professional heads (the organizational superior and planners), local government, and the police force. All of them expect remuneration, whether or not anything illegal occurs, but this mutual involvement in illegality acts as an insurance if untoward exposure is ever threatened. At one level it therefore offers support and succour to the illegal factory - but at another it limits the possibility of its potential expansion.

NOTES

(1) The study was funded by the UK Nuffield Foundation

(1980-1983).
(2)   Some 30,000 to 35,000 Jews emigrated from Georgia to
      Israel within the decade from 1973.
(3)   Socioeconomic stratifications are estimated from
      comparing Soviet statistics (Georgian SSR in 1975,
      1976) with Israeli figures of immigrants' own occupa-
      tional declarations (Litvak et al, 1981).

REFERENCES

ALTMAN, Y., A Reconstruction Using Anthropological Methods
    of the Second Economy of Soviet Georgia, Unpublished PhD
    Dissertation, Middlesex Polytechnic, Middlesex 1983.
ALTMAN, Y., MARS, G., 'The Emigration of Soviet Georgian
    Jews to Israel', The Jewish Journal of Sociology, vol.
    XXVI, no. 1, june 1984, pp. 35-45.
BAUER, R.A. et al., How the Soviet System Works, Harvard
    University, 1964.
BERLINER, J.S., Factory and Manager in the USSR, Harvard
    University, 1957.
GROSSMAN, G., 'The 'Second Economy' of the USSR', Problems
    of Communism, Sept/Oct. 1977, pp. 25-40.
GROSSMAN, G., 'The 'Shadow Economy' in the Socialist Sector
    of the USSR' in The Proceedings of the 1982 NATO Econo-
    mics Symposium, Monch Publishing Group, 1983.
KAISER, R.G., Russia: The People and the Power, Atheneum,
    New York 1976.
KATZ, D., KAHN, R.L., Social Psychology of Organizations,
    Wiley, New York 1966.
KIPNIS, M., 'The Georgian National Movement: Problems and
    Trends', Crossroads, no. 1, 1978, pp. 193-215.
LITVAK, J. et al., Georgian, Bukhara and Caucasian Jews -
    Aliyah Potential towards the 1980s, Ministry of Absorp-
    tion, Jerusalem 1981 (Hebrew).
MARS, G., Cheats at Work: an Anthropology of Workplace
    Crime, Allen & Unwin, London 1982.
MARS, G., ALTMAN, Y., 'The Cultural Bases of Soviet Geor-
    gia's Second Economy, Soviet Studies, vol. XXXV, no. 4,
    Oct. 1983, pp. 546-560.
MARS, G., ALTMAN, Y., 'Drinking and Feast Giving; Personal
    Networks in Soviet Georgia', in Douglas, M. (ed) The An-
    thropology of Drinking, Cambridge 1986.
MEAD, M., METRAUX, R. (eds), The Study of Culture at a Di-
    stance, The University of Chicago Press, 1953.
NOVE, A., The Soviet Economic System, G. Allen & Unwin, Lon-
    don 1977.
PERISTIANY, J.G. (ed), Honour and Shame, Weidenfeld & Ni-
    cholson, London 1966.
SIMIS, K.M., USSR: Secrets of a Corrupt Society, J.M. Dent &
    Sons, London 1982.
SMITH, H., The Russians, Sphere Books Limited, London 1980.
WILES, P.J.D., Anti-Systemares Verhalten in der Sowjetwirt-
    scaft, Bundes Institut für Ostwissenschaftliche und In-
    ternazionale Studien, Bois, Bonn 1980.

Case studies in second economy distribution in Soviet Georgia

GERALD MARS, YOCHANAN ALTMAN

1. INTRODUCTION

This description and analysis is based mainly on detailed data collected from the staffs of four stores which operated in Georgia during the 1960s and at least until the mid 1979s. Other shopkeepers were also questioned. Our information was then cross-checked for reliability and validity as we have explained in our earlier paper. This material was supplemented by informants who comprised a diverse cross-section of the community: manufacturers, distributors, artisans, peddlers, drivers, railway workers and of course the consumers themselves.

The four stores were selected for the following reasons:

a) Geographical location - the stores operated in three different areas of Georgia, the East, the West and the South-West.

b) Town vs Country - one was based in a village, another was situated in a busy market town, and the other two were in rural towns.

c) Size - one was a general store with 25 employees and a turnover of 250,000 rubles a month. Two stores had four employees each and an approximate turnover of 100,000 Rubles apiece. The fourth business was a one-man market stall (for which we have no details of turnover). Their illegal organization, as might be expected, varied widely:

The general store comprised eleven departments; trikotash (cotton lingerie), soft furnishings (fabrics sold by measure), men's and women's clothes, children's clothes, shoes (including stockings), perfumery, fancy goods, households appliances, electrical appliances, contruction materials and agricultural tools (this being a village store).

Surprisingly enough it did not sell foodstuffs. We inquired why this was. "I had to fight for that", was the reply. "I made it clear from the start that I wouldn't have any food in my store". Another shopkeeper remarked, "I would rather lose the shop than cater food". As a matter of fact, none of the four shops dealt in foodstuffs. There were three valid reasons for refusing to have anything to do with food:

a) The prospects for illegal earnings are limited. "How much can you overcharge for a loaf of bread?" was one comment. This informant hailed from rural Georgia, where food was abundant due to the numerous, thriving freehold plots (which produce about half of the country's output). The very poor derived additional income from home baking (Papashvily, 1973), while self-produced wine and spirits are the pride of every household.
One loaf of bread is much like another; clothes on the other hand are not, and the opportunity for overcharging on clothes is therefore enhanced. In addition, the unit cost of clothing is higher than that for food and the amount overcharged per unit can correspondingly also be higher. This necessarily reduces the risks incurred at any given level of overcharged income.

b) Dealing in foodstuffs is less prestigious than other merchandise. "You get messed up ... it's dirty work", explained one retailer. (It is worth mentioning that in the 1960s and '70s most of the foods in rural Georgia were still unpacked and distributed in bulk). Again the comparison with clothing is marked.

c) Unless he caters for exclusive tastes in ready prepared foods - wich is not usual in Georgia, the opportunity for a retailer to obtain financial and social benefits by selling foods is virtually nil. Though food is certainly used as a basis for conspicuous display, it is sold essentially as relatively undifferentiated raw material which has then to be acted upon domestically. The final products - traditional dishes - are judged more according to the quantities served and the domestic skills applied than to the nature or the source of the materials used. There is little benefit here for the retailer.

The 'display value' of clothing, on the other hand, is a matter of immediate impact and constant concern in a culture as imbued with competitive display as the Georgian. This is ideal for the retailer since it involves a constantly re-newed demand for fashions that often originate from the USSR and which can never be effectively satisfied.
One clothing retailer remarked: "On the weekday I retur-ned from the allocation centre, my friends knew they would have first choice. They would come to my shop the same evening and pick up the best". Such retailers are not only readily able to make profits by selling to close (and there-fore trusted) friends, but they also gain socially. They emerge as men of influence who, as well as offering, can also obtain scarce goods and services through exchange from people who control these in other spheres. The central role of clothing as an ideal second economy commodity is discus-sed later.

2. THE FIVE SINS OF A STOREKEEPER

X was one of the first people we approached about his second
economy activities. He was a shopkeeper and was approached
warily: "I've heard that sometimes there are strange goings-
on (Kombinatsia) in Georgian shops. Have you ever come
across any?" He found this cautious and uncertain approach
amusing.
"Sometimes! If you take law and regulations by the word then
you start breaking them the minute you open your door in the
morning. Not to mention communist morals ... (the narrator
was a Communist Party candidate). As a storekeeper I was a
true sinner".
During our investigation into the affairs of Georgia's
second economy we became familiar with five indictable
'sins', each of which is liable to grave consequences. They
can be divided into two categories: 'sins' against the State
and 'sins' against the customer.

2.1. How the system should work

Officially goods should be purchased through legal channels,
usually an Allocation Centre (which will be discussed in the
next section). In certain circumstances, eg. where the allocation centre is very remote and a major plant is considerably closer, direct access to the manufacturer is allowed.
Stores are subject to a plan which states required annual
gross income and monitors monthly accounts. The overall
monthly balance is sub-divided into various categories, in
order that departmental performance can be assessed. A plan
would usually be flexible enough to allow for seasonal
variations or any other changes. However, the scheme operated on two false assumptions: it assumed that goods were
bought and sold at the correct retail price and that the
store only catered for a particular area.
In actual fact, only some of the goods were bought and
sold at official prices. And a shop's clientele largely
depended on its reputation for stocking a good flow of
quality goods. Although the village store was supposedly
catering solely for the village community and the near
vicinity, it became well-known and attracted custom from a
much wider area than the planners anticipated. "It was
common knowledge that anything you want, you first try us.
It was said that one could even get bird's milk in my
store". The store manager was proud of his reputation for
meeting practically any customer's requirements.

2.2. Defrauding the state

2.2.1. The First Sin - Trading with Unlicensed Goods. A
store is licensed to trade only in certain items which are
clearly defined. In order to incorporate some private enterprise, the shopkeeper introduces goods for which he does not
have a licence.
Our market stallholder was licensed to trade in only
thirty-four items but had two hundred and forty in stock

when his stall was raided. Not only were these goods unlicensed and therefore acquired illegally but some had also been unofficially manufactured.

It is common practice for clothing manufacturers to design garments that imitate foreign design specifically for the private market (at the time Western jeans were being widely manufactured underground). Needless to say, these privately manufactured clothes competed with official clothes and netted a big slice of the market. It appears that sales for official clothes are rapidly declining. A report in 1978 stated that Soviet 'official' clothing and footwear had to be marked down to less than half price and had caused losses amounting to more than 1,700 million rubles. (Binyon, M., The Times, London, 16.5.80). We have not been able to obtain any figures peculiar to Georgia, but would not be surprised if its share in this exceeds the national average.

2.2.2. <u>The second sin - 'swinging' the plan</u>. Since the Plan is calculated on total sales and not broken down into individual items, it can be 'worked' in more than one way. A storekeeper explained: "Firstly, if you charge more for certain items than you should and hence obtain a private gain, you can always pass some of it to the official books. Or if you ever sell things which have nothing to do with your particular business you can still claim some of it or all of it to be items X, Y, Z. Money is money and no one can know where it comes from. But you've got to be careful to have your pockets filled with cash, so that when a sudden control comes and your books are not balanced, you can show the cash and say: 'I just happen to hold all the morning's income with me. We were so busy I had no time to register it'."

In other words, one can sell unauthorized goods and 'wangle' the Plan simply by 'swinging' the official Allocation of Goods (this will be discussed later). That is, getting hold of desirable commodities, selling them at a profit and then striking a balance by filtering a proportion through to the State. In this way, an authorized clothes shop can rise to be an exclusive sportswear store. This was the achievement of one of our informants. It is ironical that goods sold in the second economy can eventually end up as 'official' profits. Some of it would trickle back in the form of a bonus for exceeding the Plan - if this was the desired effect. In this way "... everyone was happy. I always fulfilled and usually slightly over-fulfilled my targets (2). I was considered a successful manager, my career prospects looked rosy and my boss was delighted. he also benefited from having such a good subordinate". (Greer, 1973, mentions several cases - quoting the Soviet press - in which awards for overfulfilling the Plan were won by enterprises using apparently the same method).

On the surface these 'rackets' might appear relatively easy but this is certainly not the case. Regular check-ups are carried out: every three to six months there is a stocktake and from time to time supposedly 'surprise' swoops (advance warning is usually given). Every item in stock is specified in minute detail. One informant recounted an incident where an official failed to find a specific needle. This was a genuine case of lost stock and had nothing at all to do with subversive activities (needles are too trivial). However, a 'black mark' was put on the manager's personal file together a sarcastic remark saying that the official could not understand how a store that can't produce a needle manages to effect such a good sales turn-over.

This then is the offence committed by retailers. By 'working' the Plan to their own advantage they subvert official strategy, and yet to all intents and purposes they are hardworking upholders of Soviet policy. It is a state of affairs that magnifies the intricate interwoven dependency of the economies: first and second - one mirrors the other.

2.3. Defrauding the customer

2.3.1. The third sin - selective sale. Selective sale is the key to successful trade for a second economy retailer. The reason being that allowing unselective access to goods might be disastrous: one should always consider the implications of an unknown customer or an excessive price. The principle itself is well established in the formal economy. Soviet official trading does differentiate between higher and lower ranking customers to such an extent that there are 'special' shops for an élite circle.

The second economy retailer adopts this concept inasmuch as he too selects. "The safest to sell to are family and close friends. Then to friends of friends", explained an informant. It is in this respect that the network comes in as a selection criterion. And one measure of how good a network is depends upon how many scarce commodities it has to offer its members.

2.3.2. The fourth sin - falsifying trade descriptions. This is one of two ways in which the customer is swindled. It could be argued that the onus is on the customer to beware when hastily buying scarce goods. An informant explains how it works:

"Let's take an example - towels. There are three sorts of quality (many products have three sorts of quality). Each sort is recognized by its label (3). Differences, especially between the first and second, would sometimes be insignificant and difficult for an unexperienced person to notice. The easiest way to differentiate between the sorts of towels is by weight. Sort A should be 230g., sort B 195g. and sort C 185g. The difference in price between each classification would be 50-70 Kopeks and that is a lot of money, especially if you sell in considerable amounts."

"There would be enough work to occupy a person for days just taking off labels. From clothes this would be relatively easy, from china a special blend of acetone would be used and sometimes you can't help it. On certain items the details are imprinted, like cutlery, irons, mixers."

One of our informants once had a huge quantity of galoshes (rubber boots) to sell which were in great demand as it was winter time, but his rate of sale was determined by the time needed to take off the identifying labels. After taking off the labels, the merchandise was being sold as a higher grade product. Usually it would be 'upgraded' one stage. An informant explains:

"We would specialize in cotton-wool, sold for 1.60 rubles, 1.30 rubles and 0.90 rubles per unit. There were only slight differences between them and as it came loose it was difficult to distinguish. We would normally stock the third and second grades only and sell the third as second and the second as first quality."

2.3.3. The fifth sin - overcharging the customer. Overcharging for selected goods is another common method of swindling the customer. It is an unavoidable consequence of the second economy system. The retailer has to pay his superiors 'licensing fees' and protection ('hush') money. He also has to make the manufacturer or middle-man an attractive offer for good quality and scarce commodities. Thus he 'rolls' the excess in price over to the customer. This is to be expected where a buyer has to chase for goods. The customer is the last link in the chain and, therefore, has to bear the costs. Usually the customer is only too glad to have obtained the goods and, therefore, has no qualms about over-paying but this is not always the case - overcharging by stores is the most common of citizens complaints.

The practice of overcharging is more common in villages than in towns, the main reason being that stores in towns usually have direct access to manufacturers who will sell them under-the-counter goods at cut prices, as we saw in the previous paper's discussion of the factory. Once goods have been obtained in this way there is no need to take further risks as sale at the official price still yields an adequate profit. In the case of stores dealing with the biscuit factory, this amounted to a safe 15%.

The village stores, however, are often remote from industrial centres and in order to survive they have to opt for this method. Also, since their staff know their customers more intimately than do the staffs of city stores, they face less risk of complaints. It is in the customer's interests too to keep their local store going. Otherwise, they will have 'your own man' to approach when in need, even if this means regularly paying more than the going rate.

3. OBTAINING ILLICIT GOODS

There are basically two ways of obtaining illicit goods: either directly from manufacturers, or through intermediary sources. Both methods will be described.

3.1. Obtaining goods from manufacturers

Both town stores had regular contacts with three to five manufacturers at time. The factories were local or located a short distance from the town, although in one case an informant used to travel regularly over 100 km to obtain particularly desirable merchandise. Informants would normally go once a month to collect goods which had been requested over the telephone or ordered the month before. Sometimes this would not be necessary - certain manufacturers preferred to send their representatives with samples (as is normal practice in the West). Representatives frequently called at the market where one of our informants ran a stall. Not only was it lucrative from the manufacturer's point of view (there were fifty-five shops and stalls in the market) but it was absolutely essential for informants who ran their businesses single-handed. Unlike the other stores in our sample, where at least one member (usually the most senior) would be mostly away from the premises chasing goods - this informant worked alone (with occasional assistance from various members of his family) (5).

The purchased goods were transported either by the retailers themselves or by the factory's official transport. This would be relatively easy since illicit goods cannot be distinguished from official merchandise.

When, however, the illicit produce is not the same, there is no point in changing the use of official transport. Under these circumstances private cars or taxis would be used, the latter having the flexibility of short-notice availability and relative immunity from road patrols. A patrol would be considered paranoid (or have been 'tipped-off') to search a passing taxi.

3.2. Obtaining goods from intermediary sources

As with illicit production and transportation, illicit distribution too exploits the formal system - bending regulation to meet its needs and subjecting the centrally controlled bureaucracy to Georgian market forces.

Most goods are purchased, formally, at specially designated Allocation Centres (in Russian Tsentral Bazi). Goods are purchased not with money but Bills of Allocation denoting only a general commodity (eg: footwear, textiles, perfumery) and total price. The bills are issued by the organization to whom the shop belongs, and when it is transferred from the store representative to the allocation clerk (Tovaroved), it become a proof of purchase.

Since only a category and a total price are given, the content of the transaction is dependent upon the needs of the purchaser, on the one hand, and availability on the other. And so they are indeed. Only that store's needs are determined by the (informal) potential of making a good profit and availability is largerly dependent on the Tovaroved's good will, which is measured in purely monetary terms.

A retailer would come to the allocation centre with three

aims in mind:

(a) To obtain everyday goods for the routine running of the store - accessible items which require no extra cash to obtain or sell them. However, he would not buy goods for which there was no market as this would necessitate unnecessary labour and space and spoil his achievement record (the Plan).

(b) Secondly, he would bring a list of 'orders' - not necessarily customary products but 'orders' from clients' families for scarce products or unusual goods.

(c) Thirdly, a purchaser comes with the idea of laying hands on anything worth having - i.e. anything that can be sold at a high profit.

The allocation official has two aims in mind: to sell the unusual and quality goods at as high a price as possible and to get rid of the poor quality items and those not in demand, so that his Plan's (which includes sundry goods that must be disposed of) requirements are met. A customer who agrees to give extra cash will get the better products - consequently (since there is a zero total sum) somebody else will get the inferior goods. He is thus able to apply 'stick/carrot' pressure so that the person who bids higher for unusual products will also get ordinary goods 'free of charge'. An informant explained:

"I would get a periodic allocation to purchase a certain amount of goods (according to the Plan). Take for instance, clothes. They are, according to Soviet standards, divided into: cottons, wools, linen and synthetics. Now in each category I could purchase for an overall amount during the given period, with contents and time of purchase at my discretion. So I would get say half a million Rubles allocation for cottons. And I prefer to purchase with it only underwear because it sells well".

"But why should the Tovaroved agree?"

"Either because I do him a favour and accept some stuff no one wants, or because I make a deal with him on other matters - or simply because I pay him to allow me to choose the contents of my allocations".

The Tovaroved is indeed in a prime position since he deals with a closed circle of clients, who cannot risk losing him as a source of informal supply. He is a 'King' - an expression often used to decribe the holder of this position. In negotiations one would, therefore, have to adopt a humble approach:

"... there could be a negotiation on the extra price to be cashed, but very gently and with respect. Because if he gets furious with you, you get nothing. He has another million clients besides you".

For the purchaser and his store, the Tovaroved is a vital

link. Since this is essentially a sellers' market, the
storekeeper's capacity to survive depends upon his relations
with this official. The village store manager who had few
contacts with producers was indeed obliged to spend most of
his time at the allocation centre:

"Almost every day I used to go to ... I knew nothing to
do there - and still I would feel an urge to go".

On some occasions, the allocation centre turned into a
meeting place and became a social club. These social gather-
ings were an arena for gossiping, exchanging information
and a natural bargaining ground for business matters.

Performing similar functions to the allocation centre is a
certain type of travelling broker - the expenditor - who
supplies to village stores whose staffs are unable to regularly attend the allocation centre; or to one-man businesses
where the proprietor is unable to leave his premises. He
would take orders from the storekeepers and, like his senior
colleague the Tovaroved, would be remunerated for any extra
service or just for carrying out his regular duties. As with
the Tovaroved, each transaction would be negotiated separately and paid for on an ad-hoc basis.

4. THE ORGANIZATION OF THE INFORMAL STORE

The organization of informal activities in the four stores
differ widely in important aspects. In large part these
reflected differences in social and physical factors such as
size and location. We found that these affected the nature
and extent of employee participation which were widely di-
vergent, and affected too the extent of managerial involvement with influential figures in the outside hierarchies.

4.1. Three types of informal structure

The four stores discussed in this paper had different organizational structures - legal as well as illegal (see Figure
1 and 2). We concentrate in this section on the situation of
their managers.

4.1.1. <u>Appointment</u>. The village store manager was appointed
by his superiors in the regional headquarters. Incidentally,
this was a village general store. On the surface there seems
to be nothing unusual about the selection process. But in
reality things were different. Not only was he well-suited
because of his formal qualifications (Diploma in Trade) and
his experience as assistant manager, but he also satisfied
the informal criteria on several bases. Firstly, it was
thought he would be grateful to his superiors for advancing
his career faster than usual, his gratitude expecting to
yield extra returns. Secondly, and linked to that, his
personal support network was mediocre (6). It was expected,
therefore, that he would have only a limited ability to
develop local autonomy. In addition, he hailed from the

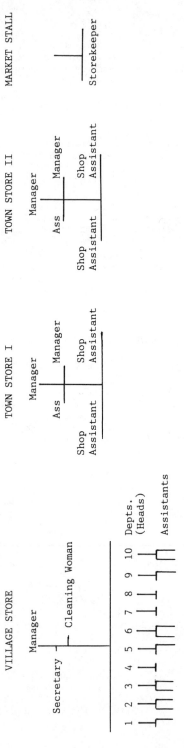

VILLAGE STORE

Manager

Secretary — Cleaning Woman

Depts. (Heads)

1 2 3 4 5 6 7 8 9 10

Assistants

TOWN STORE I

Manager

Ass ⎯ Manager

Shop
Assistant

Shop
Assistant

TOWN STORE II

Manager

Ass ⎯ Manager

Shop
Assistant

Shop
Assistant

MARKET STALL

Storekeeper

Figure 1: Formal Structure of the Four Stores

228

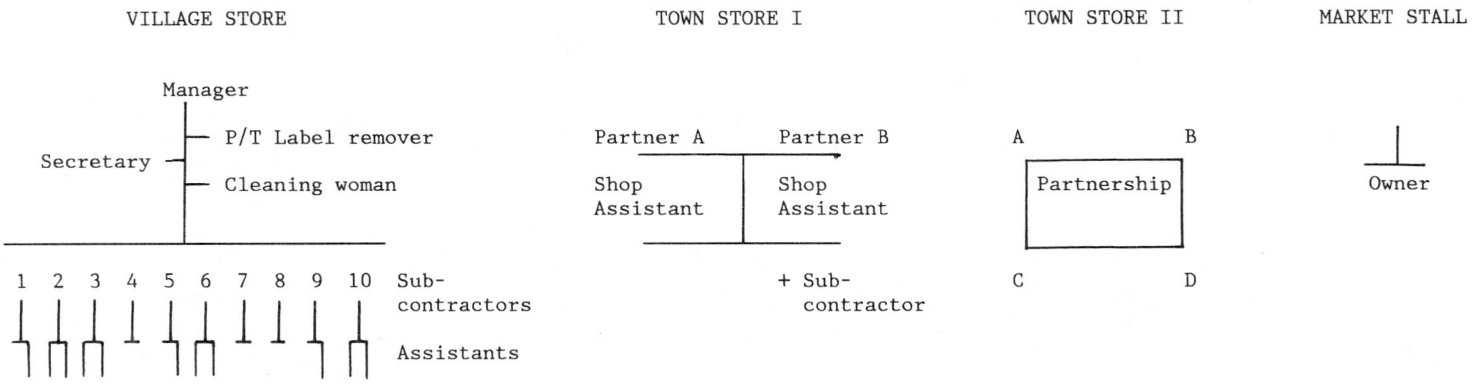

VILLAGE STORE   TOWN STORE I   TOWN STORE II   MARKET STALL

Figure 2: Informal Structure of the Four Stores

229

village and knew the local community intimately - he was
therefore considered 'their man' - very important in a local
village setting where a profitable business is dependent
upon local support. Needless to say, it was most desirable
to have the residents' implicit trust in order to avoid any
trouble.

In a case similar to that of this village store manager, a
person with a particularly weak network core (6) was also
appointed to a powerful position - as a head of an import
warehouse. This unofficial 'qualification' for the post was
considered paramount in his selection. In appointing him,
his superiors could keep a tight grip on how he ran the
warehouse and potentially opposing power-base was avoided.
They were thus able to ensure control over the informal
spin-offs that came to the holder of such a powerful post.

Both cases are further example of symbiotic-interactive
bonds between the first and second economies in Soviet
Georgia.

4.1.2. Ownership. Three of the stores were, in some respects, part-owned. This was most clearly marked with the
market stallholder. There were three reasons: firstly, he
moved into the trade from a different (though not unrelated)
occupation - tailoring, while his counterparts had spent
most (Town Store I) or all (Town Store II) of their professional lives in the trade and therefore gradually progressed
to managerial position which carried a share in the profits.
Secondly, he had a particularly weak network core and as
such was unable to obtain a nomination by virtue of social
standing or through 'friends of friends'. Thirdly, the illegal network of the town's market stores had succeeded in
establishing its own 'law and customs', the customs being
that store could be bought and sold on a good-will basis
(see further details on this subject in Section 5.5). It was
for these reasons then that this man acquired a stall by,
simply, paying for it.

In 1965 he decided to move from the relatively secure services sector to the risky arena of trade (the latter being
potentially more gainful and prestigious). He was later to
regret this move, as his personal support network was not
strong enough to sustain him in this endeavour. If it had
not been for his fellow market traders, he would have been
implicated in major crisis.

The cost of the small store was 8,000 rubles of which
6,000 went to the seller and 2,000 went to the local official in charge of the market and responsible, amongst other
things, for shop allocations.

Both the seller and market official had power to impose
fees. The former had power vested in him by the market's
informal 'law and customs' commmittee - after all it was
in the interests of all stores in the market to assure an
'actual' sale as this reflected on the value of their own
properties. The latter had official power and gave authori-
zation to new occupiers for which he received 'licensing
fees'.

4.1.3. <u>Partnership</u>. Two of the four stores could be described as partnerships. Town Store II was a totally equal
partnership in that it operated whith equal shares of investments and profits. The four partners were closely connected: three were related, and the fourth was a close
friend considered to be one of the family.

Town Store I was also a partnership, but this applied only
to two of the four members operating it. Their partnership
was particularly interesting as they had established a clear
division of labour between them. One was the buyer - he
spent most of his time away from the store, chasing goods,
liaising with factories, paying out bribes. The other was
responsible for running the business, i.e. selling the merchandise. Both were close associates and they complemented
each other extremely well. One was outgoing, determined,
rather arrogant and always in a hurry. While the other
was well-known in the community as a 'white chicken': an
introvert by nature - he showed great discretion, pondered a
lot and appeared rather indecisive. Both felt they had a
very good partnership.

4.2. The employees' place in the informal structure

Unlike production line workers, shop assistants are directly
involved in the second economy. Even the most junior assistant had to help sell the goods and, therefore, had to be
familiar with prices, grades of quality, and first and
foremost, customers. They were thus closely implicated from
their initial recruitment and subsequent promotions, as well
as through the levels of their day to day renumeration.

4.2.1. <u>Recruiment and selection of employees</u>. The village
store manager 'inherited' most of his employees - they were
already employed by the store when he was appointed. When,
with time, the store grew larger and new people had to be
recruited, he aimed to "select workers with a good background", as he put it. When requested to enlarge upon this
he said: "Somebody with a large and strong family, preferably who could be influential in times of need - to the
worker as well as the store".

The same requirements applied to Town Store II. This was
a newly created store run by two partners. They gradually
expanded and employed another two staff. In choosing the
right people for the job, they looked not only for a solid
familial background but also an injection of new blood -
they specifically wanted a gentile. They hoped this would
rejuvenate the store's outlook and open up new horizons, as
well as attract a wider circle of clientele (that is
'friends of friends' of the new employee). They decided to
employ a girl, who was appointed to the ladies department.

They similary took advantage of the sex and age group
structure of Georgian society when employing a fourth assistant. He was a cousin of one of the partners and a teenager
(17 years old) when he joined.

By attracting his peers he helped to expand the store
still further.

4.2.2. <u>Involvement in the second economy</u>. In both town stores the channel through which goods reached the stores was dominated by one person. Even in the village general store, all the intake of goods for its ten departments was controlled by the manager. He would personally handle rare and espensive merchandise irrespective of which department it belonged to. Normally, however, he would sub-contract profitable goods to various departments (as shown in Figure 2 not all departments were given this privilege simply because not all of them handled consumer goods worth dealing in) (see Section 6).

Things were different in the smaller stores. Members of staff were expected to serve all clients and therefore to be entrusted with the lucrative commodities. This does not mean that employees were let in on all secrets of the trade. For instance, the gentile girl working for Town Store I was not aware of any illegal activities with manufacturers. "Was it because she was female and not Jewish?" I enquired. Our informant giggled, recalling how she couldn't understand why certain goods were not over-priced when they were in such high demand. "But why don't you take more money when you can?"she asked. "You won't believe me but I'm essentially an honest man", I used to reply. "Of course she wasn't aware that I had already made a profit by getting the stuff cheaper from the factory. And there was no point in taking too high a risk".

The village store had an employee that to all intents and purposes did not officially exist. He was engaged as a remover of labels from merchandise - an important stage in the procedure of overcharging customers or falsifying the quality and price.

According to our information, this person (a villager in his sixties) had regular work for at least one full working day per week. Thus, he was a regular part-time employee of the informal store.

4.3. Regular and irregular expenses incurred in operating the informal stores.

Table 1 summarizes the regular 'salaries' paid out by the four stores.

It would be the usual practice to pay off two types of officials: one's organizational superiors and the local police. Compared with producers, the number of payees was smaller, their formal rankings were lower and so were their remunerations.

4.3.1. <u>The regional organization</u>. In rural Georgia, in the sixties and early seventies two large organizations incorporated most retail stores: Savachroba (literally 'trade' in Georgian) and Tsentrussayooz Rykavshiri (a combination of Georgian and Russian, meaning 'regional section of the central union').

The former was a Georgian-based organization with headquarters in Tbilisi which operated mainly in the towns and townlets. The two town stores in our sample were branches

Table 1

Regular Payments of the Four Stores (Annual)

Institutiona Affiliation	Village Store	Town Store I	Town Store II	Market Stall	Powers
Regional Organization					
Direct Boss (Assistant - where applicable)	c.2000 R[2]	c.1000 R[2]	c.600 R[1] c.350 R[1]	c. 500 R[1]	Personnel selection and promotion; allocation allowances; setting and changing the Plan; granting and exempting trade areas; alarm sudden controls.
Others			Regional bookkeeper: occasional presents	Gatekeeper/ watchman: c. 150 R[1]	Much know-how of the illicit operations. Since the market stall operator is relatively weak - he is relatively powerful.
Local Police					
Head (Deputy) ODKhSS	c.600 R[1] occasional presents N/A	c.600 R[1] c.100 R[1] c.60 R[1]	c.1000 R[1] c.500 R[1] c.300 R[1]		Deal with citizen complaints Supervise road-patrols Supervise economic police Particular responsibility to fight economic crimes
Others		Officer in charge of the district c.40 R[1] Neighbourhood officer: c.20 R[1]			Some restricted local powers

Notes: 1 - Monthly Payments
2 - Periodic Payments (approx. every three months)

233

of Savachroba. The latter was an entirely Soviet organization with headquarters in Moscow, operating largely in villages - the village store was one of their subsidiaries. The market store was governed by the regional council.

The local representatives of the organizations had considerable autonomy in running their affairs: i.e. recruiting and promoting personnel, expanding, merging or moving of stores, allocation of resources, setting-up and supervising the plan, and specifying trade responsibilities (for instance, exemption from sales of foodstuffs).

Due to these powers, the regional senior officials (who usually supervised local stores) netted a large proportion of the stores' regular 'pay-outs'.

This was particularly the case in the village store where the manager owed his promotion to his superior, but it is also a reflection of the size of the store and its anticipated illicit earnings. A characteristic of the stores' regular pay-outs is that there would be an agreed sum to be paid monthly and it would tend to fluctuate according to trade. In most cases, it reflected how much the direct boss knew about what was going on. In the market, for instance, the official in charge of the market would spend several hours a day scrutinizing activities. Consequently he was able to tell from first hand experience how a store was doing - he even charged extra fees for giving his consent to take leave on High Holidays and Sabbath. In the other stores, however the director was largely dependent on the cooperation (or fear) of his store managers. "I would actually determine the illegal earnings of my boss," said one informant. "In a sense, I was my boss's boss".

One of the town stores also used to bribe the regional book-keeper with small gifts: "Just in case. He might always mess up his books". But this seems to be a unique variant, reflecting a particularly powerful personality, or lack of skill in double book-keeping.

The market stall had an additional levy, namely, paying the gatekeeper who was also the night-watchman. Although formally a marginal position it carried with it a good deal of knowhow and inside information which deserved appropriate remunaration. Since he was able to charge individual retailers (some with a week social support network) his illicit intake was considerably higher compared with his counterpart in the Biscuit Factory.

4.3.2. <u>The local police</u>. The striking fact about regular payments to the local police it that our market tradesman did not pay them. This is the only case we know where the local police were not directly involved in second econmy production and trade. This could either be because weakness of the enterprise resulted in the retailer being unable to sustain regular payments, his priorities being limited to essentials - the direct supervisor and the gatekeeper/watchman - or because the business was so small it would be too demeaning for a senior policeman to accept bribes. As we shall see, keeping only lower ranking officers on the pay list would be pointless. Without the backing of local seniors, a store could not be guaranteed protection.

Yet another possibility is that the market with its huge potential for illicit profits was dominated by powerful enough individuals to exclude the police from direct involvement. This does not mean to say that officials were unable to obtain some illicit gains, but these would have to be channelled through a key figure among the market traders or more likely as part of the payouts of local representatives to their superiors. Our informants estimate the illicit annual income of the officials running the market as in excess of 40,000 Rubles from 'salaries' alone. Though informants had no evidence, they believed it most unlikely that such a large sum went into one pocket only. Among the main beneficiaries, they said, had to be the highest echelons of the police.

With the other three stores one finds, as would be expected, regular payoffs distributed up the hierarchical ladder, with the head of the local police sitting on the top rung. His 'salaries' were far in excess of any of his subordinates, the reason being that: "The big boss is a big man. The bigger he is, his word counts more. Besides, it's important that the 'small ones' know I am a friend of the boss. But though the 'small ones' hadn't much power, I wanted them to be good to me - so they were paid as well".

Town Store I, in particular, gave pay-offs to all the minions - the reason being that the store was situated close to a tourist resort and therefore catered for a passing trade. Consequently, it was a more vulnerable target than usual for customer complaints. By paying off every policeman it hoped to 'tie up all loose ends' and diffuse such complaints at as early a stage as possible.

The village store, on the other hand, had only limited expenses as the local police force consisted of only two policemen. It is interesting to note that while the store manager was willing to pay a regular 'salary' to the junior policeman as well, the senior police officer objected. Apparently, he wanted exclusive rights on the local store (as a way of asserting his seniority). So our informant used to give the junior occasional presents, to ensure his good will without upsetting the local balance of power.

4.3.3. 'Ad hoc' payments. Although most expenses incurred in running the illicit store were in the form of 'ad hoc payments' not 'salaries', our informants did not consider them to be bribes or dishonest in any sense. In fact these payments were expected when trading in illicit merchandise, as reflecting "the real value of goods".

The largest pay-off went to the broker at the allocation centre, who would usually charge about 10% of an item's price. To this one had to add additional levies imposed by road patrols (the mobile militia) and the customary few Rubles to the driver who transported the goods.

4.4. The organization and sale of goods in the second economy

Unlike factories, stores work on an 'open door' principle - anyone is free to wander in and browse. This calls for strict control to ensure that illicit activities are not exposed to the wrong people.

In this section, we examine how goods are displayed and stored and how the sale of second economy merchandise works.

4.4.1. <u>The lay-out of the informal store</u>.

All our information suggests that in the typical - not the exceptional - Soviet Georgian store, two different but interlinked enterprises operate simultaneously under the same roof and at the same counters: one is legal, the other illegal.

One informant explained the relation between the two as follows: "Anything in demand would go under the counter - everything without demand would be dispayed on the shelves". This is a reverse of the position in the West and a sharp manifestation of the main differences between the two markets: one is a buyer's market, the other a seller's. One is an open market (money will buy anything), the other is a market within a market with only limited access.

A retailer who had a new store built told the following revealing anecdote about a conflict between a law-abiding ('straight') store designer and the informally inclined locals. "He came from Moscow", stated our informant, as if this explained it.

The new purpose-built store consisted of two floors. The store designer suggested that maximum display space was desirable. He had all the merchandise stored on shelves and he installed a self-service system. Each floor had only one desk, where shop assistants would help with enquiries and packaging of goods, whilst the customer paid his bill at the cash desk. In fact it had a similar layout to Western stores. The manager, on the other hand, wanted a more ortho-dox organization of display counters, whereby merchandise would be exhibited in a display cabinet and be handed over by the assistant at the customer's request - a far more personal service. Having this kind of arrangement meant ample storage space for hiding 'under the counter' merchan-dise and ensured that quality goods were under the auspices of staff and were sold only at the right price to the right people.

An essential requirement for the illegal sale of goods is personal contact between customer and retailer. The manager thus wanted a decentralized system whereby each department had its own cash register. Separate cash registers had the added advantage of complicating audits - when officials made a swoop they would have to check six sets of accounts, as opposed to only one in the proposed system. However, the manager's proposals contravened the ethos of central com-mand.

The way the disagreement was resolved is particularly significant. On his boss's advice our informant stopped arguing with the store designer and allowed him to do as he pleased. When he had finished and authority was back in local hands, this informant altered the premises to his own requirements (this was sanctioned by his superiors) claiming that the original design was not practical for the store's purposes. The local powers did not question this.

Yet another common hurdle is where to hide illicit merchandise, especially since supply is erratic and retailers cannot plan their store's intake. This is a major concern for town stores who tend to obtain specially manufactured goods, not only imitations of legal merchandise. One informant solved the problem by acquiring a local residential property. The owner agreed to rent out a room to him which was turned into a 'warehouse' for 'hot' merchandise. he paid the owner a monthly rent (10 rubles) and, more importantly, offered him the opportunity of access to sought-after goods at somewhat reduced prices. Our informant felt the landlord was well pleased with this arrangement.

4.4.2. The strategy of illicit sales. To sell or not to sell: that is the question. This is the Achilles Heel of illicit sales and if a storekeeper is careless or unfortunate he can end up in great trouble. The main risk lies in overcharging (8). With small quantities there is usually no problem. They can be sold to trusted associates. Difficulties occur when off-loading large quantities, especially in town stores which lack the rapport that exists between locals and their village storekeeper. An informant explains:

"Say I got 300 pairs of fine shoes. It's a real opportunity to make some money - but I handle it cautiously. First, I wait a couple of days to see who else has the same stock and how much they are sold for. If I'm lucky and the only one in the area, I will start selling 20-30 pairs for a day or two at the official price so that the rumour will spread that my store can get quality shoes cheaply."

"It normally doesn't take longer than a day to have people queueing for the goods. And then I can select. Either I sell (for more than the official price) or I say: "Sorry we've sold out". And if a 'big shot' comes in I may tell him: "Sorry I'm sold out - but leave me your shoe number and I'll try my best to find a pair for you." And then I gain twice. First I do him a special favour and he owes me now. Second, I can always call him as witness (if a control is made) that he just got the last pair".

Another common problem with customers who present themselves as 'friends of friends' (Boisserein, 1968) is that networks can proliferate to hundreds of people. Obviously circumstances vary, but one informant claimed he never took chances. "I would say I haven't got the goods right now: come tomorrow and we'll see. In the meantime I check his references".

4.5. The retailers unofficial organization

It is their vulnerability, more than anything else, that forces storekeepers in a given area to band together. This tendency was particularly clear among market traders, to the extent that they frequently established their own codes of 'custom and practice' which they were able to collectively impose on their memberships.

These unofficial associations of retailers had a say in the running of stores. Any new store, for instance, had to have at least the silent approval of fellow storeholders and of the local market, especially if the new business aimed to vie in a competitive trade area. On one occasion a forum of all interested parties gathered to discuss a claim put forward by one member, who argued that an adjacent store had taken on a new line of products similar to those he was dealing in. The assembly decided against the complainant and the dispute was settled.

The strength of market associations stems from familiarity, through having to work in close proximity ,and also (at least for some of them) from having very weak social support networks. By joining forces they overcome weaknesses: they thus form a coalition of, the weak.

With the other stores, close associations were marked through payment of bribes, because unlike factories, 'salaries'were not paid out directly by individual stores but collectively and through a collective representative, who acted as a 'linking pin' between officials and stores. An informant explained: "... the reason being the Head of Police, for instance, doesn't want to get too dirty; he doesn't want to be everyone's pal - so he does not take from everyone. Only from the biggest.

This phenomenon also applied to manufacturers. The small producers had a similar problem and they solved it in a similar way. It was considered dishonourable to take from them since in exchange for this money they were owed a favour - it was unthinkable to be indebted to such nonentities.

Consequently the town store managers formed groups of 10 to 15 stores (9) wo passed their 'contributions' via a representative who was considered respectable enough to deal with the authorities. The fee was a fixed sum, but varied according to the size and location of each store. Although the official would not receive bribes from individuals, he would be informed who had paid and how much.

Another function of unofficial groups of retailers is the communication of reliable information. In such an unstable millieu, business contacts are essential - one has to be well-informed about the whereabouts of scarce commodities and of the likelihood of official swoops and mingle with people who possess such information to "... develop antenna about what goes where" as one informant put it.

5. THE FIVE RULES OF INFORMAL TRADE

Bearing in mind the principles and practices governing the operation of unofficial stores in Georgia, the question one may ask is how do these principles and practices determine the retailers choice of merchandise? Five rules of thumb were proffered by our informants.

5.1. First rule: pricing

'Trade with medium priced products. Don't deal with either very cheap or very dear goods'.

There is no point dealing in products with a very low market price, since even excessive overcharging will not yield a worthwhile profit. Further, the large number of transactions required to make a reasonable profit would increase the risks of exposure. On the other hand, it is not advisable to handle very dear products as there is a big initial outlay and the possibilities for a potential market are limited. Consequently, the target should be a medium sized product in reasonable demand from which one could make a fair profit.

An example of the first negation concerns perfumery. Every brand available was Soviet-produced and very cheap. It was in reasonably high demand and the stores would supply it accordingly However, no attempt was made to decrease its availability and, in so doing, raise the market price because it was too insignificant and profit margins would have been negligible.

A reason for not dealing in too rare and expensive items was put by one informant:

"One day I was approached by an old acquaintance who wanted to sell an antique piece, which had been in his family's possession for some years. It was a nicely shaped jewellery box, or perhaps it was originally made for tobacco or even fire-powder, made of fine wood, artistically silver-plated and inlaid with precious stones. The seller asked a fortune for it - about 5.000 rubles - and it was probably worth it. But I couldn't find a buyer. It seemed crazy to put so much money into the purchase of one small box'.

5.2. Second rule: supply and demand

'Trade with goods which are neither rare nor common, but which are in reasonable demand'.

It is not a good idea to deal in products which are in high demand and very scarce because it is difficult and dangerous to overcharge. On the other hand, handling very rare items might leave one open to pressure and blackmail by prospective customers eager to acquire these products as precious status symbols. Consequently, the trader should therefore aim at products which are neither rare nor easily accessible.

An example of the complications pertaining to such scarce commodities is ZIL refrigerator (10). This Russian-made appliance was considered one of the best: it was of good quality, had a powerful motor, a strong freezer and was nicely designed. Needless to say, it was in extremely high demand. An informant explained why he didn't like to speculate with them:

"We only got two every three months, which was our official allocation. It was supplied directly from Moscow. No intermediate agencies - therefore it was very difficult to establish connections and arrange for more items. But, say I got the connections and pay extra money and arrange to get some more, where would I put them? They're too big to hide - so I'll have to display them in the open display space, which would make it more difficult to sell for an excessive price. But that's not the main problem. If people in the area would hear that one can get a ZIL refrigerator at my place I would expose myself to extreme pressures to supply - both from informal and formal channels. So that the best was the simplest: to get what I am formally authorized to, to sell it at the formal price and only to those who are supposed to get it. Which means to the 'big ones'. My boss would tell beforehand - since he knew when an allocation was due - to whom to designate the fridges and sometimes I wouldn't even bother to pass them through my store, but rather advise the clients to get them from the area central warehouse".

Products which are in plentiful supply and therefore easy to obtain are not worth discussing - they would not be sold 'under the counter' because they could be purchased at the store over the road for the official price.

5.3. Third rule: the size

'Stock the smaller items - they are safer'.

The thinking behind this rule is that large items can draw unwanted attention and land one in trouble. Large items require special transportation and storage arrangements, and the likelihood of detection by a road patrol or any other interested parties increases. The village store manager used to inform his superiors of any large illegal transactions he made - for instance furniture - which meant they had to get a share too. "Even a large profit wasn't worth the effort", he concluded.

5.4. Fourth rule: durability of goods

'Trade with consumer goods that have a good turnover'.

This rule refers to the way in which goods are purchased and

sold. Indeed it is an intrinsic principle of networking. To
establish a network for limited, if infrequent use, would be
very expensive and impractical. A network needs constant
nourishment in social and monetary inputs. Only a regular
ongoing process would therefore be beneficial. This applied
to both the process of acquiring the goods and selling them
- both require a network. An informant explains:

"There were a lot of goods in high demand, in which one
could specialize. But that was only worthwhile if working
on very large scale: at least regionally and certainly
not confined to a townlet or a number of villages.
For instance, a piano is a must for any Georgian who
respects himself. The sought-after makers are Russian:
Bielorus or Krasnaya Octyabr. But how many can you distribute among your friends or among customers you trust?
Sooner or later you have to expose yourself to a larger
market and eventually your supply sources dwindle. After
all, how many pianos does a man buy in his lifetime?
The same was true even for smaller items. Czechoslovakian
china and crystal were renowned. But once again, once you
sold someone a dinner set, it satisfied his needs. You
can't sell him another set the following year!"

Networks, then, can be 'saturated' by expensive immovable
goods.

5.5. Fifth rule: selecting one's customers

'Deal with regular customers. They have a vested interest in
keeping you going'.

There was an immense difference between the way the village
store and the town stores selected their customers, and it
has been explained how this influenced the kind of illicit
dealing a store could operate, e.g. overcharging (country)
versus obtaining cheaper supplies from manufacturers (town).
We have shown the impact this has had on the informal meta-
structure: the number of policemen on the regular 'pay roll'
was the largest in the tourist resort centre.
   The village setting is ideal for covering-up illicit activities.
Firstly, strangers can easily be detected and, secondly,
the store manager is considered by the locals as 'one of
us'. An informant said that to the customer's way of thinking, "He's also got to make a profit. But we trust him".
And indeed the manager confirmed that he would not exploit
them: "I would never squeeze them. We have established a way
of living with mutual trust as its foundation".
   The vested interest of customers in having 'their store'
is self-explanatory. Firstly, they know they will be overcharged - but not too severely and not very often. Secondly,
they have somewhere to go for 'special requests'. For instance, one of the town stores specialized (as an additional
source of income) in introducing engaged couples' families

to their suppliers in order that they could obtain supplies
of food and clothes for the wedding ceremony.

5.6. Clothes - the ideal commodity

A summing up our informants' rules of thumb confirms that
the best policy is to:

Trade with medium-priced products, which are neither rare
nor easily accessible, but which are scarce, consumable and
preferably small. Finally, sell only to regular customers.

One can now see that certain merchandise fits very well
into the desired paradigm. Clothes, as we have indicated,
probably fit best of all:
    Firstly, clothes go out of fashion, wear out and constan-
tly have to be replaced. This is a good reason for developing a supply network for regular clients over a long period
of time. Secondly, they are easy to transport and to conceal: they are basically small, flexible and light items.
    Thirdly, they are at the right profit level - not too dear
to require a large investment and not too cheap to make
profit levels negligible. Fourthly, they are not too rare to
become status-linked commodities and thus cause risks, and
not too common (because of their diversity) to be of no
trading value.
    In addition, clothes are a natural focus for conspicuous
display - a cultural must in the Georgian style of living.
It should not be surprising, therefore, that clothes should
prove a major source of illicit profits in Georgia.

6. Postscript

Given the official restraints in catering for consumer
needs, it is not surprising that we should find a fertile
ground for the development of illicit production and distribution. This can be more successfully geared to accommodate
local taste, adapt to the rapid changes of fashions and
respond to requirements for design and personal style.
    With the removal of the planner's influence on production,
as it occurs in Soviet Georgia's second economy, we find two
factors permitting an increased influence of consumer
choice. Firstly, that producers having a greater degree of
local involvement can more readily cater to specific de-
signs; and secondly, the storekeeper for his part is able to
influence production by reflecting his customers' demands.
In this way, consumers' preferences as these are mediated
through the stores which can influence production. Stores
therefore acquire a standing in the second economy that
brings them closer to the position of their counterparts in
Western economies.

Though the people in Georgia would appear to have an
insatiable demand for consumer goods and though there is

some evidence that unofficial supply expands to meet it (as evidenced, for instance, in the quick and steady expansion of road freight as compared to both rail and air), the possibility of the second economy being for ever able to effectively expand must be limited. First and foremost an effective expansion in supply depends upon an output that benefits from economies of scale. It appears that increases in supply are necessarily limited, however, not because of lack of effective demand but because distribution is reduced to a radius that is bounded by the effectiveness of personal networks. It is this distributional limit that limits production to safe levels. This perhaps explains why Mars in 1982, was able to observe a factory in Tbilisi that produced a whole range of different consumer items, each of which he considered was being produced at well below their optimum output levels.

By producing a multiplicity of small output for local markets, managements maximize security but at the cost of operating without the benefits of scale. We believe we can now go some way in explaining why the Georgian Second Economy should be larger in real terms than the second economies of other Soviet type republics. To be sure other Soviet type economies display the same kind of informal economy practices. They too depend for much of their informal economic activity on 'friends of friends'. But it is the degree to which networks in Georgia are institutionalized as a means of linking individuals through trust-based honour commitments that forms the cornerstone of Georgia's second economy. The difference may appear to be merely one of degree but is based on a fundamental cultural distinction.

We hope to have demonstrated how retrospective reconstruction can work. How a concern with the central interest of anthropology - the idea of culture, the application of the concept of personal support networks and the alliance of these to the anthrolpolgical method of patient participant observation, can produce both understanding of an economic system and hard data that would otherwise be unobtainable. Other Soviet-type economies based on different cultural core values may well display high levels of second economy activity. Our present work, for instance, suggests that this is the case in Central Asian republics - known to be second only to Georgia in this respect. It is not sufficient, however, to consider merely the overall outcome of second economy activity. If this phenomenon is to be understood, it must be examined in the context of its local cultural setting. Recourse to the methods and concepts of anthropology are, we believe, the way this can be achieved.

NOTES

(1) We use the term "Kombinatsia", a common expression referring to the Second Economy Activity.
(2) There is no point in excessively and regularly over-fulfilling the Plan, as this would indicate some basic error in planning, and consequently the targets will be

re-adjusted upwards. Unless of course this is exactly what the shopkeeper wants to achieve - that is expanding the store. One of our informants extended three times in this way, by simply showing that he supplied growing needs.

(3) Each sort bears a different colour label. Sort 1 is red, sort 2 is blue and sort 3 is green. The other specifications given in the label indicate the type of product and the price.

(4) Unless their products do not compete with the state goods, in which case they may get whatever the market forces dictate.

(5) Although in emergencies one could rely on fellow traders to give a hand. The business was always kept open, even if the storekeeper was absent due to illness.

(6) The personal support network is a man's power base, consisting of the adult males within the nuclear family of origin and of marriage, as well as of close friends and associates. See Mars, Altman, 1983.

(7) Suggesting cowardice, feebleness.

(8) Falsifying the quality, the other common method of defrauding the customer, is a safer way of maintaining client ignorance.

(9) This number is the largest adequate to function effectively as an intimate social group.

(10) ZIL stands for: Zavod Imena Lenina, (name of the manufacturer).

REFERENCES

ALTMAN, Y., 'A Reconstruction Using Anthropological Methods of the Second Ecomony of Soviet Georgia', Unpublished PhD Dissertation, Middlesex Polytechnic, Middlesex 1983.

ALTMAN, Y., MARS, G., 'The Emigration of Soviet Georgian Jews to Israel', The Jewish Journal of Sociology, Vol. XXXVI, vol. 1, June 1984, pp. 35-45.

BAUER, R.A. et. al, How the Soviet System Works, Harvard University Press, Cambridge 1964.

BERLINER, J.S., Factory and Manager in the USSR, Havard University Press, Cambridge 1957.

BOISEVAIN, J., Friends of Friends, Blackwell, Oxford 1968.

DOUGLAS, M., Cultural Bias, Royal Antropological Institute, Occasional Paper, no. 35, London 1978.

Georgian SSR in Figures in 1975, Godu, Tbilisi 1976, (Russian).

GOLDMAN, M.I., Soviet Marketing, The Free Press, New York, 1963.

GOLDMAN, M.I., 'The Reluctant Consumer and Economic Fluctuations in the Soviet Union', Journal of Political Economy, vol. 73, no. 4, 1965, pp. 366-380.

GREER, T.V., Marketing in the Soviet Union, Praeger Publishers, New York, 1973.

HANSON, P., The Consumer in the Soviet Economy, MacMillan, London 1968.

LITVAK, J. et al., Georgian, Bukhara and Caucasian Jews-

Aliyah Potential towards the 1980's, Ministry of Absorption, Jerusalem 1981 (Hebrew).

MEAD, M., METRAUX, R., (eds), *The Study of Culture at a Distance,* The University of Chicago Press, Chicago 1953.

MARS, G., *Cheats at Work: An Anthropology of Workplace Crime,* Allen & Unwin, London 1982.

MARS, G., ALTMAN, Y., 'The Cultural Bases of Soviet Georgias Second Economy', *Soviet Studies,* vol. XXXV, no. 4, Oct. 1983.

MARS, G., ALTMAN, Y., 'Drinking and Feast Giving; Personal Network in Soviet Georgia', in Douglas, M. (ed), *The Anthropology of Drinking,* Cambridge 1985.

NOVE, A., *The Soviet Economic System,* G. Allen & Unwin, London 1977.

PAPASHVILY, G. H., *Home and Home Again,* Harper & Row Publishers, New York 1973.

ROBIN, K., 'Soviet Set New Goal: A Better Mousetrap', *US News,* no. 84, 1978, pp. 88-91.

SHAPIRO, J.P., 'The Soviet Consumer in the Brezhnev Era', *Current History,* vol. 75, 1978, pp. 100-103.

SKURSKI, R., 'The Buyer's Market and Soviet Consumer Goods Distribution', *Slavic Review,* vol. 31, 1972, pp. 817-830.

WILES, P.S.D., *The Political Economy of Communism,* Blackwell, Oxford 1962.

Effects of the new anti-Mafia law on the proceeds of crime and on the Italian economy

PINO ARLACCHI

1. CONFISCATION OF ILLEGALLY ACQUIRED ASSETS UNDER THE 'LA TORRE' LAW

On 13 September 1982, the Italian authorities enacted law No. 646, just a few days after the assassination at Palermo of General Dalla Chiesa, who had been sent to Sicily by the Government to fight against the mafia. This law is known to Italians as the 'La Torre Law', named after one of its founders, Pio La Torre, a member of Parliament who was also assassinated at Palermo by the mafia five months prior to Dalla Chiesa.

The La Torre Law, which represents the most recent anti-mafia regulation of the Italian State, includes two fundamental innovations:

(a) The introduction in the legal system of a new crime - the mafia conspiracy;

(b) The possibility for the courts to seize and to confiscate the goods of the persons belonging to the mafia conspiracy, as well as of relatives, partners and cohabitants who in the past five years have played a 'front man' role or cover-up role for the mafia.

With the inclusion of the mafia conspiracy crime in the Italian Penal Code, a serious regulation gap has been filled. In spite of its obvious danger, the mafia conspiracy had not been recognized by the Penal Code as a criminal phenomenon. As a result, many judges had not considered it a criminal association. The provisions contained in article 416 of the Penal Code concerning criminal association were suitable to cope with local and limited phenomena of associated delinquency, but not with organized crime (Macri, Macri, 1983; Turone, 1984).

The provisions of the La Torre Law with respect to seizure and confiscation of illegally acquired property are based on the updated analyses and knowledge of the modern mafia phenomena. The provisions of this law are intended to deal a blow to the accumulation of wealth by the mafiosi, which is the principal motivating force of the criminal activity on a large scale.

To arrive at the point of confiscation, the following procedure has been established: the District Attorney or the Chief of Police requests the police force to make inquiries into the standard of living, the financial status and the possession of property of the individuals who are suspected of belonging to criminal associations. Such investigations are directed to find out whether or not the property of the investigated person has been acquired legally. If sufficient circumstantial evidence indicates that the suspect's property has been acquired illegally, such property will be proposed for seizure. The proposal for seizure is either accepted or rejected by the court set up to judge such cases, and if such a proposal is accepted, the property is seized. Within a year, the same court must conclude the case and decide either to release the property or to order its definite confiscation.

2. PREMISE OF THE LA TORRE LAW

The premises of the La Torre Law should be considered in conjunction with the emergence of two phenomena that have modified the Italian economic structure over the past 10-15 years. The first was the establishment of an illegal sector of the economy which was brought about by the growth of the criminal activities of the Calabrian and Sicilian mafia and by the development of a vast internal illicit market of heavy drugs. As a result, the demand for criminal work increased. Such demand has been readily met by an increased supply of criminal work, favoured by two factors: unemployment among young people and the worsening of the situation in the South. While it is not appropriate in this article to elaborate on the most profitable branches of the illegal economy, it should be noted that in some areas of Western Sicily, for example at Palermo and Trapani, the income derived from illegal activity is estimated at approximately 15 to 20 percent of the total gross income, and that the illicit sale of drugs nation-wide exceeds 10,000 billion lire.

The second phenomenon is the increase in the number of mafia firms and entrepreneurs in the emerging sectors of the economy in the southern peninsula and Sicily. This development has taken place since the early 1970s. In the legitimate business, an increasing number of mafia entrepreneurs have moved into those branches of the economy that are characterized by weak technological and economic entrance barriers, by high profit rates and by high internal competition. Businesses having relations with mafia have managed to achieve particularly strong positions in the following market sectors: building trade, motor transport, agriculture, wholesale trade, various types of service activities and tourism. In Sicily, an attempt to revise the register of public contractors in 1980 enabled an estimate to be made of the percentage of owners of building firms with previous criminal records: there were 2,500 such firms out of 6,000, or 42 percent of the total number for the province (Corriere della Sera, 1980).

The element that played a crucial role in the expansion of the mafia power in the Italian economy is a very high level of interrelation between the legal and illegal sector of the economy. Labour, capital and methods of organization of the illegal sector have been transferred without great difficulty to the legal sector of the economy with the ordinary economic competition, endowing the mafia firms with an extensive capacity. Profits obtained from the legal sector of the economy have in turn been reinvested in the further expansion of criminal activities marked by very high entrance costs, such as the production and the distribution of heroin on a large scale. Each of the two sectors has functioned as an additional resource for the other.

Compared with the firms that do not belong to the mafia, one of the most important competitive advantages of mafia firms operating in the legal sector is the greater availability of their financial resources. The money necessary for the ambitious investment programmes conceived and in part accomplished by the mafia business during the 1970s and 1980s has not come from the accumulation of profits, as in ordinary business firms. The mafia entrepreneur has not saved to obtain the goods he needed, nor has he accumulated goods before starting his production. He has invested resources coming from elsewhere besides his personal patrimony. In his case, illegal activity has carried out the function of the banking system.

The impressive growth of the criminal activities of the mafia, which has taken place over the past 15 years at both the national and international levels, has enabled the mafia firms present on the legal markets to have a self-financing supply much greater than their own current dimensions and much larger than those of ordinary firms, which have often been suffocated by scarcity of funds and by the consequent subordination to financial capital.

3. RESULTS OF THE ENFORCEMENT OF THE LA TORRE LAW

The following few paragraphs present an examination of the impact of the La Torre Law on the illegal economy in Italy during the first 21 months of the enforcement of this law, covering the period from 1 October 1982 to 30 June 1984. It should be noted that the adoption of this law was followed by very harsh reactions on the part of those individuals whose interests were threatened. During 1983 there was a considerable downturn in the deposits of shares and currency in Sicilian banks. The withdrawal of capital from Sicilian banks was publicly revealed by the Chief Anti-mafia Commissioner; the amount of capital withdrawal was estimated at hundreds of billions of lire. Simultaneously, a strong legal and political counter-campaign was waged against the law, which was accused by the defending counsels of the _mafiosi_ of being unconstitutional and by some local politicians of being 'northern' and anti-Sicilian. In his report, presented on the occasion of the second anniversary of General Dalla Chiesa's death, the Chief Anti-Mafia Commissioner made the following comment on reactions to the enforcement of the La Torre Law:

"Resistance, sometimes evident, sometimes hidden, was not

lacking on the part of ... individuals, groups and economic environments ... because they, themselves, being
mafiosi, connected or associated with the mafia, were
afraid of the positive effects of the enforcement of
regulations aimed at revealing and destroying the profits
that had been acquired over the years through criminal
activity" (Alto Commissariato, 1984, p. 3).

In spite of such opposition and resistance, an assessment
of the results obtained during the first 21 months of the
enforcement of the La Torre Law shows that it cannot be
defined a failure. Table 1 shows that in four provinces -
Calabria, Campania, Lombardy and Sicily - property of suspicious origin was seized on 352 occasions during that period.
The total value of the seized property was estimated at 650
billion lire. In 108 cases, illegally acquired property was
confiscated and handed over to the State.

Table 1

Number of proposals for seizures, seizures carried out,
and confiscation of property according to the La Torre Law
during the period from 1 October 1982 to 30 June 1984

Proposals for seizures	Seizures carried out	Confiscations
1,183	352	108

Source: Alto Commissariato, Palermo, September 1984.

Taking into account the innovation established by the La
Torre Law within the particularly rigid penal system that
existed in Italy and the bulk of economic interests that
were affected, the enforcement of this law unexpectedly
achieved quite positive results; many people had anticipated
a reaction of rejection on the part of the legal institutions, who could have chosen to obstruct the enforcement of
this law for various reasons in a rather traditional legal
culture.
Table 1 indicates, however, that the courts were very
selective in deciding whether to accept or reject the proposals to seize property; the proposals were made by the
office of the District Attorney and the police. The courts
decided to order seizures in 29.7 percent of the proposals
for seizures, and investigations ended in the confiscation
of property in only 9.1 percent of the cases. This fact
probably implies a need for greater precision in the preliminary investigations and a greater concentration on assets
and on criminal activity of larger dimensions.
The analysis of the geographical distribution of the sei-

zures and confiscations carried out in accordance with the
La Torre Law reveals another interesting aspect of the
enforcement of this law. Table 2 shows that 98 percent of
the seizures were carried out in only four Italian provinces. Three provinces, Calabria, Campania and Sicily, are in
the South and Lombardy is in the North of Italy. In the rest
of the country, in spite of the recent diffusion of the
mafia and the establishment of its 'enclaves', as well as
its illicit investments and profits in many areas of central
and northern Italy, the new law has been substantially
ignored by the investigating authorities.

Table 2

Number and percentage of proposals for seizures, seizures
carried out and confiscations, by province, during the period from 1 October 1982 to 30 June 1984

Province	Proposals for seizures		Seizures (carried out)		Confiscations	
	Number	%	Number	%	Number	%
Calabria	471	39.2	31	8.1	8	7.4
Campania	165	13.8	56	15.6	–	–
Lombardy	177	14.8	19	5.3	11	10.2
Sicily	370	30.8	246	68.5	89	82.4
Other provinces	17	1.4	7	2.0	–	–
Whole country	1,200	100.0	359	100.0	108	100.0

Source: Alto Commissariato, Palermo, September 1984.

In two provinces, Calabria and Lombardy, the law was
effectively enforced. The government bodies of these two
provinces followed a strategy of using the investigative
resources against some of the most consistent criminal proceeds. The power and the prestige of one Calabrian family,
the most powerful among mafiosi, was seriously jeopardized
by seizures carried out by the local authorities. The seizure orders included the blocking of real estate and firms,
the value of which was estimated at approximately 44 billion
lire. This amount is estimated to be approximately half of
the entire assets that allegedly belong to some 100 members
of the mafia group called cosca.
   The greatest seizure of illegally acquired assets ever
carried out took place in Lombardy in February 1983. In this
action, all of the property owned by a Milan-based financial
group that was connected to the Sicilian and American mafia
was seized. The seizure included companies, hotels, commer-
cial and industrial firms, and banking and real estate

deposits, the value of which was estimated at approximately 250 billion lire.

4. POSSIBLE LONG-TERM CONSEQUENCES OF THE LA TORRE LAW

In the light of the analyses that have been carried out, possible long-term consequences of the developments in both the legal and illegal sectors of the economy in which the mafia firms operate in Italy can be predicted, and some of the consequences have already become evident. The new law has finally been able to set up a barrier between the legal market and the illegal market. Such a barrier was lacking in the Italian economy, which largely contributed to the competitive success of the firms and entrepreneurs of the mafia. The two markets (illegal and legal) might continue to operate, but under radically different conditions. The supply of additional resources represented by the use of capital and services of the mafia, and other components of the legal economy that originate in criminal activities, are likely to be exhausted or reduced to a minimum, and with such a development more just conditions for competition between mafia firms and other firms in the labour, money and goods markets should be re-established.

The division between the legal and illegal sectors of the economy is expected to coincide with the establishment of a hierarchy between them. If this law is effectively enforced, one of its effects is expected to be a strong increase in the risk inherent in any illegal business activity, with a consequent downflow from the market of the illicit investments of individuals active in the legal and respectable world of business. Such elements flowed together into the accumulation of the mafia's wealth during the boom years. Participation, even irregular or part-time, in mafia activities was made attractive by greater possibilities for economic mobility. Individuals who are prone to enter into such activity are, however, particularly sensitive to the threat of arrest and to the prospect of a clash with the legal system. Furthermore, they have fewer possibilities of defense and of manipulation than the actual mafia entrepreneurs (Arlacchi, 1983, pp. 167-173). This means that such individuals, unlike the professional criminals who run the increased risk of arrest with lesser intensity than other members of society, will be to a great extent influenced by the effects of the La Torre Law. The law can have the most painful consequences for such individuals, forcing them to rely on their own activities and, by accepting their own identity, to make a clearer distinction between the criminal economy and the legal economy, as well as between the mafia entrepreneurs and the world of law-abiding entrepreneurs. Finally, the La Torre Law may trigger a tendency among the mafia groups to move into more legitimate activities, a tendency which has not yet been seen among the Italian mafia.

The persistence in illegal activity for long periods of time can be convenient for the mafia entrepreneur only as

252

long as the regularity of the transactions and the security of ownership of property are guaranteed, and the advantages derived from the high profits of illicit production and trafficking are not eliminated. However, it is believed that in a prolonged situation of intense internal conflict caused by an uncertain distribution of markets and authority, and by growing pressure applied by the police and the magistracy, the risks involved in remaining in the illegal market may outweigh the interest to gain profits. Such a situation, in the long run, can help prevent the mafia from becoming more deeply involved in illegal activities and in the economy of the country.

It should be borne in mind that the mafia entrepreneurs, unlike other business entrepreneurs, cannot depend on the security of exchanges and on the rights of property guaranteed by laws and formal institutions. Society does not supply them with the services of law enforcement, such as the police and the courts, who are able to guarantee the respect of the contracts and to impose some essential rules to be followed in the business field. For this reason, the illegal markets operate on the basis of the relationships of trust and fear, of traditions, codes and conventions that have the aim of avoiding the costs of a continuous resort to force, which might result in interruptions in the flows of transactions. Such a situation is characterized by uncertain solutions with the constant danger of failure, which represents one of the most heavy restrictions to the growth of any illegal business activity.

In fact, there is no sense in continuing to reinvest forever in the circuit of the illegal market. Even if the rates of remuneration of invested capital are very high, the risk inherent in the practice of an entrepreneur's activity, which is not legally protected and which cannot be legally transferred, becomes too high at a certain point, so that it may automatically trigger a tendency towards the conversion of the assets and of the illicit activities into property shares protected by legal means. Therefore, the presence of an effective barrier between the illegal (or semi-legal) circuit and the sector of the economy has the following effects: it helps to control the acquisition and the reinvestment of the criminal wealth, and it reduces the amount of goods of illegal origin that become legitimate and that can be passed on by inheritance. The inquiries carried out in the United States of America into property passed on through inheritance by mafia leaders revealed that a surprisingly small amount of goods was inherited by the descendents of such individuals (Rogovin, 1983). This can perhaps help to explain the tendency among mafia leader to invest in higher education for their children to enable the children to enter into the respectable world. This was practised by many American mafiosi of the classical period.

The enforcement of the La Torre Law is a powerful means of reestablishing the equilibrium of relationships between the legal and illegal sectors of southern economy. The provisions in this law relating to the seizure and confiscation of assets illegally acquired can have disastrous effects on the security and on the business activities of the mafia entrepreneurs in both the illegal and legal economies. As a result, there could be a substantial shrinkage of the criminal economy in the entire southern peninsula and elsewhere (particularly with regard to heavy drug trafficking), and there could also be a general movement towards legitimate business activities on the part of mafia firms that operate in the legal markets.

The principal mafia groups should, therefore, be forced to make a rapid transfer of resources from the criminal to the legal sector, even if they are able to pass on to their own descendents the largest possible amount of those resources. A possible trend towards more legal business activity on the part of the mafia families might to a certain extent be explained by the entry of their own descendants into the élite of the normal economy as result of higher education and marriages with descendants of the more respectable strata of society, factors which seem to have played such an important role in the history of the American mafia (Bell, 1965; Ianni, 1972).

With regard to the mafia in Sicily and Calabria, however, the situation seems to have been somewhat different. The prevailing tendency here seems to have been the practice of a tight status endogamy. According to the author's research, out of 50 marriages of members among Sicilian and Calabrian families belonging to the mafia that took place from 1970 to 1980, 35 intermarriages occurred between descendents of those families, whereas 10 women and 5 men from families belonging to the mafia married descendants from families that did not belong to the mafia.

5. CONCLUSION

As result of the La Torre Law, there is a certain movement away from illegal activities and in the direction of legal activities and investment in financial affairs, rather than in more traditional areas such as real estate, agricultural and tertiary assets. Attention has been drawn to this tendency by magistrates who operate in the most important Italian financial markets. There are some proposals to modify the La Torre law by putting more emphasis on that part of the proceeds of crime which remain in the form of cash.

It is not likely, however, that such a tendency can be encouraged to the point of provoking a change of identity on the part of the mafia entrepreneurs. The mafiosi will most probably continue to keep their unique social and cultural features. They may not be inclined to give up easily their old territorial power, their intervention in the concrete political and economic life in order to transform themselves into financiers and speculators. The confiscation of the illegally acquired property and profits of crime will, consequently, remain for a long time the cornerstone of every effective struggle against the mafia.

NOTES

* The views expressed in this article, and selection and interpretation of facts, are the responsibility of the author and do not necessarily represent the views of the Italian Government.

REFERENCES

MACRI, C., MACRI, V., La Legge Antimafia, Jovene, Napoli 1983.
TURONE, G., Le Associazioni di Tipo Mafioso, Giuffré, Milano 1984.
Corriere della Sera, 10 October, 1980.
Considerazioni dell'Alto Commissario sullo Stato di Applicazione della Normativa Antimafia, Alto Commissariato, Palermo 1984.
ARLACCHI, P., La Mafia Imprenditrice l'Etica e lo Spirito del Capitalismo, Il Mulino, Bologna 1983, pp. 167-173.
ROGOVIN, G., Personal communication to the author, 1983.
BELL, D., 'Crime as an American Way of Life', The End of Ideology, Free Press, New York 1965.
IANNI, F., A Family Business, Routledge & Kegan Paul, London 1972.

Political trade-offs, collective bargaining, individual tradings: some remarks on industrial relations in Italy

BRUNO GRANCELLI

1. INTRODUCTION

Industrial relations in Italy operate in a socio-economic setting which seems to make the 'neo-corporative' solutions as impracticable as the 'neo-liberist' ones. The contradiction between the need for economic accumulation and maintaining social stability exists here perhaps more than in other countries, and in recent years has induced intense and even dramatic social conflicts. Yet a basic stability exists in this country.

How then is the problem of governability resolved? With what instruments of economic-social regulation? And how do such instruments complement one another in the present situation?

The studies of political exchange and trade-union activity, although numerous, give on the whole partial or unsatisfactory answers to these questions. It seems to me that the reason is to be found in the poor capacity to grasp the implications of current changes both in the economy and in the intentions and behaviours of social actors.

In the first part of the paper, I shall briefly review some aspects and problems of the Italian economic and social reality wrongly ignored or underestimated in the literature on political exchange. In the second part, I will point out some methodological weaknesses found in this literature - whether they concentrate on the state's role or on trade-union strategies. Finally, I will try to propose some short and fragmentary remarks that go beyond 'the neo-corporatist horizon'.

2. SOME FEATURES OF SOCIAL CHANGE IN THE 1970's

A great deal of important information on the social and economic changes is available in the annual reports of CENSIS and in the so called 'social-territorial analysis'. A first observation suggested by such research reports is that it would not be quite exact to say - as Tarrow (1960) does - that there was a 'challenge to capitalism' in Italy in the 1970's.

Indeed, at that time, the system of industrial relations underwent radical changes which were reflected to a certain measure even in the political equilibrium, opening the way to a relatively pro-labour government. (Accornero et al., 1977; Caloia, 1976); but this is only one side of the coin. At the same time, a series of phenomena were also taking shape which show that the 'challenged capitalism' has turned into a burgeoning capitalism. We shall remember, in particular, some which happened in production, the labour market and lastly in the attitudes and behaviour of the social actors.

In the industrial system, especially between 1972 and 1977, a series of mechanisms of adaptation were activated which have been gathered together under the heading of 'underground economy'. The fundamental process in this regard was undoubtedly the one of subcontracting from large to small enterprises: a process by which firms regained flexibility with respect to the changeable demands of the market and to the contractual and legislative constraints on the use of the labour force. Research on this subject, done mainly in the 1970's, has pointed out a great variety of productive situations and typologies (Varaldo, 1979; Ferrero, Scamuzzi, 1979; Luciano, 1979). For our argument, it may be sufficient to refer to two salient aspects of the functioning of small enterprises. The first is that the small enterprise born from subcontracting, decentralizes some entrepreneurial functions in its turn (administration and marketing, but also production), thus creating a variety of societary cross-breeds which bring about rather complex local economic systems characterized by flexibility and innovation capacity. (Saba, 1980; Ferrero, Scamuzzi, 1979; Luciano, 1979; Varaldo, 1979).

The second aspect is the absence of the typical hierarchies of capitalism, since the figures of the workers and entrepreneurs are not distinct, and passage from the former to the latter is rather common. In fact, many workers, having a qualification in demand in the labour market, may perform another activity which might constitute an intermediate stage in the transition from the status of dependent worker to the one of entrepreneur or artisan (Saba, 1980; Potestà, Barsotti, 1983).

It seems evident that not one, not two, but no less than four 'representative enterprises' exist in our productive system: the traditional capitalist enterprise, the public one, that of 'assisted capitalism', and the small enterprise with less than 15 dependents. We may note that in the past decade it has been this last type of enterprise in particular which has shown the greatest dynamism and capacity to make increases in industrial employment. And this has also happened by taking advantage of the failures of the state-assisted capitalism: a process which is particularly evident in certain areas of the South where the selection of enterprises to which incentive would be granted occurred not on the basis of entrepeneurial capacity, but rather of political and client-oriented criteria. The consequences, in brief, have been: the formation of a frail and corrupt industrial fabric, the diffusion of corruption and parasitism, and chain failures of subsidized enterprises. Yet, paradoxically, it was precisely the failure of the traditional model which laid the conditions for a diffusion of the 'submerged' industry, even in certain zones of the South. In fact, the crisis of the assisted enterprises and the consequent diffusion of the Cassa Integrazione Guadagni (Fund for the Integration of Earnings) has made a good many qualified workers available in the unofficial market, for whom payment of social security was not necessary (Saba, 1980).

So, in the past decade, the productive system has developed a series of adaptation mechanisms which have assured a certain 'flexibility amidst precariousness' by means of subcontracting production as well as developing a tertiary sector through small enterprises and forms of cottage industry (CENSIS, 1982, 1983).

3. MOONLIGHTING AS SOCIAL SHOCK ABSORBER

The phenomena briefly reviewed above provoked in their turn some transformations in the labour market. Among the most important and significant, the growth of the various forms of non-institutional work should be highlighted. We may in fact note that in the analyses of the labour market and its transformation, the prevailing tendency is to take into consideration only the government and trade-union interventions in the matter of employment and use of the labour force. In any case, there are several studies which throw light on the fact that the decision-making centers are not only found at the institutional and trade-union level. Family is equally important because it emerges that it does not exclusively fulfil the function of reproduction of the labour force, but that it also controls the quantity, times and modes of distributing the labour services. In other words, the family unit, on the basis of its own needs, divides the time of its members between production and domestic reproduction in terms of salaries earned and services produced (Paci, 1979).

Between the family and the local productive system, then, a sort of 'reciprocal reinforcement' is exercised, in the sense that even the weaker quotas of the labour force (young and elderly people, women) may exercise a productive function and contribute to increasing the family income. At the same time, the family guarantees a reduction in the costs of reproduction of the labour force, as well as flexibility in the supply of manpower (Barsotti, Potestà, 1983). More generally, we may say that in Italy the combination of resources offered by welfare, the market and family members - quite different from one territory to another - appears to be one of the fundamental mechanisms of the survival of a Welfare System in crisis (Balbo, 1981).

But the family fulfils yet another function regarding the productive system based on small enterprises in that it provides micro-entrepreneurial energies wherever the socio-cultural contexts encourage the head of the family to assume the role of self-employed worker (Ardigò, Donati, 1976; Paci, 1979). And, as has been seen, an intermediary stage in this direction often seems to comprise the second jobs of

the heads of family employed in small or middle-sized enterprises. It should be added, however, that the diffusion of a
second job is certainly not a peculiarity of local systems
based on small enterprises. Even in the areas where big
public and private corporations dominate, second jobs appears to be widespread, provided that productive structure,
organization of services and infrastructures, characteristics of the labour force and family models, create favourable conditions (Barsotti, Potestà, 1983).

Some observations should be made regarding the characteristics of the labour force, bearing in mind the informa-
tions provided by recent research. The first regards the
quantitative aspect: on the whole, the estimation is that
from a fifth to a third of all dependent workers have a
second job. The second observation relates to the socio-
professional characteristics of the worker with a second
job, who is generally male, between 26 and 35 years old in
the urban- industrial context, or between 40 and 50 years
old in the 'suburban' one, has completed obligatory school-
ing, is paid slightly above the average in the first job,
and possesses an average-to-high level of qualification
(Barsotti, Potestà, 1983; Gallino, 1982).

The explanations proposed by the authors who have investigated the phenomena of 'moonlighting' are also quite
interesting. Such phenomena perform three types of
functions. The first is that of a functional substitute for
the career, measured in terms of income, professional prestige, autonomy and qualification in the main profession (L.
Gallino, 1982). In fact, the profile of the double worker
which emerges from this research is that of a subject able
to organize his own resources efficiently in terms of time
and information. Furthermore, a subject of this type appears
to belong to political parties more than the average - at
least in some areas. An interpretive hypothesis relative to
these two apparently contradictory facts is that in Italy
political parties control an increasing amount of resources
and information. Belonging to parties which govern at the
central or local level means, therefore, having an additional quota of opportunity for upward mobility (Milanaccio,
1982).

The function of the second job as a vehicle for social
mobility is tied to one aim of containing industrial conflict and maintaining social integration. The workers who
perform a second activity may thus enjoy at the same time
the advantages of the system of guarantees on one hand, and
socio-economic opportunities supplied by the unofficial work
market on the other:

"Industrial relations in public and private sectors are
thus rid of the burden of the political trade-union
demands and the relative conflictuality which could originate from this minority group ... Thus some space is
left for the individualistic mechanisms of consensus next
to the collective ones, and almost as to their guarantee,
with great benefit from a political system like the
Italian one, which has sustained its own fortunes and

standstills on the balanced dosages of both mechanisms". (Gallino, 1982, p. 352)

A third function performed by the second job is that of modifying social stratification, which passes from a pyramid form to one like a spinning top, typical of post-industrial societies:

"So, the second job appears to be one of the instruments, even if distorted, submerged and ungoverned, of a process of modernization which the families practice with respect to institutional opportunities which are offered to them". (Gallino, 1982, p. 228)

From the research on informal economy one may draw the conclusion that the qualities of articulation and flexibility in the socio-economic fabric have been shown to be just as decisive in facing the economic crisis as the inadequacy of state institutions. But these are not only mechanisms of adaptation. The variety of social interests, the diverse motivations of individual and collective social actors have brought about a true evolutionary process which may be summarized in the following terms.

Beginning with the late seventies, the intense action of the four fundamental factors in the process of adaptation of the preceding years was consolidated. These factors are interwoven and reciprocally reinforced, inducing an unplanned process of development made up of adaptation, familyism, small dimensions, localism: all factors which are deeply rooted in Italian history. It follows that the economic and social system acquired a continuously more articulated and polycentric character, appearing as an archipelago of local realities (CENSIS, 1982; Bagnasco, 1977).

4. THE 'RUSTING' OF POLITICAL INSTITUTIONS AND THE 'POLYCEN-
   TRISM OF SOCIAL POWER'

The above-mentioned processes are important from our point of view for two fundamental reasons. The first is an increase in the number of decisional centers which influence economic and social development. The second is that references for individual and collective decisions fall more frequently at the local rather than national level. At this latter level, a series of phenomena defined as 'rusting' of the institutions has taken place. Its causes are diverse and they go back in time. In short, we may say that these take us back to the ways in which the direct and indirect costs of disorderly economic development have been reversed back to the state, just as in governative methods in which assistential-clientary logic has always been dominant (CENSIS, 1982). It happened, for example, that the employment difficulties regarding especially educated young people were confronted, on the one hand, with laws which proved to be ineffective, and, on the other, with mass hiring in the public sector. The purely quantitative development of state

bureaucracy could not in its turn but accelerate the contradiction between the institutional objectives of state administration and the interests of public employees defended by
a corporative trade-unionism (CENSIS, 1983). Furthermore, an
analysis of the functioning of state institutions illustrates the general situation characterized by a multitude of
organisms, each of which is capable of resisting coordination but not of imposing it on the others. Consequently, the
different institutional subjects act in a disarticulated way
and pursue area interests in a context of generalized anarchy (Ferraresi, 1983).

For an institutional situation such as in Italy, the
social and cultural conditions are lacking which in other
countries favoured the emergence of programmed experiences
and 'neo-corporative' models. Instead, a social structure
and political culture developed which favoured the emergence, in the second half of the sixties, of a 'contracted
democracy' characterized by joint practices at the par-
liamentary level without a complex of government institutions being able to orient the economic development with
legitimate and effective decisions (Rusconi, Scamuzzi,
1979). We could say that a political trade-off took place,
but 'without the state', since the latter was not able to
guarantee that the counterparts maintain their promises, nor
to stipulate independent bilateral agreements with the interest groups (Ferraresi, 1983). The essence of this type of
political exchange was the compensation with public funds of
the various subjects harmed by the failure to solve the
economic and social problems. The state asked the entrepreneurs not to let the enterprises adopt decisions which might
fuel the collective conflict. In exchange, immunity regarding transfer of financial resources and in general various
forms of illegal behaviour was offered. In addition, several
types of compensation were conceded for the 'improper'
burden born by the enterprises for the solution of certain
social problems. On the whole, we may speak of a long series
of 'assistential trade-offs' oriented towards the realization of pro tempore consensuses (Caselli, 1983). The results
have been tangible in terms of containing social conflicts
but were nonetheless paid for in terms of inefficiency and
waste of resources.

The whole of the phenomena which we have rapidly alluded
to gives rise to a type of society in which more and more
numerous and vital actors interact economically. Yet in the
face of this 'polycentrism of social power' it becomes more
and more evident that there is a crisis of roles and identity, not only in public institutions but in intermediate
subjects as a well, such as parties and trade-unions which
constitute the basis of the relationship between society and
government institutions (CENSIS, 1982). The definition of
'anarchic centralisms' for the Italian institutional system
seems therefore appropriate (Gallino, 1979).

The absence of a central power capable of stabilizing
beforehand the objectives and rules of the game of political
exchange, and of verifying interests and behaviour of the
social actors on this basis, exposes the society to the risk

that the less positive aspects of individualism and parti-
cularism prevail. In other words, Italian society runs the
risk of becoming a 'society of compliance' in which "shel-
tered from the law, far from power, one may make a little
space for small illegalities and the sweetness of living"
(CENSIS, 1982, p. 51).

In the face of the tendencies quoted above, however,
tendencies of a different sort are taking shape. The most
important event concerning our arguments was the agreement
of January 1983 between government, enterprise associations
and trade-unions. This agreement seems to mark a change in
industrial relations and political exchange for two basic
reasons. In the first place, triangular negotiation is set
in motion on the themes of labour and employment policies.
In the second place, among the different parties, control
procedures on the dynamics of salaries are agreed upon. Thus
a significant step towards policy-making is made, based on
accords between big interest groups and the government (Cella, 1983).

What significance does this triangular negotiation have,
which has provoked and continues to provoke so many pole-
mics? Does it really mark a turning point in industrial
relations? Are political trade-off and agreements destined
to assume more and more relevance and systematicity?

Here, no answers will be directed to the above questions.
I will simply confine myself to proposing some preliminary
methodological considerations which may perhaps be useful in
underlining several analytical weaknesses which may be found
in the literature on political exchange.

5. BEYOND THE NEO-CORPORATIST HORIZON ...

Some socio-economic processes, which have taken place in
Italy in the past decade and which I have briefly alluded
to, have induced some scholars to express the need to go
'beyond the neo-corporatist horizon' (Carrieri, Donolo,
1983). These authors set out with some considerations on the
changes in the scenario of political trade-offs and collective bargaining currently in progress. We shall briefly
review them, and in so doing we may detract something from
the analysis in terms of coherence and formal rigour, but
add perhaps a greater degree of realism.

The state, because of its enormous budget deficit, finds
itself in the face of growing difficulties in managing
welfare policies and distributing financial resources to the
economic system. On the other hand, the demand of the market
encourages the enterprise, whether small or medium-large,
towards a recovery of competitivity and flexibility which
provokes the elimination of numerous workers from the productive process.

Faced with these events, trade-unions used to acting in
relation to state intervention in the economy find themselves deprived of substitute resources right at the moment
collective bargaining becomes much less practicable than in
the past. In the political market, a transition to a 'reces-

sion trade-off' is going on. The consequences are reduction
(or non-increases) of the salaries on the one hand and
maintenance/readjustment of some social guarantees on the
other (Carrieri, Donolo, 1984). But that is not all. The
government also tends to 'immunize' itself in some way
against trade-union pressures by resorting to different
intermediaries for the organization of consensus. The same
thing happens even at the enterprise level where the entrepreneurs tend more and more to manage the new phase of
productive restructuring independently.

To sum up, the employment crisis, and the demands of the
political system regarding the costs of labour, bring the
trade-union to a crisis of representation, which means a
crisis of effectiveness due to the limitation of their
internal resources.

In their turn, the diminished representativity and poor
effectiveness of action are linked to the orientation crisis
due to the scarce capability which trade-union officers demonstrate in understanding mutations in Italian society.

This sort of analysis is important because it throws light
on the reasons why state and industrialists manage to 'immunize' themselves against the trade-union, thus determining
a more marginal destiny for it. But this analysis is also
partial because it passes over the different behaviours of
working people.

According to Carrieri and Donolo, in the face of the
representation crisis of trade-unions, three basic types of
grass-root unionism seem to emerge. The first is the 'hyper-
responsible' type, ready to accept centralized negotiation
and forms of agreement. The second is the 'irresponsible'
type, made up of workers who manifest free-rider attitudes
and behaviour. Finally, the third is a non-worker type of
unionism - for social extraction, culture and claimant menta-
lity of rank and files. In this third case, we have subjects
who often perform new types of activities similar to those
of self-employed workers, which implies preference for flexibility, autonomy in the market and appreciation of professionality. These are subjects who manifest a propensity for
non-union, non-collective protection.

Carrieri and Donolo point out that in the eighties, the
three types of unionism will tend to co-exist together with
a plurality of individual ways for safeguarding living and
working conditions. Yet they do not provide any conceptual
or methodological indications for the analysis of these new
situations. Therefore, I would like to propose here some
preliminary remarks on the subject.

6. ... BEARING IN MIND THAT A LOT OF WAGE EARNERS ARE POLICY
   KEEPERS AND MARKET PARTICIPANTS AS WELL

If we consider the 'neo-corporatist' literature as a whole,
we may observe that throughout the sixties a shift in perspective takes place. In an early phase, in fact, the attention is prevalently concentrated on the state considered as
the agent who assumes initiative at the political and econo-

mic level, involving major interest groups in the decision-making process (Lehnbruch, 1961; Panitch, 1981). Afterwards, criticism of the presumed 'functionality' of the neo-corporative assets leads to shifting attention from state interests and initiatives to the objectives and strategies of the trade-union and worker movement.

Now, even though the two perspectives quoted above present diverse analytical points of view, they share some postulates. One is that which relates the practicability of political exchange to the autonomy of the representatives from the represented (Pizzorno, 1977). On the basis of this postulate, organizational devices and centralization of bargaining allow union representatives ample autonomy in interpreting and defending the interests of the represented. The possibility for organizations to formulate strategies in the field of the political market is derived from this autonomy (Mutti, 1983).

The postulate of autonomy of the representatives from the represented is doubtlessly acceptable. The fact is that it seems to be accompanied by another implicit postulate, namely, that the represented do not have substantially any autonomy in relation to the representatives, so that, in the event of dissatisfaction, they would be limited to protesting or withdrawing from the organization. In reality, it is not so, or rather it is not exclusively so, because even the represented have often sufficient resources for developing strategies of self-protection and improvement of material conditions. Departing from this fact, one may begin to develop a third analytical perspective which also considers strategic behaviours which social actors set in action without the mediation of state institutions and representative organizations.

A first step in this direction should be the analysis of the processes of industrialization and modernization, focusing in particular on the consequences of the balance between the articulation of social demand and its politico-institutional management.

Important steps in this direction may be found in studies which attribute the same importance to state, associations, the market, and habit as mechanisms for allocating resources (Streek, Schmitter, 1983; Trigilia, 1981, 1983). In these studies, the specific character of each society is reconstructed, beginning with the degree of development and role played by each of the four allocation mechanisms. Concerning the state's role in economic and social regulation, how the political centralization/decentralization may be put in relation to characteristics assumed by the labour movement is emphasized. For each country considered, the concrete interactions which have taken place historically between labour and institutional structures are thus studied.

The novel element in these studies lies in the fact that the variables used in the research of the labour movement are no longer only those typically found in 'neo-corporatist' literature, such as degree of centralization, relations between unions and pro-labour parties, etc. The strength or weakness of labour is evaluated above all in relation to characteristics of the social context using variables of a high degree of generalization, such as the 'proletarization degree' of social structure. The dimensions used have been objective rather than subjective types. Among the first, the expropriation of the means of production from the property is considered, as well as the degree of autonomy in the labour process and community uprooting. Among the second ones, subjective perceptions concerning the possibility of modifying the socio-economic situation with collective action, space for social mobility, possibilities of increasing earnings and professionality through insertion into the informal economy, etc. (Trigilia, 1982). As to the institutional tradition, factors examined are the structure and functioning of the channels of political representation, local government and centralized bureaucratic organizations.

On the basis of the criteria of analysis mentioned above, the Italian situation has been characterized by a dichotomy between two fundamental areas. The first, called 'areas of proletarization', in which big enterprises as well as big urban areas prevail, would see the prevalence of collective claims by the organized labour movement. The second, called 'area of non-proletarization', is where the small enterprise prevails, access to autonomous work is facilitated, and the family performs the significant role of not only social reproduction but also of production. In this field, forms of 'individualistic mobilization and local political trade-off would prevail as the outcome of a 'class compromise' at the territorial level, given the impractibility of a 'Keynesian compromise' at the national level (Trigilia, 1981, 1983).

This sort of research has the merit of underlining the importance of the territorial dimension in tranformations of the national political system. The movement towards 'politicization of territory' with forms of local political exchange would then be the outcome of two trends, namely, a weakening of the union, and crisis of the welfare state. But the socio-territorial analysis has another methodological advantage: it introduces the distinction between extension and the actual weight of the politico-administrative mechanisms in allocating resources. This means that in each national context, one has to verify how wide the field of action of state intervention is in social economic regulation with respect to the action mechanisms of the market or community structures. But it also means that the distinction between center and periphery can be proposed on the inside of politico-administrative allocation (Trigilia, 1982).

What does not appear very convincing, however, is the dichotomization between two areas: one where the centralized political exchange and collective bargaining have more power, and the other where individualistic mobilization of the social actors prevails together with political trade-off on a territorial basis (Mutti, 1983).

Recent research throwing light on new forms of social differentiation stemming from the informal economy focuses on the behaviour of social actors with more precision than the social territorial analysis. This new acquisition is in fact relative to the possibilities of individuals to participate in a variety of social dimensions and functions. This acquisition derives from the surpassing of marxist and functionalist foundations - according to which the processes of industrialization and modernization tend to nullify all pre-existing forms of economic and social organization. In reality, many of these forms are preserved by subjects involved in economic and social transformations in order to maintain certain freedom of action in work and free time (Gallino, 1979; Capecchi, Pesci, 1983). This is an important methodological point, since it permits us to understand relations among social actors, interest groups, and state institutions with greater precision and realism.

Italian society today appears quite differentiated. This differentiation assumes the aspect of a variety of professional roles due to the development of the social division of labour. But research on the informal economy highlights another important factor, namely, the opening up of social spaces in which individuals move. This means that professions no longer identify the class standing of individuals, from which certain consequences would be derived in terms of orientation, needs and interests (Gallino, 1979).

The notion of social differentiation requires a level of analytical depth which neither functionalist nor marxist sociology are able to provide (Capecchi, Pesce, 1983). Let us consider, for example, the concept of social formation. Today a rather widespread agreement exists in individuating the co-presence of different social formations in contemporary Italian society. According to Gallino, we may individuate four, known as 'traditional', 'capitalistico-entrepreneurial', 'capitalistico-oligopolistic' and 'state formation'. The latter is characterized by the fact that the 'productivity' option has been substituted with the 'employment' option, and by the fact that political and administrative criteria for allocating resources clearly prevails over those of the market. The political organization, mode of production, and socio-cultural reproduction present a unique specificity on the inside of the four formations, even if common traits exist due to the ordering of the state (Gallino, 1979).

What methodological suggestions may be drawn from the research on the informal economy? Is seems to me that the analysis of industrial relations could gain advantages at two levels. The first concerns the relations between representational organizations and the individuals represented, and the second the state's role in the Italian society used to "surviving without a government".

Some studies on the politics of interest groups highlight how the formation of representational organizations make these politics possible but also precarious. Possible, because it provides formal and stable intermediaries; precarious, because its presence transforms the nature of interests, introducing new ones which are not identical to the preference of the individual. From here, a growing possibility for changing the demand and therefore giving unsatisfactory responses to the needs of the represented (Pasquino, 1983).

The areas where the action of interest groups brings about changes are numerous. A reference to those changes which interfere with the identity of social actors may be sufficient for pointing out a further methodological deficiency in the analysis of political exchange.

According to Schmitter (1983), recent history indicates a tendency towards increasing institutionalization of interest groups, and there is nothing to object to in this statement. This author adds, however, that organizations manage interests which were previously managed by individuals with the help of natural collectivities (families, relatives, etc.). And here one may object. It has already been sufficiently demonstrated that the institutionalization of interest representation has not at all substituted the traditional forms of self-protection. Different forms of interest intermediation co-exist and are combined by the social actors according to the constraints and resources available in their field of action - that is, according to the degree of autonomy they have. A typical example is the phenomenon of double jobs, which often appears as daily commuting from one social formation to another, and assures the satisfaction of needs of people involved which the union is not able - or does not have the interest - to guarantee, like professionality and social mobility (Gallino, 1982; Gruppo di Pisa, 1983; Milanaccio, 1983).

At the methodological level, it follows - as has already been said - that it is not enough to postulate only autonomy of the interest groups with respect to the state. Autonomy of the represented from their representatives must also be taken into consideration. This new acquisition enables us to point out two other limits in the 'neo-corporatist' theories. The first is that of considering only the main socio-economic groups of producers on the basis of their standing and function in the division of labour. This limit has been emphasized in critical analyses of 'neo-corporatist' literature (Mutti, 1983). But this analysis is not able to overcome another weak point in the approach which has been criticized, namely, that of considering the trade-union and pro-labour parties as the only resources of workers.

But what emerges today is that social actors do not express their demands only in their professional field, but also by taking into account their role as customers, consumers, etc. (Gallino, 1979). Moreover, for many of them, organization, ideology and collective participation are less and less important because they are interested not only in the strengthening of their collective identity but also in the affirmation of their individual identity. This affirmation may be realized by means of personal initiative in the market (official or unofficial). In other words, many unionized workers are not only policy-keepers but also market participants (Paci, 1981).

To sum up, from the methodological remarks mentioned above, we may draw a research strategy on industrial relations which takes into account information supplied by research on different territorial realities, and on the informal economy. More precisely, the possibility of develop-ping intermediate interpretative models should be verified, which associate formal and informal aspects of social relations in specific areas (Bagnasco, 1981). Such models should bear in mind the following facts:

a) the existence in Italy of different social formations;
b) the different relative influence that local and centralized political exchanges have in every social formation;
c) political trade-off and collective bargaining have not historically overcome the atomistic trade-off, but rather they intertwine themselves with it;
d) social actors tend to adopt a wide variety of instruments for improving their living and working conditions, and do not have the union and pro-labour parties as the sole resource.

These models should then take into account that the Italian reality is two-faced, where the emerged and submerged facets intertwine in a complex fashion (CENSIS, 1982), a reality that cannot be understood by analyzing only the behaviour of collective actors - the state and interest groups - but which also requires an analysis of individual behaviour in specific social and organizational contexts.

REFERENCES

ACCORNERO, A., et al., Movimento sindacale e società italiana, Feltrinelli, Milano, 1977.
ARDIGO', A., DONATI, P.P., Famiglia e industrializzazione. Continuità e discontinuità negli orientamenti di valori in una comunità a forte sviluppo endogeno, F. Angeli, Milano 1976.
BAGNASCO, A., Tre Italie. La problematica dello sviluppo territoriale italiano, Il Mulino, Bologna 1977.
BAGNASCO, A., 'La questione dell'economia informale', Stato e mercato, vol. I, 1981.
BALBO, L., 'L'organizzazione familiare in alcune situazioni urbane', Inchiesta, vol. 49-50, 1981.
CALOIA, A., 'Industrial Relations in Italy: Problems and Perspectives', British Journal of Industrial Relations, vol. 2, 1979.
CAPECCHI, V., PESCE, A., 'Se la diversità è un valore', In chiesta, vol. 49-50, 1983.
CARRIERI, M., DONOLO, C., 'Sindacati e sistema politico (Italia: 1975-1983)', Giornale di Diritto del Lavoro e di Relazioni Industriali, vol. 22, 1984.
CARRIERI, M., DONOLO, C., 'Oltre l'orizzonte neo-corporatista. Alcuni scenari sul futuro politico del sindacato', Stato e mercato, vol. 9, 1983.
CASELLI, L., 'Scambio politico: l'impresa', Prospettiva Sindacale, vol. 3, 1983.
CELLA, G.P., 'Relazioni industriali: segnali di svolta', Prospettiva sindacale, vol. 3, 1983.
CENSIS, Gli anni del cambiamento. Il rapporto sulla situazione sociale del paese dal 1976 al 1982, F. Angeli, Milano 1982.

CENSIS, XVII rapporto sulla situazione sociale del paese, F. Angeli, Milano 1983.

FERRARESI, F., 'Uno scambio politico senza stato?', Prospettiva Sindacale, vol. 3, 1983.

FERRERO, F., SCAMUZZI, S., L'industria in Italia: la piccola impresa, Editori Riuniti, Roma 1979.

GALLINO, L., 'Effetti dissociativi dei processi associativi', Quaderni di Sociologia, 1979.

GALLINO, L., Occupati e bioccupati. Il doppio lavoro nell'area torinese, Il Mulino, Bologna 1982.

HIRSCH, J., Developments of the Political System of West Germany, in Scase, R. (ed), The State in Western Europe, Crom Helm, London 1980.

LANGE, P., TARROW, S., Italy in Transition. Conflict and Consensus, Cass F. & Co., London 1980.

LUCIANO, A., 'I rapporti non competitivi fra le imprese', Politica ed Economia, vol. 3, 1979.

MILANACCIO, A., 'Gli orientamenti politici dei bioccupati', Il Mulino, vol. 4-5, 1982.

MUTTI, A., Stato e scambio politico, Ed. Lavoro, Roma, 1983.

PACI, M., 'Struttura di classe e complessità sociale', Inchiesta, Nov.-Dec., 1981.

PACI, M., Famiglia e mercato del lavoro in una economia periferica, F. Angeli, Milano 1979.

PASQUINO, G., (ed), Le società complesse, Il Mulino, Bologna 1983.

PIZZORNO, A., Scambio politico e identità collettiva nel conflitto di classe, in Crouch, C., Pizzorno, A., (eds), Conflitti in Europa. Lotte di classe, sindacati e stato dopo il 68, Etas Libri, Milano 1977.

RUSCONI, G.E., SCAMUZZI, S., 'Italy: An Eccentric Society', Current Sociology, vol. 1, 1981.

POTESTA', L., BARSOTTI, O., (eds), Segmentazione del mercato del lavoro e doppia occupazione. Il doppio lavoro nell'area pisana, Il Mulino, Bologna 1983.

SABA, A., L'industria sommersa. Il nuovo modello di sviluppo, Marsilio, Padova 1980.

SCASE, R., (ed), The State in Western Europe, Crom Helm, London 1980.

SCHMITTER, P.C., Organizzazioni degli interessi e rendimento politico, in Pasquino, G. (1983).

STREECK, W., SCHMITTER, P.C., 'Private Interest Government: Order Beyond or Between Community, Market and State', report to the Sixth Colloquium of the European Group for Organizational Studies, Firenze, 3-5 Nov. 1983.

TRIGILIA, C., 'Struttura di classe e sistema politico: neo-corporativismo o neo-localismo?', Inchiesta, vol. 46-47, 1980.

TRIGILIA, C., 'Modernizzazione, accentramento e decentramento politico', Stato e mercato, vol. 4, 1982.

VARALDO, A., (ed), Ristrutturazioni industriali e rapporti fra le imprese, F. Angeli, Milano 1979.

WIRKLER, J.T., L'economia corporativa: teoria e gestione, in Maraffi M., (ed), La società neo-corporativa, Il Mulino, Bologna 1981.

The informal work of industrial workers. Present situation, trend prognosis and policy implications

J. JESSEN, W. SIEBEL, C. SIEBEL-REBELL, U.–J. WALTHER, I. WEYRATHER

I. INTRODUCTION

This paper reports on an empirical project about household strategies. Our research deals with the so called informal economy in the self-provisioning of working-class households. In our research we look at four questions. Firstly, what kinds of informal work can be found? Secondly, in what way has informal work changed? Thirdly, to what extent does informal work cause an internal differentiation between industrial workers? Fourthly, what subjective experience do the workers associate with formal and informal work, and to what extent are both fields of work experience referred critically to each other?

This paper does not discuss our particular research questions. Rather, it takes issue with two central theses which, in our view, govern the discussion about the informal economy:

1. The first thesis states that the so-called informal sector is growing quantitatively. At least implicitly, it has been argued that a radical change is taking place in the process of socialization. Social change used to be described in terms of more and more state involvement, and less and less _oikos_, i.e. self-provisioning at home. Now the thesis is advanced that the informal sector is growing, namely relatively to the formal sector. This, however, assumes that the process of socialization has been reversed.

2. The second thesis is the assumption that informal economy is an alternative resource, with the help of which labour market problems and socio-political problems could be solved.

On both theses we take the opposite view: The change of informal work is to be described as a _qualitative change_ rather than quantitative growth. And while this change is taking place, informal work _loses its independence_ of the formal economy.

The informal economy is a very diffuse object. There is only little reliable information available on the different forms of informal work and on its reasons and motives on the micro-analytical level. This lack of knowledge can give rise

to very far-reaching and speculative theses which are illustrated with spectacular phenomena: new self-employment,
increase in illicit or "black" labour. The first part of the
paper attempts to throw some light on the different forms of
informal work. It should be emphasized that we treat informal work as a very common and rather traditional phenomenon.
Our research is on the work industrial workers do outside
formal employment. For them informal work has always been a
natural part of their self-provisioning. Thus, if our
results differ in parts from those often presented in the
discussion on the informal economy, this certainly is also
due to the specific part of the broad spectrum of informal
economy that we examined. We conducted qualitative interviews with 120 shipyard workers which lasted between two and
five hours. Our sample is split twice, according to work situation (skilled and semi-skilled categories) and living
situation (urban and rural areas). The statistical limits of
this kind of empirical base are obvious. After all, the
study is not finished yet and we can only present working
hypotheses.

2. PRESENT SITUATION - WHAT KIND OF INFORMAL WORK DO IN-
   DUSTRIAL WORKERS DO?

Informal economy is usually divided in three parts: illegal
production, legal household production, community production. Our results confirm the outstanding importance of
household production, which is that part of productive work
outside the company where unit of production and unit of
consumption are identical. Only 15 percent of our interviewees are involved in illicit work in order to increase their
income. But more than half of the interviewees is busily
employed in big projects of household production mobilizing
considerable and complex resources, most of all, of course,
with regard to house-building but also regarding the building of big boats, hothouses and the like.
   When looking at the spectrum of informal work, a steady
range of "basic" activities becomes obvious, which are done
almost without exception by everybody. This range of activities includes maintenance, repair and improvement work on
one's flat, car and consumer durables.
   Apart from this there is a manifold spectrum of work
activities outside formal employment. The time spent on
these activities varies from very sporadic to a second full
working day. Correspondingly, the economic effects range
from marginal savings to larger possessions. In extreme
cases, workers have thus acquired two houses or receive an
income more than doubling their wages. Beyond the basic
range of work activities this spectrum of informal work
varies, less so according to the individual's working situation in the company and the phase in his life cycle. Informal work varies primarily according to his living conditions, i.e. urban or rural area, city or country. As expected, house and garden are the main places of activity (workshop) the main object (expanding and rebuilding) and goal of

informal work: hardly any of the shipyard workers got a house of his own without contributing his own work and substantially mobilising informal networks. During this very long phase of mobilising all resources, holidays, shift work and overtime are often adjusted to the demands made by the informal work as to time and money. This means that the generally assumed determination of the living situation by the work situation is reversed - as far as there is room for this reversal (viz. overtime, shift schedules, holidays).

When using variations in living conditions as a central explanation for the considerable differences in informal work done, do we point to more than the trivial difference between the spatial and legal possibilities of flat tenants and houseowners? Pointing to house and garden as the points of crystallization of a specific rural way of living, however, implies more than this triviality. Owning a house is not just the material prerequisite for this way of living but its most frequent and conspicuous result. This way of living, which makes it possible for the worker to acquire a house and garden of his own, includes very heterogeneous components:

- Obviously low real estate prices are required, a steady earned income, trust in the soundness of the social network, i.e. a number of objective conditions without which even rural inhabitants do not venture to build or purchase a house.

- A specific rural form of post-adolescence is required. Even after marriage young workers in the country often continue living with their parents until their first child is born, having to pay only little for board and lodging, which enables them to save up a lot of money. In the city this phase of life is characterized rather by extensive consumption.

- Marriage partners must be conceived as cooperating producers; husband and wife are ready to save and work towards one goal for up to 20 years.

- A social capital in the form of kin networks, making it possible to procure qualified labour, workshops, tools, materials, money.

- Specific concepts of action like "the growing house" gradually being built according to one's money and working potential.

Thus, in the case of shipyard workers, city and country are not just two types of residence but two modes of living, in the course of which individual factors, in the long run, form a pattern of biography and the result of which usually is the house or other material possessions.

In so far as the more important and bigger projects of household production in particular are to be understood as an integral part of a certain lifestyle, they cannot be explained in terms of the classical model of homo economicus. Using a term developed by Thompson, we therefore speak of the informal labour of industrial workers as being part of a moral economy. That is to say, an economy partly or even primarily based on rules of conduct, on notions of the right way of living, thus on economically relevant acting guided by social norms, and in this respect only partially based on economic-rational considerations.

This thesis also applies to other forms of informal work, even to parts of illicit work, which is normally considered as the example of market-controlled informal labour. To give a short explanation: The scientific discussion (see PAHL, 1984) usually differentiates between three types of productive activity after work: illegal work, household production where the oikos-type of production and consumption unit are identical, and, thirdly, communal or joint production (gratuitous activities in organisations like the voluntary fire-brigade).

This differentiation concentrates on the economically relevant aspects of the so-called "informal economy". It distinguishes between relationships of production and of exchange. The fact that informal labour, in the first instance, is differentiated according to economic criteria is justified not only by a special scientific interest of political economy. At least for industrial workers, who, as compared to other groups of the population, have always had to economize, informal work is a traditional part of a household's means of self-provision. Thus it is for economic reasons, among others, that workers do informal labour. However, on the micro-analytical level of studying the self-provisioning of individual households, a purely economic view conceals important differentiations.

Concerning "black" labour, one has to distinguish between two forms. On the one hand there is illegal selling of one's working capacity for money, with no specific supply problem of the household existing. The point here is to enlarge the income to be spent on further goods and services. This kind of illicit work depends on a market. The subjective considerations of the person doing illicit work orient themselves towards the model of "homo economicus" calculating different possibilities of selling his working power so as to optimize the relationship between work and earned income.

This is the type of illicit work the theses of a positive relationship between degree of state involvement and informal economy are based on - theses that dominate the economic discussion on the shadow economy (see Langfeldt, 1984).

In our sample only a minority is involved in illegal work. But half of this minority does a different type of illegal work. They exchange their labour power against "payment in kind": working power for working power, material, permission to use production facilities and certain services. This type is almost exclusively found in the context of larger projects of household production (house-building).

For instance: after having installed a heating system in his house, a worker hires himself out for 3 days to a fitter. He receives material in return and a certificate saying that the heating system was installed and approved by that firm. This form of illicit work is a traditional and integral part of household production. Without possibilities of this kind many larger projects of informal work would never be started. Thus, any attempt to repressively control illicit work would abolish parts of household production without increasing formal production at the same time.

This means that this form of illicit work is not based on the individual's considerations of advantageous alternatives to the use of his working power but based on a "moral economy" (Thompson, 1980). It allows the persons concerned e.g. to cultivate a garden, build a house as a matter of course and, in doing so, help each other with whatever one has. For workers the latter primarily means to help with their capacity to work.

From the workers' point of view, this type of illicit work is a form of help between neighbours, relatives, members of societies. In the context of a moral economy of the working-class household, it is characterized by norms of solidarity and mutual exchange.

The moral economy of informal work can also be explained by examples of what we have termed basic activities. They are characterized by two rules typical of workers:

Firstly, whenever skilled handiwork is concerned, workers first of all think that they are competent to do the job themselves. This often leads to a deeprooted distrust of the skilled handiwork offered on the formal market.

Secondly, it is characteristic for workers to think in terms of their working capacity instead of their buying capacity. As opposed to a finite earned income, one's work potential is considered as a permanently available resource. It is limited by qualification and lack of production facilities rather than limited by time.

Within the scope of this basic range of maintenance and repair work, the formal economy has subsidiary functions. The people concerned first of all think of their own capacity to work, subsequently of the social networks available and ultimately, when there is no other choice, of the formal economy. They do not even bother to compare the costs of formal and informal work. Thus, the basic activities of informal work cannot be considered as a reaction to rising taxes or as a result of changed values. To put it in a nutshell: They are the exact opposite of a post-industrial phenomenon.

3. TREND PROGNOSIS - THE FURTHER DEVELOPMENT INFORMAL ECO-
   NOMY

In the beginning, we referred to two assumptions, the one of a relative growth of the informal economy and the one that the informal economy is a possible alternative to formal work. Certain hopes that the informal economy could contribute to solving existing crises of a 'labour society' are based on both assumptions.

On the first assumption: As far as quantitative changes can be ascertained at all, our results rather suggest a decline of extra-professional work. Certain activities are gradually given up, in particular activities that have limiting and structuring effects on people's private life, such as keeping cattle on a small scale in rural areas. For the rest the range of activities is fairly stable.

In our sample the extent of informal work as to time, as well as its relative economic relevance for the households' self-provisioning, has decreased. This fact runs counter to most macro-analytical indicators of a relative growth of the informal sector. Clearly these deviations may be due to the peculiarities and the small size of our sample. However, in our opinion this reveals the long-standing and fundamental problem of measuring economic activities outside the socially institutionalized economy of market and state.

Looking beyond a society's capacity to work as institutionalized in the form of state and economic system necessarily leads to the question in what way economically relevant and productive activities differ from other forms of activity. What activities out of the inumerable manifestations of life given by individuals outside their companies and offices are contributions to informal economy? Thus the discussion about informal economy leads back to an old problem which neither political economy nor domestic science have been able to solve as yet, i.e. the problem of distinguishing between productive and non-productive work. "It will be difficult to find any two words on the right use of which the opinion of political economists is more divided than on the two words productive and unproductive, no matter whether they are referring to work, consumption or expenditure". John Stuart Mill's introductory words to his essay "On the terms productive and unproductive" (1976, p. 103) are still valid today, at most with the reservation that, seeing the theoretical difficulties, political economists have given up any further attempt at clarifying the terms productive and unproductive (see Nutzinger, Introduction to Mill, 1976, p. 97). One is content with a formal definition of economic activity; a definition, however, that remains external to its particular qualities. According to this logic, the object of economy is whatever is socially institutionalized in the form of market-oriented or administratively organized work. Mill already warned of the arbitrariness of this kind of classification: "From this it would follow that the same work and the same expenditures would have to be called unproductive when made available free of charge and productive as soon as money is charged" (106). As long as social science explicitly deals with work only, and in so far as it is defined in detail in society as an economic system of market and state, this arbitrariness does not have any major effects. However, as soon as the theses of an absolute or even relative growth (relative in proportion to market and state) of the informal economy are advanced and the limitations of this object of research are thus removed, a measurable definition of informal work must be found. With this definition missing, there is no basis for statements on quantitative changes. Time budgets, for instance, will have completely different results regarding the amount of time used when one accounts for the material results of manual work alone or when one accounts for the immaterial effects of services as criteria of productive work, too. The same applies to measuring economic effects for the budget or the welfare of a nation.

As already mentioned, this is a very old, notoriously debated problem. Depending on the historical situation and prevailing economic theory, the definition of what is productive varies; for the physiocrats it is agriculture alone, for Marx it is the specific form in which work is organized in a society so as to produce surplus value. According to Mill, "The wealth of a country consists in the sum total of its permanent sources of material or immaterial enjoyment. Any work or expenditure aimed at enlarging or preserving these sources, in our opinion, ought to be called productive. Any work done for the purpose of immediate pleasure, e.g. the work of someone playing a musical instrument, we call unproductive" (Mill, 1976, 108). After so many and so very different attempts, it is not surprising, then, that the question in what way productive activities differ from non-productive activities causes frustration rather than curiosity.

Any statement, however, on quantitative changes of informal work in comparison to formal work requires a measurable definition, unless we are willing to do without statements which can be tested empirically. As already mentioned, for a long time all kinds of considerations have been made in all kinds of areas of science in order to solve this problem, and as a result of these efforts we can only repeat the conclusion drawn by Schettkad: "As a matter of fact, there is no theoretical criterion allowing a satisfactory differentiation between consumption and production" (Schettkat, 36).

Conclusion: It is not possible to give a positive, theoretically sound definition of informal economy as against the non-economic areas of everyday activities. This means that the category of informal economy is faced with the same dilemma as all residual categories, that is to say both can be defined only negatively, and informal economy is indeed a residual category for it is defined negatively only as an area of production that is neither organized by the state nor shaped by market forces. However, without a theoretically sound and positive definition of the formal economy, any calculations concerning the economic results of informal economy are tautological in essence. What one gets is exactly the same as what was put into it previously by way of definition. And the systematic criteria for what may be put into it are lacking.

We can see only one way out of this dilemma, which in principle is unsolvable: to do without the global sector model. I.e. the solution would be to stop comparing the rates of economic growth in the informal market and state sector and measure the changes in clearly defined bundles of

activities and products instead. And that is how we proceeded. Because of the generalizability of the explanations
given for the change ascertained, any generalizations going
beyond this observed part of informal activities, on the
whole are possible in theory only. We tried to show for
instance that the model of homo economicus does not reach
very far in explaining even illegal black labour.

We have shown at some length now, why we cannot say anything theoretically or empirically sound with regard to
theses of a relative growth of the informal sector. Based on
our study, we are able, however, to make empirical statements on the second assumption, according to which informal
work is an alternative to formal work. Here we have formulated the following anti-thesis: Informal work is not an alternative but a complement to formal paid work in a company. Informal work depends on formal work.

This point requires further explanation. A central characteristic of informal work outside the company as a means
of self-provisioning of the household is its material and
social dependence on paid work within the company. This
connection between informal and formal work is mainly based
on the simple fact that for informal work, too, resources
are required:

- material ones (workshop, tools, machinery, material)
- social ones (social networks and connections)
- technical and moral qualifications (skills, work discipline).

As far as industrial workers are concerned, these resources are, to a large extent, bound up with their job.
Because of their wages they are in a position to acquire
means of production for more qualified informal work. Often
the social network existing between the workers in a company
is far superior, as far as qualification and information are
concerned, to the networks existing between neighbours and
relatives. Moreover, access to the company also gives access
to a variety of material, tools and machinery. Our present
results permit us to formulate the thesis that the company
as source of wages, raw materials, reservoir of qualification and labour, and as source of information is a central
prerequisite, especially for the more humane qualities of
the informal work done by the shipyard workers. When a
worker loses his job, he has more time, but the scope,
standards and returns of his informal work will decrease. At
least with regard to existing tendencies of dividing employed persons from those unemployed, the thesis can be held
that instead of alleviating inequality the informal economy reinforces it.

Correspondingly, the workers interviewed by us did not
consider work outside the company as an alternative to paid
work within the company:

1. Neither in an economic sense: only 10% consider it to be
   an economic alternative in the sense that their work
   outside the company reduces their being dependent on
   their wages; in periods of short-time work or unemploy-

ment they cannot fall back on it.

2. Nor in the sense of <u>defining their place in society</u>: all of the interviewees call themselves workers. Hardly any of them responded to the possibility suggested by us in the interview to define their place in society differently because of their activities after work and their property.

3. Nor in a <u>psychological</u> sense: We have found hardly any indications in support of the theses on changing values. These theses suggest that the centre of identity is shifting from the area of professional work to the extra-professional areas of life. Professional work continues to be valid as a central standard of self-estimation. The logical background for understanding the reasons for work being done outside the company is to be found mainly in problems of self-provisioning of the individual household. The shipyard workers' experience in the company are of secondary importance only. And, nevertheless, the ways in which work outside the company is interpreted are changing; this does not mean, however, that orientations for which there was no room in the context of one's professional work are given asylum, as it were in work done outside the company. Rather, these productive activities outside the company, which the shipyard workers have always done, are more and more backed up by further motives such as: recreation by means of non-committal activities, development of skills, realisation of use-value standards and conceptions of an ideal self etc. These humane qualities of informal work, however, are dependent on the prerequisite that working outside the company is relieved of existential needs by means of paid work. And all interviewees are aware of this. Even those 10% who conceive of their informal work as reducing, to a limited extent, the dependency on wages are of the opinion as one of them put it: "... this wouldn't be much of a life anymore".

Thus, extra-professional work does not constitute an alternative, neither economically in the context of household strategies nor subjectively in the consciousness of the workers. Its significance is due to the very fact <u>that the workers are employed and paid on a regular basis by their company</u>. For employees in East Frisia, wage labour brought wealth. We have formulated this somewhat emphatically to the effect that, to them, industrial work to a certain extent meant liberation. When referring to the political potential of informal work as a subjective alternative to industrial work, the fact has to be considered that in the lives of many of our interviewees this background still is of immediate importance. Particularly those activities which are close to rural subsistence production are associated with the unpleasant recollection of former bad times; whereas work in the shipyard is associated with recollections of the time when everybody was better off earning good money, good in a threefold sense: it was sufficient, regular and paid for qualified work.

However, the complementarity of informal and formal work is _ambivalent_. On the one hand informal work became _more humane_ in the course of social and economic developments. All of the following factors contributed to making extra-professional work _more productive, qualitatively better and more complex as to its motives_:

- people gained access to industrial work and thus to a regular paid income, to professional qualification, to the company as a basis for extra-professional work;

- the network of social securities was expanded and public infrastructure was improved;

- consumer goods and household capital goods were reduced in price.

But calculated market strategies, developing technologies and production processes contribute to _restricting the play of informal work, too_. Growing technical complexity, black boxes, built-in wear and tear _reduce_ the possibility for people to repair electrical appliances themselves. The development of machine tools and materials which are inexpensive and easy to handle has offered new opportunities for productive activities, but for acquiring these spending power is required, that is to say regular wages. With the new possibilities these machines offer for working, they also force _certain work processes_ and _certain ways of using them_ upon those who employ them. Thus informal work, too, is pushed into pockets intended for this purpose by the market, meaning that informal work is more and more integrated into the market.

This tendency of _integrating the informal economy into the market_, i.e. its very disintegration as an autonomous sector, is concealed by the model of the three sectors of market, state and informal economy. The model alleges that social change is to be understood as a process of substitution and that it can be measured as a shifting of clusters of activities between separate sectors of society. As a rule, however, those productions that move away from the market sector do not, on re-entering the sector of private household production, return to a state of innocence as before the Fall of Man, as it were, i.e. to state and market production of goods and services. On the contrary, household production _assumes a new quality which is determined by what is produced on the market and by political and administrative factors_, for instance when people produce services themselves by using sophisticated household machines or when the government mobilizes social networks for rehabilitating people suffering from psychological strain. This social change is not to be understood as a shifting of weight between the separate sectors of formal and informal economy. Rather, we have to take into account an increasing interconnectedness and mutual penetration of the sectors combined with qualitative changes in politics and ways of living. To put it in terms of a catch-phrase: We believe that to ask for the quantitative growth of the so-called informal sector and to compare it with the formal sector is putting the question in the wrong way. We also believe that it is hardly possible to answer this question. Rather, what is happening at the moment is a change of quality of informal work and a tendency towards its market integration.

4. POLICY IMPLICATIONS

The activists of informal economy mainly are those workers who are integrated into the formal labour market, who are qualified and well paid. Informal economy does not constitute an alternative to formal work, at least not with regard to the mass of industrial workers or a whole region. The existing tendencies of a change in quality aim at a stronger integration into the market of extra-professional work. Both these tendencies, as well as the complementarity of informal and formal work, are arguments against overestimating informal economy, no matter whether this is done by conservatives or progressives. The informal economy is anything but a soft feather-pillow, cushioning the fall of those who have slipped through the coarsely tied meshes of the net of the welfare state after having been thrown out of the labour market. Neither is the informal economy an autonomous sector in which a transformation of the capitalist system is under way. It, rather, is an increasingly integrated part of the latter. Even the shipyard workers themselves consider their working activities outside the company as a different but totally private counter-world to the factory. By no means do we intend to suggest that work within the company is being instrumentalized or that professional values are being shifted to the extra-work sphere. Rather, the trend is to be characterized as a further differentiation of demands made on work. Work in the company maintains its validity as a point of crystallization of the individual's identity.

For politics, this means something negative to begin with. Informal economy is no resource-saving strategy, unemployment policy or social policy could fall back on. A policy trying to functionalize the informal economy as an alternative to formal employment and government-provided securities will probably lead to opposite results, that is to say to cumulative negative effects even in the area of informal economy.

To the extent that positive consequences can be drawn from our results, two demands can be made: A redistribution of the formal work available, i.e. reduction of working hours, on the one hand, meaning an equal distribution of formal work as the basis on which informal work can develop. And, on the other hand, the potential for real appropriation of the built environment needs to be improved, both with regard to space and material available and the legal possibilities of disposing of one's living conditions.

REFERENCES

LANGFELDT, E., Ursachen der Schattenwirtschaft und ihre Kon-
    sequenzen für die Wirtschafts-, Finanz- und Gesellschafs-
    politik, Kiel 1983.
NUTZINGER, H.D., (ed), John Stuart Mill. Einige ungelöste
    Probleme der politischen Ökonomie, Frankfurt 1976.
PAHL, R.E., Divisions of Labour, Oxford 1984.
SCHETTKAT, R., Das Bruttosozialprodukt und die Produktion
    von Haushalten, Berlin 1982.
THOMPSON, E.P., Plebejische Kultur und moralische Ökonomie,
    Frankfurt 1980.

PART IV
CONSEQUENCES AND
INCOME DISTRIBUTION

Measuring hidden personal incomes in the USSR

GREGORY GROSSMAN, VLADIMIR G. TREML

An international committee of experts charged with compiling a list of conditions that maximize the potential for a large underground economy would invent the Soviet Union. In that country:
- nearly all economic pursuits are barred to private activity, and the few that are not bear the brunt of heavy and steeply progressive income taxes (excepting private agriculture);
- indirect ('turnover') taxes on many goods of everyday use can be extremely high; but there are also large subsidies, inviting illicit abuse and arbitrage;
- nearly all prices are controlled and centrally fixed, generally below market-clearing levels, which causes widespread goods shortages and rent-seeking activity; multiple prices for a single good are quite common, inviting arbitrage;
- there is chronic excess aggregate demand in both the socialist and the household sector with reference to the fixed prices;
- domestic price ratios diverge sharply from those of every other country, which invites smuggling; exchange rates are 'artificial';
- planning and management of the economy and the goods distribution system work poorly, contributing to chronic shortages of goods and services, lack of variety, and sluggish adjustment to needs, fashions, and tastes;
- as a matter of deliberate policy, some final demand is left unsatisfied in such areas as the arts, literature, intellectual and spiritual endeavors, religion, traditional rites and customs, ethnic values, youth culture, etc.;
- the whole society is heavily controlled, regulated, and bureaucratized.
Finally, there is yet another condition, second to none in importance, namely, the ubiquitous presence of state (socialist) property, easy to steal, misappropriate, embezzle, exploit for private profit, and misuse in every conceivable way. A very common practice, often on the scale of even a whole factory, is the use of a socialist facility by insiders as a facade for a private business. This kind of crypto-private operation typically depends on resources stolen from the socialist sector, such as materials, equipment time, labor time, and even customers. It is a major cause of private income, especially on a large scale (Gross-

man, 1979).

Needless to say, personal incomes from illegal activities are not reported to the authorities; they are hidden incomes. Yet income from activities that are per se legal may also be hidden (i.e., deliberately concealed or simply statistically unobserved) for a variety of reasons, such as: tax evasion, reluctance to reveal activities and incomes which are system-alien albeit technically legal, fear of inviting demands for "squeeze" from officials, and failure on the part of the government to collect complete, if any, data on certain legal market transactions. An example of the last is the significant underenumeration - and, hence, understatement in published statistics - of food sales in the legal open market, the so-called kolkhoz market, as discussed below.

Although Soviet publications carry voluminous descriptive and anecdotal information about the underground economy - activities "on the left" in Soviet parlance - and although the files of certain Soviet institutions must be bulging with relevant data, no aggregate figures or generalizing analyses have appeared in the USSR, to our knowledge. Nor are we aware of any comprehensive scholarly effort in the USSR to study the underground economy as an economic or social problem, as distinct from a legal or police problem. The outside observer has to generate his own aggregate and partial data, and to provide his own analysis. In doing so he has the obvious disadvantages of an outsider trying to peer behind veils, yet also certain distinct advantages over scholars and institutes in the USSR. He does not represent any Soviet authority.

Thanks to the valuable systematic surveys of methods of measuring hidden economies for which we are in good measure indebted to the indefatigable Bruno Frey, Werner Pommerehne, and Hannelore Weck of Zurich (see References), we can tick off the measuring methods which are not applicable or practicable for an outsider in the Soviet case. Thus, the currency-ratio and the transactions approach will not do for two reasons: (1) the USSR does not publish data on currency (virtually the only form of money in the household sector), and (2) the chronic state of repressed inflation would in any case render these methods even less accurate than they have proved to be in the West. Nor can the outside observer conduct audits of business and household accounts within the Soviet Union. And if he attempted a door-to-door canvas of consumer budgets or labor participation rates, he would get neither the permission of the authorities nor the cooperation of the potential respondents.

Published (official) statistics tell us very little if anything about the main sources of hidden personal incomes, such as legal and illegal inter-household transactions, massive theft and embezzlement from the socialist sector (mostly from the state), and a wide range of illegal production activities.

1. QUESTIONNAIRE SURVEYS

In the USSR, hidden incomes are a mass phenomenon; hence their measurement calls for methods of mass data collection by the scholar. In the West, the questionnaire survey method has been successfully employed under similar circumstances. As in the West, the main objects of inquiry in the Soviet case would be household incomes, expenditures, wealth, and labor-time utilization, plus a certain amount of detailed information, e.g. the levels of some black-market prices.

The use of the questionnaire survey among Soviet emigrants to generate data about the household sector was pioneered by Gur Ofer and Aaron Vinokur in Israel in the 1970s. Hidden incomes were not the primary object of their study originally but gained in importance as the work went on. At this writing, only partial findings of the Ofer-Vinokur (OV) project have been published (see References to this paper); for a brief description of their sample and method see (OV, 1981, pp. 135-137). A similar questionnaire survey, in part inspired by and patterned after the OV survey (2) but expressly focussed on the "second economy" (legal private and illegal production activities and related phenomena), is currently being conducted by the present authors as part of their larger project on the Second Economy of the Soviet Union (3). The rest of this paper briefly describes the Grossman-Treml survey and reports on our preliminary and provisional findings in regard to one magnitude, the size of food purchases by the urban population from private persons.

2. THE GROSSMAN-TREML SURVEY

Our questionnaire survey is part of our broader on-going project on the Second Economy of the USSR. Before launching the survey itself, we conducted several dozen non-questionnaire ('open ended') interviews with well-informed Soviet emigrants (former defense lawyers, prosecutors, judges, underground businessmen, police officials, journalists, etc.), and familiarized ourselves with the relevant Soviet and emigré literatures, and the relevant official statistical data. This preparation was valuable for designing the questionnaire and the sample.

The Sample. The unit of observation is threefold: the household (usually, family) for most variables, every adult income-earner within the household for personal income, and every adult in the household, regardless of past income earning, for 'perceptions' of side-incomes by the public at large. Following the OV survey, our sample is limited to the urban population; but unlike the OV survey, ours covers southern as well northern republics of the USSR. All questionnaire interviews took place in the United States. The interviewers were Soviet emigrants themselves.

Recent Soviet emigrants in the United States are, of course, not representative of the 'parent' Soviet urban population in a number of important socio-economic respects. Thus, by nationality, they are predominantly, though far

287

from exclusively, of two nationalities, Jewish and Armenian. Accordingly, in our sample we made a determined effort to give additional representation to other nationalities (including mixed-Jewish families), to blue-collar as against white-collar income-earners, to less as against more highly educated families, and to emigrants from other than the largest cities (except Leningrad, as explained below), and fron southern rather than northern republics.

Our sample includes 1,007 households (families). The geographic breakdown of families is as follows: R.S.F.S.R. - 446, Ukraine - 119, Baltic republics - 45, Belorussia - 37, Moldavia - 28, total for northern republics - 675; Armenia - 210, Georgia - 46, Azerbaidzhan - 38, Uzbekistan - 38 (including 5 from southern Kazakhstan), total for southern republics - 332 (4). By city size (1977): over 1 million population - 52.7 percent of families (of these, 57 percent from Leningrad, as explained below), 500,000 to 1 million - 27.8 percent, below 500,000 - 19.1 percent.

The number of individuals within the 1,007 households is 2,824, of whom 2,097 were adults (16+) in the last normal year before emigration. Of the adults, 52.2 percent are Jewish, 23.9 percent are Armenian, and 19.7 percent are Russian, Ukrainian, or Belorussian. (Nationality is here defined according to the internal Soviet passport). Number of income-earners interviewed - 1,819; number of persons filling out the questionnaire on 'perceptions' of side incomes of various occupations and jobs - 1,970. Last normal year of household's material conditions in the USSR: mean and median - 1977, mode - 1978, with the years 1974 through 1979 accounting for 95 percent of the sample.

Two geographic locations, Armenia and Leningrad, constitute special case studies within our survey, the two together accounting for half the families in the total sample. The Armenian sub-sample accounts for half the families in the total sample. The Armenian sub-sample accounts for 20.9 percent of the sample, and 90.5 percent of it consists of ethnic Armenian families, very close to the proportion in the republic as of 1979. Since the ethnic Armenians are the only contingent from a southern republic consisting of persons of the titular nationality, in our sample it must perforce stand as proxy for the whole South, a region that plays an important and distinctive role in the Soviet second economy.

All Armenian families in our sample came to the United States from Soviet Armenia proper (though there is also a large Armenian population in the rest of the USSR). However, because of Soviet emigration policy, almost every Armenian family contains at least one 'repatriant', i.e. one of the over 102,000 who immigrated into Soviet Armenia, mostly from the Near East and SE Europe, in 1946-1948 (Mouradian, 1979). Many of those who recently re-emigrated were very young when they repatriated just after the War. The non-repatriants among the Armenians in our sample are, typically, members of the repatriants' later-formed families. For some purposes the fact of being a repratriant or a member of his/her family may significantly set such a person apart from the bulk of Soviet Armenia's population, but we do not believe this to be a serious problem for our purposes.

The other special case, Leningrad, accounts for 30.0 per-cent of the sample. Here, in addition to the full, working families that are our exclusive object for all other locali-ties, we collected sub-samples of other types of household, namely, single working males, single working females with children, single working females without children, and pen-sioner families. We hope that the relationships for the relevant variables between these various kinds of household from Leningrad will give some insights into the correspon-ding relationships in the USSR as a whole.

On the advice of our survey-research consultants we used the 'snowball' technique of collecting interviews, con-strained in the just-mentioned ways, rather than random sam-pling. To hold down the risk of 'sample inbreeding' (our term) in the course of questionnaire collection, we inter-viewed in a large number of American cities using different interviewers. (An exception to the statement relates to Armenians, who were all interviewed in the Los Angeles area, where they are highly concentrated).

3. THE QUESTIONNAIRE

It consists of two main parts. The first (in order of answe-ring) deals with individual perceptions of the size of unofficial ('left') incomes as supplements to the official earnings of 36 occupations, professions, and jobs listed in the questionnaire. Respondents were asked to place a mark against each occupation, etc., in one of eight columns representing class intervals. The class intervals range from zero to "over 300" rubles per month. We deliberately included occupations, etc., where we expected very low side incomes (e.g. librarian) as well as those where we expected high ones. In this we have not been disappointed, though there are a few surprises, such as the very high assessment of side incomes of directors of funeral parlors. Altogether, over 1,900 persons answered the 'perceptions' part.

The 'perceptions' questions were asked somewhat diffe-rently of respondents from northern and southern republics. The former were asked to provide estimates for the USSR as a whole; the latter, only for their own (southern) republic, which we expected to be considerably higher given the puta-tive high development of the second economy in the South. We find that for each of the 36 occupations the means of esti-mates by southern respondents (N = 300) are higher than those by northern respondents (N = 667). In the case of none of the 36 occupations does the ratio of the 'southern' mean to the "northern" mean fall below 1.24; in the case of 22 occupations it falls in the range of 1.24-2.50, 6 occupa-tions - 2.51-5.00, 7 occupations - 5.01-10.00, and for one occupation (elevator operators - sic!) the ratio is 14.5 (5). These inter-regional differences in our respondents' perceptions of unofficial incomes are in general agreement with a number of other scholars' findings regarding the second economy in the Soviet South (cf., e.g. Mars and Altman, 1983).

The rest of the questionnaire pertains mainly to the composition of the household and to its expenditures, income, and wealth in the "last normal year" (LNY) in the USSR. LNY is defined as the last calendar year in which the household's material circumstances were not yet significantly affected by the prospect of emigration; it is not necessarily a typical year in the family's experience.

In regard to expenditures, the questionnaire asks for considerable detail regarding payments to private individuals for goods and services purchased, for repairs performed, tips and bribes given, rentals paid, and so forth. These data, we expect, will allow us to estimate - albeit approximately - the dependence of the urban population on private sources of supply. At a further remove, the expenditure data should help throw light on the aggregate hidden incomes of private producers and traders who sell to the urban sector, including the incomes of those outside the direct purview of our survey, such as agricultural producers.

In this connection, a serious problem of estimation is created by incomes from the aforementioned crypto-private production, that is, private activity that hides behind the facade of a socialist enterprise. Such incomes are many and can be quite large individually, but are not likely to be reported by our respondents as payments to private persons. The reason is that, typically, the products of crypto-private production are indistinguishable, physically or by price, from identical products sold on the state's account, and in fact are sold side by side with them (6). This effectively protects the private operation - and fools the customer, too, to think that he is buying 'socialist' (say) soap. Unless we find a plausible way to estimate crypto-private sales and corresponding hidden income, our estimates of total hidden income from private expenditure data may be significantly understated.

Still in regard to household expenditures, the questionnaire dwells on a number of special problems, such as privately owned housing and related matters; private automobile ownership and outlay on repair, gasoline supply, etc; alcohol purchase, consumption, and use, including illegal home distillation and the use of vodka as a means of payment. We also inquire into methods of circumventing goods shortages that were practiced by our respondents (such as exploiting personal connections, paying under the counter, travelling some distance to obtain goods, using 'closed distributors'). In addition, the questionnaire asks for information on current saving during the LNY, and stocks of liquid savings and other property at the end of the LNY broken down by major items.

In the income and work sections of the questionnaire, emphasis is placed on second-economy components of income and of time utilization. As noted, this information has been sought of all members of households who had significant income, from whatever source, during the family's LNY, 1,816 persons in our sample altogether. Our data show that the Soviet people earn supplementary income in the most diverse, ingenious, and unexpected ways. Grey is the Soviet man's visible tree of life, but green and lush are its subterranean roots!

A perennial question is the size and importance of hidden income relative to observed income. Students of the Soviet economy are inundated with anecdotal material from both Soviet media and emigrants describing ingenious illegal operations and schemes producing tens and hundreds of thousands of rubles of private income. It is usually impossible to ascertain from internal evidence how characteristic and frequent are such operations. The study of the second economy in the USSR would be in danger of degenerating into a mere collection of amusing and tantalizing stories, were it not for the questionnaire survey.

While the emigrants constitute a far-from-representative sample of the total Soviet population, yet with the help of purposive sampling and re-weighting, one may be able to approximate the general Soviet population in some relevant respects. Nevertheless, serious problems remain. Re-weighting is hampered by the (increasing) paucity and unreliability of Soviet official statistics, while on the subjective side one must guard against respondent bias, poor recall, and the like. We try to deal with the sample's 'Jewish bias' by referring to the size of a household's alcohol consumption. Insofar as problems can be kept within reasonable limits, the survey technique harbors considerable promise of obtaining, for a given time period, estimates of hidden personal incomes, total and by social groups and regions, and a large amount of detail. Most importantly, survey findings may be combined with incomplete data from official statistics to estimate hidden income and underground activity in specific sectors and markets.

A case in point is the following recomputation on the basis of our questionnaire returns of the urban population's purchases of food from private persons, i.e., not from state-owned or cooperative outlets. Our recomputation can be thought of as pertaining to the year 1977, which - as already mentioned - is both the mean and the median year of the relatively narrow range of years to which our sample data refer.

4. HIDDEN INCOME FROM PRIVATE FOOD SALES

One of few types of legal income from private economic activity in the USSR is the income, in money and in kind, earned from private agricultural operations (so called private plots). Income in kind consists of food produced and consumed by the same households; money income is derived from sales mainly at so-called urban kolkhoz markets but also in a non-organized way (here termed 'off-market' sales or purchases). Income so earned is included in Soviet national income accounts and in Western estimates of Soviet GNP.

Some Western students of the Soviet economy, including the

authors of this paper, have for some time believed that sales of agricultural products on urban kolkhoz markets are understated in standard Soviet statistical reporting and so was the income (7). Our questionnaire survey provides us with an estimate of the value of these sales and, by implication, also of more accurate estimates of the value of privately produced agricultural output and of private income therefrom.

Soviet official sources report the value of sales on urban kolkhoz markets for 1977 as 7,300 million rubles, or 45 rubles per capita; our estimate on the basis of the emigré survey is 33,800 million rubles, or 210 rubles per capita. Soviet statistics are silent regarding off-market private sales or purchases, which we estimate at 3,200 million rubles for the urban population, or 20 rubles per capita per year. Total private purchases by the urban population by our reckoning are thus 37,000 million rubles, or 230 rubles per capita, for around 1977. The difference between the official sales figure and our estimate is therefore a remarkably high 29,700 million rubles. Most of it must represent hidden (gross) private income.

In all probability a large share of the hidden sales are of produce from private plots. However, some of the foodstuffs are stolen from farms or the food industry, produced by crypto-private enterprises using stolen raw materials, or purchased in official retail stores at low, often subsidized, prices and resold by speculators. Because of uncertainty of the origin of these products and the difficulty of accurately estimating the cost of material inputs into private agriculture, we are not in a position at this time to estimate the net portion of gross income, but it would probably fall between 18 and 22 billion rubles. Not all of it went to the agricultural population proper, of course. Brief explanations of our estimates follow.

The figure of 7,300 million rubles includes 5,800 rubles of sales directly by private persons and 1,500 million rubles of sales of foodstuffs through the cooperative retail network, which procured these on a commission basis from agricultural producers. The cooperative network operates small stalls alongside private vendors at kolkhoz markets and Soviet shoppers generally do not distinguish between the two. Accordingly, we have combined the two figures for a total of 7,300 million rubles for comparability with purchases reported by our respondents.

Our questionnaire asked specifically about purchases of food from private off-market vendors, but in all probability our respondents could not have always distinguished between a private vendor and a small stall operated off-market by a state or cooperative retail organization. The error, if any, is probably quite small.

The figures of purchases at kolkhoz market and 3,200 million rubles of food purchased from off-market vendors were estimated as follows. Our survey covers 10 out of 15 republics. For each republic, the mean per capita value of purchases reported by our respondents was multiplied by the population of the republic. Since per capita kolkhoz market

sales are smaller in larger cities, for each republic separate estimates were made for major cities (2 in RSFSR, 4 in
the Ukraine, and 1 each in other republics) and for the
remaining urban communities. The per capita purchases in
Riga and the rest of the Latvian republic were used as
proxies for Lithuania and Estonia which are underrepresented
in our sample. Average per capita purchases in Uzbekistan
and southern Kazakhstan were used as proxies for Kirgizia,
Tadzhikistan, and Turkmenistan, which are not in our sample.
Normalization for the entire urban USSR for purchases of
food from ex-market vendors was done in the same manner. For
major cities, mean per capita purchases in kolkhoz markets
ranged from a high of 570 rubles in L'vov to a low of 140
rubles in Leningrad. Purchases in urban communities ex-
cluding the 14 major cities range from 631 rubles in Armenia
to 128 rubles in the RSFSR.

In terms of republics, RSFSR has the lowest mean per
capita purchases of 135 rubles, while Armenia has the highest - 584 rubles. The former is probably explained by the
fact that RSFSR in the most urbanized of Soviet republics,
i.e., has the highest number of urban dwellers purchasing
food in markets supplied by a relatively small rural population, by the poor state of RSFSR agriculture, and by the
distance of many cities from significant food production.

Per capita kolkhoz-market food purchases by republics
calculated from our sample and expressed as percent of the
USSR average fall remarkably close to the corresponding
ratios based on official Soviet statistics (for the few
republics for which such are available). For instance, average per capita food purchases in the RSFSR are 64 percent
of the USSR figure according to our sample, and 70 percent
according to official Soviet data; for Latvia, 1.49 and
1.45, respectively.

Unfortunately, official Soviet data on kolkhoz-market
sales are scarce for the 1970s, except for a set of such
data for most large cities for 1963. Expressing per capita
purchases in each of 13 large cities in our sample as a
ratio of the USSR average, once again we find a high degree
of similarity with the corresponding ratios obtained from
Soviet data (of some 14 years earlier) (8). This similarity
might be taken to suggest both stable regional patterns of
kolkhoz market purchases over time and a certain degree of
accuracy of our survey-based estimates.

Generally speaking the dispersion of reported purchases
around the mean is not great, as can be seen in the following:

	Mean	Std. Dev.	Std. Error of the Mean
		(rubles)	
Per capita purchases in urban markets	303.68	311.16	5.86
Per capita purchases from ex-market vendors	31.14	79.59	1.50

One possible upward bias in our estimate which cannot be corrected at this time must be mentioned. Food purchases are, as a rule, income inelastic, but given their higher quality and higher prices, food purchases from private sources are probably positively correlated with income. Since our respondents on the average have a moderately higher (official) family income than the average for the USSR, they could have been conceivably purchasing more in kolkhoz markets than an 'average' Soviet urban family would.

Purchases at kolkhoz markets and from urban off-market vendors do not exhaust food purchases from private sources by the urban population. There are in addition, first, purchases of food while vacationing in rural or resort areas (while at dachas, to use the Russian term). In our sample, families comprising 524 persons, 18.5 percent covered by the survey, purchased an average of 161 rubles' worth of food per capita per season (year) in this manner. This figure is not part of our other estimates. Such food sales to dachniki might add, on the all-union scale, another 1.2 - 1.6 billion rubles per year to hidden incomes from private plots.

Second, by all accounts, a not insignificant amount of the food sold in official outlets as 'socialist' merchandise at regular prices is in fact 'crypto-private' in the aforementioned sense. It is sold on private account behind the front of a state-owned or cooperative establishment, and is not perceived as being on private account by the buyer, that is, by our survey respondent. Its retail value goes into the pockets of private individuals all along the production and distribution chain, stretching from the collective or state farm to the retail store. At this time we have no way of estimating the hidden incomes arising from crypto-private production and sale of foodstuffs.

Finally, the urban family also grows and consumes its own food to a considerable extent. Thus, it has been reported that, as of 1978, some 8.3 million urban families had individual garden plots (Trud, September 2, 1978). Our survey includes data on the value of own-consumed food, but, unfortunately, they have not yet been sufficiently analyzed as of this writing.

NOTES

(1)   The authors are grateful to Professor Michael Alexeev of George Mason University for his major contribution to the larger project from which this paper derives. We are also pleased to acknowledge the research assistance of Kathleen O'Brien, Linda Ohde, and David Sedik, all of Berkeley. The larger project is "The Second Economy of the Soviet Union", conducted under grants or contracts from the Ford Foundation, U.S. Department of Defense, and Wharton Econometric Forecasting Associates (Washington, D.C.). The financial assistance of these organizations and of our two universities is appreciatively acknowledged.
(2)   We take this opportunity to cordially thank Professors

Ofer and Vinokur for their generous assistance to our project in person and for kind permission to borrow from their questionnaire and other working materials.

(3) Other questionnaire surveys of Soviet emigrants of economic import have been undertaken. The Soviet Interview Project (SIP), under the direction of James R. Millar of the University of Illinois, Urbana, is by far the largest in size and scope yet attempted. Economic aspects of life and work in the USSR are not its chief object, but a significant one. No results are yet available at the moment. Smaller but significant questionnaire surveys have been conducted on the Soviet family by Adele Nikolskaya and others on Soviet social security and social insurance as they affect households by Bernice Madison (San Francisco), and on poverty in the USSR by Mervyn Matthews (London). No published findings from the latter two have yet appeared, to our knowledge.

(4) Twenty of the families fron Armenia and all families from Georgia, Azerbaidzhan, Uzbekistan, and southern Kazakhstan, 128 in all, were locally resident 'Europeans' and not native Central Asians. We did not succeed to interview significant numbers from the Turkmen, Tadzhik, and Kirgiz republics.

(5) The ratios rest on the rather 'conservative' assumption that the mean value of the 'over 300' rubles-per-month class is 400 rubles, and are preliminary in any case.

(6) Information from interviews with knowledgeable emigrants.

(7) The understatement is probably caused both by the use of lower than actual prices in estimating the value of sales by statistical authorities and by exclusion of markets in smaller towns. Cf. Shenfield, 1984.

(8) The 13 cities are: Moscow, Leningrad, Kiev, Odessa, Kharkov, Minsk, Tashkent, Alma-Ata, Tbilisi, Baku, Kishinev, Riga, and Erevan.

REFERENCES

FREY, B.S., POMMEREHNE, W.W., 'The Hidden Economy: State and Prospects for Measurement', Review of Income and Wealth, vol. 30, pp. 1-23, 1984

FREY, B.S., WECK, H., 'Estimating the Shadow Economy: A 'Naive' Approach', Oxford Economic Papers, 35: 23-44 March 1983.

GROSSMAN, G., 'Notes on the Illegal Private Economy and Corruption' in US Congress, Joint Economic Committee, Soviet Economy in a Time of Change, Washington US GPO, pp. 834-855, 1979.

MARS, G., ALTMAN, Y., 'The Cultural Bases of Soviet Georgia's Second Economy', Soviet Studies, vol. 35, no. 4, pp. 546-60, October 1983.

MOURADIAN, C., 'L'immigration des Arméniens de la diaspora vers la RSS d'Arménie', Cahiers du Monde Russe et Sovietique, vol. 20, no. 1, pp. 79-110 Jan.-March 1979.

OFER, G., PICKERSGILL, J., 'Soviet Household Saving: Study of Soviet Emigrant Families', Quarterly Journal of Economics, vol. 94, no. 3, pp. 121-143, August 1980.

OFER, G., VINOKUR, A., 'Earning Differentials by Sex in the Soviet Union: A First Look.', in Rosefielde, S. (ed), Economic Welfare and the Economics of Soviet Socialism: Essays in Honor of Abram Bergson, Cambridge University Press, Cambridge 1981, pp. 127-162.

OFER, G., VINOKUR, A. 'The labor-Force Participation of Married Women in the Soviet Union: A Household Cross-Section Analysis', Journal of Comparative Economics, vol. 7, no. 2, pp. 158-176, June 1983.

SHENFIELD, S., How Reliable are Published Soviet Data on the Kolkhoz Market? Unpublished paper at the Centre for Russian and East European Research, University of Birmingham, 1984.

Some problems of the expansion of the second economy in Hungary

ANDRAS HEGEDÜS

In Hungary the legitimation of the Second Economy is an integral and important part of the current reforms in that country. This also means the expansion and enrichment of its forms. With regard to specific characteristics of Hungary one may refer to the paper of Eva Szita within this volume. In my paper I deal with some social and economic consequences of the legitimation of the Second Economy. When looking at this process one must take into careful consideration the obvious and profound differences that exist between Eastern and Western Europe.

Firstly we can see the main economic consequences of the legitimation and expansion of the Second Economy. They are as follows:

- Through the mobilisation of one part of the individual capital and free time, the offer of goods and services is increasing. Therefore, the extent of shortages of goods will decrease. This is very important in Eastern European countries where the shortage economy is a basic component of the general economic crisis that is striking these economies.

- The 'price' to be paid for the advantage of a decreasing intensity of shortage is that of increasing inflation, due to the system of income tax which is unable to control or restrict incomes to the same extent as the state salary controls of the old system. The expansion of the Second Economy plays a considerable role in the inflation rate of Hungary which now stands at 9 percent, three times greater than that of neighbouring capitalist Austria.

- The attainable wages within the Second Economy are twice if not three times higher compared to that of the First Economy. Therefore, there has been a large shift of workforce from the First to the Second Economy, thus having a serious and grave effect on heavy and military industries.

The legitimation and expansion of the Second Economy has its main socio-economic consequences on living standards. In this respect three main situations have to be singled out in which this process of legitimation and expansion is taking place: increasing, stagnant and decreasing living standards.

The third is true in Hungary at present. Living standards have deteriorated at a steady and considerable rate since 1980. However, as a consequence of the economic reform, decreasing living standards have had different consequences for the various social strata.

The legitimation and expansion of the Second Economy offers good opportunities to the young and forward-thinking people, in particular, to change their situation and even to improve permanently their living standards. There is also an opportunity for a few, mainly among the elderly, to mobilise their unutilized personal capital and make large profits.

However, those within the large social strata without personal capital, who cannot participate in the Second Economy are the ones who suffer. There is a large difference between those who benefit from the reforms and those who cannot do so and the gap is widening. However, even the young workers who benefit the most from Second Economy pay dearly for it. They forfeit hours for supplementary paid work that could be utilized for self-education and recreation.

It is too early yet to appreciate exactly what the negative effects of the reforms are, due to the lack of a thorough sociological analysis.

The social and political consequences of the legitimation and expansion of the Second Economy clearly have both a positive and a negative side, the characteristics of which are discussed below.

A considerable part of the dynamic social groups now have a better base from which to reach their ambitions. The political activity of regular moonlighters has decreased. Consequently the danger of any significant political opposition is restricted. For the power-holders this complex process means that political tension will decrease and the danger of a political crisis is averted.

In this development a peculiar contradiction is hidden: it deprives political pluralism of its social basis because mainstream social activity is diverted to non-political areas. At the same time economic pluralism stemming from the legitimation of the Second Economy provides an economic basis for political pluralism, including the development of a political opposition.

These developments cause the power structure to be divided into two parts: the pro-reformists and the anti-reformists. Rezso Nyers in 1982 stated in a Newsweek interview that two parties exist within the one-party system in Hungary: the Reform Party and the Anti-reform Party. Consequently there is constant fighting between the two sides, the outcome of which will depend to a large extent on the political events of the other East European countries. But it must be said that Hungary's situation with regard to other East European nations is now more favourable than it was in the sixties.

After the invasion of Czechoslovakia in 1968, the leaders of the socialist countries, with the exception of Hungary, criticised sharply the Czech reforms, the Prague Spring and the conception of Ota Sik. This was also seen as an indirect attack against the Hungarian reform and therefore helped the antireform trend in Hungary, the victory of which duly happened in November 1972. Remarkable reform activities are now occurring in Poland, though within the shadow of that country's deep political and economic crisis. It may also be seen in an experimental form in the Soviet Union, in Bulgaria and in the Federal Republic of Germany, though in a rudimentary state.

The legitimation and expansion of the Second Economy is consistent with the existing ethos and official ideology. Since World War Two, the ethos has changed considerably in East European countries. I prefer to use the notion of ethos rather than ideology in order to characterize the cognitive motivation of the economic activity and avoid the naive economic determinism that stressed economic interests.

The main types of ethos existing now within Hungarian society are as follows:

1) Post-socialist bureaucratic ethos fostered by the media as the only socialist ethos.

2) Protestant ethos according to the Weberian interpretation. It was an ethical behaviour of entrepreneurs in past time but is now experiencing a positive comeback.

3) Quasi-hedonism, existing mainly among young people and entrepreneurs, who often lead lavish lives because of their existential insecurity. Hostility against this stratum of entrepreneurs is intensified by their way of life. This is understandable because of social inequality and is strengthened by the media on the basis of quasi-socialist bureaucratic ethos.

The contradiction between official ideology and reform is also important. The dominant ideology in Hungary is so-called Marxism-Leninism (post-Stalinism). It does not claim to have a monopoly but is the dominant ideology. Therefore, other ideologies have freedom of existence and this situation of restricted pluralism can help the process of reform.

The official ideology occupying a dominant position is hostile towards the legitimation and expansion of the Second Economy. The latter cannot be accepted and built into the official ideology. To this end an interiorization of the official ideology. To this end a modernization of the official ideology is not sufficient; a true revision would be necessary. So revisionism (of the dominant ideology) is a historical necessity in Eastern Europe.

The reassessment of the socialist image of Marxism-Leninism is of particular importance. In doing this the inconsistency of the original Marxist prophecy on the future of socialism must be overcome. Marx's prophecy claims that national socialist economy works like (a) one large industrial plant and is (b) an ensemble of free producers' associations.

The Hungarian reform is close to the second conception.

At this point the question arises whether it is possible to implement a reform like the Hungarian one in only one East European country. This is paraphrase of the old issue, whether it is possible to build socialism in one country only. According to Hungarian experience the answer to the former question is positive, but only with the following realistic restrictions:

- There is a contradiction between the institutional system of COMECON and the legitimation and expansion of the Second Economy, but there are several economic sectors (goods and services for the local population in particular) where this contradiction is not experienced. In these sectors, methods are likely to be found to build the second economy into the COMECON co-operation.

- The military economy and heavy industry are serious obstacles in the way of the legitimation and expansion of the Second Economy, though ways are available to foster reforms such as the small workers' collectives within large firms in Hungary. These collectives are forms of transition from the First to the Second Economy.

- Another serious obstacle is the rigid official ideology of neighbouring socialist countries, as discussed by O. Vladimirov in his article in <u>Pravda</u> on 21st June 1985. This ideology is a source of the criticism against the Hungarian reform. By ridding the theory of socialism from its dogmatic components, positive changes could be brought about. The need for such a theoretical activity is particularly strong in China and in Yugoslavia.

I would also like to consider as a last question the prospects and possibilities of the Hungarian reform. Three basic developments may occur:

1) A new anti-reform period may begin similar to the one of 1972-1978. This would mean a return to the model of Soviet state management. Today's reformers would either be forced into a marginal position, or, through exercising 'self-criticism', would be executioners of the anti-reform policy. At this moment this development is not supported by economic considerations, but political aims and interests push it in this direction.

2) The reform comes to a standstill at the present level. That is, neither an efficient political reform nor a revision of the post-Stalinist ideology will be carried out. If we use the old Marxist terminology, we could say that there would be a clash between the basis (the pluralised economy) and the superstructure (monolithic political system). However, we must not be dogmatic when regarding the possibility that this contradictory system may last even for several generations. Yugoslavia is a good example of this.

3) As a result of the reforms, a third version will develop, whose essence may be explained by the Gramscian concept of 'historical blocks'. This means that an authentic civil society will be born, in conjunction with the power. Its authenticity consists in that it will have its own institutions and will be able to move and develop independently from the actual power, without claimimg to be all-powerful and therefore hinder the activity of the institutional power.

I hope to witness the realisation of the third possibility.

Some observations on the welfare economic aspects of the unofficial economy

ARNOLD HEERTJE

1. INTRODUCTION

In this chapter I approach the unofficial economy from the perspective of the broad concept of welfare. According to this interpretation, welfare refers to the level of satisfaction of wants, in so far as this level depends on the allocation of scarce resources. Welfare in this subjective and formal sense has a broader scope than is the case in most other writings on the unofficial economy.

According to this view, it does not matter whether the allocation of resources is expressed in terms of money or not, is registered or rooted in illegal activities. The essential feature from an economic point of view is the allocation of resources. What is often called the official economy, defined in one way or another, is then a sub-set of a much broader economic system, in which all kinds of activities take place. In the unofficial economy one encounters market transactions outside the sphere of the market. To the first category belong black labour, barter exchange and the buying and selling of goods without paying taxes. Activities outside the market sphere are production within the household, consumption within the firm, labour of volunteers, tax avoidance, hidden employment and the internal allocation in the bureaucracy of the public sector and the firms in the private sector. In short, the unofficial economy covers much more than just 'black money' and 'black labour'.

2. R.H. COASE

In our approach to the unofficial economy, the allocation of resources within the firm is part of it. In this respect, it is of some interest to refer to Coase's famous article, of 1937, on the nature of the firm (1).

Coase looked at the firm as a type of coordination, alternative to the coordination by the price mechanism. In the case of the firm the allocation is brought about by the manager. The transaction costs of these two types of coordination can be compared and considered with regard to the benefits of both. The outcome of the cost-benefit analysis explains why economic activity is divided into allocation within the market and within the firm. Not only within the firm, but also in the household, in institutions and within

303

the public sector, internal allocation of resources takes place. All these examples of internal allocation belong in my view to the unofficial economy.

Coase rightly points out that it is easier for the government to link its policy to the market mechanism than to comparable transactions that take place within households and firms. Measures in the sphere of taxation can be expressed in terms of market transactions, but cannot be applied in a meaningful way in case of internal allocation. In so far as individuals have a negative preference for the interference of the government, a positive welfare effect will be involved if allocation shifts from allocation through the market mechanism to internal allocation.

Without the role of firms and households the market mechanism does not exist. However, to what extent producers and consumers take care of the allocation of scarce resources themselves depends on the transaction costs of the use of the market and on the benefit of the internal allocation. The allocation of resources in the informal sphere and households is, therefore, not marginal to the allocation through the market, but reflects an alternative method of decision making of which the benefits increase.

Without the explicit allocation or implicit acceptance of property rights, the allocation of resources will be the result of orderly anarchy (2) or dictatorship. The freedom of exchange is based on a system of property rights.

In the strict sense those rules have a legal character, and in a broader sense we refer to the class of all social behaviour rules that have a tendency to restrict actual social behaviour.

In the formal sphere of the economy, economic activity largely depends on the financial transaction rooted in legal rules, while in the informal economy, economic activity highly depends on mutual trust.

3. THE EDGEWORTH-BOX AND THE CORE

In a barter economy without the interference of the government, individuals may reach optimal allocations in the core through a process of exchange, starting from an arbitrary initial position. It is a well-known proposition in welfare economics that a point in the core will be reached by means of a market mechanism. Now, if a movement from an initial position to the core is blocked by taxation, frustration will emerge and participants have a tendency no longer to accept the official pricing. Two developments may take place. Firstly, people may no longer accept the official price which involves a certain tax level, and start to individualize prices, through which they try to reach optimal points. Secondly, they may go back to barter exchange and try to negotiate deals without using prices.

In reality both developments take place. Individuals try to maximize welfare by abstracting from the public element in the price structure and they have invented all types of exchange without money.

4. SHOULD PREFERENCE FOR ILLEGAL ACTIVITIES BE ALLOWED TO COUNT IN THE SOCIAL WELFARE FUNCTION?

Sandmo has developed a well-known model on tax evasion (3). A question raised by Sandmo may throw some light on questions of a welfare theoretical nature. Sandmo himself does not defend an ethical position in this respect. He is just looking at the analytical consequences of a positive answer to the question. Within the framework of Paretian welfare economics, I can only adhere to such an attitude.

The individuals attach utility to their black activities. Whether this will bring about an increase in social welfare depends on the answer to the question whether, due to the black activities, one or more individuals undergo a decrease in welfare. One may assume that at both sides of the black market people attach a positive welfare effect to their behaviour. According to the Paretian principle, welfare, then, will increase in case of black labour. But it is also possible to look at the welfare position of others in society. If they have to pay more taxes, they suffer a welfare loss, and the application of the Pareto principle no longer allows us to make a statement on social welfare. In this case, it is possible to apply the compensation principle in the hypothetical version. A potential Pareto-improvement is at stake if the gainers from the black labour activity are able to compensate the losers. It seems probable that this is the case.

Now, if the social welfare function is the starting point for the policy of the government, the question arises whether the utility that the agents derive from black labour has to be taken into account. I am inclined to answer this question in a positive sense, as the government cannot deny the fact that black activities produce individual utility and, therefore, contribute to social welfare. The social welfare function then describes the welfare of both tax payers and tax evaders, who have determined their optimal positions. The agents take into account a certain level of taxes, the fine in case of cheating and the probability of being caught. The government may maximize welfare by choosing the rates of taxation, the fine in case of fraud, and the probability of being caught.

This welfare theoretic approach does not exclude the possibility that the government makes clear that it is against illegal activities. This raises the interesting question whether social welfare will be increased from the point of view of efficiency if the government fights tax evasion (4). The answer to this question depends on the ratio of the marginal costs of producers who evade taxes and those who do not. If the marginal costs of the evaders are higher than those of the other producers, as they have to make costs in order to conceal their tax evasion, it is from a welfare point of view optimal to prevent tax evasion. If marginal costs are lower, tax evasion does not hamper optimal welfare in Schweizer's model.

The further development and refinement of models on the behaviour of the government as to the reaction patterns of the citizens to rules and regulations, may throw light on the effect of both the government and the individual behaviour on the allocation of resources and therefore on welfare. It is, in particular, important to study the influence of the interference of the government on Pareto-optimality in the private sector, by comparing the allocation of resources with and without the role of the government.

5. DISEQUILIBRIUM

Let us start from a Pareto-optimal situation, brought about by large numbers of individual consumers and producers, who take prices as given. May we expect an informal economy under these circumstances? The answer crucially depends on the assumption we make on the optimal labour time. Activities in the informal sector of the economy take time. If the labour time in the formal sector is not exogeneously given but is the endogeneous result of the welfare decisions of the individuals, then two cases are particularly important. If we exclude the possibility of black labour, labour time and full employment in the formal sector of the economy are determined according to the preferences of the economic agents, in such a way that room is left for work in the household, do-it-yourself activities and the labour of volunteers. We then face a modest informal sector.

It is, however, possible that the optimal formal labour time also depends on the possibility to offer black labour in the informal sector of the economy at a higher wage rate than received in the official economy. In that case, labour time and full employment in the formal sector correspond with the preferences of the individuals and with technical possibilities, so that there remains room for legal informal activities and black labour. The market mechanism then not only allocates goods and factors of production, but also labour times in an optimal way. So far, we may conclude that even in case of equilibrium on all markets in the informal economy, an informal and even black sector can exist. However, the emergence of a black labour market is not very probable and the situation implies a modest role of the government and economic flexibility. The modest advantage in income derived from black labour in general does not outweigh the disadvantages and the lack of social security. Black labour turns out to be a very risky activity if official labour and social benefits in case of unemployment do not exist.

The assumption that an optimal structure of working hours will emerge through the market mechanism is rather unrealistic, as "hours of work are a little in the nature of what economists call a public good" (5). If the choice of the optimal labour time is determined in the market by heterogeneous technical possibilities and pluriform individual preferences, serious problems of communication and information arise, the solution of which may lead to excessive costs. These external effects of the implementation of the labour time indicate that an average labour time will be

determined in a more or less collective way through a decision process outside the market. As the collective outcome
of the decision-making cannot in all respects reflect individual preferences, a source for informal or black labour
springs up.

A more general framework for the pattern of formal and
informal economic activities provides the modern theory of
disequilibrium. This theory is a natural side line of general equilibrium models à la Walras, Arrow and Debsen, particularly if one starts to look for stability. The discussion
about the stability of the general equilibrium provides us
with insight into the behaviour patterns of the economic
agents, outside equilibrium. Of major importance is the
introduction of expectations (6), so that temporal equilibrium emerges, during which prices do not change. The decisions of the economic agents depend on current and expected
prices, so that in the next period there may be shortages of
demand or supply. The economy passes through a chain of
temporal equilibria; in each period equilibrium is brought
about by an adjustment of quantities and, from period to
period, prices change. At first sight, such an approach is
compatible with the empirical evidence that prices and wages
are sticky downwards, which leads to unplanned stocks and
waiting times. However, Drazen rightly observes that we are
in need of models of endogeneous price formation, "showing
that prices don't move to clear markets, not because they
are exogeneously constrained from doing so, but because no
price selling agent finds it in his interest to change
prices" (7). In order to explain Keynesian unemployment with
sticky wages, this vision is of particular interest. The
essence is to provide an endogeneous explanation for unemployment and stickiness of prices and wages. The theoretical
discussion has lead to the conclusion that the price mechanism does not establish full employment, because economic
agents have an interest in sticky prices and wages. As far
as prices are concerned, one may refer to monopolistic and
oligopolistic market structures and to the phenomenon of
administered prices (8). Many actual market structures are
characterized by a cooperative behaviour as to other components of the marketing-mix. Alongside these endogeneous
levies the combination of sticky prices, overcapacity and
surpluses can be explained. The modern theory of the implicit labour contract is capable of explaining the relative
stickiness of wages with respect to employment.

Individual behaviour of economic agents on the markets of
goods and labour results in an inflexible economic process,
with unemployment on one hand, and shortages of specific
types of labour and stocks of some, and shortages of other
goods. The economic agents are governed in their micro-
economic behaviour by individual targets and motives, and in
the end they are confronted with an unexpected and unintended macro-economic result which no longer correspond to
their individual preferences (9). Pressure groups of consumers, producers and workers further strengthen the in-
flexibility in the economy by asking for privileged positions (10). In so far as resources are directed at the

acquisition of those monopolistic and protected positions, they form the costs of the rent-seeking behaviour of individuals and groups (11).

For all these reasons, the actual picture of the formal economy deviates from the general equilibrium scheme. Oligopolistic market structures and bureaucratic and politic behaviour make the economy depart more and more from a Pareto-optimum. The power structure on the markets weakens the allocative function of the price mechanism, makes fluctuations in quantities more important, and undermines the general equilibrium.

In these imbalances, one can see an important cause for the emergence and growth of the informal economy. Productive capacities that remain unused in the formal economy are being used in the informal sectors. The unemployed, secured by social payments of a minumum income, offer their labour on the informal labour market, on which they meet a demand for black labour. The allocation in the informal economy is governed by a Walrasian price formation.

Transaction costs in the informal economy may be higher than in the formal economy, the advantages of activity in the informal sector are still higher. There is no power structure at either side of the labour market; direct negotiations are involved and no rule of the government plays a role. The market structure, then, is that of perfect competition; wages and prices reflect scarcity and the allocation corresponds to preferences of the consumers and is therefore Pareto-optimal. In the informal economy, no surpluses crop up, as prices adjust in order to get an equilibrium position. From the point of view of the economic agents, the macro-results of their micro-behaviour corresponds to their individual preferences.

In short, we face a dual economy: a formal sector characterized by sticky wages and prices, regulation by the government, a high level of social payments and taxation, working hours determined collectively, unintended stocks of goods and means of production, and long waiting times; and an informal sector characterized by flexible wages and prices, decentralized decision-making, a low level of the public burden, working hours determined individually, and planned stocks. Small scale production and technical change seem to stimulate the informal economy, so that a general equilibrium will be less and less reached. The total economy has a schizophrenic character, as equilibria with full-employment and under-employment and tendencies in the direction of a Pareto-optimum and a non-Pareto optimal situation develop themselves side by side. Looking at the formal and informal sector together, the allocation is nearer to a Pareto-optimum than could be the case without an informal sector. Through spending, both sectors are linked to one another. Informal income is at least partly spent in the formal economy. This compensates for the fact that part of the formal productive capacity remains unused. The actual level of consumption in the total economy is higher than in the formal sector.

6. CONCLUSION

A discussion of the welfare-economic aspects of the unofficial economy is still in its infancy. In our approach a
starting point has been to avoid moral statements and opinions and to concentrate on the allocative and distributional effects of the existence and growth of the unofficial
economy.
Another line of approach would be to look at the implementation of law and order as public good with positive and
negative external effects. Against this background a welfa-
re-theoretical analysis of the unofficial economy seems to
be possible.

NOTES

(1) Coase (1937).
(2) Buchanan (1975), pp. 4-6.
(3) Sandmo (1981).
(4) See Schweizer (1984), pp. 247-258.
(5) Hahn (1979), p. 79.
(6) See, in particular, Patinkin (1965), (1972).
(7) Drazen (1980); Cippa, Guidi (1982).
(8) Means (1961); also Weiss et al. (1977).
(9) The situation may be compared with the situation de-
     scribed by Hirsh (1977), p. 3, in which individuals all
     buy a car in order to drive; an aim made impossible by
     the fact that all consumers buy a car and try to drive
     on the roads.
(10) Olson (1982); Mueller (1983).
(11) Buchanan, Tollison, Tullock (1980); Tollison (1982).

REFERENCES

BUCHANAN, J.M., The Limits of Liberty, Chicago 1975.
BUCHANAN, J.M., TOLLISON, R.D., TULLOCK, G., (eds), Toward a
    Theory of the Rent-Seeking Society, Texas 1980.
CIPPA, R.F., GUIDI, V., 'Temporary Equilibrium with Ration-
    ing' in Baranzini, M., (ed), Advances in Economic Theory,
    Oxford 1982, pp. 90-112.
COASE, R.H., 'The Nature of the Firm', Economica, 1937, pp.
    386-405; reprinted in Boulding, K.E., Stigler, G.J.,
    (eds), Readings in Price Theory, Chicago 1952, pp. 331-
    351.
DRAZEN, A., 'Recent Developments in Macro-economic Disequi-
    librium Theory', Econometrica, 1980, pp. 283-306.
HAHN, F., The U.S.A. in the World Economy, edited by
    Heertje, A., San Francisco 1979.
HIRSH, F., Social Limits to Growth, London 1977.
MEANS, G.C., 'Administered Prices' in Mark, S.M., Slate,
    D.M., Economics in Action, San Francisco 1961.
MUELLER, D.C., (ed) The Political Economy of Growth, New
    Haven 1983.
OLSON, M., The Rise and Decline of Nations, New Haven, 1982.

PATINKIN, D., <u>Money, Interest and Prices</u>, New York, 1965.
PATINKIN, D., <u>Studies in Monetary Economics</u>, New York 1972.
SANDMO, A., 'Income Tax Evasion, Labour Supply and the Equity Efficiency Trade-off', <u>Journal of Public Economics</u>, 1981, pp. 265-288.
SCHWEIZER, U., 'Welfare Analysis of Excise Tax Evasion', <u>Zeitschrift fur die gesamte Staatswissenschaft</u>, 1984, pp. 247-258.
TOLLISON, R.D., 'Rent-Seeking; A Survey', <u>Kyklos</u>, 1982, pp. 575-602.
WEISS, L.W. et al., 'Administeres Prices', <u>The American Economic Review</u>, 1977, pp. 610-610.

Optimal income taxation and the untaxed sector

INGEMAR HANSSON

1. INTRODUCTION

The literature on optimal income taxation examines the tax pattern that optimally balances the desirability of an even distribution of utilities and the cost of distortionary taxes. Typically, individuals are assumed to differ with respect to their income earning capacity in the taxed sector only, and distortions only arise for the allocation of time between the taxed sector and leisure (1). Available studies show, however, that households spend almost as much time in home-production and other types of untaxed production as in taxed production. Moreover, capacity obviously differs across individuals also for untaxed activities. Traditional studies of optimal income taxation hence neglect both an important source of distortions in the allocation of time and an important source of differences across individuals.

The purpose of the current paper is to extend this literature by recognizing the importance of untaxed production. In particular, the optimal tax schedule for redistributive income taxation is estimated numerically when untaxed production is incorporated in the analysis. A comparison with the corresponding result in the special case when untaxed activities are ignored reveals the potential error in the traditional analysis.

The literature on optimal income taxation applies two conceptually different approaches for the determination of the optimal tax pattern. Early studies such as Feldstein (1973), Cooter and Helpman (1974) and Stern (1976) motivate redistribution by ethical judgements about the importance of equality. Typically, social welfare is measured as a weighted sum of individuals' utilities, where the weights reveal the importance of egalitarian considerations in the social welfare function.

A more recent strand in the literature interprets redistributive taxation as a system of social insurance for risk-averse individuals with imperfect information on their future capacities to earn income, (Varian, 1980; Persson, 1984; and Hansson, Stuart, 1984). Progressive taxation in the form of a negative income tax functions as social insurance, since individuals who are unlucky and have low realized incomes are compensated via a net redistribution from the public sector. Given risk aversion, this social insurance is valuable. Providing insurance, however, also generates moral hazard in the form of distorted factor supply incentives. The optimal pattern of taxation balances the insurance effects and the distortions caused by greater tax progressivity.

In order to get some type of neutral or objective basis for the determination of optimal redistributive taxation, some of these papers apply a Rawlsian conceptual experiment, where individuals are made identical by being placed behind a 'veil of ignorance'. More specifically, individuals who have yet to enter society are identical in that they face the same probability distribution of their future capacities. While these capacities are uncertain prior to entry, they will become known afterwards, when the individual must determine how much labor to supply. Maximization of expected utility then determines the optimal tax pattern. Since all entrants have the same probability distribution of capacities, the decision is unanimous.

The current paper applies this more recent approach. Expected utility for risk-averse individuals is, however, equal to 1/I of the sum of the ex post utilities of the I individuals of society. Maximization of expected utility is, therefore, equivalent to maximization of a social welfare function with equal weights for all risk-averse individuals. Therefore, the current model also represents the traditional approach with a utilitarian social welfare function.

Recognition of untaxed production has several potentially important implications for the analysis of optimal income taxation. At first glance the most striking effect is that income measured for tax purposes may be a poor measure of the sum of an individual's gainful activities. This may decrease the scope for redistributive taxation. A closer analysis reveals, however, that this argument is misleading. Instead, several countervailing effects are involved. In the traditional simple model, utility is related to income earning capacity as measured by the wage rate in the taxed sector. The tax base is, however, the product of this wage rate and the optimal labor supply in this sector. The scope for redistributive taxation then depends on how well the tax base approximates the wage rate in this model. In the current extended model, utility instead depends on what we will term 'capacity' in the taxed and the untaxed sector. The question is then how well the tax base approximates these two capacities. The crucial issue for the scope of redistributive taxation in the two models is hence how well an imperfect measure, the tax base, approximates variations in the single and the two capacities respectively. The fact that the tax base may provide a poor measure for the value of all gainful activities in the extended model is less relevant.

If a higher capacity in the untaxed sector implies, say, lower labor supply in the taxed sector ceteris paribus, low supply in the taxed sector signals high capacity in the untaxed sector. This may decrease the scope for redistributive taxation when the untaxed sector is incorporated in the analysis. A related factor is that variations in capacity also in the untaxed sector involve an additional source of uncertainty that may call for more insurance, i.e., an increase in the optimal tax rate.

Finally, capacity in the untaxed sector is likely to be correlated with capacity in the taxed sector. A high wage may then signal high capacity in another respect, which is also relevant for utility. This is another reason why recognition of variations in capacity in the untaxed sector may imply a higher optimal tax than in traditional analysis, where individuals are identical except for different capacities in the taxed sector.

The current paper examines the importance of these effects in a simulation model, which determines the optimal income tax when untaxed production is taken into account. The traditional model with no untaxed production raises a special case. A comparison of the optimal tax rates in the two cases illuminates the potential bias in the traditional analysis.

2. THE MODEL

2.1. Introduction

The analysis takes place in a general equilibrium model of an open economy with I individuals and a government that collect taxes and redistributes tax revenues as lump-sum transfers.

The model includes two sectors. Sector One is the taxed sector. In this sector, taxed labor produces output that is sold on a market with low transaction costs. Sector One output is the numeraire.

Sector two is the untaxed sector. This sector includes home production and activities that are untaxed due to tax avoidance and tax evasion. Market exchange of goods and services in this sector typically involves tax evasion. Therefore, this sector is characterized by high transaction costs. This gives a strong tendency to 'self-service' in this sector.

2.2. Households

Individual i is characterized by his capacity in the taxed sector, $Xi1$, and by his capacity in the untaxed sector, $Xi2$. His endownet of time, E, is allocated to labor in the taxed sector, $Li1$, labor in the untaxed sector, $Li2$, and leisure, $E-Li1 -Li2$.

Measured in efficiency units, individual i's quantity of labor supplied to the taxed sector is $Xi1Li1$. This labor earns the wage rate W and gives a before-tax labor income of $WXi1Li1$. This income is taxed by a linear negative income tax with marginal rate T and a lump-sum transfer TR. This may be interpreted as a first order approximation of any tax schedule.

For simplicity, we assume that individuals have no capital income. Instead, government gets all capital income and may redistribute this income as a part of the lump-sum transfer (2).

313

Individual i's consumption of output from the taxed sector, Ci, is determined by the budget constraint:

$$Ci = W \; Xi1Li1 \; (1-T) + TR. \qquad (1)$$

Individual i's labor measured in efficiency units in the untaxed sector is Xi2Li2. This labor provides utility directly from home production and other tax free activities and indirectly through activities where taxes are evaded. Due to high transaction costs, output from this labor is typically not exchanged between households. Therefore, this labor is included as an argument in the utility function. This means that the utility function incorporates an implicit production function that converts this labor into goods and services. Individual i's utility function is hence:

$$U(Ci, \; Xi2Li2, \; E-Li1-Li2). \qquad (2)$$

For a given linear tax system, maximization of this utility function with respect to the budget constraint (1) determines individual i's allocation of time, Li1, Li2, and E-Li1-Li2. The budget constraint then determines his consumption Ci.

All individuals are identical except for different capacities. The allocation of time may therefore be expressed as a common function of the capacity vector (Xi1, Xi2):

$$Li1 = Li1 \; (Xi1, \; Xi2), \; Li2 = L2(Xi1, \; Xi2) \text{ for } i = 1,2,..,I.$$
$$(3)$$

If the density function for capacities is denoted f(X1, X2), aggregate effective labor per capita in the taxed sector is:

$$La1 = \sum \sum Xi1 \; Li1(Xi1, \; Xi2) \; f(X1, \; X2). \qquad (4)$$

2.3. Government

Government variables are measured in per-capita terms in order to be consistent with earlier notation. Government expenditures are lump-sum transfers and other expenditures, G. Since other expenditures are held constant throughout the analysis, the effect of such expenditures on utility and resource allocation is irrelevant, i.e., the utility function should be interpreted as being valid for the given level of G.

For simplicity, we assume that the economy is small and open. This implies that the rate of return on capital, R, is determined by a given international rate of return. If the aggregate production function in the taxed sector is homogeneous of degree one, the capital-labor ratio and the wage rate are also exogenous.

An increase in the tax on labor income that, say, decreases La1, gives a proportional reduction in capital that is _used_ in the open economy, while factor prices remain constant. Since capital owned in the country, K, is assumed to be constant, this involves a decrease in net foreign-owned capital.

The assumption of an open economy is indeed likely to be a better approximation for most developed economies compared with the more common assumption of a closed economy. This may be true also for the US in view of the ample importance of international capital flows and the fact that world economy is four times as large as the U.S. economy (3).

The government's budget is assumed to balance:

$$TR + \overline{G} = T \, \overline{W} \, La1 + \overline{R} \, \overline{K}, \qquad (5)$$

where bars indicate constants.

2.4. Determination of the optimal tax rate

For a given tax rate, T, equations (3), (4), and (5) determine the general equilibrium allocation of resources and the lump-sum transfer: Li1, Li2 for i = 1,2,...I and TR. This allocation and equations (1) and (2) determine utility for each individual.

In order to determine the optimal tax rate, consider a Rawlsian conceptual experiment, where identical individuals who have yet to enter the society are placed behind a veil of ignorance. Each individual knows the true density function for the distribution of capacities in the future society, f(X1, X2), but does not know his own future capacity. Under the von Neumann-Morgenstern assumptions such individuals would unanimously select a tax rate that maximizes expected utility:

$$E(U) = \sum \sum U \, (C(X1, X2), L2(X1,X2)$$

$$E-L1(X1, X2)-L2(X1,X2) \, f(X1,X2) \qquad (6)$$

This maximand may alternatively be interpreted as a utilitarian social welfare function, where social welfare is the sum of the individuals' utilities.

For any given tax rate, T, the model determines the allocation of resources and a value for expected or aggregate utility in equation (6). The model can be used to determine the tax rate that maximizes expected utility. This rate can then be compared to the optimal rate in a more traditional analysis that ignores the existence of the untaxed sector.

3. EMPIRICAL IMPLEMENTATION

3.1. Distribution of capacities

The distribution of capacities for activities in the taxed and the untaxed sector is obviously important for the determination of the optimal tax rate. If capital markets are perfect, such that consumption can be rearranged over the life-cycle, capacity in the taxed sector would ideally be the wage rate net of educational investments over the life-cycle. If capital markets are imperfect, this may call for a comparison of wage rates over a shorter time period.

Owing to a lack of such life-cycle data the calculations must be based on imperfect data. Figure 1 shows the distribution of hourly earnings for employees in Sweden in 1980.

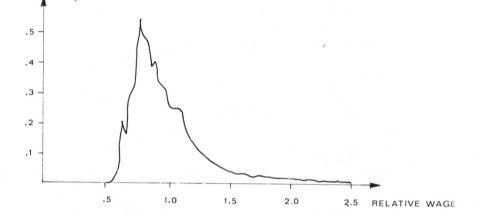

Figure 1 - Distribution of wage rates for employees in Sweden 1980.

This data involves several sources of error compared to ideal life-cycle data. Since only wage earners are included, people who do not work because of low potential wages, as well as the self-employed, are excluded. This is likely to give an underestimate of the true variance of capacity in the taxed sector. The data in figure 1 does, on the other hand, include variance that is due to education and age, by contrast with the ideal measure, thereby giving a tendency in the opposite direction.

If the agents in the model are interpreted as households rather than individuals in order to account for the averaging of consumption within households, the capacity distribution should ideally be measured over households. Since figure 1 shows data for individuals, this tends to over-estimate the true variance. This is because household formation involves an averaging over individuals, which tends to reduce the variability in the distribution of capacities.

Among non-workers, retirees and students have a distribution of income earning capacity in the taxed sector over the life-cycle that is probably reflected adequately by the distribution of wages for employees. Disabled and permanently unemployed individuals obviously have relatively low capacities in the taxed sector. Most countries, including Sweden, do, however, provide special mean-tested transfers for these groups. Therefore, these groups are not included in the current analysis. This means that the derived optimal tax system redistributes income in excess of various types of support to these special groups. Such government expenditures are consequently included in G, i.e. in other types of government expenditures.

Available data do not allow for a reliable adjustment of the raw data in figure 1 in order to take account of these and other (in some cases) countervailing sources of error. Therefore, the distribution of wages in figure 1 is simply applied as the distribution of capacities in the taxed sector, X1. The variable is measured in units such that the expected value equals unity. The potential sources of error in this data, of course, involve a source of error for the estimated optimal tax rate.

Data are even more scarce for the distribution of capacities in the untaxed sector, X2. The approach is therefore to examine the optimal tax rate for different assumed distributions. In order to examine the effects of different degrees of correlation between X1 and X2 as well as the effects of different relative variance, let Y be a random variable that is independent of X1. Moreover, the density function for this variable is assumed to be identical with the density function for X1 (figure 1). Capacity in the untaxed sector is then defined as:

$$X2 = 1 + \eta \ (\lambda X1 + (1-\lambda)Y) - 1), \qquad (7)$$

$$\text{where } 0 \leqslant \lambda \leqslant 1 \text{ and } \eta \geqslant 0.$$

The parameter determines the correlation between X1 and X2 from the value of 0 for $\lambda = 0$ to the value of 1 for $\lambda = 1$. Since both X1 and Y has a mean of unity, the expression in the bracket parenthesis has a mean of zero. A higher value of η consequently gives a higher variance of X2 but does not change the mean value.

The parameters λ and η are selected to give any desired correlation between X1 and X2 and any desired variance in X2.

As a future possible extension of the paper, the values for λ and η may be estimated as to provide the best possible fit with empirical observations of the distribution of L1 and L2 for each capacity group in the taxed sector, X1. This extension involves a potentially significant improvement in the empirical basis for the calculated optimal tax rate.

3.2. Other data and assumptions

Remaining parameters in the model are selected to give elasticities of labor supply in the taxed sector and a degree of risk aversion that are consistent with available empirical evidence. Moreover, the parameter values are selected to reproduce an equilibrium for Swedish data in 1979. In order to impose such constraints, the utility function is specified as a sufficiently generalized CES-function with a constant degree of relative risk aversion, γ :

$$U(Ci, Xi2Li2, E-Li1-Li2) =$$

$$(1/(1-\gamma)) \; (\alpha_1 C1^{-e} + \alpha_2 (Xi2Li2)^{-e} +$$

$$(1-\alpha_1 -\alpha_2) (E-L1-L2))^{(\gamma-1/e)} \tag{8}$$

The data and the assumption reported in Table 1 determine the parameters in the utility function. The elasticities of labour supply are weighted averages of median elasticities for men and women from a survey of more than 40 recent estimates for the US and the UK reported in Hansson and Stuart (1985). The assumed degree of relative risk aversion is based on a survey in Hansson and Stuart (1984).

Table 1

Data for Sweden in 1979 and assumptions.

Output (by choice of units)	1
r K, capital income	0.1
La1, aggregate labor in the taxed sector	1
La2, aggregate labor in the untaxed sector	0.80
T, marginal tax rate on labor income	0.73
G, other government expenditures	0.16
W, (implied) wage rate	0.9
TR, (implied) lump-sum transfer	0.60
γ, degree of relative risk aversion	3
Wage elasticity of labor supply	0.10
Total income elasticity of labor supply	-0.15 (3)

Source: Hansson, Stuart (1984, 1985) and Konsumentverket (1984).

4. RESULTS

Table 2 shows the optimal tax rates for different assumptions on the correlation between X and X and on the variance in X relatively to the variance in X .

318

Table 2

Optimal tax rates for different variances of X and for different correlations.

Correlation	Relative variance of X2			
	0	0.5	1.0	1.5
0	.43	.44	.45	.46
0.5	-	.48	.51	.53
1.0	-	.50	.53	.55

In a reasonable basic case with a correlation of, say, 0.5 and the same variance for the two capacities the optimal tax rate is 0.51. This rate, as well as all other tax rates in the table, are considerably lower than the actual rate in 1979 of 73 percent.

The traditional analysis, where the untaxed sector is ignored, corresponds to the case where the X2 is constant across individuals, i.e., where the relative variance is zero (implying zero correlation). The optimal tax rate is 0.43 in this case (5).

A comparison of these two results give the important conclusion that the optimal tax rate is higher when the untaxed sector is taken account of. This means that the traditional approach underestimates the optimal tax rate.

To analyze this result further, note that the optimum tax rate increases with increasing variance in X2 even when the two capacities are independent (row 1). The explanation is that L1 turns out to _increase_ in X2. A high tax base, X1L1, consequently _signals_ high capacity in the untaxed sector for a given X1. This means that a high X2 is associated with high tax payments, i.e., the income tax provides insurance also for variations in X2. Therefore, variations in X2 gives a higher optimal tax rate than in the traditional case with a constant X2.

The fact that L1 increases in X2 may in turn be explained as a consequence of an income effect. Introspection of the utility function (8) shows that a high X2 gives a high level of sector two input and output for a given L. Due to decreasing marginal utility this tends to decrease L2. This is analogous to the income effect of a wage increase in the standard analysis of labor supply. Such a decrease in L2 in turn tends to increase L1 due to decreasing marginal utility of leisure.

It should also be noted that the result that L1 increases in X1 corresponds to the observation, that the trendwise

319

increase in female labor force participation may partly be explained by increased productivity in home production.

For a given relative variance in X2, a higher correlation gives a higher optimal tax rate. The explanation is two-fold. First, a higher correlation involves a higher overall risk that tends to increase the optimal tax rate. Second, a higher correlation means that X1 is a more adequate signal for X2, implying that the tax base, X1L1, provides a more proper base for insurance against variations in X2.

The results in table 2 indicate that the underestimate of the optimal tax rate in traditional studies is especially large if correlation is high, while the variability in sector two capacity is less important.

To summarize, recognition of the existence of an untaxed sector implies a higher optimal tax rate redistributive income taxation. The explanation is that the income turns out to provide insurance not only for variations in capacity in the taxed sector but also for variations in capacity in the untaxed sector. This result holds even when the two capacities are independent.

NOTES

*   The financial support from the Bank of Sweden Tercen-
       tenary Foundation is gratefully acknowledged.
(1)   Cf. Stern (1976); Persson (1984); and Hansson, Stuart
       (1984).
(2)   This assumption is equivalent to the apparently less
       restrictive case, when all individuals possess the same
       amount of capital and capital income is taxed at a
       constant rate. This is because an increase in this tax
       rate to 100 percent, i.e., government gets all capital
       income, and a budget balancing adjustment in the lump-
       sum transfer has no effect on the allocation of re-
       sources; cf. equation (5).
(3)   Under the opposite assumption of a closed economy the
       production function and the ownership of capital must
       also be specified, as in Hansson, Stuart (1984).
(4)   Both E and B must be treated as parameters in order to
       give the desired wage- and income elasticities of labor
       supply. These wage- and income-elasticities are imposed
       for the mean individual, and parameters are selected to
       give the lowest possible variance in the wage-elastici-
       ty across individuals.
(5)   Alternatively and more directly the traditional analy-
       sis means that L and are set equal to zero a priori.
       After reparameterization this simplified model also
       gives an optimal tax rate of 0.43, i.e., these two
       formulations of the traditional approach give the same
       result. The explanation is that the parameterization of
       the two models with unchanged assumptions for labor
       supply elasticities tends to give the same response to
       changes in the tax rate and the lump-sum transfer.

REFERENCES

COOTER, R., HELPMAN, E., 'Optimal Income Taxation for Trans-
fer Payments under Different Social Welfare Criteria',
Quarterly Journal of Economics, vol. 88, 1974, pp. 656-
670.
FELDSTEIN, M., 'On the Optimal Progressivity of the Income
Tax', Journal of Public Economics, no. 2, 1973, pp. 357-
376.
HANSSON, I., STUART, C., 'Progressive Taxation as Social Insurance and as a Median-Voter Outcome: An Empirical As-
sessment', Department of Economics, University of Lund,
Sweden 1984, forthcoming in the Scandinavian Journal of
Economics.
HANSSON, I., STUART, C., 'Tax Revenue and the Marginal Cost
of Public Funds in Sweden', Department of Economics, Uni-
versity of Lund, Sweden, 1985, forthcoming in the Journal
of Public Economics.
MIRRLEES, J., 'An Exploration in the Theory of Optimum
Income Taxation', Review of Economic Studies, vol. 38,
1971, pp. 175-208.
PERSSON, M., 'The Distribution of Abilities and the Progres-
sive Income Tax', Journal of Public Economics, 1984.
RAWLS, J., Theory of Justice, Harvard University Press,
Cambridge 1971.
STERN, N., 'On the Specification of Models of Optimum Income
Taxation', Journal of Public Economics, no. 6, 1976, pp.
123-162.
VARIAN, H., 'Utility, Strategy, and Social Decision Rules',
Journal of Public Economics, vol. 14, 1980, pp. 49-68.

The inequality impact of the unofficial economy in Yugoslavia

IVO BIĆANIĆ

1. DEFINING THE UNOFFICIAL ECONOMY

The definition of what activities constitute the unofficial economy depends on which aspects are being discussed, on the institutional framework within which the economy functions, and on the nature of the economy itself. This paper is adapted to discussing the impact of the unofficial economy on economic inequality in Yugoslavia. It will include only two kinds of 'structurally incorporated' unofficial economic activities:

1.   Activities conducted completely within the legal system but not registered in national accounts or official statistics
2.   Activities which are illegal, but those participating in them run only a small risk of prosecution.

They are similar in that both are 'structurally incorporated' into the economy but not directly registered in official statistics. They differ in their relationship to the legal system in which they operate. Two notions here require clarification.

'Structural incorporation'. The unofficial economy is by its very nature ambiguous and thus it is impossible to give a completely unambiguous definition of 'structural incorporation'. In this paper we use it to differentiate between economic activities whose sudden termination would cause major short - or medium - term disruption of economic flows and those other unofficial activities which are peripheral and whose sudden cessation would pass almost unnoticed by all except those directly involved.

By 'small or even negligible probability of being prosecuted' we attempt to distinguish between those illegal activities which come to be tolerated and those which do not. A problem inherent in this distinction is that legal practice may change. Clampdowns and campaigns against activities that were once tolerated create a shifting boundary.

In spite of ambiguities, it is useful to maintain these distinctions because many people involved in the unofficial economy do not perceive themselves as criminals, while others operate in activities that it is impossible to eradicate.

Thus, as an example of the former, businessmen, when faced

with unimplementable government economic policy or unsolvable problems of bureaucratic red tape, consciously break the law to enable the enterprise to function in an unofficial activity called in Yugoslavia 'useful malpractice'. They claim to do it in the name of social goals. An example of the latter may be dealings in foreign currency, which will be described later.

2. LEGAL BUT UNREGISTERED ACTIVITIES

Official statistics in Yugoslavia register all financial transactions which take place within the socialized sector, and between this sector and private individuals (all transactions that take place through the Social Accounting Office). Economic transactions which are not covered, or are not adequately covered, or are faultily covered by the statistics, are those that take place within the private sector itself, between the private sector and the general public, and among private individuals. Some such transactions appear as estimates, but the majority are left unregistered. Even tax returns are not really helpful since a large part of the private sector pays lump-sum taxes while the taxes of others are assessed on the basis of their own bookkeeping or according to the needs of the local government administrations for funds.

3. ASPECTS OF INEQUALITY RELEVANT FOR THE UNOFFICIAL ECONOMY'S IMPACT

It is usual to distinguish three aspects of economic inequality: inequality in the distribution of income and earnings (i.e. inequality of flows), inequality in the distribution of wealth (i.e. inequality of stocks), inequality in the distribution of economic power. In the present paper, we are able to take into account only some aspects of the first two, though fully aware of the third, especially as seen in, for example, such traditions as 'the old comrade network'.
When adapting the economics of inequality to deal with the impact of the unofficial economy, two related problems must be taken into account: difficulties of measurement (indeed the impossibility of cardinal measurement), and the need to expand the area under consideration. Ideally, we should measure through two distributions: one set of points referring to the official, the other to the unofficial economy. The known difficulty is that it is almost impossible to determine the second distribution because of the very nature of the unofficial economy. The approach devised in this paper relies on the clear connection between activities and inequality. We have tried to determine the inequality impact for individuals involved in a certain form of unofficial activity, and then determine the impact of those movements on overall inequality.

4. SOME CAUSES OF ILLEGAL UNOFFICIAL ECONOMIC ACTIVITIES IN YUGOSLAVIA

Space does not permit more than a mere mention of the three most important causes for unofficial economic activities in Yugoslavia.

The first cause results from the nature of the economic environment and can be seen in the attained level of development, regional differences, and external influence on the economy.

These seem to influence the forms and variety of activities, but not neccessarily the size. The level of development also seems to have an important influence on the respect of the law.

The second cause stems from the business cycle and short term economic policy. The forms during a downswing are different from those in an upswing.

The third set of causes results from the nature of the economic system. In the Yugoslav case, three aspects are especially important. The first results from 'normative optimism' (i.e. the idea that agents behave according to the paradigm and that prescribing behaviour actually solves difficulties); the second comes from 'unimplementable' economic policy (meaning that business can sometimes function only by circumventing the law, which has led to the interesting Yugoslav phenomena of 'useful malpractices'); thirdly, the biases of decision makers (the best example for this is the notorious bias against the private sector and inequality in socialist countries).

5. THE IMPACT OF VARIOUS FORMS OF THE UNOFFICIAL ECONOMY

In Yugoslavia, the unofficial economy has a richness and variety of forms which does justice to the resourcefulness and ingenuity of the population and of individuals. Eight main forms seem to prevail. The direct influence on income and earning, and thus on income inequality of each, will be discussed in this section:

(i) moonlighting in urban professions, (ii) moonlighting and unofficial activities in agriculture including 'agribusinesses', (iii) dealings in foreign currency, (iv) real estate and the building sector, (v) renting flats and houses, (vi) retailing agricultural and industrial commodities, (vii) tourism, (viii) self-help and do-it-yourself activities.

(i) The only basic data directly related to moonlighting presently available are a series of household surveys conducted by the Centre for Marketing and a survey made by the Institute for Self-Management. Other additional data are to be found in court cases (which are unreliable due to the 'iceberg' effect), or in the traces moonlighting leaves in the official statistics.

The Marketing Centre surveys were based on a sample of the whole population in which the proportion of agricultural, mixed and nonagricultural households was determined according to the population census and regional proportions; while the choice of the over 2,200 households was otherwise random. The surveys were conducted through interviews and were usually parts of 'omnibus' surveys. The first survey to include questions on moonlighting and 'social inequality' (as economic inequality is called in Yugoslavia) was made in 1978, but the data were never published except as internal working papers of the Centre. Two more surveys which dealt with issues concerning the unofficial economy, and which were in some aspects a continuation of the first survey, were made in March and June 1984 and included data about activities in 1983. Some of these data have been published in the Centre's journal TRIN; these are papers by Marković (1984), Sirotić (1983), Maroević (1984a and 1983b) and Šrajer (1984). A short journalistic survey appeared in Maković (1984). These articles compare the two sets of surveys and present the raw data of individual surveys, remaining confined to descriptive statistics. Some of the data is still not published and therefore cannot be quoted, but the working papers were made available to the author.

The survey made by the Self-Management Institute was conducted through questionnaires among workers employed in the socialized sector in the Republic of Croatia. The most interesting data have not been made public. However, part of the survey was presented in Cimeša (1984), and all the results were made available to the author. Due to these circumstances, this paper will quote only the published data, but, in drawing conclusions, will rely on some of the still unpublished data.

The household survey dealt with the supply and demand of labour services in moonlighting data on types of services and their value. All the data refer to unofficial activities admitted to by those interviewed and should thus be treated as lower boundaries only. The actual extent is undoubtedly much larger. The phrase used to describe moonlighting in the survey was: "The supply of labour services for others outside working hours".

The survey showed that a quarter of the households admitted that some of their members moonlighted: of which 13 per cent admitted moonlighting for money, and 17 per cent had non-monetary benefits (some did both, hence they do not add up to 25 percent). Non-monetary benefits are moonlighting which implies the barter of goods, services or favours. This quid pro quo need not occur immediately but represents an obligation which can be called upon later. Among the adult population, 12 percent admitted moonlighting. 'Blown up' to national level, this implies that 1.5 million households had members moonlighting, and that 1.7 million persons of working age admitted to moonlighting (out of an economically active population of around 14 million, with 6.1 million in the socialized sector), or 312 thousand daily. Members of mixed and agricultural households were much more ready to moonlight (25 percent of the former, and 30 percent of the latter admitted) but less inclined to do so for money (only 16 percent admitted to being paid). The frequency of moonlighting varies. 1 percent regularly moonlight for money, while 2 percent regularly moonlight for non-monetary benefits 8 percent frequently moonlight for money and 11 per cent frequently moonlight without payment, while 2 percent rarely (2 to 3 times a year) moonlight for money, and 3 percent rarely moonlight without getting paid. The motivation for moonlighting is mainly a fall in living standards. In 1983, 36 percent of households estimated their incomes as insufficient to cover their expenses (a higher percentage than in previous years), the hardest hit being the urban population of towns with 2 to 50 thousand inhabitants. The second predominant motive was the satisfaction of consumers targets - purchase of consumer durables, a house, etc., for which adequate funds could not be got through regular employment or bank loans.

Comparison of the data for 1978 and 1983 shows an increase of the number of households whose members moonlight (from 21 percent in 1978 to 25 percent in 1983) and a rise in the numbers percentage of moonlighters in the population (from 9 percent to 12 percent). This data should probably be treated with care because there was a greater incentive not to admit moonlighting in 1978. In spite of this, the data reveal the expected result that falling living standards and economic crisis increase moonlighting. This fact is further strengthened by data which indicate that there was a significant increase in the willingness to moonlight for cash only - understandably enough since bills can only be paid in cash. The data also provides insight into the composition of moonlighters. The overwhelming majority of moonlighters being employed in the socialized sector.

Besides moonlighting out of working hours, there is also moonlighting during work time (mostly in urban occupations with no one, of course, admitting it) and a widespread use of sick leave to do other jobs. This kind of use of sick leave is truly incorporated, and when those surveyed could choose among the most frequent causes of sick leave, 46 percent gave illness, while 18 percent gave work in the fields, 23 percent moonlighting and 23 percent "doing something at home" (Maroević 1984a).

Since it was expected that the demand side would be less secretive, the survey also inquired into the frequency, type and value of moonlight services in demand. Moonlighting in building services were used by 7 percent of the households (an understandable fall from the previous survey due to the economic crisis). There was an increase (up to 9 percent of households) using moonlighters for household maintenance and a fall to 9 percent in moonlighting for the repair of household durables. This fall can be explained by the economic crisis, which left only major repairs to moonlighting; the minor ones being taken care of through a significant increase in do-it-yourself activities. Other unofficial labour services, such as repairs to cars or agricultural equipment, were admitted by 8 percent households (since not all have cars or agricultural equipment, the actual importance is bigger). The data, however, conceal some interesting information. We do not know when the service was supplied nor with whose tools. If moonlighting takes place during sick leave, absenteeism or working hours, the tools may well be those of the socialist enterprise.

The probable impact of urban moonlighting is to decrease inequality. In particular, it tends to increase the earnings of the lower paid, thus decreasing overall inequality in non-agricultural households. However, in spite of this, the data indicate that moonlighting did not solve the fall in incomes and standard of living caused by the economic crisis.

(ii) We turn to unofficial economic activities in agriculture and so called 'agribusinesses'.

Supplying labour service in agriculture is very likely one of the most common forms of the unofficial economy. The basic details have already been given. They are: (i) level of development (large share of peasant agriculture, which is only partly cash-oriented); (ii) the importance of the 'mixed household' (part-time peasants, one or more family members working in the socialized sector); (iii) decision-making biases against private agriculture (with the resulting constraints on production, administrative barriers, uncertainty etc.); (iv) the centuries-long tradition of peasant cooperation. All these provide a basis for the three most common forms of the unofficial economic activity in agriculture. The first is the cultivation of land during the peak agricultural seasons regardless of other obligations; the second is devious forms of renting and leasing land so as to cultivate areas above the permitted minimum (which being 8 hectares is technologically suboptimal); the third is selling produce to unauthorized retailers. Disregarding the long discussions on the costs and benefits of 'mixed households', and also the fact that official policy makers are not inclined to further and ease their livelihood, it remains a fact of life that over a third of Yugoslav households are mixed. Such households have thus become an important feature of the economy, which is especially interesting from the standpoint of the unofficial economy, since without it this kind of household could not exist. Indeed, perhaps the mixed household is the best example in Yugoslavia of structurally incorporated unofficial economic activity.

In the peak agricultural seasons there is a labour bottle-neck and the entire family works on the land. Since by definition some of these in mixed households will have regular jobs in industry, they cannot get paid or unpaid leave, and there is a strong stimulus to resort to sick leave or absenteeism. In 179 enterprises that were surveyed, 72 percent registered a disruption of production during peak agricultural seasons through sick leave or absenteeism (Maroević 1984a, p. 46). Similarly, when being asked to name the cause for high sick leave, 23 percent admitted taking such leave to work on the fields and 23 percent to "doing something at home", while less than half were actually sick during sick leave (Maroević 1984a, p. 45). The short dura-

328

tion of the average sick leave , its distribution during the
calendar year, and the immense number of hours thus lost,
all validate the above. Lastly it must be mentioned that
mixed households show the greatest propensity to moonlight
(over 25 percent do so) with an equal preference for paid
and unpaid moonlighting.

The impact on inequality of moonlighting in agriculture
can be appreciated after the inequality measured for different types of households has been presented. The official
statistical office conducts a large household survey concerning the income and expenditure of over 20,000 households.
They have been conducted as two-stage random samples every
five years since 1963. The most recent one was made in
January 1984 (data 1983) but has not yet been published.
Thus, the Gini coefficient could only be calculated for the
15-year period of the four available surveys (1963, 1968,
1973, 1976). This data show a definite duality between urban
(nonagricultural) and rural (mixed and purely agricultural),
with the level of inequality in the former being significantly greater and much less stable. A second interesting
duality is between households connected to the socialized
sector (non-agricultural and mixed) and the private sector
(where agricultural dominates). The inequality among the
former is larger and moves differently from the latter.
Taking each kind of household on its own, the highest level
of inequality and greatest instability is in nonagricultural
households. Inequality in mixed households is smallest and
most stable, but the small changes which do exist follow the
pattern of nonagricultural households. Agricultural households show medium changes and inequality levels, somewhat
larger than those among mixed households, but significantly
smaller than the inequality levels among nonagricultural
households.

The overall inequality level is the same as that of the
nonagricultural population and so is the pattern of change,
which shows a major increase in inequality from 1963 to 1968
and an equal fall to 1973, which is followed by a very small
rise in inequality, Lorenz curves of the levels with the
distribution for 1963 and 1978 intersecting. Other measure-
ments (Bićanić 1984) and decomposition by regions (Bićanić
and Miljanović 1985) confirm this pattern, the only regional
exception being the Republic of Slovenia in any of the
senses mentioned. In Slovenia the differences in inequality
among various kinds of households is negligible, and almost
the same as overall inequality whose changes they completely
follow.

As far as average income per household member is concerned, the mixed ones have the lowest average and the urban
ones the highest.

Illegal land cultivation and leasing and selling produce
to unauthorized retailers both increase inequality. The
first appears in two forms, the second will be dealt with
later. Illegal land leasing occurs both among peasants and
between peasants and other professions. Among peasants it is
done for purposes of tax evasion and/or attempts to till
more land than the maximum 8 hectares (in the plains, in the

mountains or infertile land, it is somewhat higher but still below the estimated economically feasible size for modern agriculture). Tax paid by peasants is determined on the basis of an estimated income for the kind of land and cultivation in question. Tax avoidance takes the form of the owner leasing the land for cultivation while paying tax as if it were in its original state (usually declared as uncultivated land). The extent of this activity is impossible to estimate, but the large increase in land registered as fallow, the increase of the average age of households to over 60, and the fact that more and more women till the land when coupled to the increase of agricultural production in the private sector can only mean that there is a very lively system of leasing and renting with inequality increasing effects.

Another form of unofficial economy in agriculture is the 'agribusiness'. It is a term which does not overflow with obvious meaning, but is used to describe the organization of agricultural production by persons not possessing the necessary permits and thereby not paying taxes on it. Members of the most varied professions and occupations have been convicted or are on trial for this kind of activity, from doctors and lawyers to employees of the local government and managers of enterprises. Frequently they lease land from peasants but very often cultivate fallow land from socially owned agricultural estates or even usurp it. They then organize agricultural production without registering it at the tax office. Production is completely cash oriented and it is not unknown for the agribusinessmen to use their social influence to lower costs and find labour, even using their authority to divert labour from socially owned farms during working hours. This kind of activity increases inequality since the income flow generated by moonlighting does not outweigh the sizeable fortunes made.

(iii) The third unofficial activity mentioned was dealings in foreign currency. Since the early seventies the government has attempted to attract the foreign currency savings of Yugoslav workers 'temporarily working' in Western Europe by allowing any Yugoslav citizen to open a foreign currency saving account in a Yugoslav bank. Interest (also in foreign currency) was even higher than in Western banks, and savers were not asked questions about the source of their money. The idea was supposed to apply only to Yugoslavs working abroad, or members of their families they supported by sending remittances, or to those with pensions in foreign currency, but in practice the system quickly changed and Yugoslavs started to buy foreign currency and build up savings deposits in it. Thus the dinar value of foreign currency savings increased dramatically - outstripping the value of dinar savings. The number of foreign currency savers also increased dramatically, the number of accounts even more, as the savers, aware that they were entering the unofficial sector, usually opened more than one account. Today this presents an inflation-proof, highly liquid form of saving, and with the rapid devaluation of the dinar provides savers with capital gains. Moreover, slowly an intricate system emerged in which many transactions essential for the normal functioning of households came to be based on the illegal buying and selling of foreign currency, either from 'foreign' workers and their families or from tourists. The most interesting fact about these activities is that they were completely 'laundered' by the banking system. Once the money entered savings deposits, it was completely within the official economy. Changes in the way interest is paid since Jan. 1, 1985 may check this, since now interest in foreign currency can be paid only on the accounts of genuine workers abroad. Moreover, the dinars to buy foreign currency have recently become severely reduced.

Income inequality effects for those able to build up such savings accounts is quite obvious.

(iv) The fourth dimension discussed relates to land and housing. Real estate trading among individuals has become a very lucrative source of wealth which completely by-passes official channels. The main reason for this is the widespread system of double-contracting. One contract is presented to the authorities and registered; the other is an arrangement according to which actual payments are made (frequently in foreign currency -itself illegal). The system has adapted to this kind of business by determining the tax on real estate not according to the value of the contract but according to the officially estimated value of the property (which opens up vast areas of bribes to valuers). This system, of course, allows for a complete untaxed transfer of capital gains.

The second aspect of real estate dealing within the unofficial economy refers to the acquisition of building permits. For various reasons, there are great delays in issuing such permits (development plans not made, official foot-dragging etc.). Thus, side payments are made to speed up the process. Until recently this was part of the unofficial economy; within the last two years in some areas attempts are being made to prosecute - thus shifting the boundary between acceptable and unacceptable law breaking. Another aspect is building without permits at all. In the case of one Adriatic commune (Zadar and surroundings), 1,200 summer houses were built without permits, 500 of them on socialized land (Cimesa 1984, p. 80). In the Republic of Croatia, which includes most of the Adriatic coast, the courts during 1984 passed 1,326 demolition orders for such houses (Črnjaković, 1985). To what extent these houses have become permanent can be illustrated by data from the coastal commune of Split which has the longest coastline and greatest fame for tolerating houses built without permits. There were 22,000 such houses in 1969 and 38,000 by 1984 (Črnjaković, 1985).

The spinoff effects of real estate trading and house building have, of course, provided room for a great expansion of unofficial building activities. Since most second homes are out of town, they are very frequently a source of income for the nonurban population, which even if they are not qualified builders still retain the peasant tradition of knowing how to build a house. Furthermore, there is the private sector, which, like the rest of the private sector, can employ up to six individuals, a number frequently over-shot by employing unregistered workers.

(v) The fifth form of the unofficial economy is the renting of flats and houses. The unregistered (hence unauthorized and tax free) letting of flats/rooms in which the rentee has no protection is induced by: the tax system (and the appli-cation of the socialist principle that nonlabour incomes should be highly taxed); the legal system (which legislates the maximum number of flats or houses an individual can possess, but does not do so for the family as a unit); the housing system (which allows the employees of enterprises to get rent-subsidized socially-owned flats with inheritable tenancy rights); the inflated price of private flats (where the consumer gets charged for all delays and price rises); the rapid urbanization; the delayed baby-boom (which took place in the mid-fifties); the transformation of the tradi-tional into the nuclear family (even though the present economic crisis may have reinstated the importance of the former). When all this is connected to the relatively small supply of flats and houses, then it can be seen that being in a position to let is an important source of inequality both of income distribution (imputed rents, unregistered renting) and the distribution of disposable wealth (since socially owned flats only allow for the inheritance of tenancy rights, there is a significant discrepancy between the distribution of wealth and disposable wealth).

(vi) The sixth important form of unofficial economic activi-ty with inequality effects takes place in the retailing trade. Two different types of activity are involved: the first is the retailing of agricultural produce, and the second concerns the distribution of goods in shortage.
The basis of the retailing business in agriculture is in the legal constraint that peasants can only sell their own produce on the market (i.e. to the consumers directly) or to authorized dealers (usually to representatives of the socia-lized sector but in some cases to private individuals such as butchers). This, given the wholly inadequate system of authorized dealers and their pricing policy, would greatly reduce the mobility of agricultural produce (in the sense that the individual peasant would not have the capacity or time to travel longer distances) so that the very old tradi-tion of local cooperative arrangements (by which one peasant takes the produce of the village to market) was tolerated as a vital part of the distribution system. However, a new form of retailing has recently appeared. Entrepreneurs with sufficient cash, vans or lorries, and storage space buy directly from the peasants in the village during harvest time (i.e. at low prices) and sell it later in the town market, frequently a very distant one. It does not seem unusual for them to have the information and enough market power to determine the price in the local market. The reason for this is that the retail entrepreneurs are registered as

peasants selling only their own produce, and pay taxes as such even though they are in fact in the retail trade and selling other produce which is illegal. This activity, nick-named the 'green mafia', has control over the largest part of the local markets. Only rarely are its participants fined, and then in sums which do not deter them; as an unofficial activity they are beyond doubt structurally in-corporated and move large quantities of produce over di-stances covering the whole country.

Only very circumstantial evidence exists concerning the quantities involved (i.e. in court case, fines and amount of produce confiscated in the wholesale part of their trade) but everything indicates that large fortunes are made this way, which have a definite income inequality increasing ef-fect; a situation quite different from the local traditional cooperatives which probably left the distribution unchanged.

The second aspect of retailing is connected to industrial goods in shortage. Through unofficial channels the popula-tion can get supplies of goods in temporary shortage (like detergents in the early eighties, like coffee, and more importantly, spare parts for household durables and cars) or those in chronic shortage (which especially exists for im-ported spare parts, but not only them).

The mode of supply is very varied and the common forms are smuggling, prearranged auctions, stealing, stockpiling goods in shortage etc. The distribution system is intricate, with the last person in the chain usually being a moonlighter who makes the least money in this very lucrative chain. As in some previous cases which had the largest inequality increa-sing effect, it must be stressed that most of this activity occurs at points of contact between the socialized and pri-vate sector.

(vii) Inequalities arising in tourist regions have been touched upon already, and demand wider treatment. Tourism on the Adriatic coast has undoubtedly brought hitherto undeve-loped regions into the rank of developed ones. Inequalities have arisen from a number of causes, but one statistic certainly worth noting is that concerning the syphoning of foreign currency into private hands - later laundered by the banking system as already described. The only estimate for this exists for 1980, when the estimated inflow of foreign currency was 1.65 billion dollars, of which only 1.15 was the official and registered inflow representing legally exchanged currency, which means that 32 percent was outside the official economy (Car, 1984, p. 2).

At the end of this section, it may be interesting to pre-sent the results found in the survey when the interviewers were asked to estimate the importance of illegal payments and moonlighting (defined, as was mentioned previously, as 'working for others outside working hours') on social ine-quality (which is the term used for economic inequality in the surveys). When asked to determine the importance of illegal payments on social inequality, 64 percent thought they had a large influence, 17 percent thought the influence was medium, 4 percent thought it small, and 15 percent did

not know. Taking a narrower aspect, when asked to estimate
only the effect of moonlighting, then 31 percent of the
interviewed thought the influence was large, the same percentage thought it medium, 20 percent thought it was small
and 18 percent did not know (both sets of figures are from
Srajer, 1984, the first on p. 16 and the second from p. 10).
Similarly a local survey conducted in Belgrade showed that
28 percent of the respondents thought the unofficial economy
was a way of making a fortune and 10 per cent a way of
making ends meet (Zlatić 1985).

The survey also allowed the interviewed to choose the five
most important sources of inequality and then to decide only
on one most important source. In both cases they could
choose from a list. This data were presented by Marković
(1984), and are reproduced in the following Table 1:

Table 1

The most important sources of inequality
in income distribution (*)

	five most im- portant causes of inequality		the most important source
Illegal income	62		32
generally		62	
bribes and corruption		48	
retailing commodities		32	
High personal incomes	51		12
generally		51	
privileges in employment		23	
use of car		11	
better health care		11	
more agreeable jobs		10	
better supply of goods in shortage		10	
quicker completion of jobs in administration		7	
easier access to schooling		6	
getting tenancy rights in socialized flats		4	
Living conditions	45		5
generally		45	
tenancy rights in social- ized flats		30	
living in more agreeable neighbourhood		13	
owning a flat or house		7	
Family connections	21		4
Living standard in general	21		8
Working conditions	20		2
generally		20	
travelling abroad		11	
highly specialized office jobs		5	
working in warm and closed premises		4	
Other	1		1
Don't know	99		12
There are no differences	1		1

(*) The figures quoted refer to the percentage distributions
and all three types of households were interviewed.

REFERENCES

BIĆANIĆ, I., <u>Analiza-raspona i raspodjele osobnih primanja od 1983. do 1981. godine</u> (Analysis of the inequality in the distribution of population earnings from 1963 to 1981), unpublished doctoral thesis, Zagreb 1984.

BIĆANIĆ, I., MILJANOVIĆ, O., 'Razlike nejednakosti raspodjele ukupnin primanja stanovnistva po republikama i pokrajinama' (The inequality of the distribution of population earning among regions), forthcoming in <u>Ekonomska politika</u>.

CAR, K., 'Devizni turistički priliv u 1983. i metodologija njegovog iskazivanja i utvrdjivanja' (Foreign currency earnings in tourism in 1983 and the methodology of its calculation and presentation), <u>Turizam</u>, vol. 32, no. 2, 1984, pp. 2-11.

CIMEŠA, M., (ed), <u>Uzroci i posljedice socijalnih razlika na nekim podrucjima društvenog života</u> (Causes and consequences of social inequality in some areas of social life), Radničke novine, Zagreb 1984.

CRNJAKOVIĆ, A., 'Bagerom ili mudrovanjem' (To bulldoze or to pontificate), <u>Vjesnik</u>, 1985.

MARKOVIĆ, Lj., 'U četiri oka i dva džepa' (Business among four eyes and two pockets), <u>Vjesnik</u>, 18 Nov., 1984.

MARKOVIĆ, M., 'Pogledi na socijalne razlike' (Views on social inequality) <u>TRIN</u>, no. 2, 1984, pp. 2-10.

MAROEVIĆ, T., <u>Radna aktivnost stanovništva SFRJ</u> (The economic activities of the Yugoslav population), mimeo., ZIT/CEMA, Zagreb 1984a.

MAROEVIĆ, T., <u>Mišljenja i očekivanja stanovništva o vlastitoj i široj ekonomskoj situaciji</u> (Opinions and expectations of the population concerning their own and wider economic livelihood), mimeo., ZIT/CEMA, Zagreb 1984b.

SIROTIĆ, S., 'Mogu li se prihodi nositi s troškovima života' (Can earnings "keep up" with living costs?), <u>TRIN</u>, no. 3, 1983, p. 3-8.

ŠRAJER, K., 'Uticaj prihoda na socijalne razlike' (The influence of earning on social inequality), <u>TRIN</u>, no. 2, 1984, pp. 11-20.

ZIATIĆ, M., 'Ilegalni društveni ugovor' (The illegal social contract), <u>Ekonomska politika</u>, no. 1718, 1985

Some proposed methodologies to quantify the influence of macroeconomic disequilibrium on the size of the second economy in Poland

LEENDERT COLIJN

1. INTRODUCTION

Since the beginning of research on the hidden, irregular, black, etc. economies, macroeconomists have attempted to quantify the phenomenon under study. Here are mentioned two, suggested a third and elaborated a fourth methodology.

1.1.1. Already in 1962, Kalecki (at that time working at the Planning Commission) proposed a study of 'economic crime' in Poland to the authorities. In a preparatory study of family budgets and survey under Kalecki's supervision, it was estimated that <u>at least</u> 2 percent of consumer goods' sales (6 percent for meat products) was paid for by, but not delivered to, the buyers. This stealing from the consumers by a 'criminal bourgeoisie' was made possible by the forced industrialization drive, its excess demand and seller's market, and the low living standards. One of its effects is mutual tolerance in society of such crimes: "there are no thieves, only people steal" is the attitude Kalecki reports. The research proposal was not accepted by the authorities. (See for an account of events surrounding this proposal Kalecki, 1984, pp. 359-63.).

1.1.2. Another methodology attempts to apply Feige's monetary method to a centrally planned economy. Simon (1982) tries to measure the zloty value of hard currency circulation for Poland in 1980. For 1980, the hard currency in circulation was estimated at an equivalent of US $200-300 million. In private savings account another US $600 million was placed. Total supply then is $900 million. The average black market exchange rate for that year is estimated to amount to 120 zl/$, which makes the zloty value of $ circulation reach the level of 110 billion zloties. Official currency in circulation was around 300 billion zl. If it is assumed that black and official currency have the same income velocity of money (black income /black money supply = registered income/ registered domestic supply of money) then black and official incomes relate 1:3, or 25% of total incomes is black.

In fact it is not clear what is actually estimated: maybe all black transactions where dollars are actually used, but there also exist SE (Second Economy) transactions where the dollar is only the implicit unit of account. It is also debatable whether the hard currency savings should be included in the dollar supply, and the accuracy of the dollar supply itself is subject to doubts. One might moreover expect "Gresham's law" to be operative, in which case "bad zloties drive out good hard currency" as a means of payments. This would mean a much lower income velocity of hard currency money. But without assumptions, nothing black can indeed be measured.

1.1.3. Perhaps an alternative method would start with Fisher's equation MV = PT which can be rewritten as

$$M1*V1 = P1*T1 \qquad (1)$$

and

$$M2*V2 = P2*T2 \qquad (2)$$

The total official money supply M is known and it consists of

$$M1 + M2 = M \qquad (3)$$

The relative price levels are

$$P1 = P(off) \qquad (4)$$

and

$$P2 = k*P1 \qquad (5)$$

which should be estimated empirically.
The sales volume in the first economy (FE) is also published

$$T1 = T(off) \qquad (6)$$

The normal FE equilibrium (absence of inflationary gap and monetary overhang) velocity of money could be inferred from a method used by Birman (1981) for the USSR:

$$V1 = V \text{ (normal)} \qquad (7)$$

Now a rather strong assumption needs to be introduced in order to make the model determined. The assumption is that the velocity of money in both economies of the country are equal:

$$V2 = V1 \qquad (8)$$

This crucial assumption does not seem however to be justified in a period of economic and social turmoil which has affected Polish consumer behaviour so much in the last years.

2. A MULTIPLIER APPROACH

A multiplier approach is here proposed and elaborated. The method restricts itself to the measurement of income earned in the second economy, because of the existence of macroeconomic disequilibrium in the first economy. Thus the results should be seen as <u>additional</u> to the normal level of SE incomes which exists in a situation of a macroeconomic equilibrium. In the absence of FE macroequilibrium (and this is what can be observed in 'realised socialism') the SE is likely to be larger in size and range.

The model on which the attempted quantification is based could be called Keynesian in line but borrows many insights from a Kaleckian model presented by Brus and Laski (1983).

The SE is defined as the aggregate of all activities with the aim to get monetary incomes which are not reported /registered statistically in the income/expenditure balances and other official publications. In this approach, therefore, part of the SE is the legal private sector. The basic or normal level of SE activities is <u>i.a.</u> due to partial disequilibria on the official consumer goods markets. But this method draws the attention to the SE incomes which are due to a general disequilibrium on the official consumer goods market.

3. THE MODEL

The national economy is divided in two sectors: the first economy and the second economy. They are indicated with the respective subscripts 1 and 2. The second economy is a market-type flexible-price economy. The first economy is only partly producing for markets where money-backed demand is exerted. The FE production for the market is covered by consumer good production mainly, of which the prices are fixed at the center. Also money-wages and the aggregate national wage fund are determined centrally. It is assumed that for the FE in the short run (e.g. annual plan period) aggregate money wages and market supplies as well as prices are insensitive to developments in the more flexible SE.

The SE is vertically integrated, which means that for its material inputs it is not dependent on the FE. There are no exchanges between the SE and the FE of intermediate products and/or investment goods. Material inputs consumed in SE production processes are either 'free' goods, stolen from the FE production and storage units, or produced in the SE itself.

The equilibrium situation on the FE market for consumer goods is the starting point of the analysis. Aggregate demand equals aggregate supply of FE goods:

$$W1 - C1 - S1 = 0 \qquad (1)$$

where:
$W1$ = net FE incomes;
$C1$ = expenditures on FE consumer goods at official prices and
$S1$ = voluntary savings out of $W1$

The initial situation of the SE is similar. Flexible prices have established in the previous period an equilibrium of income and spendings; thus

$$Y2 - C2 - S2 = 0 \qquad (2)$$

where:
Y2 = SE incomes
C2 = expenditures of SE incomes on consumption
S2 = voluntary savings out of SE incomes.

Now, due to an exogenous shock (e.g. planned output under-fulfillment, increased investment or defense spending) excess demand develops in the FE. Since the prices remain at their fixed levels a so-called inflationary gap arises:

$$W1 - C1 - S1 = IG > 0 \qquad (3)$$

where:
IG = inflationary gap.

This excess money is from the consumers point of view unspendable on the FE market. They are forced to increase their stock of savings with IG, or they can divert it to the SE, where the prices are generally higher. Holders of excess 'unspendable' money are therefore reluctant to 'bring' all the IG into the SE. Moreover, they can hold on to their excess money, speculating on the future availability of the desired goods on the low priced FE market. Consumers do also take account of their stocks of accumulated savings (MO), when directing their excess demand to the SE. That part of the IG which is brought to the SE is called the inflationary demand (ID). Its complement consists of the speculative (demand for) cash (SC). The relationships between these magnitudes can be written as follows:

$$ID = a * IG + b * MO \qquad (4)$$

$$IG = ID + SC \qquad (5)$$

where:
ID = inflationary demand directed to the SE;
MO = accumulated nonvoluntary savings (monetary overhang);
SC = speculative (demand for) cash and
a,b = are coefficients (a,b < 1)

In case of excess demand originating in the FE, equation (3), by substituting from (5), can be rewritten as

$$W1 - C1 - (S1 + SC) = ID > 0 \qquad (6)$$

A next step is joining the FE and SE into one income

equation. This is justified, since in this aggregate model (official) money is the only link between the two separate spheres. In the initial situation holds:

$$W1 - C1 - (S1 + SC) + Y2 - C2 - S2 = ID \qquad (7)$$

Hence after substituting (6) in (7):

$$Y2 = C2 + S2 \qquad (8)$$

Aggregate demand in the SE has however increased by ID

$$AD2 = C2 + I2 + ID \qquad (9)$$

where:
AD2 = aggregate demand for SE goods & products
I2 = demand for SE investment goods
C2 = demand for SE consumer goods

In this short run model investments in the SE are insensitive to changes in demand

$$I2 = I02 \qquad (10)$$

and the consumption function is described in a Keynesian manner

$$C2 = CO2 + (1 - s2) * Y2 \qquad (11)$$

where:
CO2 = autonomous consumption and
s2 = marginal propensity to consume.

The equilibrium condition is

$$AD^e 2 = Y^e 2 \qquad (12)$$

From the equations (1), (9) - (12) the new level of SE incomes can be derived

$$Y^e 2 = \frac{1}{s2} (CO2 + I2 + ID) \qquad (13)$$

The initial level where ID = 0 was

$$Y2 = \frac{1}{s2} (CO2 + I2) \qquad (14)$$

Substracting (14) from (13) shows the increase of SE incomes as a multiple of the inflationary demand originated in the FE:

$$\Delta Y2 = \frac{1}{s2} * ID1 \qquad (15)$$

341

Further remarks seem relevant:

a. It is important to repeat that <u>not</u> total SE incomes are
   modeled, but the increase of it which can be ascribed to
   a demand impulse caused by 'unspendable' money on the FE
   markets.
b. Although the initial disequilibrium of the FE is absorbed
   by an increase in semivoluntary savings (SC) and an
   increased volume of SE transactions (Δ Y2) the equilibrium of the FE is artificial and unstable. Firstly,
   holders of (accumulated) speculative money balances are
   permanently ready to activate their purchasing power on
   the FE. If they do so, consumers' frustration due to
   increased queueing, forced substitution and spending
   might transform itself into pressures for political changes, as Polish postwar history clearly teaches. Secondly,
   SE prices are generally higher than FE prices. A decreased consumer willingness to pay the higher SE prices
   might have similar political effects.
c. The increase in SE incomes is measured in nominal terms.
   In case the volume of SE production is not sensitive to
   prices, then 1/s2 reflects the <u>pure price multiplier</u>. The
   functioning of the price multiplier is similar to the
   Keynesian nominal income multiplier of a demand shock in
   a full employment market economy (cf. Brus, Laski, 1983,
   pp. 22 ff.). More realistic seems a combination of output
   and price increases creating the new level of nominal
   incomes, where both income and price multiplier do their
   work.
d. In equilibrium, both income and savings in the SE have
   increased. The cause of this increase (FE excess demand)
   is transformed into increased voluntary SE saving (for SE
   investments), semivoluntary FE speculative money balances
   and SE transaction money. Earlier authors have stated
   that "in the second economy, prices tend to be high
   enough to eliminate any overall 'monetary over-hang'"
   (Grossman, 1979, p. 39) and "excess money supply (...) is
   removed in the short run; partly by increasing prices in
   the second economy; partly by a renewed rise in the
   demand for liquid assets" (Hartwig, 1983, p. 104). This
   model can be interpreted as incorporating a 'moderate
   Grossman-Hartwig effect': the SE is only partially absor-
   bing the current inflationary gap.
e. At the same time this model takes explicit account of the
   role of the accumulated inflationary gap (monetary overhang). From this it results that even if in the FE there
   are no forced (current) savings, there can be still
   excess demand activated from the stocks of formerly 'unspendable money'.
f. The increased SE incomes distort the official income
   distribution figures. Not all individuals are likely to
   get a proportional part of aggregate SE incomes. The net
   gain of SE income earners is the increased SE income
   minus the value of sales to the FE (Δ Y2 - ID). If this
   is available to a small group in society, it might create

Table 1

Tentative calculations of the national income share of second economy incomes in Poland due to the existence of an inflationary gap

Years	1978	1979	1980	1981	1982	1983	1984
First Economy							
W1	1270	1400	1535	1970	3295	4080	4490
C1	1160	1280	1400	1490	2655	3690	4240
IG	110	120	135	480	640	390	250
MO	200	225	250	270	510	810	900
Second Economy							
a*IG (a=%33)	35	40	45	160	210	130	80
b*MO (b=%25)	50	55	60	80	130	200	225
ID	85	95	105	240	340	330	305
$\triangle$Y2 (=1.75*ID)	150	170	185	420	595	585	530
% - share	10.5	11.0	10.5	18.0	15.0	12.5	10.5
SS (= IG-ID)	25	25	20	240	300	90	-55
Income shift from FE to SE (= $\triangle$ Y2 - ID)	65	85	80	180	255	235	255

Source: Own calculations on the basis of data (for incomes W1 and sales C1) from Raport, Warsaw, 1981 (p. 127) and Rocznik Statystyczny, Warsaw, 1983. The data for 1983 are not fully comparable and those for 1984 are planned figures.

The monetary overhang MO is calculated as follows; Mot = MOt-1 + IGt-1 - IDt-1 or MOt = MOt-1 + SSt-1. As starting value is chosen 200 billion zloties for 1978.

W1 = net incomes;
C1 = sales to the consumers;
IG = inflationary gap;
MO = monetary overhang;
ID = inflationary demand;
SS = speculative savings;
$\triangle$Y2 = increase in SE incomes due to the inflationary gap.

social tensions or give rise to FE wage rise pressures. A
vicious circle (inflationary gap - higher SE incomes -
wage pressures - inflationary gap - etc.) may be the
result.

4. AN EXAMPLE WITH ARBITRARY PARAMETER VALUES

In Table 1 (using some official Polish data) the results of
tentative calculations, based on the following arbitrary
assumptions, are presented:

1. the value of the multiplier is chosen as 1.75 or implicitly the marginal propensity to save s2 = 0.57;
2. only a third of IG is directed to the SE: a = 0.33;
3. every year one quarter of the monetary overhang is directed to the SE: b = 0.25 and
4. the starting value of monetary overhang is chosen as 200
   billion zloties for 1978.

Further, for the calculation of the monetary overhang over
the years the following equation is used

$$MO_t = MO_{t-1} + IG_{t-1} - ID_{t-1} \qquad (16)$$

or $\qquad MO_t = MO_{t-1} + SC_{t-1} \qquad (16')$

REFERENCES

BIRMAN, I., Secret Incomes of the Soviet Statbudget, Den
    Haag 1981, pp. 122-8.
BRUS, W., LASKI, K., Repressed Inflation and Second Economy
    under Central Planning, paper presented at the Bielefeld
    Conference on the Second Economy, October 1983.
GROSSMAN, G., 'The Second Economy of the USSR', Problems of
    Communism, vol. 26, Sept.-Oct. 1977.
HARTWIG, K.H., 'Involuntary Liquid Assets in Eastern Europe:
    Some Critical Remarks', Soviet Studies, vol. 35, no. 1,
    1983, pp. 103-5.
KALECKI, M., 'Proba wyjasnienia zjawiska przestepczosci
    gospodarcwej' (1962) and 'Przypisy i Dodatki', in Kalec-
    ki, M., Dziela 4: Socjalizm, wzrost gospodarczy i
    efek tywnosc inwestycji, Warsaw 1984.
SIMON, C., 'L'economie polonaise en mouvement: reformes,
    inflation et recherches de l'equilibre', Revue d'études
    comparatives Est-Ouest, vol. 13, no. 4, 1982, pp. 35 ff.